Using Literature in English Language Education

ALSO AVAILABLE FROM BLOOMSBURY

Children's Literature and Learner Empowerment, Janice Bland

Children's Literature in Second Language Education, edited by Janice Bland and Christiane Lütge

Reflective Language Teaching, Thomas S. C. Farrell

Teaching and Learning the English Language, Richard Badger

Teaching English to Young Learners, edited by Janice Bland

Using Literature in English Language Education

Challenging Reading for 8–18 Year Olds

EDITED BY JANICE BLAND

BLOOMSBURY ACADEMIC

LONDON · NEW YORK · OXFORD · NEW DELHI · SYDNEY

BLOOMSBURY ACADEMIC
Bloomsbury Publishing Plc
50 Bedford Square, London, WC1B 3DP, UK
1385 Broadway, New York, NY 10018, USA

BLOOMSBURY, BLOOMSBURY ACADEMIC and the Diana logo are trademarks of
Bloomsbury Publishing Plc

First published in Great Britain 2018

A catalogue record for this book is available from the British Library.

A catalog record for this book is available from the Library of Congress.

ISBN: HB: 978-1-3500-3425-9
PB: 978-1-3500-3424-2
ePDF: 978-1-3500-3427-3
eBook: 978-1-3500-3426-6

Typeset by Newgen KnowledgeWorks Pvt. Ltd., Chennai, India
Printed and bound in Great Britain

To find out more about our authors and books visit www.bloomsbury.com
and sign up for our newsletters.

You don't have to burn books to destroy a culture.
Just get people to stop reading them.

RAY BRADBURY

The unread story is not a story; it is little black marks on wood pulp.
The reader, reading it, makes it live: a live thing, a story.

URSULA LE GUIN

For Reinhold,
and our inspiring family

Contents

Figures

Foreword

Peter Hunt

Professor Emeritus, Cardiff University, UK

It is my conviction [...] that literary reading is the single most important cultural and educational activity we all – adults and children – engage in. [...] I hold that in literature we find the best expression of the human imagination, and the most useful means by which we come to grips with our ideas about ourselves and what we are. (Chambers 1985: 16)

As the form of the object to be read is one of the crucially important aspects of reading, what is available or is made available for children to read is highly significant. [...] What is available is laden with the meanings of [... the surrounding] culture. Making sense of the world happens in a world already laden with sense. (Kress 1997: 58–9)

Literature in education and English Language Teaching (ELT) have had a fraught relationship over the years.

One school of thought, which might be called, without any derogatory intent, the 'mechanistic' approach, saw (and sees) literacy as *functional*, reading in the ELT classroom as *informational*, and facilitated through *reading comprehension questions* (see Janice Bland 2018a: 5–7, this volume), the processes of achieving it controllable, and the outcomes, measurable. The other, possibly the 'humanist' approach, sees the process of learning to read (and to read in a second or subsequent language) as less fathomable – literacy as a more complex, culturally embedded phenomenon encompassing *literary*, *critical* and *visual* literacy, and the outcomes as potentially dialogic, with dynamic interpersonal communication. The first sees 'difficulty' as something that must be carefully managed in complex contexts, the second sees the processes and transactions in the use of literature, with its unregulated challenges, as highly productive freedom.

The educational and political pendulum swings, decade by decade, between these extremes, and the current situation is one which this book attempts to address and redress. But all is not lost: if resources in many Western countries – notably the UK – for introducing challenging and provocative texts to young readers have been reduced within educational systems, the parallel development of Children's Literature as an academic discipline opens up new vistas of help. This wide-reaching discipline is growing rapidly worldwide, and explores every aspect of the relationship between the developing reader and the texts that they read or are designed for them. Thus the discipline provides an as yet mostly untapped resource for ELT researchers, students and teachers wishing to investigate the challenge of literature in education.

Frank Smith, in his highly influential *Reading* (1978, 2nd edn 1985) saw himself as writing at a point when the 'programmatic approach to reading instruction has clearly failed'. His key thesis was that the then current research had

confirmed what many experienced teachers have known intuitively, that children become readers when they are engaged in situations where written language is being meaningfully used [...]. The implications of this research have been slow to break through at decision-making levels of education, primarily because they would replace stringent outside control of classroom activity with trust that teachers can teach and that children will learn if both are given reasonable autonomy. (Smith 1985: vii–viii)

One of the underlying principles of this line of thinking was that for depth of understanding and true literacy – *literary* literacy – the child should be surrounded by books from birth and throughout the school years. As Brian Alderson noted of a bestselling manual of the 1980s, New Zealander Dorothy Butler's *Babies Need Books*: 'She lays down with conversational ease an incontrovertible case for the wedding of books to every stage of a child's development' (Butler 1982: Back Cover).

But not, as it turned out, incontrovertible. By 1993 in the UK, there had been a political backlash, summed up by Michael Rosen, later the British Children's Laureate, as follows:

But let's be clear, this government, in spite of all the rhetoric concerning literacy levels, has declared war on the reading of books [... by] the closing of public libraries [...] the elimination of the library support services [and] the forced amateuring of school librarians. [...] The elimination of the expertise [...] has meant that teachers [...] have lost the leisure, and for some, the will to gobble up the latest children's literature in their spare time. (Rosen 1993: 108–9)

This makes the assumption that 'real' books are essential for promoting reading, and it is obviously one that would be hotly disputed, not least by publishers of textbooks for the worldwide ELT market. To some it may appear that this lack – even though literature is often assumed to be essential to unlocking the love of reading – is more than met by the availability of 'quality levelled readers' (Oxford University Press 2017).

Whichever side of the argument you take, Michael Rosen was (and is) right that in the UK – and in many countries worldwide – the resources that can help teachers and parents to navigate the great world of fiction (and poetry and picturebooks and graphic novels) and to mediate this world to children have been stripped away. What can be done?

Even at its most abstract – and it can be very abstract – children's literature scholarship recognizes the essential presence of the child in the book, and equally recognizes the sophistication of even the *apparently simplest* text and the complexity of children's responses to texts. Thus the problem addressed in the current book, of introducing developing readers to wide and difficult issues, in complex and challenging contexts, will find resonance in hundreds of scholarly books on children's literature. A glance along my own shelves encounters titles such as *Language and Ideology in Children's Fiction*; *Children's Fiction about 9/11: Ethnic, National and Heroic Identities*; *Left Out: The Forgotten Tradition of Radical Publishing for Children in Britain 1910–1949*; *A Past Without a Shadow: Constructing the Past in German Books for Children*; *Children's Literature and Capitalism*; *Radical Children's Literature*; *Ethics in British Children's Literature*; *Over the Top: The Great War and Juvenile Literature*; *Take Up Thy Bed and Walk: Death, Disability and Cure in Classic Fiction for Girls*; *Children at War* and so on.

Help is there for those who need it, to support students of language and literature in relating to the very many difficult issues that surround them.

This current book brings together strategies for providing a context for deep reading (as opposed to superficial reading comprehension) and the spectrum of literacies that are crucial for a differently sophisticated generation of emerging readers. Their electronically influenced mindsets, their modes of learning, are increasingly different from those of their forebears, and they live in a world in which even the primacy of story as we have known it is challenged. This is a transitional period, moving between book-literacy and Web-literacy. As the novelist Terry Pratchett put it,

First you build a library, then build the school around it. You make sure that the kids can read adequately, write coherently if simply […]. Then you show them how to use the library, and you *don't* let them loose on the net until they *can* read and write and have grown up enough not to confuse data with information, otherwise they're just monkeys in a banana plantation. (Pratchett 2015: 297–8, emphasis in the original)

More than ever before, the contexts of the word are the essence of literacy.

References

Bland, Janice (2018a), 'Introduction: The challenge of literature', in Janice Bland (ed.), *Using Literature in English Language Education: Challenging Reading for 8–18 Year Olds*, London: Bloomsbury Academic, pp. 1–22.

Butler, Dorothy (1982) *Babies Need Books*, Harmondsworth: Penguin (Pelican).

Chambers, Aidan (1985), *Booktalk, Occasional Writing on Literature and Children*, London: The Bodley Head.

Kress, Gunther (1997), *Before Writing. Rethinking the Paths to Literacy*, London: Routledge.

Oxford University Press (2017) https://global.oup.com/education/content/primary/series/treetops/fiction/?region=uk (accessed 2 November 2017).

Pratchett, Terry (2015), *A Slip of the Keyboard*, London: Corgi.

Rosen, Michael (1993), 'Books and schools: Books in schools', *Signal: Approaches to Children's Books*, 71: 103–14.

Smith, Frank (1985), *Reading*, 2nd edn, Cambridge: Cambridge University Press.

Contributors

Evelyn Arizpe is Senior Lecturer at the School of Education, University of Glasgow, UK, where she coordinates the MEd programme in Children's Literature and Literacies and supervises doctoral students working in these fields. Her teaching and research attempt to bridge the gap between children's literature and literacy and she has taught and published widely in both these areas. Evelyn has worked on a number of studies related to reading and response, involving both children and adolescents in various international contexts. She co-authored *Visual Journeys through Wordless Narratives* (2014) and a new edition of *Children Reading Picturebooks* (2016).

Janice Bland, originally from London, is Professor of English Education, Nord University, Norway, having worked previously in teacher education in Germany for many years. Her core interests are concerned with creativity in ELT with primary and secondary-school children: creative writing, children's literature, visual and critical literacy and global issues, intercultural learning and drama methodology. Her publications include *Children's Literature and Learner Empowerment – Children and Teenagers in English Language Education* (2013) and the edited volume *Teaching English to Young Learners: Critical Issues in Language Teaching with 3–12 Year Olds* (2015), both with Bloomsbury Academic. Janice is editor of the open-access *CLELEjournal*.

Sonja Brunsmeier trained as a primary teacher at the University of Education Freiburg and holds a master's degree in 'Teaching Languages to Young Learners'. She has worked in primary schools in and around Freiburg and as a research fellow at the University of Education Freiburg, and currently works in the position of school principal. In her PhD project, she investigated the development of Intercultural Communicative Competence in the primary EFL classroom. Her further research interests include using literature and media in language education.

Werner Delanoy is Associate Professor of ELT in the Department of English and American Studies at the University of Klagenfurt, Austria. His main areas of research are inter- and transcultural learning perspectives, literature teaching, language education and contemporary British culture and literature. His main publications include *Fremdsprachlicher Literaturunterricht: Theorie und Praxis als Dialog* (2002), *Cultural Studies in the EFL Classroom* (2006; with Laurenz

Volkmann), *Future Perspectives for English Language Teaching* (2008; with Laurenz Volkmann) and *Learning with Literature in the EFL Classroom* (2015; with Maria Eisenmann and Frauke Matz).

Sam Duncan works at the UCL Institute of Education, University College London, UK, in adult literacy studies. Sam has a background in literature, film and community education, and now teaches on research methods and teacher education modules to do with literacy, language and lifelong learning. She is the author of *Reading Circles, Novels and Adult Reading Development* (2012) and *Reading for Pleasure and Reading Circles for Adult Emergent Readers* (2014). Sam is currently the recipient of a UK Arts and Humanities Research Council (AHRC) Fellowship to research contemporary adult reading aloud practices across Britain.

Gail Ellis MBE is Adviser Young Learners and Quality for the British Council and based in Paris, France. Her publications include *Learning to Learn English*, winner of the first Frank Bell Prize, *The Primary English Teacher's Guide*, shortlisted for the Ben Warren Prize, and *Tell it Again!,* as well as *Teaching Children How to Learn*, co-authored with Nayr Ibrahim, which won an award in the 2016 English Speaking Union English Language Awards. Her main interests are children's literature, young learner ELT management and inclusive education.

Geoff Hall is author of *Literature in Language Education* (2nd edn, 2015) and further chapters and articles on this topic, such as 'Using Literature in ELT' in *The Routledge Handbook of ELT* (2016). Geoff was editor of the journal *Language and Literature* until 2016. He has taught students and teachers of English since 1978 across a wide range of contexts and countries, in Europe and Asia principally. Currently Professor of English and Dean of Humanities and Social Sciences at the University of Nottingham Ningbo China, China, his recent research collaborations have included colleagues in China, Singapore and Japan.

Tzina Kalogirou is Professor of Modern Greek Literature and Literature Teaching in the School of Education/Department of Primary Education at the National and Kapodistrian University of Athens, Greece. She is the author, editor or co-editor of academic texts in Greek, English and French published in international and national refereed journals, edited volumes and conference proceedings. She is the editor of the Greek edition of Rosenblatt's seminal book *The Reader, the Text, the Poem* and of the volume *Aspects of Time and Memory in Texts of Childhood: Mnemosyne for Children*.

Annika Kolb is Professor at the English Department of the University of Education Freiburg, Germany. She holds a doctoral degree in EFL from Hamburg University. In her dissertation, she investigated the use of portfolios in the primary EFL classroom. She has worked as a language teacher in primary and secondary school in Germany and Spain. Her main research interests are teaching English to young learners and literature (especially picturebooks) in language education. Current research projects include the use of story apps (digital picturebooks) in primary ELT, multilingualism in language teaching and teacher education in a blended-learning programme.

Johanna Marks is Lecturer in the TEFL department of Westfälische Wilhelms-Universität Münster, Germany. She is a certified teacher for English, German and Educational Studies and has taught at a number of secondary schools prior to her current position. Her research interests include foreign language teacher education, teaching methodology and the role of literature in the language classroom. Johanna is currently completing her doctoral thesis on the growing impact of standards and competencies on ELT teacher education.

Thorsten Merse is a postdoctoral research assistant in the field of TEFL at the University of Munich, LMU, Germany. In his research and teaching, he engages with cultural and global learning, literature, multiple literacies and media in ELT. In his PhD from 2017 titled *Other Others, Different Differences: Queer Perspectives on Teaching English as a Foreign Language*, he conceptualizes a broadening of culture, literature and gender-oriented approaches in TEFL and suggests the inclusion of sexual and gender diversity as a relevant content dimension of teaching and learning English.

Marek Oziewicz is the Sidney and Marguerite Henry Professor of Children's and Young Adult Literature and Professor of Literacy Education at the University of Minnesota, USA. He teaches courses on speculative fiction, fantasy, and other literatures that help young people become global citizens of a multicultural world. His publications explore how stories empower readers to seek equity and challenge injustice. His most recent monograph, *Justice in Young Adult Speculative Fiction* (2015), offers a cognitive history of justice and examines how non-factual narratives help young people develop an understanding of real-life justice issues in the modern world.

Amos Paran is Reader in Second Language Education at the UCL Institute of Education, University College London, UK. He started his career as an EFL teacher in secondary schools in Israel, later moving to the University of Reading, UK, and then London. His current interests are literature and reading in EFL, and he is co-presenter of the MOOC, *Teaching EFL/ESL Reading: A Task-Based Approach*. He is the editor of *Literature in Language Teaching and Learning* (2006) and co-editor of *Testing the Untestable in Language Education* (2010). He is co-author, with Pauline Robinson, of the teachers' handbook, *Literature: Into the Classroom* (2016).

Michael Prusse is Professor of ELT and English Literature at the Zurich University of Teacher Education, PHZH, Switzerland. His academic interests include English in professional contexts, bilingual language teaching, reading in and outside the ELT classroom and literatures in English. Both in his teaching and his research there is a particular focus on children's and young adult literature. His contribution to a volume, dedicated to the uses of *Harry Potter and the Philosopher's Stone* in the classroom, consists of hands-on teaching materials for ELT teachers; he has also published on Philip Pullman and Kevin Brooks.

Sadie Ryan is a PhD candidate at the University of Glasgow, UK. She works between the department of English Language and Linguistics and the department of Education, looking at the acquisition of Glaswegian speech norms by adolescent migrants from Poland. She is particularly interested in the role of self-perception and identity in second language acquisition, and also in the role of language attitudes and ideologies in the acquisition of stigmatized linguistic features. Alongside her doctoral research, she produces a non-academic podcast about language attitudes and identity; the podcast, *Accentricity*, can be accessed at www.accentricity-podcast.com.

Jean Webb is Professor of International Children's Literature and Director of the International Forum for Research in Children's Literature at the University of Worcester, UK. Her publications include: *Introducing Children's Literature: Romanticism to Postmodernism* (2002; with Deborah Cogan Thacker) and 'Reading as protection and enlightenment in Marcus Zusak's *The Book Thief*' in Evelyn Arizpe (ed.), *Children as Readers in Children's Literature* (2015).

Jürgen Wehrmann teaches English and Philosophy at Graf-Anton-Günther School in Oldenburg, Germany. His doctoral thesis on meta-historical Irish plays won the CDE Award for the best monograph study in the field of contemporary drama and theatre in English in 2010. He has published on Irish literature, science fiction and English language teaching and has worked as a lecturer of English Literature and ELT at the Universities of Tübingen, Mainz and Oldenburg. Currently, he is concentrating on finishing his second book, which is intended as a handbook for teaching utopias, dystopias and science fiction in the ELT classroom.

1

Introduction: The challenge of literature

Janice Bland

The topic of this volume is English literature in language education in school settings. It is argued that an emphasis on the aesthetic value of literature, and its challenging, provocative content, is of great significance wherever the school curriculum requires meaningful content in addition to focusing on the language itself. Content-based learning is on the increase, as students now learn English in many countries worldwide throughout their school careers, and the content of instruction slips ever more into focus. In the language–literature classroom, young learners and teenagers take part in language-dependent activities that include reading, creative writing, viewing, talking around the texts and a multiplicity of text-related tasks. As this volume will show, literary texts afford wide educational benefits in addition to language benefits, for example intercultural understanding, empathy, multiple literacies, an understanding of the connectedness of the world and global issues, tolerance, cognitive and affective gains and self-reliance.

English learning is a worldwide phenomenon, with hugely different stakeholders, contexts, needs and nuances, and a narrow understanding of English language teaching (ELT) should consequently be critically overhauled. In school settings, two extremes might be identified as follows:

- Contexts where students have a great deal of access to out-of-school English, so that English is a second or additional language (L2) rather than a foreign language. This is usually the case where English is the majority language while many students have a different home language, for example emergent bilinguals in the United States. As plurilingualism in classrooms becomes increasingly common, and multicultural awareness increasingly respected, there is a huge interest in all teachers being able to work on literacy development with linguistically diverse children. Simultaneously, the majority of school students in European countries such as the Netherlands and Norway, where the media are seldom dubbed and where there is wide access to the Web, can increasingly be considered as ongoing bilinguals.

- Another extreme is the context where children are trying to learn the language with next to no access to out-of-school English and no access to motivating English language books through well-stocked school or community libraries. Clearly here the learning outcomes are very different from those in the previous category, except for the lucky few students who can spend time in an English-speaking country.

A major argument of this volume is that, in all such ELT contexts, the earlier children can start reading autonomously the better, which could help towards closing the gap between the two extremes described above. A second, equally urgent argument is that out-of-school or in-school extensive reading and viewing, with possible fluency as an end result, must be complemented by critical literacy, deep reading and the aim of developing a reading community. The contributions to this volume illustrate that the narrow repertoire of texts currently employed in ELT settings must widen dramatically in order to mirror the hugely differing interests and the cognitive and emotional needs of school children aged between eight and eighteen; and the term *challenging* must be understood in multiple ways according to the different contexts and ages of the reader. The following chapters set about describing these different challenges for the participating students as well as for the teachers implementing multiple educational goals in ELT. It is never the text alone that is in focus but how we deal with the opportunities for challenge in the classroom community.

Quality education embraces two essential principles: 'cognitive development as the major explicit objective' and 'promoting values and attitudes of responsible citizenship and in nurturing creative and emotional development' (UNESCO 2004: 2). Exploring the humanistic and educational role of literature is a highly valuable undertaking: it is then all the more surprising that the informed use of literature hardly plays a role in most handbooks on ELT. Curricula worldwide will vary – however, at least in school settings, ELT offers prodigious opportunities for the language-learning context to become a hive of dialogue characterized by interdisciplinary and intercultural activity.

The studies and discussions in the chapters that follow argue for a serious consideration of children's and young adult literature in ELT with students to circa the age of sixteen, an age range when many if not most learners are usually confined to the limitations of a textbook. In addition there are new perspectives on literature teaching with canonical texts in the highest grades, with sixteen-year-olds and above. Notably, the complexity of selecting challenging reading for ELT entails a huge challenge for the teachers (see Duncan and Paran 2018, this volume, for a study of teachers' perspectives).

Why take up the challenge of literature with young learners and teenagers?

The importance of widespread quality education can hardly be disputed, nor can we dispute the need for human ingenuity and creative solutions that must be 'sustained by a populace constantly contributing original ideas and receptive to the ideas of others' (Bronson and Merryman 2010: np). However, ELT in school settings seems to carry a particular burden in this respect: the responsibility for intercultural learning. For English as a lingua franca does not belong to individual national cultures but rather to all those cultures worldwide – the huge majority – where English now plays a role. Intercultural competence calls for an approach to language education 'that takes into account the actual, the imagined and the virtual worlds in which we live' (Kramsch 2011: 366). Narratives are an important pedagogic medium; they metonymically represent cultures of the language learner's own world or cultures unfamiliar to them. At the same time, stories support humankind's drive to construct coherence and meaning and they take the reader on educational journeys: 'Storytelling is central to humanity because it is through narrative that we learn about ourselves and prepare ourselves for the future in an evolutionary sense' (Hunte and Golembiewski 2014: 75).

If we accept that materials for language education are significant cultural artefacts with an ideological impact on our students (Gray 2016: 99), our research into meaning-making in language classrooms will also draw on areas such as cultural studies, literary studies, postcolonial studies, cognitive criticism and critical pedagogy. All texts are ideology-laden, just as our mental representations of experience are 'value-laden, perspective-taking movies in the mind' (Gee 2001: 715). For this reason, when choosing texts for language education, it makes sense to include many experiences from around the world, so that no one particular perspective predominates. Thus, one of the ways of avoiding reductive, one-sidedly stereotyped topics in the language classroom is through discussion of a wide range of literary texts: 'Books are sometimes the only place where readers may meet people who are not like themselves, who offer alternative worldviews' (Tschida, Ryan and Ticknor 2014: 29). Clarke and Clarke (1990: 36) have maintained in addition, 'it is in TESOL textbooks published in the west for the world market that we find a major instrument for cultural transmission and a source of concern for the effect which stereotyped images may have'. Relying on a textbook alone – even with young learners – must limit children's imaginative scope, while 'recent research into the nature of the human brain pleads an evolutionary advantage to our capacity for narrative' (Hunte and Golembiewski 2014: 73). Stories elicit an engaged response, and empathizing with characters in compelling stories is important for initiating the pleasure of literature (Krashen and Bland 2014: 8).

Our language learners have always brought culture with them into the classroom – the 'common imaginings' (Kramsch 1998: 10) of their generational, family, social class, ethnic and national cutures. In this volume, culture is understood as meanings and practices ranging beyond national cultures, to include, for example, family, social class and school cultures. Intercultural understanding should now, I argue, also encompass intra-cultural learning: 'sociologically speaking there is no difference in principle between inter- and intra-cultural communication' (Byram 1997: 41). This is surely particularly relevant for language education two decades later, as language-learning settings become increasingly diverse, heterogeneous, multilingual and multicultural – children having often crossed borders themselves before arriving in our classrooms. Both in children's literature scholarship and applied linguistics there is concern about the 'representation of the world and the *mis*representation and/or erasure of specific categories of people and the consequences this may have for students' (Gray 2016: 97, emphasis in the original). As Tschida, Ryan and Ticknor maintain (2014: 28): 'Scholars of children's literature have long stressed the need for turning a critical eye to the stories we tell, who is doing the telling, and who gets left out.' The misrepresented or Othered in texts, but equally the hidden ideology of materials used in classrooms, must receive critical attention and be made visible – whether the materials were specifically published for language teaching or not. Suggestions to this end are made in this volume (e.g. Bland 2018b, Delanoy 2018, Marks and Merse 2018, Prusse 2018).

Critical literacy leading to critical pedagogy

Experienced readers do not tend to aim for total comprehension when enjoying literature but rather a critical transaction with the text. Exploration is part of the joy and challenge, and *reading is not a passive skill* – a misnomer that hopefully no longer haunts ELT. Cognitive science has now revealed how reading and listening to language is experienced in an embodied way: 'While we listen to or read sentences, we simulate seeing the scenes and *performing the actions* that are described' (Bergen 2012: 16, my emphasis). Comprehension questions, however, imply that reading is about knowledge transmission rather than dynamic response: reading comprehension questions should thus never be seen as the main point of a literacy event with a literary text.

The need for a wider understanding of literacy is ever more apparent in the twenty-first century, with the hugely influential role of social media and the dangers of 'a culture where a few claims on Twitter can have the same credibility as a library full of research' (Coughlan 2017). Consequently the understanding of literacy has become fluid – we talk of multiple literacies, which are socially and culturally embedded, 'reflecting not one standard literacy but diverse literacies. The emphasis [is] on context, purpose, language, actors and the relations between them' (UNESCO 2017: 60). Clearly, ELT is highly involved not only in children learning to read and write (functional literacy) but also their learning to use the Web wisely and skilfully for information (information literacy), learning to read the aesthetic nature of a literary text (literary literacy), learning to read all texts critically and understanding their manipulative power (critical literacy) and also reading pictures for information both deeply and critically (visual literacy). The aim of teaching multiple literacies is reading at a deeper level, and it is undoubtedly the ELT classroom that offers most opportunities for this training due to the enormous diversity of English-language texts. The current preoccupation with 'alternative facts' in the political sphere highlights the vital importance of both comprehension and critical interpretation. The ability to interpret the choices made in verbal and visual text is essential: particularly literary texts prompt the reader to consider language formulations deeply, as well as connotations in verbal and pictorial text and cultural meanings.

It follows that the tendency in ELT to teach and explain literature meant for an adult audience – even when shortened and simplified in graded readers – to less experienced younger readers, rather than to allow them to empathetically and critically interact and transact with a narrative suited to their developmental level (age as well as language), is counterproductive to the rich cognitive development literature can support. Scholars of children's literature make the claim that the most successful children's literature 'challenges its audiences cognitively and affectively, stimulating attention, imagination, memory, inference-making, empathy and all other elements of mental processes' (Nikolajeva 2014: 227). Children of the twenty-first century are faced with complexity, diversity and challenge. They need the opportunity for a serious engagement with literature that will help them realize their agency and the power of imagination to prepare the world for change.

This is where critical literacy moves into critical pedagogy, which 'deals with questions of social justice and social change through education [... and seeks to] take steps towards social change in such a way that there is more inclusion and representation of groups who are left out' (Akbari 2008: 276–7). Language and literature teaching has sociopolitical implications – as education generally has – and critical pedagogy strives to support the potential of students whatever their background. This involves overcoming unfair challenges misguidedly or selfishly lain down by adults, it involves students being empowered to recognize their self-worth and gain resilience and – importantly if improved social justice is a goal – becoming autonomous and self-reliant in their learning. Children come to school with different knowledge sets from their home and out of-school lives, known as the *virtual school bag* (Thomson 2002). However, these are not equally valued, and some children are not invited to open their bags and access such assets as additional languages and cultural knowledge. Students' voices must count, and if 'education in general and ELT in particular are going to make a difference, then the *totality* of the experiences of learners needs to be addressed' (Akbari 2008: 278, emphasis in the original).

Deep reading for deep learning in ELT

This book argues for both compelling and challenging reading in order to entice a literacy apprenticeship that will reach all students to improve their language and cognitive development chances. From the language perspective, the more reading the better, in that literary texts offer contextualized access to stretches of authentic discourse that sensitize learners to grammatical relations and the semantic associations of words (Hoey 2005). Reading is key because it 'provides many different contexts, episodes and experiences which, over time, sum to a rich and nuanced database about a word, its connections to other words and its lexical history within an individual's experience' (Nation 2017: 2). Consequently reading can contribute to a dynamic and multifaceted repertoire of knowledge both of the word and the world. Yet more dramatic is the finding that 'childhood reading is linked to substantial cognitive progress between the ages of 10 to 16' (Sullivan and Brown 2013: 2). Thus it is clear that reading truly affects chances in life: 'those who do not develop the pleasure reading habit simply don't have a chance – they will have a very difficult time reading and writing at a level high enough to deal with the demands of today's world' (Krashen 2004: x). Leland, Lewison and Harste demand 'a new educational mantra that shifts the focus from raising text scores to raising readers' (2013: vii) and Tomlinson argues succinctly: 'If you read forever you can continue to learn forever' (1998: 184).

Literary cognitive criticism searches for an explanation *why* literature is such a powerful instrument of human thought, serving to expand cognitive abilities. It appears we simulate an experience described by words by literally engaging those parts of our brain that we use for perception and action, so that our experience of narrative is embodied, igniting empathy. This is particularly significant when fiction offers vicarious ethical experience, placing characters 'in situations where ethical issues are inescapable, and moreover, in fiction these issues can be amplified and become more tangible' (Nikolajeva 2014: 178). The process of deep reading frequently involves encouraging the community of readers to contemplate an ethical issue in empathy with a protagonist – rather than the teaching of a moral lesson through the text (see, e.g. Bland 2018c, Delanoy 2018, Ellis 2018, Webb 2018 and Wehrmann 2018 in this volume). Overall, the aim of this book is to illustrate a deep, participatory reading of a broad range of compelling literary texts.

Now, in the twenty-first century, we can be sure that the *majority* of readers of literary texts in English are not reading in their first language. While readers across the world are increasingly characterized by a hybrid cultural identity, 'moving in the borderlands between cultures' (Macleroy 2013: 304), literary texts are increasingly diverging from the monomodal novel format, to 'something woven, textured, connected to strands that may lead beyond the single text to contexts, intertexts, and subtexts' (McGillis 2011: 349). The more complex, the more interwoven and intertextual these multimodal texts are, the more opportunities arise in the classroom for talking around texts – leading to potential acquisition of multiple literacy through cognitively demanding, contemplative deep-reading processes.

Deep reading is considered to be slow and meditative (Birkerts 1994: 146). It not only goes beyond the reading comprehension questions associated with intensive reading in ELT but also comprehends more than recognizing stylistic devices. Rather, deep reading means 'inferential and deductive reasoning, analogical skills, critical analysis, reflection, and insight. The expert reader needs milliseconds to execute these processes; the young brain needs years to develop them' (Wolf and Barzillai 2009: 32). We use our real-life experience to understand the narrative, and the storyworld itself helps illuminate and explain the real world, so that 'cognitive engagement with fiction is a two-way process: life-to-text and text-to-life' (Nikolajeva 2014: 25).

For ELT the training of reading is particularly important. On the one hand, creating a mental model of the storyworld while reading is more difficult to attain – but also most desirable – in a second language: 'The ability to turn words into mental images distinguishes deep reading with understanding and pleasure from merely decoding words on the page' (Bland 2015b: 26). On the other hand, the acquisition of information literacy is most essential in English, the lingua franca of the Web: 'In the last few years, we've moved from an information-scarce economy to one driven by an information glut. [...] The challenge becomes, not finding that scarce plant growing in the desert, but finding a specific plant growing in a jungle. We are going to need help navigating that information to find the thing we actually need' (Gaiman 2013: np).

The pluralism of literature

Howard Gardner, in discussing the demands of education for the future, writes that 'elders have a responsibility to introduce instances and systems that operate according to different rules – utopias, dystopias, alternative numerical systems, counterfactual historical accounts [...]. The adolescent mind can take it from there' (Gardner 2006: 87). Yet adolescents' language learning is still mostly restricted to the scope of traditional textbooks which 'feature magazine-style reading passages exclusively, ignoring news reporting, prose fiction, poetry, or anything else' (Brown 2009: 243). Since the cultural turn in the last decades of the twentieth century, the understanding of literature has been re-conceptualized to become broader and pluralistic, and the inclusion of literature in ELT may embrace postcolonial and migrant literature as well as an exciting and still developing array of formats (see Bland 2018d). It is now understood that literary texts form a gateway to new perspectives and intercultural awareness through the many literatures in English from nations throughout the world.

At the same time, attention has shifted from a literary product to the communicative process of reception: 'One of the more welcome developments in literature study in L1 contexts, and now in ELT, is the rapid growth and popularity of literature as "doing", something to try for yourself, as well as something to study in the work of expert published writers' (Hall 2016: 465). Creative writing and hands-on approaches allow for more autonomy and agency of the adolescent participant in a literacy event that understands texts as 'cultural products, with the notion of culture seen as increasingly dynamic and co-constructed interactively, as an emergent and specifically linguistic process rather than as a completed product' (Carter 2015: 316). However, pre-service teacher education in ELT worldwide is often designed by applied linguists with a focus on language alone, who may have little knowledge of literature or the educational requirements of school settings, and no knowledge at all of children's literature. Consequently the chapters in this volume will attempt to debunk some myths still prevalent in many language classrooms.

Myths in literature teaching current in ELT

Differing theoretical stances underpin the chapters in this book – for example reader-response criticism (Delanoy 2018), philosophy (Wehrmann 2018), creativity (Bland 2018b), multilingual learning (Arizpe and Ryan 2018) and multiple literacies (Ellis 2018). Despite this variety of perspectives, all chapters tend to repudiate certain beliefs that are still prevalent in many ELT classrooms and assessment regimes.

Myth 1: A literary text is an artefact with clear boundaries and students must find the correct interpretation

In ELT, there still seems to be a dominant belief among teachers and their students that there are absolute meanings in texts that must be taught: 'the default position continues to be that of the text as "container" of meaning and of the reader as a "comprehender" who extracts meaning from texts' (Paran and Wallace 2016: 447). A more exciting perspective for language students is surely to deliberate on the shifting meanings of texts, on 'how the text explodes and scatters. [...] Our goal is not to find *the* meaning, nor even *a* meaning of the text' (Barthes 1988: 262, emphasis in the original). Readers' perspectives evolve, and Widdowson discusses reading as 'adaptive and emergent conceptualizations that shift and vary as a function of the process of interpretation itself' (2017: x). Similarly Kalogirou, this volume, writes 'the literary text is multifaceted and therefore cannot be considered as a preconceived and stable entity but as a space that offers multiple pathways for exploration' (2018: 230).

Myth 2: Students should identify with characters

Experimental evidence has recently established the advantages of narrative for the development of Theory of Mind (ToM), which refers to the understanding that others have beliefs, thoughts and feelings that are different from one's own (Kidd and Castano 2013). In order to support ToM, teachers should encourage students to empathize with characters rather than identify with them. Nikolajeva refers to the 'identification fallacy', which can lead to an uncritical alignment with a fictional character, and delay the development of ToM and empathy: 'To be a successful mind-reader, you need to be detached from the mind you are reading' (2014: 86). This argument is highly important if language education is to support the development of critical literacy and empathy. The best time for this training is childhood through to late adolescence: 'If empathy is acquired gradually and is not fully developed until late adolescence, and if fiction is to serve as a training field for the social brain, fiction should logically offer challenge, not comfort' (Nikolajeva 2014: 87).

Myth 3: Students should discover the author's intentions

While the context is important in understanding meanings in a literary text, an author is part of that context and cannot stand outside of it: 'A large part of any book is written not by its author but by the world the author lives in' (Hollindale 1988: 15). Authors cannot entirely escape their cultural influences and confines, and may scarcely realize the ideological perspective woven within their writing. The reader will find it most difficult to discover bias, for example, when the cultural background of an author is close to their own. In this volume, authors recommend 'appreciative *and* resistant, ideology-critical readings' (Delanoy 2018: 143).

Myth 4: Only language is a stumbling block for accessibility of texts in L2 reading

The challenge of literary texts is complex. In Duncan and Paran's study with teachers of advanced teenagers (2018, this volume), reference was made by the teachers both to conceptual and linguistic challenges. With younger children, unfamiliar cultural and conceptual content is likely to play an even greater role. This is particularly a danger with simplified literature (graded readers) not written specifically for children – it is easy to underestimate the confusions posed by content from the experienced adult world for children and teenagers. Children's literature, on the other hand, takes into account the needs and age-related schemata of its audience, but must be carefully vetted for linguistic accessibility in addition. Schmitt, Jiang and Grabe (2011: 29) identify a wide number of variables that, alongside vocabulary, have been shown to affect comprehension: 'involving language proficiency (e.g. grammatical knowledge and awareness of discourse structure), the text itself (e.g. text length, text difficulty, and topic), and those concerning the reader (interest in topic, motivation, amount of exposure to print, purposes for reading, L1 reading ability, and inferencing ability)'.

Myth 5: Only the linguistic mode is relevant for literacy

Literacy is the qualification required for the interpretation of texts with confidence, mindfully and critically – whether canonical literature, the Web or other multimodal texts. Few can become experts at any skill without practice, and this is certainly true for the skills of the literacy spectrum. Children are generally immersed in a digital world outside of school – educators do their students a major disservice if there is no apparent connection between ELT in school and the students' world beyond. The reimagining of literary texts in different formats and media is very much a part of empowered learning through literature, with text-related and language-dependent activities in ELT, beginning already in the elementary school. The visual and audio modes of communication are hugely important, and must be included in ELT for the practice of visual and critical literacy (pictures, Web pages, film, TV series and so forth). However the spatial, touch-related and gestural modes of communication are highly important for humanistic approaches such as drama (see Bland 2015a), and must not be neglected in language education – particularly when social interaction is becoming ever more virtual.

Myth 6: Literature for young people is not sufficiently challenging

A large body of international scholarship on children's literature – its cultural and educational relevance as well as the opportunities it affords for literary analysis – examines the huge differences in literature for young people. Roderick McGillis writes that the possibilities for interpretation of children's literature are 'as varied as they are for any literature. This is an important lesson because many books for the young are disarming in their ostensible simplicity. Theory has taught us that what appears simple does so because we have not looked closely enough at that simple thing' (2010: 14). The theory of children's literature now belongs increasingly to ELT teacher education although there is still much work to be done in connecting conceptual and empirical research in ELT with young learners and teenagers. However, school libraries with a certified librarian scarcely exist anywhere except in private schools. Some countries formerly had many well-stocked libraries with school librarians, such as Canada and the United States, Australia, New Zealand, Malta, Croatia, Hong Kong and the UK, but it seems with few exceptions that the situation is rapidly deteriorating. Consequently teachers have a heavy burden in selecting the most suitable texts for their students, and mostly without the opportunities of guidance.

Ten criteria for selecting texts for deep reading in ELT with adolescents

It has been discussed so far that deep reading is important for intellectual, emotional, ethical and social development. Thus the emphasis in this volume is on deep reading, for example as an attempt to counteract the increasingly splintered attention spans of young people, identified in Hayles (2007) and discussed in several chapters (Bland 2018b: 52–3, Bland 2018c: 181, Brunsmeier and Kolb 2018: 109 and Delanoy 2018: 148). Deep reading in combination with self-selected extensive reading is seen as an ideal, and Brunsmeier and Kolb focus particularly on the latter approach in order to initiate elementary school learners into L2 pleasure reading at the outset. While it is argued that the rewards of literature in English language education are multifarious, the issue of access to suitable literature is the greatest stumbling block both for classroom and out-of-school reading. As noted above, this places a huge burden on teachers, many of whom well understand the advantages of reading in English but enjoy little support, if any. As a consequence, the following criteria are hopefully a useful, if idealized guide, which will need adjusting to each age group:

1   The text should be generative – providing material for deep reading and genuine communication on complex dilemmas.

2   The text should possess literary merit and the teacher should also enjoy the text.

3   Accessibility is essential, and this refers not only to language but also to culture-related and age-related schemata.

4   Some empathetic and appealing characters must be involved.

5   The text should be a compelling read, involving the emotions – for example through surprising, humorous, tragic or heart-warming features.

6   The text should be imaginative, well researched and informative, throwing light, for example, on different periods of history, different nations or diverse cultures within nations.

7   The text should be potentially schema refreshing, challenging readers to re-examine their beliefs.

8   The text should offer gaps, and opportunities to speculate on creative solutions to problems.

9   The text should be packaged in an inviting, attractive way and not too long for the relevant age group. Connected opportunities for autonomous, extensive reading or viewing would be ideal.

10   Teenagers prefer books they can discuss with their friends so that ideally the text should have renown with the peer group.

Finally, and this is reflected throughout this volume, the issue of age should carry huge weight when selecting texts:

> We know adolescents like young adult novels because, unlike classical, canonical works, these novels have been written *about* adolescents, *with adolescent readers in mind*. It is these books that teachers should use in the classroom if today's adolescents are to see school as relevant to their lives and experiences. [...] Teenagers' reading habits and their out-of-school lives *must* matter in today's classrooms if we don't want to further students' disengagement with school. (Groenke and Scherff 2010: 2, emphasis in the original)

The structure of *Using Literature in English Language Education: Challenging Reading for 8–18 Year Olds*

As volume editor, I have looked for contributions that throw light on areas where major opportunities for literacy development in language education are being missed. Part One, 'Multimodal challenges', focuses on still underexplored formats that are full of promise for ELT, including the picturebook, the graphic novel and the screenplay. Part Two, 'Provocative and compelling', focuses on challenging genres: for example inclusive and diversity-oriented love-themed fiction, science fiction, environmental dystopia and Shakespearian intertexts for young adults. The building blocks that distinguish different formats and narrative genres in print and screen media are important in structuring teaching and learning, just as they structure this volume. Thus the book begins with a contribution that throws light on definitions (Oziewicz 2018), and ends in Part Three, 'Embracing the challenges', with an annotated bibliography on literary texts recommended for children and young adults in ELT (Bland 2018d), which is organized in ten categories, from story apps to young adult fiction.

In order to make an informed selection within the wide range of graphic novels for booktalk in the classroom, it is important to understand the variety of constellations of pictorial and verbal elements they offer. In his contribution to this volume, Marek Oziewicz (Chapter 2) first examines the spectrum of multimodal literary works that encompasses graphic novels, comic strips, comics and picturebooks in order to propose a taxonomy of the graphic novel. Following Eisner, he finds sequential art an appropriate umbrella term for these texts that blend the pictorial and the verbal. Oziewicz examines, together with his students, how the graphic novel format works, for '*how* is exactly what the format is all about' (2018: 30). Brian Selznick's magical works are examined in order to illustrate the complicated mechanisms by which students are enticed by Selznick's storytelling method into becoming participants in the story, 'requiring a significant effort on the reader's part' (Oziewicz 2018: 35).

Following this, Janice Bland (Chapter 3) examines opportunities for creativity and critical literacy in ELT, taking examples from work around the playscript *Harry Potter and the Cursed Child* (Thorne, Rowling and Tiffany 2016) and *Fantastic Beasts and Where to Find Them, Original Screenplay* (Rowling 2016). Drama conventions are introduced that help students shape their thinking – by scripting and then voicing characters' thoughts that are unrecorded in the original script. Bland describes how drama conventions, such as the gossip circle, intrapersonal role play, role-on-the-wall and subtext strategies, potentially reveal absences in a story, which, once noticed, can be critically analysed. Students respond with active reflection, challenging questions and creative writing, from different perspectives and potentially resisting. The use of mentor texts for students' own creative writing is exemplified, with the outcome that 'a magical combination of Rowling's screenplay, overflowing with ingenious ideas in *Fantastic Beasts*, and David Almond's musical language in *Mouse Bird Snake Wolf* (Almond, illus. McKean 2013) makes for an excellent partnership' (Bland 2018b: 55).

The next two chapters illustrate that the construct of challenge is woven within the literacy event rather than only inherent in the text. Evelyn Arizpe and Sadie Ryan (Chapter 4) focus on wordless picturebooks – how can this be challenging? The researchers show how an active and aware engagement with David Wiesner's award-winning books can have a significant impact on students in multilingual educational contexts. In the studies with children and teenagers documented in this chapter, it was found that Wiesner's *Mr Wuffles!* (2013) and *Flotsam* (2006) raise the themes of intercultural understanding, invite co-authoring, inspire creative writing and teach metacognitive strategies involved in learning a language. These rich findings illustrate that 'meeting the challenge of the wordless picturebook is more than worthwhile in language learning because it provides the opportunity to develop metacognitive strategies and metalinguistic thinking' (Arizpe and Ryan 2018: 77). Gail Ellis (Chapter 5) continues with a consideration of the educational affordances of picturebooks and the development of multiple literacies. She notes that children's ideas and aspirations will not be limited just because their English is limited: 'Real success depends on having the right story for the linguistic and cognitive ability and interests of the children in order to maximise their enjoyment, involvement and learning' (Ellis 2018: 84). Her study with an ELT class of nine-year-olds shows that, even with this young age group, the agency of the language learner can be supported, so that 'children feel active and powerful in their role' (Ellis 2018: 86).

Gathering reading experience through extensive reading of self-selected texts could initiate an important start to lifelong literacy. However with younger elementary students, it is a challenge to make any autonomous reading a realistic possibility. Sonja Brunsmeier and Annika Kolb (Chapter 6) focus on a very recent development in narrative texts. Their chapter describes the potential of the interactive features and the supportive elements of story apps in fostering autonomous reading. Again, the agency of the child was a key factor: 'The different types of comprehension support proved to be especially beneficial if the children were able to activate them themselves, choosing the moment when they wanted the audio narration and the animations to start because they were ready for the input' (Brunsmeier and Kolb 2018: 112). Not only were the more interactive story apps motivating but they also seemed to foster the development of reading strategies. In some cases, however, it was found that animations distracted children from the audio story narration.

Michael Prusse (Chapter 7) turns our attention to transmedial reading and critical cultural literacy with Tim Winton's *Lockie Leonard* young adult book trilogy and TV series. Series and seriality are discussed as well as the evolving and adapting nature of children's literature. Historical paintings are brought into the transmedial discussion to add another layer to the canvas that can introduce ELT mid-secondary school students to a multifaceted picture of Australia. Prusse examines the quest pattern in different narrative formats, illustrating how students may learn to comprehend adaptation as a creative cultural practice, and how adaptations extend meanings. Finally, the challenge of transmedial reading is illustrated by passages from *Lockie Leonard*, in which 'surfing challenging waves [...] becomes a metaphor for adolescence' (Prusse 2018: 133).

As an opening to Part Two, Werner Delanoy (Chapter 8) outlines the complex discussion of 'literary, language-related, educational and sociocultural demands' made of literature in language education (2018: 141). The author emphasizes going beyond the tried and tested in literature for ELT, and establishes the intricacy of the discussion, matching a multiperspectival approach to the multidimensional complexities of literature in language education. Delanoy maintains that standardization is a threat to the inclusion of complex content, and illustrates moving beyond the single text approach, with the example of a text ensemble inspired by Beverley Naidoo's short story collection *Out of Bounds* (2001) and a multimodal literature project design for secondary-school students.

Johanna Marks and Thorsten Merse (Chapter 9) continue the narrative of intercultural learning by discussing the importance of avoiding the equation of culture with nation. They argue for a 'balanced representation of cultural diversity in the ELT classroom' (Marks and Merse 2018: 162), opening up ELT to the challenge of potentially explosive global issues, and moving teachers and learners out of their comfort zones. The authors make the case for learners examining their experience of Otherness through highly successful love stories set in the context of LGBTQ identities (Levithan's short story 'Princes') and disability and disease (Green's *The Fault in Our Stars*). The ELT classroom must give voice, they argue, to underrepresented sociocultural difference. Language learners can engage with these utterly compelling stories and will experience 'specific literary representations of love as a universal, yet culturally contingent, human experience' (2018: 170).

Janice Bland (Chapter 10) then examines the opportunities of teaching with Collins's *The Hunger Games*. She begins with a discussion of possible reasons why the dystopia genre is so attractive to the current generation of teenagers. Concentrating on the second book of the trilogy, *Catching Fire* (Collins 2009), Bland considers the twenty-first-century themes that are woven so well into the dystopia. The chapter details how urgent contemporary topics that concern young people deeply are addressed in the books: 'reality television and celebrity culture, the theme of social justice, the theme of education and mental enslavement, idealism and realism, and the theme of the environment' (2018c: 179). It is shown how these serious issues can be meaningfully exploited for 'engaged reading' in ELT.

Following on from this, Jürgen Wehrmann (Chapter 11) begins by differentiating romantic reading, close reading and wide reading of science fiction, and *speculative reading* – which preserves 'the important element of wonder in the genre' (Wehrmann 2018: 194). He then explains the plot elements that science fiction and thought experiments have in common. The analysis concentrates on Ursula Le Guin's 'The Ones Who Walk Away from Omelas', and Wehrmann suggests additional short science-fiction narratives for thought experiments in advanced ELT. The author makes the highly significant point: 'Without including utopian thinking, political education could only aim at fostering understanding and accepting societal arrangements and not at shaping them and developing them further' (2018: 200). Jean Webb (Chapter 12) contributes on environmental fiction for younger teenagers who themselves will have to grapple with the ongoing environmental damage caused by current irresponsible practice. The author argues that fiction is 'a space where these matters can be contemplated; where awareness can be raised and possible futures can be posited in creative and imaginative ways unrestricted by reality but related to actual conditions' (Webb 2018: 209). This accords with the views of ecocritics: Murphy (2000: 52), for example, considers the 'really salient feature of environmental literary work may be its impact on the reader's point of view, which can be accomplished through fictional stories as well as non-fictional ones'. In the selected texts Webb introduces, the leitmotif seems to be 'fighting not only against the weather but also against the savagery into which society has descended' (Webb 2018: 213). The teen fiction introduced here confronts readers and classroom communities with speculative scenarios that challenge them to reconsider real-life concerns. Such topics would fit well into Content and Language Integrated Learning classrooms, for example in the mid-secondary school.

Tzina Kalogirou (Chapter 13) introduces a highly engaging one-act play that convincingly dramatizes the rebellious adolescence of Hamlet, Ophelia and Laertes at the corrupt court of Denmark. The educational affordances of this material, commissioned by the London National Theatre, are immediately apparent. While Shakespeare's *Hamlet* is challenging literature par excellence, but beyond the scope of most ELT school settings, Lesslie's *Prince of Denmark* is a far more accessible, standalone piece that examines the characters and themes of Shakespeare's play, thus preparing for it – as well as challenging in its own right. However the author describes a project in Athens where her students in fact read both texts, where they 'opted for a deeper, more insightful reading of both works leading to a profound understanding of the intertextual reading process itself. The students were encouraged to delve into the Shakespearean pre-text so as to examine more profoundly its contemporary adaptation' (Kalogirou 2018: 230).

Part Three begins with Sam Duncan and Amos Paran's report (Chapter 14) on their research study, which aims to achieve an empirically based understanding of how literature is actually used in the classroom with advanced secondary, higher level students in three European countries. Important understandings of the sense of challenge as experienced by dedicated teachers, including the challenge that students' expectations may pose on teachers, are delivered in this chapter. The teachers were enthusiastic about teaching literature, and selected 'engaging topics, texts they were passionate about themselves, texts that they felt students, or particular groups of students, would relate to or enjoy' (Duncan and Paran 2018: 247). The study evidences that even in the highest grades the selection of suitable texts is highly complex, with choices being motivated in multiple ways. This points to the pivotal role of teacher education in supplying teachers with the knowhow to select the most suitable text for the language–literature class – particularly as teacher autonomy in making such choices is highlighted as highly desirable in this study. This desideratum of teacher education is yet more urgent for teachers of lower secondary and elementary schools where the selection is more difficult due to widespread lack of knowledge of potentially suitable children's literature.

Geoff Hall (Chapter 15) reflects back on the volume, and reflects forward on the needs of the current times. His message mirrors the message of the book – that stronger readers are needed – and will hopefully fall on fertile ground, and seed reflection and action among administrators, parents, teachers, teacher educators and publishers. Hall sums up the understanding of challenging reading from the perspective of education: 'Challenging reading may be thought of as some kind of travel into a wider world than we are familiar with just as much as (in its other sense) challenging reading may involve a resistant reading to a familiar story or other text with familiar yet questionable values' (2018: 262).

Finally this volume offers an annotated bibliography of literary texts recommended for children and young adults in ELT (Bland 2018d). The bibliography is divided into ten categories that offer manifold stimulating text-related activities: story apps, picturebooks, poetry books, chapter books, graphic novels, short stories, verse novels, playscripts, screenplays and young adult fiction. This is hopefully a useful aid to teachers as well as student teachers who must nonetheless take each decision with due cultural sensitivity in their own sociocultural context as well as considering the age and language level of their students. English-language children's literature is not for the most part published for a particular market, and some works can be controversial in some contexts. Young adult literature largely escapes the self-censorship that troubles the international ELT graded reader and textbook industry – international ELT publishers often insist that their authors avoid politics, alcohol, religion, sex, narcotics, isms and pork – known as the PARSNIP policy (Gray 2002: 159). The lack of self-censorship in children's literature is a huge advantage, not only for young adults' reading (for teenagers positively like 'dangerous' topics) but also for critical literacy approaches and intercultural learning. And surely we agree with Ravitch (2003: 159) 'that minds grow sharper by contending with challenging ideas'.

The approaches represented in this volume offer a richly differentiated, multiperspectival view of the opportunities of the language–literature classroom in school settings. An argument is made that an understanding and appreciation of wide or extensive reading as well as in-school deep reading and critical literacy should accompany all pedagogical, administrative and financial decisions on teaching English to young learners and teenagers. The volume cannot satisfy all teachers, teacher educators, student teachers and scholars in all possible contexts but it does, I hope, bring us closer to the meaning of challenging reading for eight to eighteen-year-olds in English language education.

Bibliography

Almond, David and McKean, Dave (illus.) (2013), *Mouse Bird Snake Wolf*, Somerville, Massachusetts: Candlewick Press.

Collins, Suzanne (2009), *Catching Fire*, London: Scholastic.

Green, John (2013), *The Fault in Our Stars*, London: Penguin.

Le Guin, Ursula (1975/2004), 'The Ones Who Walk Away from Omelas', in *The Wind's Twelve Quarters: Stories*, New York: Perennial, pp. 275–84.

Lesslie, Michael (2012), 'Prince of Denmark', in *Connections 2012. Plays for Young People, National Theatre*, London: Methuen Drama, pp. 163–201.

Levithan, David (2008), 'Princes', in *How They Met, and Other Stories*, New York: Alfred. A. Knopf, pp. 131–61.

Naidoo, Beverley (2001), *Out of Bounds. Stories of Conflict and Hope*, London: Puffin.

Rowling, J. K. (2016), *Fantastic Beasts and Where to Find Them, Original Screenplay*, London: Little, Brown.

Thorne, Jack (script), Rowling, J. K. and Tiffany, John (story) (2016), *Harry Potter and the Cursed Child*, London: Little, Brown.

Wiesner, David (2006), *Flotsam*, New York: Clarion Books.

Wiesner, David (2013), *Mr Wuffles!*, New York: Clarion Books.

Winton, Tim (1990/2007), *Lockie Leonard, Human Torpedo*, Camberwell (Victoria): Penguin.

References

Akbari, Ramin (2008), 'Transforming lives: Introducing critical pedagogy into ELT classrooms', *ELT Journal*, 62/3: 276–83.

Arizpe, Evelyn and Ryan, Sadie (2018), 'The wordless picturebook: Literacy in multilingual contexts and David Wiesner's worlds', in Janice Bland (ed.), *Using Literature in English Language Education: Challenging Reading for 8–18 Year Olds*, London: Bloomsbury Academic, pp. 63–81.

Barthes, Roland (1988), *The Semiotic Challenge*, trans. Richard Howard, Oxford: Blackwell.

Bergen, Benjamin (2012), *Louder Than Words: The New Science of How the Mind Makes Meaning*, New York: Basic Books.

Birkerts, Sven (1994), *The Gutenberg Elegies. The Fate of Reading in an Electronic Age*, Winchester, MA: Faber and Faber.

Bland, Janice (2015a) 'Drama with young learners', in Bland, Janice (ed.), *Teaching English to Young Learners. Critical Issues in Language Teaching with 3–12 Year Olds*, London: Bloomsbury Academic, pp. 219–38.

Bland, Janice (2015b), 'Pictures, images and deep reading', *Children's Literature in English Language Education*, 3/2: 24–36.

Bland, Janice (2018b), 'Playscript and screenplay: Creativity with J. K. Rowling's Wizarding World', in Janice Bland (ed.), *Using Literature in English Language Education*, London: Bloomsbury Academic, pp. 41–61.

Bland, Janice (2018c), 'Popular culture head on: Suzanne Collins's *The Hunger Games*', in Janice Bland (ed.), *Using Literature in English Language Education* London: Bloomsbury Academic, pp. 175–92.

Bland, Janice (2018d), 'Annotated bibliography: Literary texts recommended for children and young adults in ELT', in Janice Bland (ed.), *Using Literature in English Language Education*, London: Bloomsbury Academic, pp. 277–300.

Bronson, Po and Merryman, Ashley (2010), 'The creativity crisis', *Newsweek*, 10 July 2010 <http://www.newsweek.com/creativity-crisis-74665> (accessed 12 June 2017).

Brown, Dale (2009), 'Why and how textbooks should encourage extensive reading', *ELT Journal*, 63/3: 238–45.

Brunsmeier, Sonja and Kolb, Annika (2018), 'Story apps: The challenge of interactivity', in Janice Bland (ed.), *Using Literature in English Language Education*, London: Bloomsbury Academic, pp. 105–19.

Byram, Michael (1997), *Teaching and Assessing Intercultural Communicative Competence*, Clevedon: Multilingual Matters.

Carter, Ronald (2015) 'Epilogue: Literature and language learning in the EFL classroom', in Masayuki Teranishi, Yoshifumi Saito and Katie Wales (eds), *Literature and Language Learning in the EFL Classroom*, Basingstoke: Palgrave Macmillan, pp. 316–20.

Clarke, Jane and Clarke, Michael (1990), 'Stereotyping in TESOL materials', in Brian Harrison (ed.), *Culture and the Language Classroom*, The British Council, pp. 31–44.

Coughlan, Sean (2017), 'What does post-truth mean for a philosopher?' *BBC News*, 12 January 2017 <http://www.bbc.com/news/education-38557838> (accessed 24 September 2017).

Delanoy, Werner (2018), 'Literature in language education: Challenges for theory building', in Janice Bland (ed.), *Using Literature in English Language Education*, London: Bloomsbury Academic, pp. 141–57.

Duncan, Sam and Paran, Amos (2018), 'Negotiating the challenges of reading literature: Teachers reporting on their practice', in Janice Bland (ed.), *Using Literature in English Language Education*, London: Bloomsbury Academic, pp. 243–59.

Ellis, Gail (2018), 'The picturebook in elementary ELT: Multiple literacies with Bob Staake's *Bluebird*', in Janice Bland (ed.), *Using Literature in English Language Education*, London: Bloomsbury Academic, pp. 83–104.

Gaiman, Neil (2013), 'Why our future depends on libraries, reading and daydreaming', *The Guardian*, 15 October 2013 < https://www.theguardian.com/books/2013/oct/15/neil-gaiman-future-libraries-reading-daydreaming> (accessed 24 September 2017).

Gardner, Howard (2006), *Five Minds for the Future*, Boston, MA: Harvard Business School.

Gee, James Paul (2001), 'Reading as situated language: A sociocognitive perspective', *Journal of Adolescent & Adult Literacy*, 44/8: 714–25.

Gray, John (2002), 'The global coursebook in English language teaching', in David Block and Deborah Cameron (eds), *Globalization and Language Teaching*, London: Routledge, pp. 151–67.

Gray, John (2016), 'ELT materials: Claims, critiques and controversies', in Graham Hall (ed.), *The Routledge Handbook of English Language Teaching*, Abingdon, Oxon: Routledge, pp. 95–108.

Groenke, Susan and Scherff, Lisa (2010), *Teaching YA Lit through Differentiated Instruction*, Urbana, IL: National Council of Teachers of English.

Hall, Geoff (2016), 'Using literature in ELT', in Graham Hall (ed.), *The Routledge Handbook of English Language Teaching*, Abingdon, Oxon: Routledge, pp. 456–68.

Hall, Geoff (2018), 'Afterword: Thoughts on the way ahead', in Janice Bland (ed.), *Using Literature in English Language Education*, London: Bloomsbury Academic, pp. 261–75.

Hayles, Katherine (2007), 'Hyper and deep attention: The generational divide in cognitive modes', *Profession 2007*, 187–99.

Hoey, Michael (2005), *Lexical Priming: A New Theory of Words and Language*, Abingdon: Routledge.

Hollindale, Peter (1988), 'Ideology and the children's book', *Signal*, 55/1: 3–22.

Hunte, Bem and Golembiewski, Jan (2014), 'Stories have the power to save us: A neurological framework for the imperative to tell stories', *Arts and Social Sciences Journal*, 5/2: 73–6.

Kalogirou, Tzina (2018), 'Hamlet, Ophelia and teenage rage: Michael Lesslie's *Prince of Denmark*', in Janice Bland (ed.), *Using Literature in English Language Education*, London: Bloomsbury Academic, pp.225–40.

Kidd, David and Castano, Emanuele (2013), 'Reading literary fiction improves Theory of Mind', *Science*, 342/6156: 377–80.

Kramsch, Claire (1998), *Language and Culture*, Oxford: Oxford University Press.

Kramsch, Claire (2011), 'The symbolic dimensions of the intercultural', *Language Teaching*, 44/03: 354–67.

Krashen, Stephen (2004), *The Power of Reading*, 2nd edn, Portsmouth, NH: Heinemann.

Krashen, Stephen and Bland, Janice (2014), 'Compelling comprehensible input, academic language and school libraries', *Children's Literature in English Language Education*, 2/2: 1–12.

Leland, Christine, Lewison, Mitzi and Harste, Jerome (2013), *Teaching Children's Literature. It's Critical!*, New York: Routledge.

Macleroy, Vicky (2013), 'Cultural, linguistic and cognitive issues in teaching the language of literature for emergent bilingual pupils', *Language, Culture and Curriculum*, 26/3: 300–16.

McGillis, Roderick (2010), '"Criticism is the Theory of Literature": Theory is the criticism of literature', in David Rudd (ed.), *The Routledge Companion to Children's Literature*, London: Routledge, pp. 14–25.

McGillis, Roderick (2011), 'Literary studies, cultural studies, children's literature, and the case of Jeff Smith', in Karen Coats, Patricia Enciso, Christine Jenkins and Shelby Wolf (eds), *Handbook of Research on Children's and Adult Literature*, New York: Routledge, pp. 345–55.

Marks, Johanna and Merse, Thorsten (2018), 'Diversity in love-themed fiction: John Green's *The Fault in our Stars* and David Levithan's *Princes*', in Janice Bland (ed.), *Using Literature in English Language Education*, London: Bloomsbury Academic, pp. 159–74.

Murphy, Patrick (2000), *Further Afield in the Study of Nature-Oriented Literature*, Charlottesville: University of Virginia Press.

Nation, Kate (2017), 'Nurturing a lexical legacy: Reading experience is critical for the development of word reading skill', *Science of Learning*, 2/3: 1–4.

Nikolajeva, Maria (2014), *Reading for Learning. Cognitive Approaches to Children's Literature*, Amsterdam: John Benjamins.

Oziewicz, Marek (2018), 'The graphic novel: Brian Selznick's *The Invention of Hugo Cabret*, *Wonderstruck* and *The Marvels*', in Janice Bland (ed.), *Using Literature in English Language Education*, London: Bloomsbury Academic, pp. 25–40.

Paran, Amos and Wallace, Catherine (2016), 'Teaching literacy', in Graham Hall (ed.), *The Routledge Handbook of English Language Teaching*, Abingdon, Oxon: Routledge, pp. 441–55.

Prusse, Michael (2018), 'Transmedial reading: Tim Winton's *Lockie Leonard*', in Janice Bland (ed.), *Using Literature in English Language Education*, London: Bloomsbury Academic, pp. 121–37.

Ravitch, Diane (2003), *The Language Police: How Pressure Groups Restrict What Students Learn*, New York: Alfred A. Knopf.

Schmitt, Norbert, Jiang, Xiangying and Grabe, William (2011), 'The percentage of words known in a text and reading comprehension', *The Modern Language Journal*, 95/1: 26–43.

Sullivan, Alice and Brown, Matt (2013), *Social Inequalities in Cognitive Scores at Age 16: The Role of Reading*, London: Centre for Longitudinal Studies, Institute of Education.

Thomson, Pat (2002), *Schooling the Rustbelt Kids: Making the Difference in Changing Times*, Crows Nest, New South Wales: Allen & Unwin.

Tomlinson, Brian (1998), 'And now for something not completely different: An approach to language through literature', *Reading in a Foreign Language*, 11/2: 177–89.

Tschida, Christina, Ryan, Caitlin and Ticknor, Anne (2014), 'Building on windows and mirrors: Encouraging the disruption of "Single Stories" through children's literature', *Journal of Children's Literature*, 40/1: 28–39.

UNESCO (2004), *Education for All. The Quality Imperative. Summary*, Paris: United Nations Educational, Scientific and Cultural Organization.

UNESCO (2017), *Reading the Past, Writing the Future. Fifty Years of Promoting Literacy*, Paris: United Nations Educational, Scientific and Cultural Organization.

Webb, Jean (2018), 'Environmental havoc in teen fiction: Speculating futures', in Janice Bland (ed.), *Using Literature in English Language Education*, London: Bloomsbury Academic, pp. 209–23.

Wehrmann, Jürgen (2018), 'Thought experiments with science fiction: Ursula Le Guin's *The Ones Who Walk Away from Omelas*', in Janice Bland (ed.), *Using Literature in English Language Education*, London: Bloomsbury Academic, pp. 193–208.

Widdowson, Henry (2017), 'Foreword', in Melino Porto and Michael Byram, *New Perspectives on Intercultural Language Research and Teaching: Exploring Learners' Understandings of Texts from Other Cultures*, New York: Routledge, pp. ix–xii.

Wolf, Maryanne and Barzillai, Mirit (2009), 'The importance of Deep Reading. What will it take for the next generation to read thoughtfully – both in print and online?', *Educational Leadership*, 66/6: 32–7.

PART ONE

Multimodal challenges

2

The graphic novel: Brian Selznick's THE INVENTION OF HUGO CABRET, WONDERSTRUCK and THE MARVELS

Marek Oziewicz

For over a decade now, the graphic novel has been the most contested format of contemporary literature. On the one hand, the term's wide currency suggests that it has become a permanent fixture of our literary mindscape. All undergraduates I have worked with in the United States were familiar with the term, even if sometimes unsure of its meaning. The overwhelming majority had no problems whatsoever in distinguishing graphic novels from novels or picturebooks they were shown and most were able to name at least a few graphic novels they had read previously. On the other hand, a number of literary critics, cartoonists, and authors of works considered, by many, graphic novels, have repeatedly dismissed the term. According to this line of argument, the graphic novel is nothing more than an 'ungainly neologism' for comics (Spiegelman 2010: xxii), a 'euphemistic and distinctly apologetic term' (Goggin and Hassler-Forest 2010: 2). Its popularity is due to 'marketing departments' efforts to make comics more palatable to the general public' (Abel and Madden 2008: 6).

The questions whether there is such a thing as a graphic novel and, if so, whether graphic novels are or are not comics may seem like a scholarly quibble. Yet, it has profound implications for educational practice. One of the key challenges in teaching literature is to help young people develop an understanding of how different kinds of narratives work and what their building blocks are. To label a work a novel activates a different set of expectations than those for, say, a poem, a screenplay, or a picturebook. In particular, the ability to distinguish genre from medium and format empowers young readers to better process new texts they encounter. On a more cognitively advanced level, it hones their critical literacy skills for identifying what the text seeks to achieve, and how genres and formats hybridize to create new wholes.

This chapter argues that graphic novels may be theorized as a format distinct from comics. It locates the graphic novel on a spectrum of sequential art alongside comic strips, comics and picturebooks, and offers a work-in-progress taxonomy of the graphic novel categories. The case for graphic novels as different from comics is supported by an examination of Brian Selznick's *The Invention of Hugo Cabret* (2007), *Wonderstruck* (2011) and *The Marvels* (2015). The reflection is informed by discussions with undergraduate students in two courses taught at the University of Minnesota in 2015–16 and 2016–17. I also draw on twenty-nine anonymous responses to 'The What and How of the Graphic Novel' survey I conducted in 2016. The conclusions and activities go some way to help teachers tackle the challenge of discussing graphic novels in the classroom.

Theories and approaches

The body of theoretical reflection on narratives that blend the verbal and the pictorial text is immense. Despite overlaps, it represents traditions that developed within different fields and have retained their field-specific foci. Research into picturebooks began in the mid-1970s in overlap with a growing interest in the art of children's book illustration. Joseph Schwarcz's *Ways of the Illustrator: Visual Communication in Children's Literature* (1982) was one of the first modern book-length studies in this tradition. The graphic novel was first theorized in Will Eisner's *Comics and Sequential Art* (1985). Finally, the long-overdue appreciation of comics was offered by Scott McCloud in 1993; his *Understanding Comics* was groundbreaking and remains the most widely used textbook in the field. While this study remains indispensable, McCloud's definition of comics is overreaching. Since Eisner and McCloud proposed two different frameworks for theorizing pictorial art, the bulk of modern reflection about comics and graphic novels – especially graphic novels *as* comics – has developed from a critical engagement with their claims.

The key difference between the two frameworks is not hard to grasp. Eisner proposed the umbrella term 'sequential art' to describe 'a means of creative expression [...] and literary form that deals with the arrangement of pictures or images and words to narrate a story or dramatize an idea'

(1985: 5). His premise – also expressed by the title *Comics **and** Sequential Art* – is that sequential art is not the same as comics. Rather, it operates through different outlets, among which comic strips, comic books, and graphic novels are three developmentally staggered but not identical formats (1985: 7). Although Eisner does not mention other formats, his open-ended approach allows accommodating picturebooks, illustrated books, airline safety instruction sheets, murals, photo essays, webcomics, photo booth faceshot strips and other combinations of images – or images and words – as different formats of sequential art: each unique, though sharing overlaps with others.

McCloud's approach, in turn, borrows Eisner's umbrella term but drops its inclusive meaning. Instead of *all comics being examples of sequential art*, McCloud assumes that *all sequential art is comics*. In his definition, comics are 'juxtaposed pictorial and other images in deliberate sequence, intended to convey information and/or to produce an aesthetic response in the viewer' (1993: 9). This ahistorical framework subsumes any story told in pictures – from Egyptian murals to the Bayeux Tapestry and diverse sequential modern art forms – under the name of comics.

Discussing the implications of these frameworks with my students, we have arrived at two insights. First, most students agreed that McCloud has done more than Eisner to reclaim for comics the status of legitimate art, and that his catch-all definition was an important part of that reclaiming. Even if Mayan Codices and other works that McCloud takes as comics are not comics, they feature elements of 'the picture-story' (1993: 16) that also characterizes comics, which positions comics not as an upstart art form but part of a long, venerable tradition. Second, although they appreciated the historic value of McCloud's approach, few students were comfortable with its implications. If any art form that includes two or more pictures in a deliberate sequence is a comic, then almost everything is a comic, from quick start instructions for an electronic device to clusters of icon-signs in public transport or a set of murals on a monument's plinth. Especially when it came to picturebooks, students refused to call them comics. Likewise, not one of the twenty-nine respondents in the survey answered 'yes' to the question 'Are picturebooks one special type of comic books?': 52 per cent answered 'not at all' and further 28 per cent 'rather not'. This uneasiness about conflating picturebooks and comics – albeit qualified by caveats that the two cannot be distinguished in any absolute way – was most vocally expressed by a panel uniting four scholars (Annual MLA Convention, 7 January 2012) on 'Why Comics Are and Are Not Picturebooks'. Perry Nodelman suggests that the two formats are so different that '[a]pproaching comics with the meaning-making strategies I have derived from my experience of picture books is something like lacking gills' (2012: 463). Philip Nel, even while discussing key formal differences, stresses similarities. 'Comics and picture books differ in degree', he states, 'rather than in kind' (2012: 445).

This 'difference-in-degree' position is widely shared and appears to be more aligned with Eisner's than McCloud's framework. Accordingly, I have found it more productive to use sequential art rather than comics as the umbrella term for a variety of art forms that blend the pictorial and the verbal text. This does not mean that sequential art is the only possible general label: any among several terms proposed so far may do – graphic narratives, 'graphica' (Kiefer and Tyson 2013: 80), picture stories, visual or pictorial narratives, 'sequential visual narratives' (Cohn 2016: 1) or others. The advantage of these terms is that they are relatively neutral, fuzzy categories. Comics, by contrast, is a culturally loaded term hard to disentangle from its troubled, albeit exciting history. As 'literature' is a vague yet handy umbrella term for various formats, genres and articulations of narrative fiction, 'sequential art' appears a convenient, open-ended umbrella term for a range of art forms that blend the pictorial and verbal 'to narrate a story or dramatize an idea' (Eisner 1985: 5).

Differentiating comics and graphic novels

Within sequential art, is there a difference between comics and graphic novels? That, obviously, depends on what framework one adopts. In my experience, scholarship aligned with McCloud's assumptions is either hostile towards the graphic novel or tolerates it as a highbrow synonym for comics. The more radical scholars in this group completely ignore the term. Paul Gravett, for example, opens *Graphic Novels: Everything You Need to Know* by stating that 'there is nothing to be gained by defining it' (2005: 9). Others denounce it for obfuscating the true nature of comics. In *On the Graphic Novel*, Santiago García insists the graphic novel has 'no a priori stylistic features' that set it apart from comics (2010: x) and adds that 'the well-intended insistence on viewing comics as literature by authors like Eisner has done nothing more than harm to the general view of comics, since it has made it possible to judge comics using criteria proper to literature, instead of criteria specific to comics' (2010: 14). A more nuanced inflection of this position, exemplified by Charles Hatfield, takes the graphic novel to be 'a term of convenience [...] increasingly used by booksellers to bracket a dizzying range of disparate comics' (2005: 30). According to Hatfield, the graphic novel is a 'long-form comic' (2005: 5) that differs from the open-ended, serialized comic book in being a format that accommodates 'genres of the self-contained story, the novel, or the memoir' (2005: 6). This line of thought, in which graphic novels are 'comic books that deal with more literary topics' (Yang 2014: 125), acknowledges graphic novels as literature and finds ample support among literary critics. All definitions of the graphic novel as 'a longer and more artful version of the comic book bound as a "real" book' (Schwarz 2006: 58), or 'an extended comic book' (Tabachnick 2009: 2) project the graphic novel as a type of comics.

Built into the notion that graphic novels are comics is an assumption that the graphic novel must necessarily be crafted in what has variously been called the comic or cartoon style: featuring multiple panels per page, gutters, speech and thought bubbles, motion lines and other structural conventions characteristic of the comic page layout. Indeed, this is often the case. However, what is one to do with a body of literature that relies heavily on the pictorial narrative but does not draw on the comic style, as is the case with Selznick's work? How should one classify chapter books in which the pictorial narrative – sometimes two or more illustrations per page – is integral to the story, as in Obert Skye's *Wonkenstein* (2011), André Marois and Patrick Doyon's *The Sandwich Thief* (2013) or Dasha Tolstikova's *A Year Without Mom* (2015)? What term best describes picturebook-novels such as those by Matt Phelan, Peter Sis and Shaun Tan or wordless woodcut-novels by Lynd Ward? An alternative may be found in a taxonomy based on Eisner's approach, which strives to recover elbow room for formats other than comics. This line of inquiry is a recent development, informing, among others, Francisca Goldsmith's *The Reader's Advisory Guide to Graphic Novels* (2010) and Jan Baetens and Hugo Frey's *The Graphic Novel: An Introduction* (2015). Both works locate the graphic novel on the continuum of sequential art that comprises comics, but whose closed-endedness and other formal features set it apart from comics. From this perspective, comics can no longer be a 'simple shorthand for a comic strip, comic book, or graphic novel – or for a picture book divided into panels ...' (Op de Beeck 2012: 472–3).

What then is a graphic novel?

In Eisner's framework, the graphic novel is one of the four key formats of sequential art, alongside comics, picturebooks and comic strips. The format is the vehicle of the story's delivery, independent of content and type of narrative, which are described by the term genre. As a 'publishing format' (Hatfield 2005: 4) with 'some definable responsibility to "bookness": that is, to the conventional form, history, or authority of the book' (Joseph 2012: 466), the graphic novel is 'a mode of production' (Op de Beeck 2010: 11) that gives rise to specific material commodities called graphic novels. In their materiality, these commodities are 'scriptive things' that prompt – or *script* – a specific kind of bodily performance (Bernstein 2011: 71) – in this case, a reading protocol for the narrative experience. As Joe Sutliff Sanders has demonstrated, one way to distinguish picturebooks from comics is to compare them as scriptive things: these formats are different, Sanders contends, because they anticipate 'different reading situations' (2013: 59). Likewise, I suggest that the graphic novel differs from picturebooks and comics primarily as a scriptive thing. When compared to the other three formats of sequential art, the graphic novel accommodates most extended, self-standing works of fiction and nonfiction published in the form of books and albums. Like all sequential art, it is predicated on the primacy of the visual medium – one that has to be seen to be fully appreciated – but has fewer restrictions on design, style, content and formula of picture–word interaction than the other three formats.

Thus, prototypical comics and comic strips employ panels and gutters as their primary means of expression, but graphic novels may forego panels in favour of single- or double-page spreads and ignore the affordances of the gutter. Also, in prototypical picturebooks the pace of the story is set primarily through page turns, but graphic novels may rely on that effect only in part or not at all. Lastly, graphic novels can handle any amount of verbal narrative, which is not the case for comic strips, comics and picturebooks. There is no such thing as a graphic novel that is too text-heavy.

An additional advantage of discussing the graphic novel as a format is increased clarity on its relationship to the term genre. Genre is a fluid category, of course, but it refers primarily to *the type of story content* the reader will experience – historical fiction, fantasy, romance and so on – rather than to *how* that story will be delivered. And the *how* is exactly what the format is all about. Since any format of sequential art can accommodate almost any genre combinations, the graphic novel's generic range spans memoir, biography, historical fiction, contemporary realistic fiction, fantasy, romance, ghost stories and many other genres.

Finally, given the wide diversity of graphic novels, I found it helpful to postulate three non-exclusive categories. Graphic Novel Firsts (GNFs), such as Eisner's *A Contract with God*, are works envisioned and originally created in the graphic novel format – works dubbed 'one-shot "novel" [graphic narratives]' (Baetens and Frey 2015: 56). Graphic Novel Compilations (GNCs) – a category of 'novel-length volumes that had originally been serialized' (Hatfield 2005: 29) – include collected volumes of previously serialized comic books such as Jeff Smith's *Bone*. Lastly, Graphic Novel Adaptations (GNAs) comprise graphic novel versions of pre-existing works such as Craig Russell's adaptation of Neil Gaiman's *The Graveyard Book*. Although many graphic novels fall into two or three categories at the same time, this taxonomy helps distinguish signature markers of each category, such as the execution of the complete story arc in GNFs, the stamp of episodic structure, with opening recaps and end-of-chapter cliffhangers, that characterizes most GNCs, or the constraints of the pre-existing original that impacts the creation of GNAs.

Brian Selznick's graphic novel 'invention'

To examine the graphic novel as a format helps reveal how pictorial storytelling conventions – developed in comics, comic strip, picturebook, book illustration and even film traditions – may hybridize with the verbal narrative to create new constellations. And it is in this sense that Brian Selznick's novels offer perhaps the best example of how graphic novels may come to be and how they work. The challenge of reading Selznick's books as graphic novels is all the more exciting because they have so far been taken as unclassifiables. The publisher's website for *The Invention of Hugo Cabret* quotes Selznick's statement that the book is 'not exactly a novel, and it's not quite a picture book, and it's not really a graphic novel, or a flip book, or a movie, but a combination of all these things' (Selznick 2007, 'About': np). In the taxonomy proposed above, however, *Hugo Cabret* is clearly a GNF. And if *The Invention of Hugo Cabret* is taken as Selznick's own graphic novel 'invention' – modelled on his expertise as a picturebook artist – *Wonderstruck* and *The Marvels* represent Selznick's continuing experimentation with the affordances of the graphic novel format.

In discussing the three books, I invite students to reflect on the following true story. On 22 September 2015, I sat in the audience at the University of St Thomas in St Paul, MN, listening to Selznick's talk on his newly released *The Marvels*. Recalling the creative journey, Selznick said that he had initially written *Hugo Cabret* as a novel: the contract with Scholastic projected it as an up to a 100-page text. Only after completing it, Selznick thought of replacing chunks of verbal narrative with image sequences. He sent the first batch of pictures to the editor with a suggestion to substitute them for a specific descriptive passage. The editor liked the idea and Selznick began drawing other episodes until the book ballooned to 530 pages.

Based on this account, I ask students to identify traces of this creative process – the replacing of verbal with pictorial text. Invariably, they find (1) action sequences that depict movement, and (2) panoramic-and-action sequences that provide context about time and setting for events. What all these sequences share, they notice, is lack of dialogue. This allows pictorial representation to capture the scene in a non-verbal mode and provide visual details that would otherwise be lost in a dialogue-focused account. To appreciate the difference, students create and compare verbal descriptions of an action sequence: Hugo looking around the bookstore and finding a specific book (Selznick 2007: 178–85), chased by the Station Inspector (416–51), or watching the incoming train before being yanked out of the tracks (460–9). In each case, they find that even detailed descriptions have a qualitatively different feel than the 'suspended animation' mode of presentation, which, through page turns, creates an experience of 'a sort of extracinematic montage'

(Op de Beeck 2010: ix). They likewise comment that the night sky sequence which opens the first chapter (Selznick 2007: 2–45) not only establishes the story's time, place and the protagonist's exact location but also sets the tone and raises questions about the story in the reader's mind. Again, it is possible to tell this story in words, but the pictorial narrative – with its shifting focus and zooming – offers a different context than words ever could.

Upon closer inspection, students also spot three other types of pictorial representations: (3) single-picture images, (4) photographic inserts, and (5) book-in-a-book or film-in-a-book artwork. A number of single-picture images are illustrations. Some could, potentially, be eliminated without diminishing the story – like Isabelle's face framed by the lines 'then he recognized the girl' (100) and 'It was the girl from the toy booth' (102) – albeit there is never complete redundancy because of the difference in mode. Other images include the level of detail – such as Hugo cranking the station clock (78–9) – that add specifics even to a lengthy verbal description in which they are couched (76–80). Selznick also employs single-picture illustrations for a dramatic effect to reveal objects or characters for the first time, as is the case with the automaton (110–11), or Etienne (170–1). Some single-picture images are photographic inserts, like the photo of the 1895 train derailment at Gare Montparnasse (382–3) or the Harold Lloyd still from *Safety Last* (174–5). In fact, students quickly realize that most photographic inserts – single-picture or sequences – are stills from early silent films (348–9, 352–3), including those by Georges Méliès (498–505), reproductions of his original sketches (284–7) and stills illustrating Méliès' 'substitution trick' effect (355). All of these reinforce the book's themes of celebrating Méliès' pioneering work and the art of film as a modern form of magic. The intermedial quality of *Hugo Cabret* – its representation of film through the pictorial mode – is likewise highlighted through book-in-a-book artwork (52–9), in which the reader sees Papa Georges reading Hugo's notebook, and through film-in-a-book artwork (194–201) in which characters watch a film. The filmic feel is additionally pronounced through the novel's opening and closing pictorial sequences as well as by the thick black framing of all pages.

With all those pictorial elements being integral to the book's effect, does *Hugo Cabret* retain markers of being a novel? Would it perhaps be correct to call it an illustrated book, or a picturebook – as the Caldecott committee did in 2008? Students felt that the two latter labels are inadequate. If anything, *Hugo Cabret* is a novel, but also something more. The key features of the novel that the students were able to name include the material form, especially the book trim size, structural division into chapters and/or parts and a complex, self-standing story recounted in a verbal narrative. *Hugo Cabret* has all these but is also, as Selznick states on the title page, 'a novel in words and pictures'. These pictures, in turn, reshape the prototypical novel structure. Specifically, although the chapter division is retained, the pictures are unpaginated picturebook-style double-page spreads. Such formatting privileges narrative movement through page turn (Selznick 2007, 'About': np) and trumps the mode of page breakdown typical for novels. Thus, when the amount of text between two pictorial sequences is less than what fills two pages, the verbal narrative is laid out as two symmetrical half-pages of text blocks (120–1), in some cases only two or three lines in length (108–9). This clean separation of the pictorial from the verbal represents 'the classic arrangement' tradition in children's book illustrations (Schwarcz 1982: 13). It forces the reader to attend to the two modes one by one, even though the total effect of *Hugo Cabret* depends on their integration. The amount of white space dictated by varying text lengths and elaborate decorations of chapter openings – always on the recto page with the verso page black – adds to the effect of images in drawing the reader's attention to the material, visual experience of the book.

The novelistic exposition is not lost though. As students realize when asked to look at examples of text-to-pictures and pictures-to-text transitions, the two modes flow seamlessly into one another. The description of how Hugo 'undid the knot' (Selznick 2007: 135), followed by an image of his hand holding a handkerchief with ashes (136–7) and transitioning to 'Hugo touched the ashes' (138) is an example of mode couching that Selznick employs to the best effect. This technique, called 'alternate progress', refers to narrative movement in which 'text and picture tak[e] turns in continuing the story, with some of the steps in the plot presented only once, by either of the two' (Schwarcz 1982: 15). Selznick himself calls it the 'relay race' (2016: np) and employs this technique to achieve the effect, in which, upon finishing the book, 'the reader wouldn't remember what parts of the story had been told in words and what part in pictures' (np). And that is how, in *Hugo Cabret*, Brian Selznick invented his own articulation of the graphic novel format.

Continuing experimentation with *Wonderstruck* and *The Marvels*

Selznick's experiment did not stop there. When students look at *Wonderstruck* and *The Marvels*, they note that each work introduces a new constellation of pictorial, verbal and other textual elements. *Wonderstruck* – which, referring to the method of *Hugo Cabret*, has been called 'a sequel of method, and a test of it' (Gopnik 2011: np) – offers interlaced stories of Rose and Ben, with Rose's story told only in pictures and Ben's story narrated only in words. The stories of Part One and Two blend in Part Three when the characters meet, at which point the book resumes the alternate progress method developed in

Hugo Cabret. Unlike *Hugo* though, *Wonderstruck* features two protagonists, two settings and two time periods: 'Gunflint Lake, Minnesota, June 1977' for Ben – told in words – and 'Hoboken, New Jersey, October 1927' for Rose, told in pictures. Students are first asked to look at text-to-pictures and pictures-to-text transitions. They discover that the change of mode marks a switch from one character's story to the other, even though how exactly the stories are connected remains a guess. This is a good time to ask about their predictions: Will the characters meet? What are the connections between them? Why are their stories interlaced rather than told separately? Finally, can each story stand alone and what would be lost if it did?

One activity that helps stimulate discussion about these questions is to ask students to reread the pictorial narrative while ignoring the verbal, or scan the verbal narrative without looking at pictorial sequences. In both cases students considered each narrative coherent and self-standing. Those who read the verbal text paid special attention to text-to-text transitions between paragraphs separated by pictorial sequences rather than page turns. They noticed how smoothly Ben's narrative flows from the moment it breaks off to when it resumes several pages later. In some instances – like in the transition between 'He grabbed the red flashlight and slipped silently out of his cousin's house' (Selznick 2011: 57) and 'Water lapped at the dock, and the boats clacked against one another' (68) – the action continues with no temporal gap. In other episodes, the verbal narrative is paused by the pictorial to reinforce a temporal break and a fast-forward in the story. This is the case with Ben falling asleep in the hospital bed (177), followed by his waking up on the bus to New York City a few days later (226). Students who read the pictorial narrative of Part One, in turn, identified eleven sequences of double-page spreads totalling eighty-three pictures that recount the events of two days. Although no less coherent than the verbal narrative, the story leaves a number of questions unanswered. Except for a few notes written by characters, no words are spoken and the reader does not know why the protagonist is confined at home. The name 'Rose' may be guessed from a postcard the girl pulls out at one point and the fact that she is deaf may be inferred from the book her tutor brings, but all these are merely conjectures. Nor is it clear, despite the apparent fascination with Lillian Mayhew, why the girl escapes to New York City. All these questions, however, are part of pictorial reading: as students reflect on it, far from diminishing the experience, the images' 'visual silence' (Selznick 2016: np) draws the reader in. Most importantly, students learn to appreciate how, by silencing the girl's story, Selznick allows the reader to glimpse a deaf person's situatedness in the world 'in a way that parallels [Rose's] experience'. As Selznick puts it: 'The silence of the pictures is a metaphor for the silence of her world' (np).

If each story can stand alone, why does Selznick choose to weave them together? At this point, I invite students to identify the links between Rose's and Ben's plot lines to explain what Selznick achieves by interlacing them. The answer, invariably, is that the narrative is richer as each character's story receives a deeper context through being told against the background of the other story – especially a story told in a different mode, with each mode switch activating different narrative processing. On the level of structure, Selznick's choice of text-to-pictures and pictures-to-text transitions emerges as a fundamental strategy to connect the two stories – and characters – in the reader's mind. Ben slipping silently out of the house (Selznick 2011: 57) ushers in a picture of Rose doing the same when she climbs out through her window (58); Ben's arrival in New York City (227) proceeds into the picture of the 'Welcome to New York' sign Rose sees upon her arrival (228); the picture of lightning that tears the sky when Rose walks home after the film (155) transitions into 'When Ben opened his eyes, he was lying on the floor, staring at the ceiling' (156), following which the text offers multiple hints that the protagonist was hit by lightning. Numerous other transitions present the characters doing similar things, facing similar challenges and going through similar emotional anguish – often in the same physical space. These links create a number of thematic parallels between the characters' lives. Rose is looking for a place to belong and so is Ben; Rose is born deaf whereas Ben becomes deaf after the accident; both love museums and collecting objects: some of these objects, such as the locket and the *Wonderstruck* book, connect their lives through people who had owned them. This elaborate structure, in which pictorial sequences frame shorter verbal units, allows Selznick to eliminate traditional chapter division. In fact, the narrative moves back and forth in time, requiring a significant effort on the reader's part to understand the connections.

The Marvels presents yet another variation on the interplay of the pictorial and verbal. It is again two stories in the two modes but with no interlacing. The pictorial narrative of wordless double-page spreads encompasses the first 391 pages. It is followed by a verbal narrative in 206 pages, closed by a pictorial sequence chapter of 55 pages. While the two parts, as in *Wonderstruck*, are identified by dates, the chronology is more complicated. The initial year, 1766, marks the beginning of a story of five generations that extends until roughly 1900. Part two picks up the Marvels' family story in 1990, to develop it until 2007. More structurally complex than the first two books, *The Marvels* challenges the reader through its extended chronology. In reading the pictorial story, students particularly enjoyed five activities: One was figuring out time gaps between specific sequences or images, including discussion on why certain events are extended in narrative time – like the opening performance-and-shipwreck sequence (Selznick 2015: 1–110) – whereas others are compressed into a single page turn transition between images, such as Billy growing into an adult (147–52). Two, another group examined how Selznick uses words embedded in pictures to provide information that the image cannot convey and why he chose to do it for some episodes – as with the gravestone that names Marcus as Billy's brother (93–4) – but withhold it for others, as with details about Billy's life (111–12). Three, and no less exciting, was a search for visual details and objects that recur in the pictorial story to reappear in the verbal narrative, especially the bird locket. Four, an interesting discussion arose around the significant amount of newspaper clippings embedded in the pictorial story, especially dense on pages 213–22, as to whether Selznick cheats by smuggling in verbal narrative pretending to be images. Students commented that these textual images reveal the limitations of the pictorial narrative while paradoxically remaining pictorial – as if the reader were not supposed to read the entire text but merely steal a glimpse of its fragment. Others noted that textual images allow the author to fast-forward between significant moments of the story without getting bogged down in details of intervening years. Activity five, again on the relationship between pictorial and verbal reading, had a group of students trying to reconstruct the story Alexander tells Leo about his family (281–302), and guessing whether Leo and Alexander get out of the theatre alive when the pictorial narrative breaks off (391–2).

Primed by the pictorial story, in the second part students were keen to look for connections between the narrative present of the text and the previously recounted past. Although I am unable to address here the many themes and ways in which Selznick makes the narrative compelling – in fact, some students felt that the text *could* stand on its own as a novel – when read as part of the graphic novel whole, the second part is incomparably richer. Joseph's discovery of the house at 18 Folgate Street is a discovery of his family's history, which the reader has already glimpsed through images, but the questions of truth and authorship get complicated. Students admitted that they had never wondered about the authorship of the pictorial story in the first part: they took it, simply, as the story that happened – as if the images were a non-interpretative account. Retrospectively, however, they see them as a creative reimagining of the family story drawn by Billy Marvel. Like Joseph, they 'hear' Albert's tape recordings, which break at the same point as the pictorial narrative. They participate in Joseph's quest for truth – including learning the background of Eleonora Marvel, nee Mabel Hatch (502) – which allows them to better appreciate how the pictorial and verbal narratives complement each other. Two other aspects students identified as highlights of this part include how Selznick weaves the fictional story of the Marvels family into another fictional family, the Jervises, who inhabit the Dennis Severs House installation, and then into biographical facts in the lives of the real Dennis Severs and David Milne. 'My story is a fiction built on the truth of their lives', Selznick declares, 'in much the same way that the story-within-the-story of *The Marvels* is a fiction built on the truth of Albert's and Billy's lives' (654). This masterful mélange of truth and fiction, past and present, is epitomized in the final transition from the verbal to the pictorial (604–5), in which the image of the fire both continues the pictorial story of the first part and merges it with the verbal narrative of the second. If Dennis Sever's House is 'a three-dimensional historical novel written in brick and candlelight' (660), *The Marvels* achieves its three-dimensionality through the interplay of Selznick's signature black-and-white chiaroscuro images and a verbal narrative, whose fictionality celebrates real-life people and places.

Conclusion

Taken separately, each articulation of the symbiosis between the pictorial and the verbal in *The Invention of Hugo Cabret*, *Wonderstruck* and *The Marvels* is a cabinet of wonders. Taken together, they represent some of the compelling opportunities and challenges inherent in the graphic novel format. Exploring these with students helps them realize how our experience of any story is always mediated via a story system, how sequential art may be theorized as a system comprised of at least four main formats – graphic novels, comics, picturebooks and comic strips – and how the formats differ as scriptive things that invite, script and challenge unique kinds of reading experience. Most of all, conceptualizing Selznick's works as graphic novels rather than unclassifiable hybrids changes students' understanding of the graphic novel. They begin to see it as a format that enjoys a kinship relation with the picturebook, the novel and comics, but – as with Selznick's books – cannot be reduced to any of these.

RECOMMENDATIONS

- Brian Selznick's storyworlds are inspired by cultural phenomena in the real worlds of Paris, New York and London. Students can be encouraged to autonomously investigate and present to peers the fascinating history of pioneer moviemaking (*Hugo Cabret*), the *Panorama of the City of New York*, the jewel in the crown of Queens Museum, New York (*Wonderstruck*) and the seemingly enchanted Dennis Severs' House Installation in Spitalfields, London (*The Marvels*).

- Students might consider to what extent the different media represented in Selznick's work – print medium (pictorial and verbal narrative modes) and movies in *Hugo Cabret*, print medium and museum artefacts in *Wonderstruck* and print medium and theatre in *The Marvels* – work together harmoniously to emphasize the power of story. The meticulous craft of Selznick's narrative might be compared to *antinarrative*, discussed in Bland (2018c: 181, this volume): the world is now screened for us in multiple ways, but commonly the 'artistic integrity and carefully crafted story patterns are lacking'.

Bibliography

Eisner, Will (1978), *A Contract with God*, New York: Baronet Books.

Gaiman, Neil (2008), *The Graveyard Book*, London: Bloomsbury.

Gaiman, Neil and Russell, Craig (2014), *The Graveyard Book Graphic Novel*, New York: HarperCollins Children's Books.

Marois, André and Doyon, Patrick (2013), *The Sandwich Thief*, San Francisco: Chronicle Books.

Phelan, Matt (2013), *Bluffton: My Summers with Buster*, Somerville, MA: Candlewick Press.

Safety Last (1923), [Film] Dir. Fred Newmeyer and Sam Taylor, US: Hal Roach Studios.

Selznick, Brian (2007), *The Invention of Hugo Cabret*, New York: Scholastic.

Selznick, Brian (2011), *Wonderstruck*, New York: Scholastic.

Selznick, Brian (2015), *The Marvels*, New York: Scholastic.

Sis, Peter (2011), *The Conference of the Birds*, New York: Penguin.

Skye, Obert (2011), *Wonkenstein: A Creature from My Closet*, New York: Henry Holt.

Smith, Jeff (2004), *Bone: The Complete Cartoon Epic in One Volume*, Columbus, OK: Cartoon Books.

Tan, Shaun (2007), *The Arrival*, New York: Arthur A. Levine Books.

Tolstikova, Dasha (2015), *A Year Without Mom*, Toronto: Greenwood Books.

Ward, Lynd (2010), *God's Man, Madman's Drum, Wild Pilgrimage*, New York: The Library of America.

References

Abel, Jessica and Madden, Matt (2008), *Drawing Words and Writing Pictures: A Definitive Course from Concept to Comic in 15 Lessons*, New York: First-Second.

Baetens, Jan and Frey, Hugo (2015), *The Graphic Novel: An Introduction*, New York: Cambridge University Press.

Bernstein, Robin (2011), *Racial Innocence: Performing American Childhood from Slavery to Civil Rights*, New York: New York University Press.

Bland, Janice (2018c), 'Popular culture head on: Suzanne Collins' *The Hunger Games*', in Janice Bland (ed.), *Using Literature in English Language*

Education: Challenging Reading for 8–18 Year Olds, London: Bloomsbury Academic, pp. 175–92.

Cohn, Neil (2016), 'Interdisciplinary approaches to visual narrative', in Neil Cohn (ed.), *The Visual Narrative Reader*, London: Bloomsbury, pp. 1–15.

García, Santiago (2010), *On the Graphic Novel*, trans. Bruce Campbell, Jackson, MS: University of Mississippi Press.

Gravett, Paul (2005), *Graphic Novels: Everything You Need to Know*, New York: HarperCollins.

Goggin, Joyce and Hassler-Forest Dan (2010), 'Introduction', in Joyce Goggin and Dan Hassler-Forest (eds), *Rise and Reason of Comics and Graphic Literature: Critical Essays on the Form*, , Jefferson, NC: McFarland, pp. 1–4.

Goldsmith, Francisca (2010), *The Reader's Advisory Guide to Graphic Novels*, Chicago: ALA.

Gopnik, Adam (2011), 'A deaf boy's New York quest', *The New York Times*, 16 September 2011 <http://www.nytimes.com/2011/09/18/books/review/wonderstruck-written-and-illustrated-by-brian-selznick-book-review.html?_r=2> (accessed 28 December 2016).

Eisner, Will (1985), *Comics and Sequential Art*, Tamarac, FL: Poorhouse Press.

Hatfield, Charles (2005), *Alternative Comics: An Emerging Literature*, Jackson, MS: University Press of Mississippi.

Joseph, Michael (2012), 'Seeing the visible book: How graphic novels resist reading', *Children's Literature Association Quarterly*, 37/4: 454–67.

Kiefer, Barbara and Tyson, Cynthia (2013), *Charlotte Huck's Children's Literature: A Brief Guide*, 2nd edn, New York: McGraw-Hill.

McCloud, Scott (1993), *Understanding Comics: The Invisible Art*, New York: William Morrow.

Nel, Philip (2012), 'Same genus, different species? Comics and picture books', *Children's Literature Association Quarterly*, 37/4: 445–53.

Nodelman, Perry (2012), 'Picture book guy looks at comics: Structural differences in two kinds of visual narrative', *Children's Literature Association Quarterly*, 37/4: 436–44.

Op de Beeck, Nathalie (2010), *Suspended Animation: Children's Picture Books and the Fairy Tale of Modernity*, Minneapolis: University of Minnesota Press.

Op de Beeck, Nathalie (2012), 'On comics-style picture books and picture-bookish comics', *Children's Literature Association Quarterly*, 37/4: 468–76.

Sanders, Joe Sutliff (2013), 'Chaperoning words: Meaning-making in comics and picture books', *Children's Literature*, 41: 57–90.

Schwarcz, Joseph (1982), *Ways of the Illustrator: Visual Communication in Children's Literature*, Chicago: ALA.

Schwarz, Gretchen (2006), 'Expanding literacies through graphic novels', *English Journal*, 95/6: 58–64.

Selznick, Brian (2007), 'About Hugo Cabret', *The Invention of Hugo Cabret Official Website* <http://www.theinventionofhugocabret.com/about_hugo_intro.htm> (accessed 29 January 2017).

Selznick, Brian (2016), 'I wanted my story to exist between pictures and words', *The Guardian*, 8 November 2016 <https://www.theguardian.com/books/booksblog/2016/nov/08/brian-selznick-on-visual-novel-the-marvels-guardian-childrens-fiction-prize> (accessed 7 January 2017).

Spiegelman, Art (2010), 'Reading pictures: A few thousand words on six books without any', in Art Spiegelman (ed.), *Lynd Ward: God's Man, Madman's Drum, Wild Pilgrimage*, New York: Penguin Group, pp. ix–xxv.

Tabachnick, Stephen, ed. (2009), *Teaching the Graphic Novel*, New York: MLA.

Yang, Gene Luen, Oziewicz, Marek and Midkiff, Emily (2014), 'The "Asian Invasion": An interview with Gene Luen Yang', *The Lion and the Unicorn*, 38/1: 123–33.

3

Playscript and screenplay: Creativity with J. K. Rowling's WIZARDING WORLD

Janice Bland

One of the most attractive aspects of J. K. Rowling's Wizarding World for teenagers is its familiarity. This still expanding storyworld is full of characters intimate and dear to huge numbers of readers and cinemagoers worldwide, particularly those who grew up alongside the heroes of the seven *Harry Potter* books. Studies have shown that the series has stayed with readers more than their other reading (Kozlowska 2014). Moreover many of the millennial generation of recently qualified teachers attest to the influence of *Harry Potter* on their well-being while at vulnerable stages in their lives. Doors are magically opened in both *Harry Potter and the Cursed Child* (Thorne 2016) and *Fantastic Beasts and Where to Find Them, Original Screenplay* (Rowling 2016); and metaphorically speaking, these hugely popular works can open doors to the world of literacy. They can support creativity and literacy development, including critical literacy, at a stage when young people may be deeply immersed and experienced in virtual worlds but still lack understanding of the real world. This lack is short term, but while it lasts it is a stumbling block for the adult canon – simplified versions of adult classics included. When teachers supply lacking background knowledge and 'model interpretations' to such classics, they have unwittingly chosen a simplistic solution, blocking opportunities for dialogic transactions and deep reading. Finally, popular books such as these form a young adult canon, and offer an opportunity for bonding between teachers and their students. The enthusiasm and curiosity of the students may surprise and animate their teachers. Additionally the enthusiasm of students and teachers combined may ignite those teenagers who have not hitherto discovered that books can be a source of joy.

Creativity in the language classroom

Despite the various constraints of school curricula, creative processes, especially those without an emphasis on specific creative products, could be woven into a great deal of school subject teaching. The teaching of ELT offers huge opportunities that accord with what has been called the Four Cs of twenty-first-century education – Communication, Collaboration, Critical Thinking and Creativity (Barnett 2010). As ELT now often spans as many as ten or twelve years of schooling, clearly this space should be able to offer scope for these important goals to be developed in the medium of the target language. However, whereas communicative language teaching – the dominant paradigm of language teaching in many parts of the world for much of the last four decades – involves communication and collaboration as essential ingredients, critical thinking and especially creativity tend to lag behind.

The phenomenon known widely as the Flynn effect is described by James Flynn (2013) in his TED Talk, 'Why our IQ levels are higher than our grandparents', as follows: 'We get far more questions right on IQ tests in each succeeding generation back to the time that they were invented'. This worldwide trend of cognitive development is frequently attributed to a more cognitively challenging environment and better nutrition, among other possible factors. However, in the same TED Talk, Flynn reflects that Americans 'can't do politics. We've noticed, in a trend among young Americans, that they read less history and less literature and less material about foreign lands, and they're essentially ahistorical. They live in the bubble of the present'. Widespread political illiteracy seems to have recently been demonstrated in a number of countries that have attempted to turn back the clock to a former national identity, strongly suggesting the need for improved critical literacy in education, if democracy is to work at its best (rashly turning back the clock is a motif of *Harry Potter and the Cursed Child*).

In striking contrast to progressively higher IQ levels, educational progress in creativity development is in reverse gear (Bronson and Merryman 2010). Simonton succinctly expresses the significance of creativity for the world community: 'To a very large degree, creativity made the world we live in. Remove everything about us that was not the product of the creative mind, and we would find ourselves naked in some primeval forest' (Simonton

2006: 490). Included in the construct of creativity from a cognitive psychology perspective are mental operations underlying the creative process such as 'remote association, defocused attention, intuition, incubation, imagination, insight, heuristic thinking and divergent thinking' (Simonton 2006: 492). There are usually a variety of reasons given for the many years of ELT as a school subject, but language creativity is probably not one of the first. The following overlapping learning opportunities are frequently considered central, and may be variously identified in school curricula:

1 Competence in English outside school and in professional life is vital.

2 Intercultural learning is a key competence to develop.

3 In common with other school subjects, thinking processes, metacognition, strategies for learning or learning literacy (Ellis 2018) can be developed in ELT.

4 Language learning deepens language awareness and widens 'cultural, imaginative and cognitive horizons along with language development' (Rixon 2015: 42).

5 Literary literacy (learning to read the aesthetic nature of a literary text), creativity and creative writing can be cultivated in the language-learning classroom.

The last learning opportunity is the main focus of this chapter, for creativity as 'neither wholly domain specific nor wholly domain general' (Sternberg 2006: 2) is easily overlooked in ELT. Although domain-general elements are involved, creativity should also be a subject-specific goal, for 'to gain the knowledge one needs to make creative contributions, one must develop knowledge and skills within a particular domain in which one is to make one's creative contribution' (2006: 2). The sections that follow will study ways to develop creativity and critical literacy with *Harry Potter and the Cursed Child* (Thorne 2016) and *Fantastic Beasts and Where to Find Them, Original Screenplay* (Rowling 2016).

Harry Potter and the Cursed Child

Harry Potter and the Cursed Child is a playscript written by Jack Thorne, based on a story by Thorne, J. K. Rowling and John Tiffany. The play production in London received a record-breaking nine Laurence Olivier Awards in April 2017, including Best New Play and Best Director award for Tiffany. However, only a tiny minority of students are ever likely to have the opportunity to see the play as live theatre. Therefore the motivation to read the playscript may be correspondingly high. I found this to be the case with my student teachers at the University of Münster, 2016–17, and the ELT tasks the students developed and tried out became their litmus test as ongoing teachers of whether the material could be suitable in mid-secondary school (fourteen to sixteen-year-olds).

The playscript, set two decades after the defeat of Voldemort, has been promoted as the eighth book in the *Harry Potter* series – which has given rise to some controversy among fans. Studying a play in secondary-school ELT has a tradition in many countries worldwide, often with a particular focus on Shakespeare. However, due to the difficulty of the adult canon, plays by Shakespeare, or other playwrights such as Oscar Wilde and Arthur Miller, are generally studied as literary works on the page in the most advanced grades of secondary school, or not at all. *Harry Potter and the Cursed Child* is far more accessible for a combination of reasons. The setting is the familiar Wizarding World – students will find old friends among the characters, with no narrated text but dialogue reflecting the language of contemporary teenagers. Moreover the story includes events, places and even artefacts (the Sorting Hat, Cloak of Invisibility, Marauder's Map and Time-Turner) that are familiar from the *Harry Potter* series. Higher background knowledge tends to correlate with higher vocabulary knowledge (e.g. multiple repetition of magic vocabulary, such as wand, broomstick, potion, spell). In addition, knowledge of the *Harry Potter* films supports readers in ELT situations in generating a mental model of the text they are reading – a creative process of seeing, hearing, feeling and acting the storyworld in the mind. Schmitt, Jiang and Grabe (2011: 30) refer to adult students learning English in their study of the percentage of words known in a text and reading comprehension: 'Readers with much greater knowledge of a topic, greater expertise in an academic domain, or relevant social and cultural knowledge understand a text better than readers who do not have these resources'. For children it is at least equally true that background knowledge contributes very significantly to reading comprehension, as prior knowledge supports inferencing.

Fortunately, the play format also encourages group readings of scenes in preparation for the pleasure of dramatic readings in class. Reading aloud was found to be a favourite activity among students in advanced grades:

> they [the pupils] loved reading, they're fighting over who gets to read which part [...] I think actually reading aloud gives them a sense of security so that even kids who are very very shy feel that they can participate and join in and have a voice but don't need to worry about what they're going to say. (teacher quoted in Duncan and Paran 2018: 243–59)

Texts for deep reading should be authentic to the learner group, they should be within reach of their area of expertise and challenging – but not too challenging.

As Gardner (2006: 87) points out, during adolescence 'students need to be posed challenges where they stand a reasonable chance of success'. Certainly the playscript format demands active and curious reading – for it is challenging to conjure the staging, choreography and dramatic effects of lighting, sound and music of a complex stage production in the mind.

During the course of the play, with the help of a Time-Turner, some events of the *Harry Potter* world of the book series are revisited – particularly the Triwizard Tournament in Harry's fourth year at Hogwarts, and the scene in Godric's Hollow at the time when Harry's parents were killed. However, the play mostly centres on the close friendship between Harry's son Albus and Draco's son Scorpius, as well as difficulties between the generations, which nearly have fatal consequences. The work with the script, making use of multiple modes of communication through drama methodology, would cover at least three stages:

- *Warming up* – this is essential to begin any drama work.

- *Drama process work* – students use different drama conventions to create a drama montage to deepen the reading of the play, to try out different voices, discover richer details of characterization and theme, and potentially reveal absences.

- *Critical literacy* – absences revealed by the drama conventions are analysed, students respond with creative writing, from different perspectives and potentially resisting the subliminal ideology of the text. Resisting reading or reading *against* a contemporary text is even more challenging than resisting reading of a canonical text (see Kalogirou 2018: 225–40), for in a contemporary text the ideology may be so close to that of the reader that it seems invisible and consequently non-existent.

Warming up

It is a good idea for a group to warm up before any focused work, but essential before working with drama. There is now evidence for a suite of physiological reactions to language – a very close connection between language, perception and action (Bergen 2012) – therefore it is not surprising that students perform better in listening and speaking when they are animated and fully activated. Playing with language is both useful for warming up and helps internalize the rhythms of contemporary spoken English. As fourteen or fifteen-year-old students are at an age when they may be initially shy about using physical actions and movement in ELT, it is helpful to take a warming up activity from the script itself, so that the connection to the topic remains clear. For example, the dark prophecy introduced in Act 3, Scene 21 is exhilarating when performed as a crescendo echo with slow movement, the words of the prophecy echoed by the students and increasing in volume:

> **When spares are spared,**
> (... *spares are spared, SPARES ARE SPARED, **SPARES ARE SPARED**)*
>
> **when time is turned,**
> (... *time is turned, TIME IS TURNED, **TIME IS TURNED**)*
>
> **when unseen children murder their fathers:**
> (... *murder their fathers, MURDER THEIR FATHERS, **MURDER THEIR FATHERS**)*
>
> **then will the Dark Lord return.**
> (... *Dark Lord return, DARK LORD RETURN, **DARK LORD RETURN**)*

On other occasions students might perform one of the Sorting Hat rhymes as a rhythmical dance:

> I've done this job for centuries
> On every student's head I've sat
> Of thoughts I take inventories
> For I'm the famous Sorting Hat.
> [...] (*Harry Potter and the Cursed Child* (*CC*) Act 1, Scene 4)

A Gossip Circle is a drama convention that is useful as a warming up activity: 'The private and public behaviour of characters is commented on in the form of rumours and gossip circulating in the community; as the rumours spread around the circle they become exaggerated and distorted' (Neelands 2004: 102). This technique works very well with the tensions and conflicts in *Harry Potter and the Cursed Child*. Students could, for example, explore the bullying experienced by Scorpius, who is rumoured to be the son of Voldemort: 'I mean – father-son issues, I have them. But, on the whole, I'd rather be a Malfoy than, you know, the son of the Dark Lord' (*CC* Act 1, Scene 3), and also experienced by his best friend Albus: 'Albus Potter, the Slytherin Squib' (*CC* Act 1, Scene 4). As the students become more familiar with the play, the Gossip Circle should be repeated in order to investigate the many other conflicts and rumours. The Gossip Circle is extremely active when a soft ball is thrown to indicate who should speak next, adding the element of surprise. As a warming up activity it is creative and safe for students feeling vulnerable to peer pressure: the students are allowed and encouraged to exaggerate and distort the conflicts in the play, leading to later reflection. This has been defined by Freebody and Finneran as the 'opportunity afforded by the safe and imaginary world of drama, and the reflective space between the fictional world and the real world' (2013: 61).

Drama process work

O'Neill (2013: xix) writes: 'Study after study has shown that when the arts are given space in the curriculum, there are immediate benefits to students, schools and the wider community'. Unfortunately, there is frequently little official space for the arts, but only absences. For this reason alone, it is important to include drama methodology in tertiary ELT teacher education, so that language teachers can begin to acquire the expertise and experience needed to help compensate for restrictive school curricula, at least to some extent, by exploiting all the potential flexibility of ELT. In this section, three drama conventions are introduced that were found to be most useful for discovering absences in *Harry Potter and the Cursed Child*: intrapersonal role play, role-on-the-wall and subtext strategies.

Intrapersonal role play is an interpretative drama convention that encourages deep thinking about complex human behaviour. A number of characters are chosen, and each one is portrayed by two students, who try to express different angles of the same character. Figure 3.1 shows how several groups prepared for intrapersonal role play based on *Harry Potter and the Cursed Child* – a careful preparation for the improvised intrapersonal role play task was found to be necessary even for student teachers fluent in English.

After the student teachers had improvised a number of intrapersonal role plays, it became apparent to them that it is seldom possible to categorize opposing character facets as 'evil' and 'good', even in the Wizarding World.

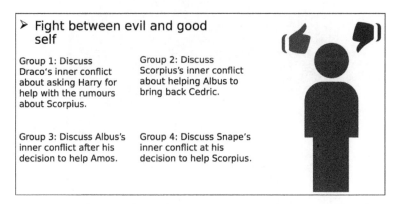

> ➤ Fight between evil and good self

Group 1: Discuss Draco's inner conflict about asking Harry for help with the rumours about Scorpius.

Group 2: Discuss Scorpius's inner conflict about helping Albus to bring back Cedric.

Group 3: Discuss Albus's inner conflict after his decision to help Amos.

Group 4: Discuss Snape's inner conflict at his decision to help Scorpius.

FIGURE 3.1 *Student teachers' design: preparation for intrapersonal role play.*

They also discovered that the scenes they had chosen happened to only portray male characters. This is further discussed in the section on critical literacy.

Role-on-the-wall is a strategy that studies the characters from the perspective of other characters. Two or three students create a large group poster of a chosen character, selecting a colour to represent their character. They then draw a spacious outline for the character, and fill it with snippets of information, qualities and thoughts, using pens of the same colour. When the outlines are full of ideas, the groups swap posters in order to annotate the other role posters – each group using the colour of their own figure and writing from their own figure's perspective – but on the outside of the other character outlines. Finally the role posters are attached to the wall, for the annotations on the various characters may be further developed as more insights arise.

The theme of generational conflict became very apparent with this task. The groups wrote either 'father issues' or 'daddy issues' within the outlines of Albus, Harry, Delphi, Draco and Scorpius. Albus was even given the words DADDY ISSUES in place of eyes (see Figures 3.2 and 3.3).

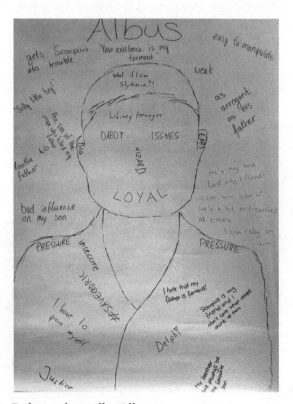

FIGURE 3.2 *Role-on-the-wall – Albus.*

FIGURE 3.3 *Role-on-the-wall – Delphi.*

The authors of *Harry Potter and the Cursed Child* wisely left open who exactly is meant as 'the cursed child'. This is an opportunity for groups of students to choose a character and formulate persuasive arguments for their character inheriting this title. Potential candidates are Harry Potter, Scorpius Malfoy, Albus Potter, Cedric Diggory or Delphi – for they are all burdened by their own or their parents' past. This motif is clearly expressed by Draco: 'There's no escaping the past' (*CC* Act 4, Scene 4). There is an opportunity here for students to learn the power they have as readers: transacting with texts and even co-creating them. For as Le Guin writes, 'the writer cannot do it alone. The unread story is not a story; it is little black marks on wood pulp. The reader, reading it, makes it live: a live thing, a story' (1989: 198).

Subtext strategies – creating and voicing characters' thoughts – allow students to reflect on, then script and speak the thoughts of characters to the audience (the class) – for characters seldom say exactly what they mean, or express all their thoughts. Creating subtexts offers the opportunity to fill these spaces – the dance of the spoken and unspoken: 'freezing a moment in time, exploring subtexts, voicing characters' inner thoughts and intentions'

(Fleming 2013: 211). Working in small groups, students could begin by creating an iceberg poster for each character. They write down snippets of text from a scene above the waterline, and then create the subtext together in the bulk of the iceberg below the waterline. They subsequently rehearse the scene, and decide on pauses when the characters' thoughts could be expressed. Finally, two students perform each character in the scene, one reading aloud the character's lines, the other voicing the character's inner thoughts. This works well at climactic moments, such as the following momentous altercation between Harry and his younger son:

Harry (*finally losing his temper*) You know what? I'm done with being made responsible for your unhappiness. At least you've got a dad. Because I didn't, okay?

Albus And you think that was unlucky? I don't.

Harry You wish me dead?

Albus No! I just wish you weren't my dad.

Harry (*seeing red*) Well, there are times I wish you weren't my son.
There's a silence. Albus *nods. Pause.* Harry *realises what he's said.* No, I didn't mean that . . .

Albus Yes. You did. (*CC* Act 1, Scene 7)

This is a devastating scene between father and son. I have had the opportunity to observe several groups create the subtext of this scene and then perform the characters and their thoughts. It was a very moving experience. Extending and examining the moment by creating subtexts takes us right inside the characters, potentially revealing troubling and very personal real-life echoes at the same time.

Critical literacy – female agency and resisting

As we have seen, there is human conflict as well as dark magic, wonder and awe in *Harry Potter and the Cursed Child*, as in the entire *Harry Potter* series. The speculative aspect of the play is imagining what might happen if we could really turn back the clock. The resulting drama is reminiscent of the butterfly effect as it appears for the first time in fiction in Ray Bradbury's short story *A Sound of Thunder* (1952), which might be read as an introduction to a central theme of the play. *Harry Potter and the Cursed Child* explores both literally and figuratively the perils of being stuck in the past, for example when Harry cannot imagine that being at Hogwarts is so completely different for his son than it was for himself. As Delphi remarks (*CC* Act 1, Scene 6): 'It's tough to live with people stuck in the past, isn't it?' The present-day fixation – which likewise seems to have seized the older generation more than the younger generation – on the rebuilding of walls and barriers as attempts to regain an assumed past stability, might be discussed in this context.

During the previously described drama activities of intrapersonal role play, role-on-the-wall and subtext strategies, a specific absence was noted: the lack of interactions between the female characters. This absence has been studied in movies particularly and found to be extremely common, following the identification of a desideratum by graphic artist and novelist Alison Bechdel: a film should have at least two named women in it, who talk to each other, about something other than a man. This has become widely known as the Bechdel test as a way of gauging the agency of women and girls in narratives (Dolan 2013: 3). In *Harry Potter and the Cursed Child*, there is no scene between sisters-in-law Hermione and Ginny, no scene between cousins Rose and Lily and no scene between teachers Professor McGonagall and Madam Hooch, for example. This is disturbing, for as Fleming points out: 'Drama's primary language mode is dialogue and it is more evident that meaning is created "between" rather than "within" people' (2001: 104). That Delphi only ever interacts with boys and men is less surprising for the sake of the plot – a woman would surely have seen through her (I will get no closer to a plot spoiler than this).

Such absences can be animated and filled creatively by having groups of students script the missing scenes – also the boys can practise writing dialogue for girls. This may help to surface any stereotypes or prejudices among students – it may be revealing, for example, when girls act out scenes scripted by boys. Gardner suggests taking risks in order to cultivate a creative mind, and recommends supporting 'exploration, challenging problems, and the tolerance, if not the active encouragement, of productive mistakes' (2006: 85). By such trial and error, young people should be given the opportunity to resist cultural conditioning. The play is ultimately only really completed in each performance – to the extent that students might also choose to perform a fluid gender identity for the close friends Albus and Scorpius, as resistance to the heteronormativity suggested in the penultimate scene when Albus and Scorpius discuss their future girlfriends (*CC* Act 4, Scene 14). Thus scripted drama can be considered a particularly powerful kind of 'literature as doing' (Hall 2016: 465). In this way, drama conventions and creative writing can be employed to create dialogic learning around scripts, involving critical literacy, creativity and resisting. This will be further explored with the aid of a screenplay in the last section.

Fantastic Beasts and Where to Find Them, Original Screenplay

J. K. Rowling wrote the screenplay to the film *Fantastic Beasts and Where to Find Them*, which was directed by David Yates. The film appeared in 2016, and the screenplay was published simultaneously. Film has an established place in many secondary-school curricula for the teaching of foreign languages. It is now widely accepted that multiple literacy, including visual literacy – reading pictures for information both deeply and critically, is an important goal in language education. The notion of teaching *literacy* in a collective and collaborative sense, rather than teaching *literature* in a knowledge-transmission sense, is centrally important: 'In teaching literacy, we are assuming a purpose or reason for reading; we are looking at reading as communication and at what readers will *do* with what they read – or what writers do with writing' (Paran and Wallace 2016: 442).

The publication of a screenplay by one of the world's favourite authors is an opportunity for ELT that should not be missed. Students recount that they found reading the screenplay was like rewatching the film in slow motion. It is this slowness, coupled with inspiring memories of the film, which is an advantage, for it is widely considered that the print medium is more able to provide for slow and steady cognitive processes than screen media. Hayles refers to this as *deep attention*, which is characterized by prolonged focused concentration on a single object, and is 'the cognitive style traditionally associated with the humanities' (2007: 187). An argument for deep attention coupled with print literacy has been made by Wolf and Barzillai:

> Until sufficient proof enlarges the discussion, we believe that nothing replaces the unique contributions of print literacy for the development of the full panoply of the slower, constructive, cognitive processes that invite children to create their own whole worlds in what Proust called the 'reading sanctuary'. (Wolf and Barzillai 2009: 36)

However Hayles (2007: 187) further documents a significant trend towards a *hyper attention* cognitive style in school and college students, 'characterized by switching focus rapidly among different tasks, preferring multiple information streams, seeking a high level of stimulation, and having a low tolerance for boredom'. Following the evidence of research on media consumption and brain imaging patterns, Hayles considers 'it is not far-fetched to imagine that the trend toward hyper attention represents the brain's cultural coevolution in coordination with high-speed, information-intensive, and rapidly changing environments that make flexible alternation of tasks, quick processing of multiple information streams, and a low threshold for boredom more adaptive' (2007: 194). Teachers need to consider carefully, in consequence, whether the school educational environment fits the students of the twenty-first century, and need to take measures to support both hyper attention and deep attention cognitive styles. Screen media such as films, TV series and story apps provide for a high level of stimulation, as is well known, but ideally should be juxtaposed with a print text or texts that demand deep attention. It seems books still have an important role to play.

Film first or book first?

We now understand more of how language is experienced in an embodied way, and that we conjure mental imagery or simulations when reading a narrative: 'Simulation is the creation of mental experiences of perception and action in the absence of their external manifestation' (Bergen 2012: 15). This depends, however, on the real world experience of the reader and the *perceptions they can activate*: an experienced reader will have more real memories and virtual memories (from previous reading, viewing, listening and so forth) than a younger reader. For example, if we read about a rushing, thundering waterfall, we both visualize and hear the water, as long as the sight and sound of cascading water is stored in our memory. I happened to read the screenplay of *Fantastic Beasts and Where to Find Them* before watching the movie, and thoroughly enjoyed the opportunity to use my New York experiences and knowledge of the historical period, and my familiarity with speculative reading, to imagine and experience the scene of magic and No-Maj (the name for Muggles in Rowling's American Wizarding World) in New York of the 1920s. Most fourteen and fifteen-year-olds, however, will lack specific cultural knowledge to feed their imagination as well as lacking linguistic resources in the second language. This would block the creative and dynamic process described by Bergen: 'Meaning, according to the embodied simulation hypothesis, isn't just abstract mental symbols; it's a creative process, in which people construct virtual experiences – embodied simulations – in their mind's eye. [. . .] It's not about activating the right symbol; it's about dynamically constructing the right mental experience of the scene' (2012: 16). For this reason it comes as no surprise that the huge majority of the 6000 reviewers, from countries all over the world, who have uploaded reviews of Rowling's screenplay to Goodreads, recommend watching the film first.

Young people are likely to watch the film several times during out-of-school hours; such repetition is highly advantageous for language learning, and also allows for differentiated and deeper readings. Repetition is far from meaningless – it is a stylistic device in creative writing (Bland 2013: 156–87), and can multiply meanings rather than reducing them, as Claire Kramsch explains:

> there is value in repetition as an educational device: utterances repeated are also resignified. [. . .] The same text, reread silently or aloud, can yield new

meanings. The same utterance, repeated in various contexts, with different inflections, can index different emotions, evoke different associations. The same poem, memorised and performed two or three times in front of the same class, yields each time new pleasures of recognition and anticipation. The same story, told to three different interlocutors, can enable the storyteller to put different emphases on the same general theme depending on the listener. (Kramsch 2009: 209)

It is not suggested here that the film itself is not worthy of study in ELT, however the combination of book and film offers more – for example, opportunities for creative writing.

Fantastic beasts and creative writing

All of the drama conventions described previously – the gossip circle, intrapersonal role play, role-on-the-wall and subtext strategies – can be used to creatively promote deep reading of any complex narrative, including *Fantastic Beasts and Where to Find Them*. However, the richly imaginative story seems predestined to inspire creative writing, an opportunity not to be missed, for as Dan Disney writes, 'L2 proto-writers expand linguistic and affective boundaries when venturing a creative response to literary artefacts' (2014: 2).

The components of the screenplay format are *screen direction* – brief descriptions of settings, visual and sound effects, characters and creatures, and their reactions and movements, and *dialogue* – the precise words the characters speak in the film. The main character is Newt Scamander, a Magizoologist, who arrives in the United States on a mission to protect and research fantastic beasts. The ecological theme is expressed with humour, warmth and urgency, and further themes emerge, including segregation and international politics in Jazz Age New York. Newt inadvertently contributes to an emerging crisis in New York when some of his creatures escape his enchanted briefcase. The case itself is reminiscent of portals to other worlds in children's fantasy (such as the rabbit hole leading to Wonderland, the wardrobe portal to Narnia, and Platform 9 ¾ to Hogwarts); the miniature world gained through the suitcase is a collection of magically realized biotopes housing Newt's endangered species. Newt's mission becomes clear when he sets out to rescue his escaped beasts: 'See, they're currently in alien terrain, surrounded by millions of the most vicious creatures on the planet . . . Humans' (Rowling 2016: 113–14). Clearly *Fantastic Beasts and Where to Find Them* also offers opportunities for critical thinking.

Students can discuss Newt Scamander's charismatic and creative career as it is revealed so far (further films are to follow), his difficulties and setbacks, his inventiveness and divergent thinking as well as his later huge publishing success in the Wizarding World. Naturally students may disagree and prefer to represent Newt differently, which is to be welcomed: 'multiple representations are grist for new ways of thinking about an entity, problem, or question: they catalyse creative questions and spawn creative solutions' (Gardner 2006: 87).

Rowling's screenplay has abundant inventive dialogue – the essence of the screenplay format – but the screen direction supplies only rather sketchy descriptions of the fantastic creatures that are to be artistically realized by the film crew. Consequently there is an opportunity for students' creative writing – supplying more detailed descriptions of their own invention. An earlier work on fantastic beasts with the same title (Rowling 2001, expanded edition 2017), purports to be based on the fictional Newt Scamander's research, and read at Hogwarts as a textbook classic. Here too, the ideas for the fantastic beasts are rich in innovation and humour. Feigning the genre of the school textbook, the descriptions are once again quasi-factual and concise. Thus Rowling's texts offer enticing gaps to inspire creative writing. While *Fantastic Beasts* provides the stimulus, the actual language model for emergent creative writers is more readily found in the poetic language associated with other writers for children such as David Almond, Carol Ann Duffy, Patrick Ness and Philip Pullman. Mentor texts can provide essential support for creative writing by supplying a model (Bland 2013, 156–87; Moses 2014). To this end, a magical combination of Rowling's screenplay, overflowing with ingenious ideas in *Fantastic Beasts*, and David Almond's musical language in *Mouse Bird Snake Wolf* (Almond, illus. McKean 2013) makes for an excellent partnership for the creative writing classroom.

Mouse Bird Snake Wolf *and the power of rhythmical repetition*

Almond's *Mouse Bird Snake Wolf* is an unusual literary format: smaller than a picturebook and more detailed than most fairy tales, vibrantly and powerfully illustrated by Dave McKean, it would qualify, according to Oziewicz (2018), as a graphic novel. It is a mystical tale about mankind's creative power, but with a dangerous edge, that destruction can follow hubristic anthropocentric creativity. Can anything be done to rid the world of a dangerous thing once it has been created? The book begins: 'Long ago and far away', and it tells of a world not quite finished. 'Like many worlds, the world they lived in was a marvellous place filled with marvellous things. It was safe and calm and rather wonderful' (Almond 2013: np). The gods who created this world became complacent and inept, so, one day, three children were inspired to creativity themselves, and invented some missing animals: a mouse, a bird, a snake and a wolf. Inventing a wolf in a fairy tale is of course asking for trouble – this is a hauntingly illustrated tale on the beauty and danger of creativity that can be read on a number of levels: 'Like an oral tale, the story progresses rhythmically through repetition and variation. It swells as it goes, gathering pace' (Mason 2013: np). The language, apparently simple, illustrates the power and suggestiveness of rhythmical repetition and multisensory storytelling. A child begins by creating a mouse:

> The mouse tottered to its tiny feet; it sniffed the air; it peeped into the sky with its little bright eyes. It squeaked, and squeaked again, and squeaked again, and scampered right away. [. . .]

All at once ambitious, an older child conjures a twisty, legless thing:

> And yes! The snake hissed. It lifted its head and it hissed again. It slithered towards them across the grass. Its scales glittered. Its eyes gleamed. It bared its sharp little teeth. It flicked its forked little tongue. (Almond 2013: np, see Figure 3.4)

This writing evokes an embodied response, which is echoed by Almond in his acceptance speech for the *Hans Christian Andersen Award*: 'For children, words don't sit still in orderly lines on the page. They work on the body and the senses. They move fluently into drama, into movement, into dance, into song. And the books that they read and love are similarly multifaceted. [. . .] The children's book world is a place of abundance, abandon, experiment and play' (Almond 2010, np).

Creativity is empowering and bestows agency on students who easily lack agency when trying to communicate in a language not their own: 'Creative writing and other forms of cultural production (e.g. art, drama, music, etc.) represent an *expression* of identity, a *projection* of identity into new social spheres and a *re-creation* of identity as a result of feedback from and dialogue with multiple audiences' (Cummins 2014, np, emphasis in the original). According to Jane Spiro, creative writing for language learners means helping them find their own voice that can be enjoyed by the classroom community: 'We trace a transition from reader-as-writer to writer-as-reader in the process of finding a writing voice' (Spiro 2014: 23). Sharing and enjoying each other's work is the essence of creative writing. The following are extracts of creative writing by student teachers from my creative writing class

It slithered towards them across the grass.
Its scales glittered. Its eyes gleamed.
It bared its sharp little teeth. It flicked its forked little tongue.

FIGURE 3.4 *Creating a snake. From* Mouse Bird Snake Wolf *by David Almond and Dave McKean (Text © 2013 David Almond, illustrations © 2013 Dave McKean. Reproduced by permission of Walker Books Ltd, London SE11 5HJ, www.walker.co.uk).*

(Hildesheim University, 2011). These descriptions of a mighty dragon, inspired by Ted Hughes's *The Iron Man* (1968), which the class used as a mentor text, illustrate the power of rhythmical repetition:

> Its sharp teeth, jagged like the blade of a saw, its sharp eyes, like piercing spears, its talons, sharp like curved razorblades, its sharp-witted glance and the sharp scent made even the bravest warrior cry out in fear. (Raffael)

His long tail swung back and forth. Back and forth. To the West of Australia. Back and forth. To the East of Australia. Back and forth. It never stopped. Swish, swash. Swish, swash. It terrified people seeing it. Swish. Somebody screamed. Swash. But the tail never hit anyone. (Andrea)

Like a colossal reptile, he crawled along the surface of the five continents, snaking through the deserts, across many mountains and valleys, and striding over the oceans. Sometimes he would stretch out his two wide and monstrous wings and would fly off, up to the sky, up through space, to reach other planets. [...] And in the starless night, the millions of bursting sparks reflected by the millions of scales that covered his body were such that the Dragon could be mistaken for the sun itself. (Julia)

This way – in becoming creative writers themselves – student teachers can learn to create their own mentor texts, to guide and support the creative writing of their future learners.

Conclusion

There are important reasons to include creativity wherever it can fit the curriculum, and ELT offers such opportunities: 'introducing new pursuits that are removed from the academic treadmill and that reward innovation and look benignly on errors' (Gardner 2006: 86). Unscripted drama conventions, critical literacy and creative writing help teachers and students of language and literature learn to cope with creative uncertainty. Too much testing, too narrow a disciplinary focus stifles creativity. Focused attention on language learning is important of course, but so is defocused attention, imagination, heuristic and divergent thinking. In order to develop creativity and creative thinking, Gardner asserts: 'Options need to be kept open – a straight trajectory is less effective than one entailing numerous bypaths, and even a few disappointing but instructive cul-de-sacs' (Gardner 2006: 84). This suggests trial and error, searching for subtexts, students thinking critically, resisting and being challenged to find their own voice.

Rowling's Wizarding World continues to be underestimated by educators. However most teenagers are highly motivated and also empowered when interacting with these texts. Sternberg writes (2003: 11), 'Successful individuals are those who have creative skills, to produce a vision for how they intend to make the world a better place for everyone; analytical intellectual skills, to assess their vision and those of others; practical intellectual skills, to carry out their vision and persuade people of its value; and wisdom, to ensure that their vision is not a selfish one'. With challenging tasks, the Wizarding World can contribute to this huge project.

RECOMMENDATIONS

- Although it is generally recognized that drama conventions and creative writing are highly motivating, they are often thought to be recreational, less serious tools. This is a misunderstanding – the challenges of creative tasks empower learners to find their own voice and allow deep reflection and a re-creation of identity in the new language. Thus creative processes should be woven into ELT.
- Student teachers should have the opportunity to practise drama and creative writing for themselves in initial teacher education to discover how to guide and support the creative writing and drama response of their future learners.

Bibliography

Almond, David and McKean, Dave (illus.) (2013), *Mouse Bird Snake Wolf*, Somerville, MA: Candlewick Press.

Bradbury, Ray (1952/1997), 'A sound of thunder', in *Golden Apples of the Sun and Other Stories*, New York: HarperCollins, pp. 203–15.

Fantastic Beasts and Where to Find Them (2016), [Film] Dir. David Yates, UK/US: Warner Bros.

Hughes, Ted (1968), *The Iron Man*, London: Faber and Faber.

Rowling, J. K. (2016), *Fantastic Beasts and Where to Find Them, Original Screenplay*, London: Little, Brown.

Rowling, J. K. (2017), *Fantastic Beasts and Where to Find Them, Newt Scamander*, 2nd edn, London: Bloomsbury.

Thorne, Jack (script), Rowling, J. K. and Tiffany, John (story) (2016), *Harry Potter and the Cursed Child*, London: Little, Brown.

References

Almond, David (2010), 'Acceptance speech by David Almond: 2010 Hans Christian Andersen Author Award winner', *IBBY* http://www.ibby.org/subnavigation/archive/ibby-congresses/congress-2010/detailed-programme-and-speeches/david-almond/?L=1 (accessed 23 June 2017).

Barnett, Meredith (2010), 'Education summit advocates 21st century collaboration, creativity', *National Education Association Today* 5 October 2010 http://neatoday.org/2010/10/05/education-summit-advocates-21st-century-collaboration-creativity/ (accessed 16 June 2017).

Bergen, Benjamin (2012), *Louder than Words: The New Science of How the Mind Makes Meaning*, New York: Basic Books.

Bland, Janice (2013), *Children's Literature and Learner Empowerment. Children and Teenagers in English Language Education*, London: Bloomsbury Academic.

Bronson, Po and Merryman, Ashley (2010), 'The creativity crisis', *Newsweek*, 10 July 2010 <http://www.newsweek.com/creativity-crisis-74665> (accessed 12 June 2017).

Cummins, Jim (2014), 'Foreword', in Christine Hélot, Raymonde Sneddon and Nicola Daly (eds), *Children's Literature in Multilingual Classrooms*, London: Institute of Education Press.

Disney, Dan (2014), 'Introduction: Beyond Babel? Exploring second language creative writing', in Dan Disney (ed.) *Exploring Second Language Creative Writing: Beyond Babel*, Amsterdam: John Benjamins, pp. 1–10.

Dolan, Jill (2013), *The Feminist Spectator in Action: Feminist Criticism for the Stage and Screen*, Basingstoke: Palgrave Macmillan.

Duncan, Sam and Paran, Amos (2018), 'Negotiating the challenges of reading literature: Teachers reporting on their practice', in Janice Bland (ed.), *Using Literature in English Language Education: Challenging Reading for 8–18 Year Olds*, London: Bloomsbury Academic, pp. 243–59.

Ellis, Gail (2018), 'The picturebook in elementary ELT: Multiple literacies with Bob Staake's *Bluebird*', in Janice Bland (ed.), *Using Literature in English Language Education*, London: Bloomsbury Academic, pp. 83–104.

Fleming, Michael (2001), *Teaching Drama in Primary and Secondary Schools*, London: David Fulton.

Fleming, Michael (2013), 'Drama', in Michael Byram and Adelheid Hu (eds), *Routledge Encyclopedia of Language Teaching and Learning*, 2nd edn, London: Routledge, pp. 209–11.

Flynn, James (2013), 'Why our IQ levels are higher than our grandparents', *TEDGlobal*, 26 September 2013, https://www.youtube.com/watch?v=9vpqilhW9uI (accessed 15 June 2017).

Freebody, Kelly and Finneran, Michael (2013), 'Drama and social justice: Power, participation and possibility', in Michael Anderson and Julie Dunn (eds), *How Drama Activates Learning*, London: Bloomsbury, pp. 47–63.

Gardner, Howard (2006), *Five Minds for the Future*, Boston, MA: Harvard Business School.

Hall, Geoff (2016), 'Using literature in ELT', in Graham Hall (ed.), *The Routledge Handbook of English Language Teaching*, Abingdon, Oxon: Routledge, pp. 456–68.

Hayles, Katherine (2007), 'Hyper and deep attention: The generational divide in cognitive modes', *Profession*, 187–99.

Kalogirou, Tzina (2018), 'Hamlet, Ophelia and teenage rage: Michael Lesslie's *Prince of Denmark*', in Janice Bland (ed.), *Using Literature in English Language Education*, London: Bloomsbury Academic, pp. 225–40.

Kozlowska, Hanna (2014), 'Can *Harry Potter* change the world?' *The New York Times* 17 September 2010 <https://op-talk.blogs.nytimes.com/2014/09/17/can-harry-potter-change-the-world/?_r=1> (accessed 14 June 2017).

Kramsch, Claire (2009), *The Multilingual Subject*, Oxford: Oxford University Press.

Le Guin, Ursula (1989), 'Where do you get your ideas from?', in *Dancing at the Edge of the World: Thoughts on Words, Women, Places*, New York: Grove Press, pp. 192–200.

McCallum, Robyn and Stephens, John (2011), 'Ideology and children's books', in Shelby Wolf, Karen Coats, Patricia Enciso and Christine Jenkins (eds), *Handbook of Research on Children's and Young Adult Literature*, Abingdon: Routledge, pp. 359–71.

Mason, Simon (2013), '*Mouse Bird Snake Wolf* by David Almond and Dave McKean – review', *The Guardian* 21 June 2013 <https://www.theguardian.com/books/2013/jun/21/mouse-bird-almond-mckean-review> (accessed 21 June 2017).

Moses, Lindsey (2014), 'What do you do with hands like these? Close reading facilitates exploration and text creation', *Children's Literature in English Language Education*, 2/1: 44–56.

Neelands, Jonothan (2004), *Beginning Drama 11–14*, 2nd edn, London: David Fulton.

O'Neill, Cecily (2013), 'Foreword', in Michael Anderson and Julie Dunn (eds), *How Drama Activates Learning*, London: Bloomsbury, pp. xix–xxi.

Oziewicz, Marek (2018), 'The graphic novel: Brian Selznick's *The Invention of Hugo Cabret, Wonderstruck* and *The Marvels*', in Janice Bland (ed.), *Using Literature in English Language Education*, London: Bloomsbury Academic, pp. 25–40.

Paran, Amos and Wallace, Catherine (2016), 'Teaching literacy', in Graham Hall (ed.), *The Routledge Handbook of English Language Teaching*, Abingdon, Oxon: Routledge, pp. 441–55.

Rixon, Shelagh (2015), 'Primary English and critical issues: A worldwide perspective', in Janice Bland (ed.), *Teaching English to Young Learners. Critical Issues in Language Teaching with 3–12 Year Olds*, London: Bloomsbury Academic, pp. 31–50.

Schmitt, Norbert, Jiang, Xiangying and Grabe, William (2011), 'The percentage of words known in a text and reading comprehension', *The Modern Language Journal*, 95/1: 26–43.

Simonton, Dean Keith (2006), 'Creativity around the world in 80 ways ... but with one destination', in James Kaufman and Robert Sternberg (eds), *The International Handbook of Creativity*, New York: Cambridge University Press, pp. 490–6.

Spiro, Jane (2014), 'Learner and writer voices. Learners as writers and the search for authorial voice', in Dan Disney (ed.) *Exploring Second Language Creative Writing: Beyond Babel*, Amsterdam: John Benjamins, pp. 23–40.

Sternberg, Robert (2003), *Wisdom, Intelligence, and Creativity Synthesized*, Cambridge: Cambridge University Press.

Sternberg, Robert (2006), 'Introduction', in James Kaufman and Robert Sternberg (eds), *The International Handbook of Creativity*, New York: Cambridge University Press, pp. 1–9.

Wolf, Maryanne and Barzillai, Mirit (2009), 'The importance of deep reading. What will it take for the next generation to read thoughtfully – both in print and online?', *Educational Leadership*, 66/6: 32–7.

4

The wordless picturebook: Literacy in multilingual contexts and David Wiesner's worlds

Evelyn Arizpe and Sadie Ryan

It is widely believed that picturebooks without words are only suitable for very young children, or perhaps for children who are at an early stage of learning a new language, and that this kind of text is of little use once 'proper reading' must be learned. However, a more careful and deeper look at what illustrators are doing in these picturebooks reveals just how aesthetically and cognitively pleasing they are, and how much they can offer an audience of all ages and at all stages of reading or language learning. In addition, research has shown that complex and well-crafted wordless picturebooks demand a heightened awareness of the role of words and images and of the reader's role in making meaning, an awareness that is crucial in developing an understanding not only of narrative but also of how 'understanding' itself works (Arizpe 2014, Mourão 2015, Pantaleo 2007). In this chapter, we argue that the active and conscious engagement demanded by wordless picturebooks can also be applied to thinking about the processes of language learning and about communication in general and that therefore it can have significant impact on children and young people involved in multilingual educational contexts.

Wordless picturebooks were used in the studies described in this chapter to open a space for English language learners (ELLs) to think about the role of words and pictures both in narrative and in language learning, encouraging a reflection on their own meaning-making processes on both these fronts. The readers who participated in these projects were also encouraged to reflect on the theme of communication across time, place and with those that are 'other'. The studies are therefore inscribed within a metacognitive approach to learning and enabled the researchers to gain insights not only into experiences, beliefs and knowledge about reading images but also about language teaching and learning processes and the contexts in which these occur. After a brief introduction to wordless picturebooks and their affordances for developing various forms of literacy, we describe the research activities and highlight findings that suggest how a pedagogical approach that uses wordless picturebooks can underpin a metacognitive approach in language learning.

Wordless picturebooks and reader engagement

In a wordless picturebook, the visual image carries the weight of the meaning but the absence of the words is significant and contributes to the overall meaning of the narrative. Many award-winning illustrators from around the world have created and received awards for their wordless picturebooks, among them Raymond Briggs, Mitsumasa Anno, Shirley Hughes, Jerry Pinkney, Tord Nygren, Istvan Banyai, Shaun Tan and Suzy Lee. They seem to fascinate both adults and children, perhaps because we are so used to word-based narratives and because they make us wonder what we must do to make sense of a purely pictorial one.

David Wiesner has become internationally known since the triumph of his picturebooks *Tuesday* (1992), *The Three Pigs* (2002) and *Flotsam* (2006), with which he became one of only two children's illustrators who have been awarded three Caldecott Medals (and he was also runner up with *Mr Wuffles!* in 2013). His books include many postmodern features such as fragmentation, intertextuality and metafiction but also humour and irony. Not all of them are wordless but the artist's intention seems to be to create images that seize the larger portion of the readers' attention. All his picturebooks encourage close viewing and invite co-authoring but Wiesner stressed the special effect of wordless books in his first Caldecott Medal acceptance speech (1992): 'A wordless book offers a different kind of an experience from one with text, for both the author and the reader. There is no author's voice telling the story. Each viewer reads the book in his or her own way. The reader is an integral part of the storytelling process'.

A review of studies on wordless picturebooks concluded that it is *the degree to which readers are expected to actively engage* that marks the difference between picturebooks with and without words and which enables the reader to become a co-constructer of meaning in the transaction with these texts (Arizpe 2014). The age of the reader and their previous experience with both picturebooks and wordless picturebooks will determine how readers act on this demand. In addition, this awareness and action can change and increase through collaborative reading with peers and adult mediators depending on the context, the aims and the strategies used in approaching and reading the text (Mourão 2015).

It is now generally established that picturebooks can be used to develop various forms of literacy; for example, they bring the aesthetic qualities of the visual image to the forefront, encouraging readers' visual literacy engagement (Arizpe, McAdam and Farrar 2017). More specifically, they help young children develop literate behaviour and an understanding of literacy itself (Meek 1988, Nikolajeva 2003). As for wordless picturebooks, Arizpe (2014) noted in her review of research that they are considered an ideal medium in educational studies for investigating language acquisition, storytelling and other skills, sometimes with children with special needs.

Picturebooks, metacognitive skills and language learning

A few studies that look at response to complex picturebooks (metafictive picturebooks in particular) refer to the ways in which these texts facilitate higher order thinking because they can increase the reader's cognizance of reading and understanding as a process (Arizpe and Styles 2003, Pantaleo 2015). Having to relate two different semiotic systems focuses the perception of the complex relationship between word and image, one of the defining aspects of the picturebook (also present in other multimodal formats). Arizpe and Styles (2003) noted examples of higher order thinking skills in the children's responses to contemporary picturebooks. Furthermore, the readers were also able to go inside their own heads to describe what they were thinking and feeling as they read the images and also as they made their own drawings in response to the picturebooks. Arizpe and Styles concluded that children's previous book and media knowledge come together with metacognitive skills when children answer questions about their expectations of a picturebook, its implied readership and their understanding of artistic techniques. This is significant, as there is ample evidence that metacognitive knowledge has a positive effect on literacy and reading comprehension (Block 2004).

In language teaching, picturebooks are often used because of the perceived simplicity and amount of words and the supportive frame provided by the pictures. More recently, however, they have been seen as a way of supporting not only language but also literary learning in an ELT context (Durant 2013, Bland 2013). Furthermore, the multiple interpretations which postmodern picturebooks invite are considered a good way to challenge language students' expectations of finding a single, 'correct' meaning in a text (Kern 2000, Hsiu-Chih 2008). However, once a certain stage has been reached in language teaching, wordless picturebooks are less frequently used, despite the fact that there are many skills required to make meaning that are similar to making sense of a new language.

A few educationalists have promoted the use of wordless picturebooks in the language classroom to develop skills such as the language of description; of temporal sequence and choice; of prediction, hypothesis and cause/effect; of judgement and of classification and concept formation (Early 1991: 245–6). Bland (2013) uses various picturebook examples with few or no words to illustrate their potential for English language pedagogy. She refers to the 'essential modelling status' which the teacher must take on (2013: 41) and which will involve 'genuine' questions and responses. Also, she notes that questions that are more open-ended will 'encourage thinking dispositions'. Given there are no 'correct' answers, students can initiate the learning discourse themselves, shifting the balance of power in the classroom (2013: 44).

Louie and Sierschynski (2015) argue that wordless picturebooks provide opportunities for developing 'close viewing' that includes effective talk but also identifying narrative conventions and reading processes that they can build on for writing tasks. Their summary conclusion covers most of the main points mentioned by others:

> What makes wordless picture books well-suited to ELs [English learners] is that visual texts display the literary conventions and complexity found in picture books with words [...] Because they remove the language input, wordless picture books allow ELs to share the critical experience of engaging with a visual text. The perceived freedom to participate in shared viewing of wordless picture books leads to a deeper engagement and guides the ELs to access more layers of meaning. (Louie and Sierschynski 2015: 106–7)

The challenge in David Wiesner's wordless picturebooks

Postmodern picturebooks tend to challenge the reader through features that do not appear in more traditional picturebooks. They are often nonlinear, for example, the words and pictures can tell different stories, and there may be references to a variety of other texts such as film or the author's other books. Although not all of Wiesner's picturebooks are wordless, he does incorporate many of these features as he plays with the concepts of reality and fiction and of worlds within worlds. Even his story app, *Spot* (2015), includes characters and spaces from his picturebooks, inviting readers to construct different stories through zooming into the images. He makes reference to the world of art in *Art and Max* (2010), and to different genres, such as fairy tales in *The Three Pigs* (2002) and detective stories in *Tuesday* (1992). By drawing the reader's attention to detail and the role of images in narrative, he makes them even more aware of the process they are going through as they co-create a story. Wiesner creates pace and rhythm through varying the size and quantity of frames, interspersed with double-page spreads for emphasizing dramatic moments.

Flotsam (2006), for example, tells the story of an old-fashioned, barnacle-encrusted camera that a boy finds washed up on a beach, and the fantastic photographs the camera contains. Bright colours, unexpected angles, framing and zooming are some of the features that invite readers into discovering the fantastic world recorded by the camera on its historical and geographical travels. As we interpret the boy's gestures and movements, we share the boy's emotional reaction to his find – surprise, impatience, wonder – and enter the game with him. *Flotsam*'s ending reveals some of the camera's secret and wordless interaction between children around the world who, throughout the entire twentieth century, had sent a picture of themselves (what we could now call a 'selfie'!) to each other.

Mr Wuffles! (see Figure 4.1) appeared seven years after *Flotsam* and sends a similar message about unexpected connections and cross-cultural communication, and again plays with frames, dimensions and perspective to involve the reader in the story. When their tiny spacecraft lands on earth, the visiting aliens' joy quickly turns to terror as a cat, Mr Wuffles, plays with their craft, turning it upside down and breaking a crucial piece of equipment. The aliens manage to run under a radiator behind which they discover a picture on the wall that describes the struggle between the cat and a group of insects. These same insects appear and although their language is different, the two groups manage to communicate through pictures and gestures. The ants help the aliens mend the broken device and get back into the spacecraft, which flies off before the very eyes of the cross-looking cat. The story plays on the idea of communicating through pictures rather than words but also raises the themes of intercultural or, more specifically, 'interspecies' understanding; making friends and working together for a common purpose.

FIGURE 4.1 *Cover from* MR WUFFLES! *by David Wiesner (copyright © 2013). Reprinted by permission of Houghton Mifflin Harcourt Publishing Company. All rights reserved.*

ELLs reading *Flotsam* in a Scottish school

Flotsam was used in the project Visual Journeys (2009–12), about journeys and intercultural experiences, in order to examine the visual literacy knowledge and practices of children with different cultural backgrounds (Arizpe, Colomer and Martínez-Roldán 2014). The group of children in the upper years of primary school in Scotland (ten to eleven years old) included children from Russia, Poland, Iraq, Congo, Afghanistan, Uganda, Pakistan and Somalia, some of whom were refugees or asylum seekers. The other wordless book used in the study was *The Arrival* by Shaun Tan, a stunning and insightful visual narrative of forced migration (for an account of the response to *The Arrival*, see Arizpe et al. 2014). The participants responded to both *Flotsam* and *The Arrival* in a variety of modes: they did a 'walk-through' of the picturebook page by page; annotated images from the book (see Figure 4.2); drew a 'graphic strip' about a journey they had taken; and took photographs. Initially developed as research tools, the strategies were also supportive in the development of literacy skills and intercultural competences (Arizpe and McAdam 2011).

FIGURE 4.2 *Illustration from* Flotsam *by David Wiesner (copyright © 2013). Annotated by participants in 'Visual Journeys'.*

All the children were intrigued by the wordless books and what was required to 'read' them. During the literary discussions (eight sessions held both in pairs and in groups during the English language support lesson times), the most frequent comments made by the participants about the wordless nature of the text contained verbs that suggest the active participation stimulated by 'reading' the picturebooks: [you have to] 'look'; 'imagine'; 'put in own words'; 'they make you think more'; 'you can make guesses'. Although Ali (all names are pseudonyms), a new arrival from Afghanistan, struggled to express himself, his close viewing and thinking processes are revealed as he talks about the objects on the title page of *Flotsam*:

> [...] it makes me think like oh, like these things they came from China, far, far away, and then someone having might have dropped it [...]. It gave me different thought, and things like that. It makes my brain think that all these things are from far away countries, like the find the sea and they came to the beach to his hands. And I think that's why he gotted (*sic*) all these things.

In the following extract from a group discussion, Sara (Kurdistan), Soraya (Pakistan) and Sadia (Bangladesh) speculate, prompted by the researcher (Evelyn), on why the author made the decision to exclude words. This was their first encounter with the book and it is striking that Sara immediately mentions its potential for the classroom and how children can take ownership of the story; presumably she has noted the potential for different stories to emerge. The other girls pick up on this and echo this interest in other people's interpretations, which do not depend on what language they speak:

Evelyn: [...] why do you think the author told the story in pictures and didn't use any words?

Sara: So they could like make their own, like words [...] like the people that buy this book. They can make their own like words or the teacher might like bring [*sic*] it for the class and [...] everybody in the class does their own story.

Sadia: It wasn't using the author's words, they could use their words.

Evelyn: Do you mean using their own words to tell the story?

Soraya: Maybe the author who would make the – draw these pictures – maybe he want [*sic*] to see other people says.

[. . .]

Evelyn: Mm. Yes, so if there are pictures – do you think everybody can understand them then? Do you think you have to know English?

Sara: No you don't need to because you could make it in my language too. You could like change it.

This exchange also shows an awareness of the authorial process and attributes a curiosity to the author for wanting to know what other people might 'say' about his pictures. It also reveals an understanding of the transcultural linguistic potential of the picturebook.

Throughout the project, however, it became apparent that the words were still considered to have more weight than images, and readers tended to 'hang' their interpretations on the few words that do appear, such as in the title or the back flap. This can be seen in the story that was spontaneously written by Sara about a family called 'Flotsam' and a boy called David. Sara proudly read us her version, which indicates the potential that wordless picturebooks can have for inviting co-authoring and inspiring the production of creative writing. Overall, the Visual Journeys project confirmed that the affordances of the wordless picturebook, along with the collective meaning making, facilitated children in thinking about language, narrative and meaning-making, in other words, they supported metacognitive awareness (Arizpe et al. 2014).

Polish students in Glasgow: Local language and social contexts

The second study took place within the wider context of the doctoral research of Sadie Ryan,[1] a linguist who investigates how immigrant students adopt the linguistic system of their new environment. Between September 2014 and November 2016, she conducted fieldwork with a group of fifteen Polish secondary school ELLs (between the ages of twelve and sixteen) all of whom attended a school in Glasgow's East End, an area of the city which has experienced a dramatic increase in the number of migrants entering the community in the past decade. Ryan's research questions focus on the factors that influence the acquisition of local linguistic behaviour in an area with a strong local dialect. When migrants move to a new area and begin to adopt the local variety of that area, they do not all do so at the same rate or in the same way. In this group of fifteen, there were some who sounded almost indistinguishable from their locally born peers within only a year or two of arrival in Glasgow, and others who still had little trace of the local accent in their speech after a much longer stay. The literature suggests that there may be extralinguistic factors at play. There has been research into the role of social networks (e.g. Meyerhoff and Schleef 2014), and whether having a positive attitude towards the local dialect or their new locality in general might lead to a faster and more full acquisition of local speech norms (Drummond 2011). Ryan's initial findings suggest that extralinguistic factors, such as cultural identity and self-perception, are key for her speakers.

The young people who participated in the study were undergoing multiple processes in their new city. They were undertaking formal language instruction in the classroom to help them learn Standard English, but they were also learning about the social norms of the local variety from their peers. They were building and negotiating new sociocultural identities, as all adolescents do, but with the additional challenge of having to do so in a new country and in a new language. The school community and the wider community where they now lived was also negotiating a shift: from being a settled, relatively monoethnic and monolingual community, a decade ago, to becoming a more multicultural community with many languages. For this reason, a group of monolingual speakers from the same secondary school was also included in the study. They were all born in Glasgow, raised as monolingual speakers of English and have been negotiating the challenges and rewards of meeting new classmates who do not (initially) share their first language.

These adolescents – both those born in Poland and those born in Glasgow – were experienced in thinking about language learning and transcultural communication. The project involved recording them in conversation with the researchers Arizpe and Ryan and with each other. Questions of how we can communicate across language barriers and how we learn language are familiar to both those participants born in Poland and those born in Glasgow. In order to probe further to find what they thought about second language acquisition and reading and learning through images, we decided to use *Mr Wuffles!*, which addresses the theme of languages and communication.

Opening a space for learners' voices using *Mr Wuffles!*

As mentioned above, there are few studies that include either the voices of the learners themselves talking about how learning a language works or their perceptions of resources and strategies for learning. We thought *Mr Wuffles!* would be an ideal book to open a space to discuss cultural and linguistic differences and thus promote deep reflection on languages, images and communication.

We indicated to the group of students Sadie Ryan was working with that we were interested in how *Mr Wuffles!* could be used to teach English to young children. Semi-structured individual interviews were held with each of the fifteen Polish teenagers and the five Scottish 'natives'. The sample questions that follow acted mainly as prompts:

> Can you describe how you would go about reading the book with a younger reader, and why you would take this approach?
>
> Do you think children would learn something from the story? What would they learn?
>
> Do you think you can use it to teach English? Imagine you are a teacher and there are many copies of the book in the classroom, some children speak English and some not very well. What would you do?

Following a grounded theory approach (Glaser and Strauss 2012), the transcribed interviews were analysed by a coding and recoding of the transcripts until the following recurrent themes were identified as key ones emerging from the data:

- The role of images and the (missing) words
- Cognitive strategies that help understanding
- The impact of language contexts on learning
- Metacognitive strategies involved in learning a language
- Language teaching strategies
- The need for guidance and mediation
- Previous reading experience
- Sociocultural identity and language learning
- Communication and diversity

In the following section, we refer to examples from the students' responses that touch on some of these themes and can help in exploring answers to the overall question: What and how can you learn if there are no words in a picturebook?

Lessons from aliens and insects

The lack of words initially baffled some of the students who had never seen a wordless picturebook before. Like Nikola, some of them projected their confusion on to the imaginary audience of 'wee children', speculating that they would not be able to understand it, especially as they would not be able to read the blurb at the back:

> I think that that book's a little bit confusing ... at the start it's, like it's *pure*[2] confusing, like, especially for the little ones. I don't understand anything [...] Like, you don't know what's happening to [the cat]. And, like, you don't know what's in the toy [...] If you read the back, like, you know what it is, but, the *wee* children won't read the back.
>
> *Nikola, thirteen, born in Poland*

However, most of the students eventually worked out the main elements of the story and conceded that it was more complex than they had initially thought and that careful viewing was necessary for any reader.

Understanding the story involved figuring out how the aliens and the insects manage to communicate through gestures and pictures in a way that allows them to make friends and work together. This led to a reflection on the strategies and dispositions that are necessary when two different groups (in this case two different species) encounter each other. Maja asked herself questions as she worked this out while she looked at one of the images (see Figure 4.3):

> I don't really get this. [Are they] trying to explain to them what happened? And then they understand there? So maybe they communicate through drawings?
>
> [...]
>
> So, like, there's another point, saying that you can speak [a] different language [and] you can look differently [*sic*] and you can still be friends.
>
> *Maja, thirteen, born in Poland*

The ability to ask herself these questions led to a thinking aloud process through which she made sense of what was happening and this allowed her

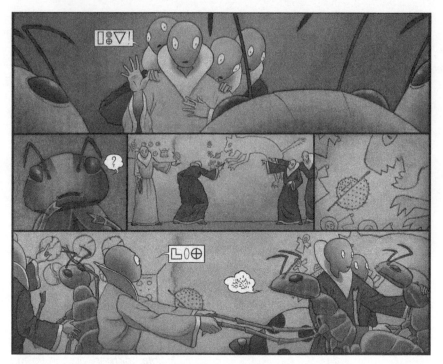

FIGURE 4.3 *Illustration from* MR WUFFLES! *by David Wiesner (copyright © 2013). Reprinted by permission of Houghton Mifflin Harcourt Publishing Company. All rights reserved.*

to reach her conclusion about what the story was trying to get across to readers. Based on this type of reflection, most of the students, both Polish and Scottish, concluded that one of the things readers could learn from the picturebook was, as Kinga (fifteen, born in Poland) succinctly put it, 'to be friends with others from different countries'.

In response to the question of whether the book could be used to teach English, again, some students were sceptical. Szymon (sixteen, born in Poland), for example, thought it would not qualify as a 'proper lesson' but that looking at it would be best as 'just, like, a warm-up exercise to get you thinking and then you can do other exercises to improve your English', although interestingly he specified that this activity would be beneficial in that it 'would probably get them positive thinking [*sic*] and then they can learn more'. By 'positive' he seemed to refer to an experience where reading is a 'fun' activity in contrast to some of his own previous experiences of directed language learning activities such as memorization. He continues:

> [...] you're basically getting them to do what you want them to do which is learning English. Except you're not giving them, like, you're not telling them

straight up. This is a more fun activity, instead of just telling them straight up [and] to give them words and tell them to learn them. I mean, come on, what kind of fun is that [. . .]? And this would be more interesting and get the people to, like, work on it more and stuff like that. It's a really good way of learning [. . .]

After talking for some time about the book and thinking about the question of teaching, some students began to describe activities that could be done with it. Zofia in particular came up with a whole range of activities. Whether she had experienced these activities before or was making them up is beside the point; the way she brings them together in the logical process of speaking, writing and presenting orally and graphically is impressive:

I would be [*sic*] like put them in the mixed groups. But with the people that speak English with the people [that speak a] different language. I would mix them up [. . .] in *wee* groups of like, say three, four people. And then give them a book to share in between. And they've to try explain to each other what they think's happening. And try, eh, like, write what they think should [be – say] on that page. And then [do a] presentation in front of the whole class what they think that should be [in the book]. So it gets their confidence up in front of the class [. . .] And they're communicating. And then it's like they can [. . .] do a *wee* book like it, like, try and make their own book. And [. . .] get wee stickers, and they can stick it on the books with the words they think that they're saying it. [You] could, like, translate that in different languages for each child who [speaks a] different language. And have it up on the wall. And, like, what it says. They'll know, like, what it – everybody will know what it means. And they're all familiar with a different language.

Zofia, sixteen, born in Poland

The Scottish students who were interviewed were mostly monolingual but had to study a language in school (usually Italian or French), so they had some idea about what it meant to learn a new language. Candice (thirteen, born in Scotland) spoke in detail about her experience of informally learning languages among her friends, an experience that perhaps made her more empathetic to the way in which *Mr Wuffles!* could be used to teach English. Her reflections include a reference to metacognitive strategies but are also based on cognitive and affective strategies related to her own experience, such as getting involved through talk, performance, guided questions and overcoming the challenges of learning new words.

Jamie also used his own reading experience of encountering a different type of text to reflect on how someone might interact with *Mr Wuffles!* He comments on his actual cognitive process of learning to read from a different direction and how it was a challenge for his brain to make this change:

> They probably would get confused, but they [would] probably get the hang of it, because that's what I was like with the Manga, 'cause I opened it, then, but I didn't know where to start 'cause my brain was always just attached to, like, starting at that that side of the page first.
>
> *Jamie, sixteen, born in Scotland*

Moving forward in language learning through wordless picturebooks

Although our research questions aimed to open a space that invited metalevel thinking skills, the participants responded to this invitation and referred to metacognitive strategies for meaning making to a level that was not expected. Many researchers agree that a learner's awareness and understanding of their cognitive processes can have a significant role in language learning and have argued that teachers should actively help learners to develop this metacognitive skill (Breen 2001, Ellis 2018, this volume). Flavell (1987) and Wenden (2001) argue, however, that this knowledge is still not fully valued or taken into account in ELT, a view confirmed by the overview of research into this area conducted by Raoofi et al. (2014).

Bernat and Gvozdenko note that language learners usually hold strong beliefs about 'the nature of the language under study, its difficulty, the process of its acquisition, the success of certain learning strategies, the existence of aptitude, their own expectations about achievement and teaching methodologies' (2005: 1). Moreover, these beliefs seem to influence what they actually do to help themselves learn. A wide range of studies, most of them quantitative and based on questionnaires, have attempted to gain insight into these beliefs and assumptions and measure this metacognitive knowledge to understand how it supports language development and performance in different contexts (e.g. Barkhuizen 1998; Narayan 2013). In the students' comments about the wordless picturebooks, it was possible to see some of these beliefs emerging in a more natural dialogic process that allowed the researcher to delve more deeply into particular topics related to language learning – something a language teacher could also do.

Raoofi et al. show that there is enough evidence to conclude that metacognition can be developed through pedagogical interventions (2014: 45), thus providing a solid argument for carrying out activities in the classroom that raise learners' awareness. We realize that with the *Mr*

Wuffles! task we were asking a student to construct a 'mini' lesson plan on the spot, which is not an easy task even for an experienced teacher. However, the conversations showed how the students were able to put their previous experiences (both positive and negative) as well as their subject and metacognitive and metalinguistic knowledge to good use. In a sense, they were able to do a 'task analysis' as described by Wenden, which involved thinking about the purpose of the task, being aware of the challenges the task posed and how they might approach it according to the demands, knowledge and skills and the difficulties it might present to younger children (2001: 51).

Encouraging learners to think about their language learning process allows them to first consider the beliefs and assumptions they have about the language in question. It can then help them make decisions about planning, selecting strategies and assessing their learning in ways that accord with their individual needs and abilities. Thinking about learning strategies in relation to different aspects of language learning (listening, reading, writing, speaking) can help understand which may need more work, how different resources (including literary texts) and approaches could work, leading to more effective learning strategies.

The empirical research referred to here strongly suggests that meeting the challenge of the wordless picturebook is more than worthwhile in language learning because it provides the opportunity to develop metacognitive strategies and metalinguistic thinking. Nikolajeva's work (2014) on cognitive literary theory and reading supports this line of enquiry because, as she argues, literary texts interact with cognition to provide readers with knowledge of the world, of other people and of themselves. In other words, the emotions provoked by words and images expand cognitive abilities, especially those of developing readers (2014: 227) and foster Theory of Mind, or the ability to understand the mental states of others (Colman 2016).

Conclusion

As the studies have shown, wordless picturebooks can provide a space for student reflection on the learning process. In addition, perhaps more importantly, they provide a space for student reflection on beliefs and assumptions about language and communication. This space can be made use of by the adults who select and mediate texts, whether it is in the home or the classroom, no matter what the age of the readers. However, further research is required on how teachers can best mediate these texts in an ELT classroom and on how the wordless picturebook links to language acquisition, intercultural learning and cultural identity in ways that enable discussion around diversity and inclusion within these and other language-learning spaces. What seems clear is that the contemporary wordless picturebook can provoke significant questions about reading and learning as well as help to transform attitudes in multilingual contexts about intercultural communication, and therefore to challenge linguistic discrimination, Othering and exclusion.

RECOMMENDATIONS

- The dialogue in *Mr Wuffles!* is mostly between insects and aliens with their own created languages (see Figure 4.3). This offers an excellent opportunity for student teachers to practise *creative teacher talk* – telling the story in their own words as teacher-storytellers (Bland 2015: 190), and simultaneously modelling language for young language learners. This activity can guide inexperienced teachers, or students in initial teacher education, in how to use repetitive and patterned language – similar to child-directed speech – in a supportive and impromptu way.
- Movies have also been made with unusual visions of the unexpectedly dramatic world of insects and other tiny creatures. Two highly recommended movies are *Microcosmos* (1996) and *Antz* (1998). *Microcosmos* is a fascinating, prize-winning documentary that shows the unexpected power and complexity of insects and other minuscule creatures in the animal kingdom – viewers might investigate the behaviour and habitat, or creatively tell or pen the creatures' stories. *Antz* is a visually striking animation, with a stellar voice cast and an intelligent and hilarious story.

Notes

1 Doctoral student in English Language and Linguistics/Education, University of Glasgow.
2 *Pure* is used as an intensifier in Glasgow; it is roughly equivalent to *really*.

Bibliography

Antz (1998), [Film] Dir. Eric Darnell and Tim Johnson, US: DreamWorks Pictures.
Microcosmos (1996), [Film] Dir. Claude Nuridsany and Marie Pérennou, France: BAC Films.
Spot (2015), [Mobile application software] David Wiesner and Houghton Mifflin Harcourt.

Tan, Shaun (2007), *The Arrival*, New York: Arthur A. Levine Books.
Wiesner, David (1992), *Tuesday*, New York: Clarion Books.
Wiesner, David (2002), *The Three Pigs*, New York: Clarion Books.
Wiesner, David (2006), *Flotsam*, New York: Clarion Books.
Wiesner, David (2010), *Art and Max*, New York: Clarion Books.
Wiesner, David (2013), *Mr Wuffles!*, New York: Clarion Books.

References

Arizpe, Evelyn (2014), 'Wordless picturebooks: Critical and educational
perspectives on meaning-making', in Bettina Kümmerling-Meibauer (ed.),
Aesthetic and Cognitive Challenges of the Picturebook, London: Routledge,
pp. 91–108.
Arizpe, Evelyn, Colomer, Teresa and Martínez-Roldán, Carmen (2014), *Visual
Journeys through Wordless Narratives: An International Inquiry with
Immigrant Children and 'The Arrival'*, London: Bloomsbury Academic.
Arizpe, Evelyn and McAdam, Julie (2011), 'Crossing visual borders and
connecting cultures: Children's responses to the photographic theme in David
Wiesner's *Flotsam*', *New Review of Children's Literature and Librarianship*,
17/2: 227–43.
Arizpe, Evelyn and Styles, Morag (2003), *Children Reading Pictures*: *Interpreting
Visual Texts*, London: Routledge.
Arizpe, Evelyn, McAdam, Julie and Farrar, Jennifer (2017), 'Picturebooks and
Literacy Studies', in Bettina Kümmerling-Meibauer (ed.), *The Routledge
Companion to Picturebooks*, London: Routledge, pp. 371–80.
Barkhuizen, Gary (1998), 'Discovering learners' perceptions of ESL classroom
teaching/learning activities in a South African Context', *TESOL Quarterly*,
32: 85–108.
Bernat, Eva and Gvozdenko, Inna (2005), 'Beliefs about language
learning: Current knowledge, pedagogical implications, and new research
directions', *TESL-EJ*, 9/1: 1–21. http://files.eric.ed.gov/fulltext/EJ1065832.pdf
(accessed 24 February 2017).
Bland, Janice (2013), *Children's Literature and Learner Empowerment: Children
and Teenagers in English Language Education*, London: Bloomsbury
Academic.
Bland, Janice (2015), 'Oral storytelling in the primary English classroom', in
Janice Bland (ed.), *Teaching English to Young Learners. Critical Issues in
Language Teaching with 3–12 Year Olds*, London: Bloomsbury Academic,
pp. 183–98.
Block, Cathy (2004), *Teaching Comprehension: The Comprehension Process
Approach*, Boston: Allyn & Bacon.
Breen, Michael, ed. (2001), *Learner Contributions to Language Learning: New
Directions in Research*, Harlow, Essex: Pearson Education Limited.
Colman, Andrew, ed. (2016) *Oxford Dictionary of Psychology*, Oxford: Oxford
University Press.
Drummond, Robert (2011), 'Glottal variation in /t/ in non-native English
speech: Patterns of acquisition', *English World-Wide*, 32/3: 280–308.

Durant, Alan (2013), 'Using literary texts in ELT: Retrospect and challenges', in
    Manasori Toyota and Shigeo Kikuchi (eds), *New Horizons in English Language
    Teaching: Language, Literature and Education*, Kyoto: Kansai Gaidai University
    Press, pp. 1–35.
Early, Margaret (1991), 'Using wordless picture books to promote second
    language learning', *ELT Journal*, 45/3: 245–51.
Ellis, Gail (2018), 'The picturebook in elementary ELT: Multiple literacies with Bob
    Staake's *Bluebird*', in Janice Bland (ed.), *Using Literature in English Language
    Education: Challenging Reading for 8–18 Year Olds*, London: Bloomsbury
    Academic, pp. 83–104.
Flavell, John (1987), 'Speculation about the nature and development of
    metacognition', in Franz Weinert and Rainer Kluwe (eds), *Metacognition,
    Motivation and Understanding*, Hillsdale, NJ: Lawrence Erlbaum, pp. 1–29.
Glaser, Barney and Strauss, Anselm (2012), *The Discovery of Grounded
    Theory: Strategies for Qualitative Research*, London: Transaction Publishers.
Hsiu-Chih, Sheu (2008), 'The value of English picture story books', *ELT Journal*,
    62/1: 47–55.
Kern, Richard (2000), *Literacy and Language Teaching*, Oxford: Oxford
    University Press.
Louie, Belinda and Sierschynski, Jarek (2015), 'Enhancing English learners'
    language development using wordless picture books', *The Reading Teacher*,
    69/1: 103–11.
Meek, Margaret (1988), *How Texts Teach What Readers Learn*, Gloucester:
    The Thimble Press.
Meyerhoff, Miriam and Schleef, Erik (2014), 'Hitting an Edinburgh
    target: Immigrant adolescents' acquisition of variation in Edinburgh English',
    in Robert Lawson (ed.), *Sociolinguistics in Scotland*, London: Palgrave
    Macmillan, pp. 103–12.
Mourão, Sandie (2015), 'What's real and what's not: Playing with the mind
    in wordless picturebooks', in Janet Evans (ed.), *Challenging and Controversial
    Picturebooks: Creative and Critical Responses to Visual Texts*, London:
    Routledge, pp. 181–200.
Nikolajeva, Maria (2003), 'Verbal and visual literacy: The role of picturebooks in
    the reading experience of young children', in Nigel Hall, Joanne Larson and
    Jackie Marsh (eds), *Handbook of Early Childhood Literacy*, London: Sage,
    pp. 235–48.
Nikolajeva, Maria (2014), *Reading for Learning: Cognitive Approaches to
    Children's Literature*, Amsterdam: John Benjamins.
Pantaleo, Sylvia (2007), '"How could that be?": Reading Banyai's *Zoom* and
    Re-Zoom', *Language Arts*, 84/3: 222–33.
Pantaleo, Sylvia (2015), 'Language, literacy and visual texts', *English in Education*,
    49/2: 113–29.
Raoofi, Saeid, Heng Chan, Swee, Mukundan, Jayakaran and Rashid, Sabariah
    (2014), 'Metacognition and second/foreign language learning', *English
    Language Teaching*, 7/1: 36–49.
Narayan Shrestha, Prithvi (2013), 'English language classroom practices:
    Bangladeshi primary school children's perceptions', *RELC Journal*, 44/2:
    147–62.

Wenden, Anita (2001), 'Metacognitive knowledge', in Michael Breen (ed.), *Learner Contributions to Language Learning: New Directions in Research*, Harlow, Essex: Pearson Education, pp. 44–64.

Wiesner, David (1992), 'Why Frogs? Why Tuesday? Caldecott Medal Acceptance Speech for *Tuesday*' http://www.houghtonmifflinbooks.com/authors/wiesner/bio/bio3_cald.shtml (accessed 24 February 2017).

5

The picturebook in elementary ELT: Multiple literacies with Bob Staake's BLUEBIRD

Gail Ellis

The picturebook has had a long history in primary or elementary English pedagogy in a range of settings including ELT and multilingual classrooms, as reported in Mourão and Bland (2016). While the main focus has been on learning language, it is well recognized that using stories and picturebooks brings other gains. Ellis and Brewster (2014: 7) refer to cross-curricular goals, learning to learn, conceptual reinforcement and citizenship, diversity and intercultural gains. In addition, Enever and Schmid-Shönbein (2006) and Ellis and Brewster (2014: 14) state that the picturebook also brings authenticity and challenge to the learning experience as it can address universal themes that go beyond the 'utilitarian level of basic dialogues and mundane daily activities' (Ghosn 2002: 175).

Susan Laughs (Willis and Ross 1999) illustrates this point well. It is a short story in rhythm and rhyme that delivers a powerful message about disability. The use of the 'withheld image' means that it is not until the last page that the reader discovers that Susan is a wheelchair user (see Figure 5.1). After the picturebook was read aloud to an ELT class of nine-year-old young learners, they reflected in silence for several minutes while they assimilated this final image, relating it to what they had just heard and seen. They then began asking questions about Susan, returning to the picturebook to check their interpretations. Such experiences highlight the power of the picturebook. They

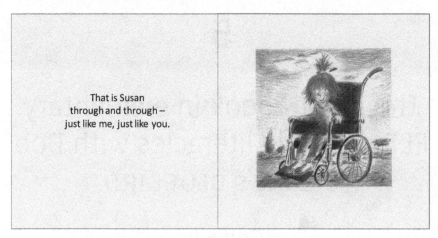

FIGURE 5.1 *Excerpted from* Susan Laughs *(text Jeanne Willis © 1999, illustration Tony Ross © 1999). Reprinted by permission of Penguin Random House.*

initiate conversations and allow children to explore questions and concerns about issues that are meaningful and real to them.

It is not surprising then, that the picturebook can provide an ideal opportunity to bring multimodal representation into the classroom and develop multiple literacies, which are such an important aspect of communication and representation of meaning in the twenty-first century, where written linguistic modes of meaning interact with oral, visual, audio, gestural, tactile and special patterns of meaning. This chapter offers a narrative account of how *Bluebird* (Staake 2013) was used to develop multiple literacies with plurilingual children in Paris.

One of the greatest challenges facing teachers using a story-based approach is selecting the most suitable picturebook for a specific class. Children may have limited English-language skills but possess ideas, concepts and aspirations relevant to their developmental age. In reality, linguistic and cultural diversity is present today in most classrooms and there is frequently a range of English language levels due to a variety of factors, such as the age the children begin learning English, the quality and quantity of teaching and the children's amount of out-of-school exposure to English. Real success depends on having the right story for the linguistic and cognitive ability and interests of the children in order to maximize their enjoyment, involvement and learning. Different picturebooks will appeal to different classes and many can be read with children of different ages and English levels, depending on the way they are used; thus it is not possible to give definitive indications regarding age-level suitability. Ellis and Brewster (2014: 19) provide systematic criteria for selection, which include reference to linguistic, psychological, cognitive, sociological and cultural aspects of the picturebook, demonstrating that, if carefully selected, picturebooks can bring other gains in addition to linguistic gains to support the development of the whole child in a language-learning context.

Picturebooks, then, provide a rich, motivating and authentic source of meaningful input to develop children's early English language learning. However, they can be used to develop much more than aural understanding, vocabulary and grammar related to the content of a story. They can also support and challenge children to develop other ways of interpreting, understanding and making meaning, through the development of multiple literacies.

Multiple literacies

The term multiple literacies embraces the notion that there are multiple modes of representation which are much broader than language alone (Cope and Kalantzis 2009: 166). Multiple literacies pedagogy 'encourages a broader perspective of the student as a learner and values diverse ways of knowing, thinking, doing and being' (O'Rourke 2005: 10). It is underpinned by multimodal theory which asserts that children create meaning using a 'multiplicity of modes, means and materials' for self-expression (Kress 1997: 97).

It can be seen that multiple literacies extend the traditional view of literacy, often referred to as functional literacy, which is the ability to read and write. This wider focus, stretching beyond alphabetical representations, brings into the classroom multimodal resources, including digital media (see Brunsmeier and Kolb 2018, this volume). Multiple literacies encompass many forms of literacy that require learning how to decode and interpret information conveyed through these multiple modes. Information conveyed through visual images is an important means of communication, and challenging children to read images deeply develops their visual literacy. They can consider the emotional temperature of the images to capture atmosphere, to feel empathy by reading facial expressions, gestures and body language and thus to develop emotional literacy. Picturebooks are full of cultural information, so noticing and understanding similarities and differences to a child's own cultural surroundings helps them develop cultural literacy, a first step in intercultural learning. Interpreting and understanding the natural world as depicted in a picturebook helps children develop nature literacy, leading towards environmental literacy. Working with animations of picturebooks helps children develop film literacy. Picturebooks offer routes into inferencing, deduction and critical thinking. So as the children seek clues to meaning via the illustrations, predict what is going to happen next, organize their learning materials, think about how they learn and review and assess their learning, they also develop 'learning' literacy.

In the primary language classroom, developing multiple literacies involves acknowledging and recognizing children's drawings, constructions, arts and crafts and actions as alternative ways of communicating with the teacher about their world. Using picturebooks allows the teacher to provide multimodal input as they offer a springboard for a range of associated activities, such as songs and chants, realia, film, digital technologies, actions and drama. These enable children to make meaning and develop and extend language.

Multiple literacies and wordless picturebooks

Children learn about narrative structure and conventions by listening to suitably rich stories, or by sharing a picturebook where the meaning of the verbal text is extended by the illustrations, such as in *Susan Laughs*. Wordless picturebooks can also teach essential narrative conventions which are as much a part of a reader's competence as the ability to decode print. These are books that children often develop a very special feeling for. As there is no printed verbal story children feel active and powerful in their role of finding words to shape the story. Where the narrative medium is solely the images, children seem more aware of their own contribution in making the pictures tell a story and feel satisfaction in the productive partnership they have entered with the artist – they begin to acquire metacognitive strategies (Arizpe and Ryan 2018, this volume). A wordless picturebook offers an open invitation where personal interpretation counts rather than finding a right or wrong answer, and they promote a sense of power, creativity and freedom. They challenge children to fully engage with their interpretation of the images and 'to reflect on the narrative resulting from this interaction' (Arizpe, Colomer and Martinez-Roldan 2015: 3).

Briggs's (1978) timeless wordless picturebook, *The Snowman*, enabled an ELT class of 9-year-old near-beginner children in a state primary school in Paris to exercise their imaginations and to become personally, actively and creatively involved in the story as they empathized with the characters. As the children interpreted the picture narrative, they were developing their visual literacy. They were developing emotional literacy as they interpreted the gestures and facial expressions in the illustrations, which enabled them to empathize with the boy in the story, especially in the final illustration where the boy is looking down on a heap of melted snow. As one child said (in French, my translation): '*The Snowman* story makes me cry. I don't want him to melt. I don't want the story to end'. The children were aware that the Snowman, a distinctive and believable character, was the boy's dream or fantasy. This enabled them to explain their sorrow at the end of the story – it was not only the melting snowman but also the end of the boy's dream. They were also developing cultural literacy as they noticed details about the setting or how the characters greeted each other, and made comparisons with their own culture. Nature literacy was supported, as they learned about winter weather, snow and how snowflakes are formed. Children also developed 'learning' literacy as they interpreted the visual narrative, predicted what was going to happen next, organized their learning materials in story envelopes and reviewed and assessed their learning. Multiple literacies, therefore, can be developed at all stages of working with a picturebook, to teach the whole child.

Bob Staake's *Bluebird* (2013)

This chapter describes how *Bluebird* (Staake 2013), a wordless picturebook, was used to develop multiple literacies with a class of sixteen

FIGURE 5.2 *Cover of* Bluebird *(Bob Staake © 2013). Reprinted by permission of Penguin Random House.*

9-year-old plurilingual children in January and February 2017. The children attend mainstream primary school in Paris, and additionally attended an out-of-school English class for two hours once a week. The shared classroom languages were English and French, and other languages spoken by the children were Russian, Korean, Arabic, Romanian, Mandarin and Italian. The main aims of the out-of-school classes were to maintain and develop the children's spoken English, which had been acquired via English-speaking parents or by attending English medium schools, either in an English-speaking country or in France, and to develop their literacy skills in English. The classes also provided a secure, stimulating space for exchange with other plurilingual children in order to expand their 'linguistic, intellectual and cultural capital' (Cummins 2014: 2). *Bluebird* (see Figure 5.2) was used over three lessons representing six hours and the final outcome task was to write a text that matched the images.

Bob Staake's *Bluebird* explores the themes of shyness, loneliness, bullying, bravery, dealing with loss and the importance of friendship and resilience. The story takes place in Manhattan and tells of a boy who has no friends and is the victim of bullying at school. He is excluded from playtime and teased in class. A small bluebird observes the boy and then follows him home at the end of the school day. A friendship between the two is established. They play hide and seek, share a cookie, sail boats on the lake in the park and daydream together. Each page is broken into smaller panels to depict the next part of the narration and the passage of time. The illustrations are distinctive, comic-like and geometrical in their structure and simplicity, shaded in black, white, greys and blues. The sky and bird are blue, but the lonely boy with the large, round head is dark grey, and shades of grey make up much of his world, while white and black are used symbolically. The muted tones combined with the lucid geometric figures create many moods. The reader follows the bird's flight past a New York City skyline filled with cones, pyramids and rectangular prisms. Vertical lines are interspersed with stylized ball-shaped trees, clocks, heads and circular forms to focus attention on a scene or character (see Figure 5.3).

Bluebird lends itself well to developing spoken and written discourse and meaning-making. As children interpret and discuss the visual narrative, they acquire metalanguage related to images, they clarify and expand ideas, discuss meaning, predict and infer, consider different points of view, activate cultural knowledge and compare and contrast. *Bluebird* is suitable for children from around age eight, and could also be used with lower secondary pupils, as it can be used to give children practice in writing at sentence level as well as practice in extended writing.

FIGURE 5.3 Excerpted from Bluebird (Bob Staake © 2013). Reprinted by permission of Penguin Random House. Stylized trees, heads, clock and circular form (iris shot) to focus attention.

Developing multiple literacies with *Bluebird*

To provide an entry point for discussion and personal connections, the sixteen 9-year-old children were shown the title and the front and back covers and asked to speculate where the story takes place, who might be the main characters, and what the story might be about. They were then shown the front endpapers and asked to comment on the illustrations. As three of the children had lived in New York there was immediate engagement. The dedication page to John James Audubon, the ornithologist and painter of *Birds of America* (1838), and the billboard in homage to him, triggered questions about what type of bird the bluebird may be.

When the children noticed the boy, this led to discussion about the theme of friendship. They were asked to think about their own friends in order to formulate their understanding of the concept of friendship, meanwhile consolidating their vocabulary. As a whole class activity, the children shared their ideas to create a concept web on the interactive whiteboard by completing the phrase, 'A friend is someone who … '. The children created a large poster of a Friendship Building and a Bully Building (see Figure 5.4) inspired by the geometric patterns of the buildings on the front and back covers. They

FIGURE 5.4 *A Friendship Building and a Bully Building.*

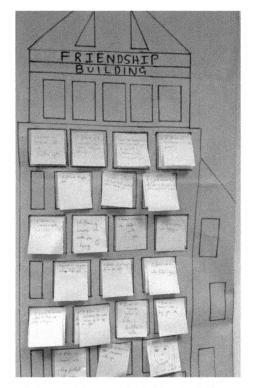

FIGURE 5.5 *Friendship Building with children's definitions of friendship.*

wrote their definitions on sticky notes and arranged them in the windows of the Friendship Building poster (see Figures 5.5 and 5.6). This tactile and hands-on writing task involving movement, contains the six types of task support described by Cameron (2001: 27) – cognitive, language, interactional, metalinguistic, involvement, physical – and it motivates the children to develop their written discourse skills at sentence level.

As can be seen from Table 5.1, the task generated a great number of definitions, and some children produced up to five definitions each. The children read out the definitions, identified duplicates and put them together in a window. After reading and interpreting the picturebook, the children wrote definitions of a bully as a follow-up task and arranged them in the windows of the Bully Building to compare and contrast friends and bullies.

Visual and emotional literacy

Emotional literacy is described as the 'ability to make sense of and apply knowledge about our own and others' emotional states with skill and competence' (Weare 2004: 2). This includes understanding ourselves and

FIGURE 5.6 *Example of a friendship definition.*

other people, and in particular to be aware of, understand, read the signs and use information about the emotional states of ourselves and others and to understand, express and manage our own emotions and respond appropriately.

In order to facilitate emotional literacy, the teacher used focused questions (Fisher 2005: 20, Ellis and Brewster 2014: 27, Arizpe, Colomer and Martinez-Roldan 2015: 187) to mediate and guide children's reading and interpretation of the visual narrative. She elicited or drew their attention to how facial expressions, such as the simple line of the mouth, the downcast eyes, the gestures, the inclination of the head and the use of arms, portray a boy who might be shy, lonely, unhappy, curious, playful, imaginative, kind and generous, mischievous, thoughtful, vulnerable and brave. This enabled the children to say how the boy felt and to reflect on how they would feel in the same situation and empathize with the boy. When the children reflected on their personal response (see Figure 5.8) they were able to express how the story made them feel:

It made me change feelings a lot: sad-happy-sad-happy. (P1)

The story makes me feel sad because the bluebird dies. It makes me feel happy because the boy makes a lot of friends with other birds. (P2)

These comments, from pupils 1 and 2, show that they empathized with the boy and his grief especially when the bird lies limp in his hands, his head is bowed and a tear marks his mourning (see Figure 5.7).

TABLE 5.1 *Children's definitions*

A friend is someone who ...	A bully is someone who ...
helps and plays with you	isn't nice to you
cares about you	is selfish
likes you	does not care about you
never lets you down	wants everything you have
is loyal	is mean
trusts you and that you can trust!!!	calls you names
doesn't insult and hurt you and betray you	is against you
is kind with you and protects you	hurts you
respects you	insults you
talks with you	is not a friend
makes you happy	doesn't like you
is always here for you	hates you
never gives up on you	makes fun of you
is like a brother or sister	beats you up
is by your side	you can't trust
plays football with you	fights you
shares with you	is a coward
risks her life for you	does not want your happiness
looks after you	kicks you and wants to annoy you
stays with you when you are sad	is not loyal to you
is always in your heart	doesn't help you
	doesn't have friends
	envies you
	scares you
	pushes you

FIGURE 5.7 *Excerpted from* Bluebird *(Bob Staake © 2013). Reprinted by permission of Penguin Random House.*

However, not all children interpreted the images as the bird dying, as revealed in their written narratives of the story:

> Then other coloured birds arrived and brought the bluebird and Paul to the sky where the bluebird lives again. (P3)
>
> The bird was nearly dead. Then many birds of different colours arrived and they took the bluebird and the bluebird flew in the sky (we don't know where). (P4)
>
> He starts crying but at one moment a red bird, a purple bird, a yellow bird and all the other coloured birds bring him in the sky and then it disappears. (P5)

Others made references to heaven and paradise: 'They took the bluebird to heaven' (P6), and 'Then he went into a cloud to paradise' (P7). Some were more explicit:

> The bullies wanted the boat and then a bully threw a stick at the boy and instead he killed the poor little bluebird. (P8)
>
> He wasn't the luckiest of people in the world because some bullies arrived and threw a stick and the bird died. (P6)

Some children recognized the boy's hope and acceptance in the final double spread as he is lifted up to the sky by multicoloured birds and described him as a 'multicoloured angel':

> Elliot cried but a lot of coloured birds came and he was very, very happy. (P9)
>
> Now he has plenty of friends but he will remember the bluebird. (P2)

One child recognized this in her personal response: 'I liked when lots of birds came to help the boy with the bird and why I like it's because the thing is to deal with loss and friendship' (P8). They read these emotions and feelings from the pictures in much the same way as they interpret other people's behaviour in real life: 'I like that there is a full story that you can understand from images and there are lots of emotions' (P10).

The teacher used questions as prompts to help children notice visual techniques such as perspective when the reader witnesses the bullying taking place at school through the eyes of the bird, the use of colour and light to indicate a change in mood and to alert the reader to danger and rescue, and the contrasting use of stark geometrical lines and shapes with circles and the gentle curves of the bluebird and the tree where they play. The children said these reflected the concrete harshness of the city compared to the beauty of nature and the happiness of the boy with his newfound friend. When asked why they thought the author had not included a written narrative for his story they replied that the images depicting the bird wordlessly interacting with the boy allowed them to imagine the conversations taking place between them and to imagine what the boy was thinking. P11 wrote in her narrative: 'As usual, some of the kids in my class start mocking me. To tell you something, I do not care, I don't mind if I don't have any friends because I have a lot of imagination'.

Cultural literacy

Cultural literacy helps develop intercultural competence by recognizing similarities and differences with one's own culture and to see oneself as part of a connected world. Furthermore:

> The role of the teacher is to encourage and help bring about this discovery, drawing attention to the fact that the differences in relation to the pupils' own habits and day-to-day lives are to be seen in a positive light. This awareness adds to the sum of pupils' knowledge of humanity and of the world. (Brewster, Ellis and Girard 2002: 146)

The illustrations in *Bluebird* are rich in information and details about Manhattan and ignited the children's curiosity. They asked lots of questions and, through prompts from the teacher, developed their skills of observation and made cross-cultural comparisons. The children noticed differences to their own environment in the architecture, street signs, mailboxes, fire hydrants, shops, a Gotham Cafe and transport and pointed out landmarks such as Central Park and the Empire State Building.

Nature literacy

Many children are spending less time exploring and playing in nature and leading more and more sedentary lives indoors with their devices and in front of screens. This may have negative effects on their emotional, intellectual and physical development. Nature literacy helps children explore and understand the plants and animals that coexist with them and recognize changes in the seasons and the weather in their local environment. It can help them develop a sense of community and responsibility for the environment and appreciation of the natural world.

Two tasks were used to develop nature literacy. The first was a craft activity to make a bluebird model which involved the children in listening, observing, drawing and cutting, all of which required precision. The bluebirds were hung from the ceiling of the classroom to create a motivating learning environment while the class was working on the picturebook. The second was a homework task that involved the children in becoming aware of bluebirds or other birds that are blue in their local environment and around the world, for example the Blue Tit, the Blue Jay, the Kingfisher, the Mountain Bluebird. They wrote a short description about one of the birds stating what it looks like, its size, the countries it is found in, where it lives, its type of song, when it breeds and what it eats. This activity enabled the children to increase their range of discourse types by having practice in writing informational text. They also began to develop their information literacy (see Krashen and Bland 2014: 7), using the Web carefully to research their chosen birds, evaluating the reliability of information, reading information texts to find specific information and make decisions.

Film literacy: First steps

In groups, the children were asked to discuss and make notes about which scenes from the story they would include in a 45-second book trailer video for *Bluebird*, which words they would include (spoken or written) or none at all and which music and/or sound effects they would include (see Table 5.2). None of the groups included any words as they felt this would not be in keeping with the wordless picturebook.

Each group presented their ideas to the class and the children were asked to vote for the presentation they felt would best entice others to read *Bluebird*. The children were then shown the *Bluebird* trailer (https://www.youtube.com/watch?v=GFWahrCXulk) and asked to identify what was the same or different from their trailer. During a second viewing, they identified the sound effects and musical instruments used to create mood and signal danger. The trailer ends with a question, *Have **you** helped a friend today?* which generated a

TABLE 5.2 *Planning a book trailer video*

Scenes	Music and sound effects
The boy meets the bird	Surprised sound effects, 3 seconds
They meet the bullies	Dramatic music, 5 seconds
They kill the bird	Very sad sound effects – violin for the sad scenes

great deal of discussion among the class as they reflected on and explained how they had personally helped a friend that day. During the final lesson children were shown extracts from Albert Lamorisse's *Le Ballon Rouge* (1956), a wordless classic short film set in the city of Paris about a boy who is also a victim of bullying. They were asked to compare the film to the story of *Bluebird*. This provided another rich opportunity to develop spoken discourse of contrast and comparison.

'Learning' literacy

'Learning' literacy (Ellis 2016: 30) is linked to metacognitive strategies and to learner autonomy. It involves developing awareness and understanding of one's own learning processes, personal cognitive preferences and learning strategies. Learning literacy is also about developing an inquisitive mindset and using resources that ignite curiosity and enable experimentation. It is an important aim of most curricula throughout the world since it underpins learning in all areas of the curriculum and life and, as 'learning to learn', is one of the EU's eight key competencies for lifelong learning (EU 2006). Children's ability to reflect on and talk about their learning should not be underestimated. They are competent, insightful and spontaneous commentators on their own learning experiences if they are given the opportunity and possess a considerable degree of metacognitive knowledge and ability (Nisbet and Shucksmith 1986; Whitebread et al. 2005).

Plan, Do, Review

In this section the *Plan Do Review* model is introduced, a framework that structured the work on *Bluebird* with the sixteen 9-year-olds and led finally to creative writing. The *Plan Do Review* model of reflection originates from the HighScope approach to early childhood education, which is a child-initiated approach to learning (Hohmann, Weikart and Epstein 2008). This model has been adapted and applied by Ellis and Ibrahim (2015) to provide a consistent, predictable routine that structures the learning sequences, and to give children a sense of control over what happens next. It contributes to a motivating environment within which children can make choices and initiate activities. The three stages parallel the familiar pre- while- and post-storytelling activities used by many teachers. They provide opportunities for systematic reflection (Plan), experimentation (Do) and further reflection (Review), thereby developing both cognitive and metacognitive learning strategies such as seeking clues to meaning via the illustrations, seeing cause and effect, predicting what is going to happen next, drawing inferences, asking questions, organizing learning, reviewing learning and assessing learning.

The Review stage involved the children in reflecting on their personal response to *Bluebird*, the learning strategies they used and assessing their performance (see Figure 5.8). Children's written responses to the first question – *what I liked about this story* – can be categorized around the theme of friendship: 'I like this story because the boy makes a friend and they care about each other' (P12), and 'I like this story because it's about friendship and kindness and I like this very well' (P3). One child, as mentioned earlier, liked the fact that the boy was able to deal with loss. Several children liked what they perceived to be a happy ending: 'I like that the boy was first sad that (*sic*) at the end of the story he is happier' (P13). One child specifically mentioned the images: 'The lovely pictures because I like this type of pictures' (P7).

Responses to the second question – *what I learned from this story* – showed that they recognized the value of friendship and the wrongs of bullying:

Friendship is important in every way and don't be a bully. (P14)

What I learned from this story is that I will never let a friend down and that you can't insult or exclude or hurt someone even if you don't like this person. You need to help him or her. (P3)

Responses also showed empathy: 'I learned to never be a bully because you wouldn't like it if you were the boy' (P1). Respecting others was also a learning point: 'I learned from this story to be nice with other people and respect them very well' (P2). Finally, hope and resilience were also reflected in the responses: 'I learned from the story that if you have no friend you are always going to find one and sometimes a friend can risk his life for you' (P13).

The self-assessment encouraged the children to reflect on the learning strategies they used, consider how much effort they had made and how well they felt they had participated. Thus, learning literacy can be developed through

Bluebird by Bob Staake

1. What I liked about this story. Why?

....

....

....

....

2. What I learned from this story.

....

....

....

....

3. How the story made me feel.

....

....

....

....

My Participation (Colour the birds blue to assess how well you did.)

I interpreted the images to understand the narrative.

I interpreted the images to understand the boy's feelings.

I asked and answered questions during the story.

I predicted what was going to happen next.

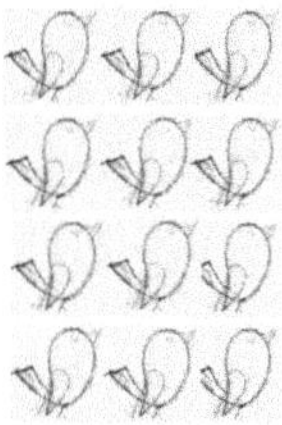

3 birds = I tried hard and did this well.
2 birds = I tried quite hard and did this quite well.
1 bird = I need to try harder next time.

FIGURE 5.8 *Personal response to a story.*

picturebooks, if children are actively involved and encouraged to reflect on their learning so they become aware of and understand the processes of learning and of their own personal interpretations, preferences and learning strategies.

The children were asked if they had enjoyed reading a book without words and how it was different for them. Written responses included:

I don't look at the pictures so carefully when there are words. Each image in *Bluebird* tells a story and they made me see things I probably wouldn't have seen if there had been words. (P3)

I liked the way I saw different things in the pictures that at first I had missed. (P6)

It was more difficult. The pictures made me pay attention. I had to concentrate and think more to find the story. (P8)

Creative writing

The final outcome task, then, was creative writing to match the images. This involved the children reflecting on and analysing the narrative structure of *Bluebird*, activating their literary knowledge and reviewing their initial interpretation of the visual narrative. It also gave practice in written discourse. To support the children in their writing, the teacher elicited how to create and structure a story, which requires:

- an opening
- characters and a setting
- a problem
- different events
- a resolution of the problem
- a closing

Some children chose to write their story as the narrator in the third person giving the boy a name, others wrote in the first person from the boy's point of view and others chose the bird's point of view. Most included the introduction of the characters and the setting in their opening and one child set the story in the future:

It all started in the street. Tom was going to school and he was sad. He had no friends to play with. (P4)

This is a story about a little boy named Brandon. He lives in New York but he doesn't have the best life. Monday 21st of April Brandon went to school just like every day. (P6)

On a hot day of summer, I was flying over the top of a building and suddenly I saw this little, lonely boy. (P15)

It was the 18 of June when I got out of school. I saw a blue bird. Oops! Forgot to present myself. My name is Theo. (P10)

In a New York school, a 9-year-old named Leo doesn't have friends. We are the (*sic*) 29/02/22 and Leo gets out of school. (P2)

The problem was almost unanimously recounted as a boy who was being bullied and as a result was very unhappy.

When he got to school everyone was bullying and laughing at him. It was a nightmare. All day it continued. (P6)

He was sad. Very sad. I went on a little tree and I looked at him. Two nasty bullies were laughing at him. (P15)

Every time he tried to get some friends, he was always rejected. (P4)

The events were related to the developing friendship between the boy and the bird, the games they played and the encounter with the bullies:

Then I went to Central Park. The bird was still following then suddenly the bird comes on my shoulder. I was very, very happy. In the park there was someone selling boats. I bought one. It was great fun because the blue bird kept on jumping on to the boat. Then I went through a bridge. Suddenly some boys in my school jumped out of the woods. (P11)

He finally noticed the bird. He was happy. He was always with him. Elliott and the bird walked in the park deeper and deeper. In the park he saw some children – the bullies!!! The child was afraid. He ran and the bird followed him. A bully threw a stick and it hit the bird. He was dead. (P9)

After the school bell had rung, I followed him. He stared at me by a mailbox. In this big New York city, he looked at me with a friendly smile. (P15)

The resolution of the problem and the closure of the story were narrated in a way that showed real empathy and happiness for the boy.

Now he has plenty of friends but he will remember the bluebird. (P2)

He starts crying but at one moment a red bird, a purple bird a yellow bird and all the other coloured birds bring him (*sic*) in the sky and then it disappears. (P5)

Elliott cried but a lot of coloured birds came and he was very, very happy. (P9)

This writing task presented children with a challenge and required a great deal of effort and concentration, drafting and redrafting. It gave them the opportunity to reflect on the visual narrative as a result of their previous interaction and organize their reflections into a structured piece of writing. They persevered and produced convincing, personal narratives, each child expressing their own original interpretation. Final versions were displayed in the classroom to provide reading practice and to value the variety of personal interpretations.

Conclusion

Many of the procedures and tasks described in this chapter develop functional literacy – reading and writing in the traditional sense. However, bringing multimodal resources and, in particular, wordless picturebooks into the classroom, allowed the teacher to also develop multiple literacies in a holistic way. In order to do this, teachers need to create a learning environment that provides a secure, stimulating space for reflection and discussion to develop visual, linguistic and intercultural competencies. In addition, using multimodal resources makes learning inclusive by accommodating children's learning differences and cognitive preferences, and enables them to express their views and opinions in their preferred mode. Through doing so, children become more engaged in their English language learning as they gradually develop an awareness and understanding of different forms of communication and representation and ways of making meaning.

RECOMMENDATIONS

- Staake's *Bluebird* is exceptionally cohesive. Children (and student teachers) might try to list all the visual and narrative patterns that hold together this close-knit, focused story.
- On the other hand, screen-based media offers so much to see in fast succession that attention often wavers. Student teachers might consider whether sharing challenging picturebooks with children can pre-empt the danger of dissolution of attention. As the celebrated film critic David Thomson writes: 'think of the agencies – from individuals and businesses to governments and ideologies – that would prefer us not to attend with too much critical concentration, but let the passing spectacle swim by without challenge. This is where watching cannot rest with mere sight. It waits to be converted into aesthetic judgement, moral discrimination, and a more intricate participation in society' (Thomson 2015: 18).

Bibliography

Briggs, Raymond (1978), *The Snowman*, Harmondsworth: Hamish Hamilton.
Le Ballon Rouge (1956), [Film] Dir. Albert Lamorisse, France: Films Montsouris.
Staake, Bob (2013), *Bluebird*, New York: Random House.
Willis, Jeanne, illus. Ross, Tony (1999), *Susan Laughs*, London: Andersen Press.

References

Arizpe, Evelyn, Colomer, Teresa and Martinez-Roldan, Carmen (2015), *Visual Journeys Through Wordless Narratives*, London: Bloomsbury Academic.

Arizpe, Evelyn and Ryan, Sadie (2018), 'The wordless picturebook: Literacy in multilingual contexts and David Wiesner's worlds', in Janice Bland (ed.), *Using Literature in English Language Education: Challenging Reading for 8–18 Year Olds*, London: Bloomsbury Academic, pp. 63–81.

Brewster, Jean, Ellis, Gail and Girard, Denis (2002), *The Primary English Teacher's Guide. New Edition*, Harlow: Pearson Education Limited.

Brunsmeier, Sonja and Kolb, Annika (2018), 'Story apps: The challenge of interactivity', in Janice Bland (ed.), *Using Literature in English Language Education: Challenging Reading for 8–18 Year Olds*, London: Bloomsbury Academic, pp. 105–119.

Cameron, Lynne (2001), *Teaching Languages to Young Learners*, Cambridge: Cambridge University Press.

Cope, Bill and Kalantzis, Mary (2009), 'Multiliteracies: New literacies, new learning', *Pedagogies: An International Journal*, 4/3: 164–95.

Cummins, Jim (2014), 'Foreword', in Christine Hélot, Raymonde Sneddon and Nicola Daly (eds), *Children's Literature in Multilingual Classrooms*, London: Institute of Education Press.

Ellis, Gail (2016), 'Promoting "Learning" Literacy through Picturebooks: Learning How to Learn', *Children's Literature in English Language Education*, 4/2, 27–40. http://clelejournal.org/article-2-promoting-learning-literacy-picturebooks-learning-learn/ (accessed 6 May 2017).

Ellis, Gail and Brewster, Jean (2014), *Tell it Again! The Storytelling Handbook for Primary English Language Teachers* (3rd edn), London: British Council. https://www.teachingenglish.org.uk/sites/teacheng/files/D467_Storytelling_handbook_FINAL_web.pdf (accessed 25 March 2017).

Ellis, Gail and Ibrahim, Nayr (2015), *Teaching Children How to Learn*, Peaslake, Surrey: Delta Publishing.

Enever, Janet and Schmid-Schönbein, Gisela (2006), *Picture Books and Young Learners of English*, Munich: Langenscheidt.

EU (2006), 'Recommendation of the European Parliament on key competences for lifelong learning', *Official Journal of the European Union*, http://eur-lex.europa.eu/legal-content/EN/TXT/PDF/?uri=CELEX:32006H0962&from=EN (accessed 25 March 2017).

Fisher, Robert (2005), *Teaching Children to Learn*, Cheltenham: Nelson Thornes.

Ghosn, Irma-Kaarina (2002), 'Four good reasons to use literature in primary school ELT', *ELT Journal*, 56/2, 172–9.

Hohmann, Mary, Weikart, David and Epstein, Ann (2008), *Educating Young Children: Active Learning Practices for Preschool and Child Care Programs* (3rd edn), Ypsilanti, MI: HighScope Press.

Krashen, Stephen and Bland, Janice (2014), 'Compelling comprehensible input, academic language and school libraries', *Children's Literature in English Language Education*, 2/2, 1–12. http://clelejournal.org/compelling-comprehensible-input/ (accessed 6 May 2017).

Kress, Gunther (1997), *Before Writing: Rethinking the Paths to Literacy*, New York: Routledge.

Mourão, Sandie and Bland, Janice (2016), 'Editorial: The Journey', *Children's Literature in English Language Education*, 4/2: ii–xi. http://clelejournal.org/contents-and-editorial-4/ (accessed 20 April 2017).

Nisbet, John and Shucksmith, Janet (1986), *Learning Strategies*, Boston: Routledge.

O'Rourke, Maureen (2005), *Multiliteracies for 21st Century Schools*, Lindfield, NSW: The Australian National Schools Network.

Thomson, David (2015), *How to Watch a Movie*, London: Profile Books.

Weare, Katherine (2004), *Developing the Emotionally Literate School*, London: Sage Publications.

Whitebread, David, Coltman, Penny, Anderson, Holly, Mehta, Sanjana and Pasternak, Deborah (2005), Metacognition in young children: Evidence from a naturalistic study of 3–5-year-olds. Paper presented at the International Early Years Conference, Warwick, March 2005, and the EARLI Conference, Cyprus, August 2005. https://www.educ.cam.ac.uk/research/projects/cindle/Cyprus%20paper%202.doc (accessed 25 March 2017).

6

Story apps: The challenge of interactivity

Sonja Brunsmeier and Annika Kolb

In elementary education, reading autonomously is often a challenging activity for children, especially in the English as a foreign language (EFL) classroom and in ELT more widely. Although picturebooks play an indispensable role in primary ELT (Bland 2013, Mourão 2015), independent reading of these texts presents major difficulties for children. The obscure phoneme-grapheme correspondence of the English language makes young language learners struggle with the pronunciation of an unknown text and this very often hinders understanding (Kolb 2013). For young learners, picturebooks are traditionally presented by the teacher in a storytelling scenario (see Brewster and Ellis 2012: 186–202). However, when reading independently, children cannot benefit from the support through facial expressions, gestures and interaction that a teacher usually provides in a storytelling session. Story apps seem to offer the potential to overcome some of these difficulties. They often include an audio narration feature that gives an oral version of the written text and allows students to read along. Additional interactive features offer comprehension support that might make up for the missing interaction with the teacher. However, story apps pose different kinds of challenges for young learners: these interactive features are not always helpful for understanding, they can also be distracting and lead children's attention away from the actual story.

This chapter presents some results from a research project that tries to find out how children's reading can benefit from story apps. It aims to shed light on the questions of what the affordances and challenges of story apps are and what the classroom setting should look like to make independent reading in English the right kind of challenge for primary school children.

Story apps – new texts for elementary ELT

Over the last few decades the rapid development of technologies has brought about new attempts to bring picturebooks on to the screen. Story apps add animations, music and background noises to the pictures and the words in the story, 'expanding to include auditory, tactile, and performative dimensions' (Al-Yaqout and Nikolajeva 2015: 1). These features either run automatically or the reader can activate them (e.g. by touching a hotspot in an illustration). Most story apps come with a 'read-to-me' audio-narration function, which provides an oral version of the narration as well as the dialogues of the stories. At the same time, words and paragraphs are highlighted as they are spoken. In addition to these multimodal storytelling features, many story apps offer interactive elements that require readers to complete tasks necessary for the progress of the story, or even let readers choose characters, settings or story paths, leading for example to different endings of the story (Bircher 2012, Cahill and McGill-Franzen 2013, Stichnothe 2014, Zheng 2016).

Nosy Crow and Ed Bryan's Jack and the Beanstalk

A truly interactive example is the story app *Jack and the Beanstalk* (2015). It presents a digital version of the traditional tale in which Jack trades the family cow against some magic beans that develop into a gigantic beanstalk. Jack climbs up the beanstalk and discovers a giant's castle in the sky. In the story app version, the many doors within the castle open onto different tasks for the protagonist (see Figure 6.1).

The more tasks Jack can complete and the more of the treasure he can steal, the better off he and his mother are at the end of the fairy tale. The text features both narrative passages and dialogue in speech bubbles. This mix facilitates comprehension even for young learners at a fairly basic linguistic level. In addition, readers can decide individually on the amount of language input: the more they tap on the characters, the more utterances the characters will produce. Animations, music, background noises and audio narration with different children's voices support the understanding of the story. Through the interactive elements, readers get to be players in the story when they are asked to help complete Jack's tasks, for example to find the goose that lays golden eggs (see Figure 6.2).

FIGURE 6.1 *Which door? Screenshot from the story app* Jack and the Beanstalk *by Nosy Crow and Ed Bryan (© 2015). Reprinted by permission of Nosy Crow.*

These contributions are necessary for the progress of the story. If the readers do not react, the request is repeated, frequently with a different wording. Through these challenges that relate to both linguistic and content-related aspects, the story app is still interesting for students who may have grown out of the typical fairy tale age. Students get immediate feedback on task completion, so that the tasks also function as a comprehension check. In addition, the readers can influence the nonlinear story path. Created in a choose-your-own-adventure format, their choices affect both the direction the story takes and the ending of the story which can support the motivation to read it multiple times: 'Once a choice is made, the interpreter will not know the other possibilities for the story's development following other choices unless he or she plays the game again and makes a different choice' (Zheng 2016: 70). This is supported by a map-format menu that allows the user to skip around in the story and try out various options.

Although research is only now starting to explore the topic, first studies with electronic stories show that story apps can increase reading motivation and lead to greater involvement with the text (Ciampa 2012, Ertem 2010). If animations, music, sound and tasks that the readers are asked to complete

FIGURE 6.2 *Where is the golden egg? Screenshot from the story app* Jack and the Beanstalk *by Nosy Crow and Ed Bryan (© 2015). Used by permission of Nosy Crow.*

match the text, they can assist word and text comprehension while they help children to link relevant details in images with textual information. The interactivity of story apps may however disturb the reading process and the understanding of stories if features are not congruent or are not presented simultaneously with the text. In these cases children tend to focus their attention on trying out the hotspots that are irrelevant to the text, which can lead to cognitive overload and distraction from the content of the stories (Bus, Verhallen and van der Kooy-Hofland 2009: 17, Bus, Takacs and Kegel 2015: 92, Korat, Shamir and Segal-Drori 2014, Miller and Warschauer 2014, Smeets and Bus 2013 and 2014, Takacs, Swart and Bus 2015: 3, Verhallen and Bus 2010).

Manresa (2015) reports that children in her study perceived a tension between the actual story and the interactive elements. These were interpreted as a parallel game that was going on, making the students choose between reading a story and playing a game (Manresa 2015: 109). This tension is confirmed by Takacs et al. who argue for a close congruency between the plot and the interactive features: 'Story comprehension and playing with hotspots or games are two fundamentally different tasks, even when their content is related, and carrying out both requires task switching. […] the more closely related the story and the interactive additions are, the smaller the cognitive cost of switching between the two tasks is' (Takacs et al. 2015: 4).

Hayles (2007) describes a similar challenge when she distinguishes between two types of attention. While deep attention is necessary to follow a narrative for a longer period of time, hyper attention is required during the reading process to switch between different tasks and multiple modes of information. Hayles hypothesizes that 'we are in the midst of a generational shift in cognitive styles' (2007: 187) and that young people need the challenge of both hyper and deep attention opportunities. The challenging interactive features together with the supportive elements of story apps might open up opportunities for independent reading in primary ELT. So far, autonomous reading is less common among young English language learners, even though reading text is a challenge that children themselves often wish to face.

Research design

The present study uses a qualitative research design to find out what features of story apps can help language learners at primary-school level understand the stories and to draw consequence for the classroom (Brunsmeier and Kolb 2017). Two classroom action research cycles (Burns 2010) have been conducted so far.

Research context

At a primary school in Germany a voluntary afternoon programme, the English Book Club, was initiated in 2015, and has since been offered once a week (60 minutes) for third and fourth graders (children between the ages of eight and eleven). In an extensive reading setting (Day 2011), a variety of both print picturebooks and story apps are provided that the young learners can choose from. The group has several tablet computers at their disposal. On each of these devices there are different story apps installed, since one purchased app cannot be used on a number of tablets. The children can read the texts on their own or together with a partner – in most cases they opt to read with a partner. For each story app, teacher-designed pre- and post-reading activities are available that focus on aspects of the content and language of the stories. These are meant to stimulate the children's use of reading strategies, for example by asking them to predict actions and events or to guess the meaning of unknown words from context. They also check the students' understanding of the plot: children are asked to note down the main facts about the story (summary of the content, setting, characters, and so forth) in a story map.

Finally, the children are invited to share their opinion of the story by rating it and deciding on their favourite character.

Data collection and analysis

We used a variety of data collection methods to find out which features of the story apps the children benefitted from during the reading processes. Video recordings documented which features the children employed when reading on their own and showed their actions (their nonverbal behaviour) as well as contextual information (what was on the screen, and what the young learners did with the story apps). Based on a micro-ethnographic approach that focused on patterns of interactions between protagonists in a specific setting, the videos tried to capture the communication between the children to further understand their reading process.

To gain additional insights into the children's thoughts, the young learners were interviewed about their reading experiences at the end of each school year. The children explained their reading experiences and were encouraged to give reasons for the course of actions they took while reading the story apps. Furthermore, the children's worksheets showcased their evaluation

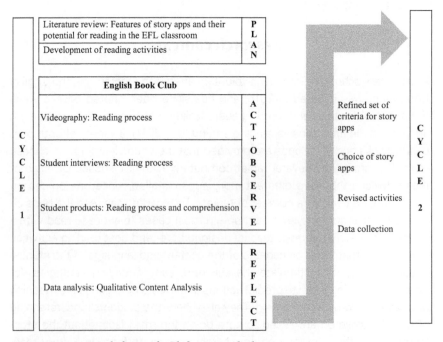

FIGURE 6.3 *English Book Club research design.*

of the story apps and their level of comprehension. Figure 6.3 provides an overview of the research design.

The video recordings, the interviews and the children's worksheets were analysed using Qualitative Content Analysis (Mayring 2014). While the interviews were analysed after they had been transcribed completely, software for qualitative data analysis allowed for the categorization of the video data without prior transcription. As a result, interesting sequences were identified which were then transcribed and underwent a detailed sequential analysis.

Benefits and challenges of interactive features of story apps

The analysis of the data allowed us to characterize the potential of story apps for the challenge of independent reading in primary ELT in more detail. Three aspects were most prominent: compared to print picturebooks, story apps

- provided new types of comprehension support for text in a foreign language
- offered innovative opportunities to foster reading motivation
- and potentially contributed to the development of reading strategies.

Providing comprehension support

Story apps offer a lot of opportunities to help students cope with unknown texts in the foreign language. A major feature is the audio narration that helps to pre-empt pronunciation problems that otherwise might prevent children from understanding text read aloud, for example by other children. In a study on extensive reading of print books in primary school carried out in Germany, many children relied on reading aloud as a strategy, which proved to be problematic: 'Although poor oral reading skills can go along with good reading comprehension results and therefore the wrong pronunciation does not automatically hinder the comprehension [...], this strategy did prevent the students from understanding the texts when they tried to read the book to each other with one partner lacking the opportunity to see the written form' (Kolb 2013: 37). Audio narration allows the students to read along and thereby connect written and spoken language, especially if the respective parts of the text are highlighted while they are being read aloud. Different speakers for different characters also facilitate understanding. In the interviews, one young learner described how the audio narration helped with the reading (all names are pseudonyms and the extracts from the interviews are translated from German):

> We read better, because we hear what they tell us, the ones that are inside the iPad, in the book. (Viktor, 15 July 2015)

In addition, the chance to have single words or whole passages repeated allowed the children to read at their own pace and facilitated their in-depth involvement with the text.

Another type of support that the children frequently used to derive meaning from the texts was the animation attached to the visuals. In story apps, actions and events are not only displayed in a static manner but also seem to come to life. This supports children's understanding as they reported in the interviews:

> Because you actually see that is what he does.

> It for example says 'The branches of the tree were moving' and that is written in English then and then the picture shows how the branch is moving. (Colin, 15 July 2015)

These animations help the students visualize actions and events in the story and therefore follow the plot, even if the language is slightly above their competence level. They also support them in making inferences and guessing the meaning of unknown vocabulary and formulaic sequences (chunks) from the context (see also Ellis 2018, this volume). In addition, animations, for example zooming in, make children focus on specific elements by directing their attention to details on the screen that may play a relevant role in the story. Some story apps provide explicit vocabulary support that is activated by tapping on objects in the picture. The respective elements of the illustration are labelled, making it easier for the children to establish connections between the content of the text and the pictures.

The different types of comprehension support proved to be especially beneficial if the children were able to activate them themselves, choosing the moment when they wanted the audio narration and the animations to start because they were ready for the input. It was also supportive if they could choose the objects in the picture they wanted to have labelled, depending on their individual vocabulary knowledge.

Sustaining motivation

Several factors proved to help children keep up their reading motivation and not give up the difficult task of coping with unknown text in the foreign language. Again, the animations were supportive, some students reported that they made them focus on the story:

Because you are more attentive, because something is happening on the screen. (Simon, 19 March 2016)

Through their interactive opportunities, story apps seem to bring about a new dimension of involvement with the text. Frequently, readers are asked to solve tasks that are part of the story, for example to look for the door which the key will open in the Giant's castle of *Jack and the Beanstalk* (2015) or mixing a potion for the wicked queen in *Snow White* (2015):

> To proceed with the story we had to accomplish a task. If you complete it successfully there is an arrow that you have to tap and then you can continue. For example, in the story app 'Nash Smasher' we had to destroy a castle. We had to draw a line and then Nash smashes a castle with a hammer. We had to do that a couple of times until the castle was completely broken. (Sascha, 15 July 2015)

These built-in tasks fulfilled two functions in the children's reading process. First, they provided an additional stimulus to understand the text since they had to be accomplished in order to proceed with the story ('then you can continue'). Therefore they helped with in-depth reading. Second, the children's reactions in our project showed that this kind of participation made them actually feel like players in the story who participated in the events rather than being observers from the outside. For example, when two boys were asked in the story app *The Three Little Pigs* (2015) to help the wolf blow down the pig's house by blowing into the tablet microphone, they remarked 'Oh, we are mean', thereby showing that they were fully identifying with their role. In another story app scene a girl repeatedly shouted at a flamingo that was trying to catch a frog 'take the fish, take the fish' as if the flamingo were a real partner in conversation and could react to her comments.

Some story apps allow children's own photos, drawings or audio recordings to be used, as yet another way to personalize a story. As seen above, readers can even influence the plot and the characters. A number of story apps offer the opportunity to decide on the amount of language input; in addition to the narration that tells the major events in the story, readers can trigger dialogues between the different characters by tapping on these. All these options allow for individual reading experiences.

Developing reading strategies

Especially when reading texts in a foreign language, reading strategies play an important role in the overcoming of comprehension difficulties (Grabe 2009, Paris, Wasik and Turner 1996). Story apps seem to have the potential to foster the development of reading strategies. In the data, different reading strategies could be observed: children made and revised predictions about the content of the story, they made inferences, they used monitoring strategies such as rereading, asking questions and identifying main ideas of the text and they established personal connections by empathizing with characters and expressing opinions about the text. Whereas many of these strategies could also be used when reading print picturebooks, some of them seem to be especially fostered through the features of story apps.

A very prominent strategy was making and revising predictions about events in the story. When in the story app *Pete's Robot* (2016) a 'heart-drive' is implanted into the robot, one child inferred for example: 'Now he has turned friendly again, hasn't he?' The young learner came to the conclusion that a missing heart must have been the cause for the destructive and unfriendly behaviour, probably based on his prior knowledge that having a heart means being loving and caring. In story apps, the animations show a lot of transformations and changes that can be predicted. Another reason why story apps seem to lend themselves well to fostering predictions is that some of them actively ask children to speculate about elements of the story. They do so by hiding objects that have to be found, by showing only parts of objects and by asking children to choose between different options. One child described the pleasure of these guessing games, referring to the picture of a shell in the story app *Mud Monster* (2013) that was not revealed in the beginning:

I found that really exciting, when you could only see the eyes, because then you could think about what that could be. (Luise, 20 June 2016)

Making inferences is a strategy that is especially relevant for reading texts in a foreign language where children will encounter numerous unknown words. Whereas in print picturebooks the illustrations help readers to understand their meaning, in story apps there are even more sources of inference support. For animations and sounds also provide opportunities to guess the meaning from context, making it easier for the children to follow the plot autonomously as this young learner explained in the interview:

It was helpful that you could get the pictures to move. If you touched them, then they started to build their house, for example. (Colin, 13 May 2015)

Another reading strategy that could be particularly enhanced while reading story apps is monitoring comprehension. The experience of participating as a player in the story did not only serve to foster the children's reading motivation but it also provided an opportunity for them to check their understanding. For example, when they were asked in *Jack and the Beanstalk* (2015) to put a certain vegetable into the soup and pick the right colour, their correct choice was instantly acknowledged – thus children were given feedback on their correct understanding of the text.

Being a player in the story also enhances readers' personal involvement with the text. At various points it could be observed that learners became very emotionally engaged in the story, which allowed them to empathize with characters and take on their perspective. In the following example, a group of students reflected on how they would have acted had the wolf in *The Three Little Pigs* (2015) knocked at their house:

Philip: What would you have done?
Fabian: I would have stayed inside.
Nicolas: I would have left at the back. (24 June 2016)

Very often they showed feelings of sympathy with characters and feelings of joy when the characters succeeded in overcoming a problem.

Distracting from the story

In contrast to these affordances, the interactive features of the story apps also proved in some cases to present disturbances for the children's reading process. Animations and sounds that were not reader-activated seemed to turn students' attention away from the text. When the students were not able to decide for themselves when the animation should start, they often did not have a chance to finish reading the text before focusing on the animation. In such cases, rather than supporting comprehension, the events on the screen prevented the young learners from understanding the text. With reader-activated animations, the call for action was paramount for the students. Especially when they were reading the texts for the first time, some children were very focused on the hotspots. Instead of listening to the audio narration and reading along, they were only looking for opportunities to trigger animations and sounds. This was also reflected in comments such as 'He's only talking here, we don't have to do anything' and 'She's talking, wait, I want to see what's happening' which show that the children pay more attention to the events on the screen than to the language. One student reported in the interview with the researcher (Sonja):

Leon: I found out something really cool when I read the 'Three Little Pigs'. When you tap on the characters and drag them, they can do somersaults.
Sonja: Does this help you to understand the story?
Leon: No, but it was fun. (15 July 2015)

Another aspect that has to be considered is the congruency of text and animations. In many story apps, the reader-activated animations are not related to the content of the story and therefore do not contribute to children's understanding but rather distract them from following the plot.

Furthermore, even if the animations provide inference support by illustrating actions and events in the story, students sometimes do not exploit their full potential. In our study, young learners started playing animations before the text had actually been spoken. The interference of animations and text being read aloud that the children were supposed to follow proved to be potentially a major stumbling block.

Consequences for the classroom

Given these challenges, independent reading in primary ELT cannot mean leaving children alone with the texts. Classroom experience shows that children need teacher-designed pre-, while- and post-reading activities to support in-depth involvement with the text, to support their understanding and to support the development of reading strategies. Several features of such activities proved to be especially productive. First, to make sure students focus on the text and not only on the animations, activities should explicitly integrate the language, so that children can only solve the activity by actually reading the text and not merely by looking at the illustrations and animations. Second, post-reading activities should also give students feedback on their understanding of the plot. When children realized that they had not understood important parts of the story, this motivated them to go back and read the text again:

I do it like this: I try to answer the questions and if I need help I go back to the story. (Luise, 13 June 2016)

Activities that modelled reading strategies seemed to be successful since various examples of strategy use could be observed in the videos. Some students were also able to reflect on their strategy use, thus demonstrating metacognitive strategies. In the interviews they reported on the employment of scanning, guessing words from the context, rereading and revising predictions. They also mentioned comprehension strategies that are specific to story apps, for example the deliberate use of reader-activated animations or audio narration as comprehension support:

You can always get the picture to move and then you can find out more or you tap on the picture and then they say more. (Luise, 13 June 2016)

Last but not least, activities should give students room for individualized reactions to the text. Activities that asked young learners to activate their personal experience and relate the content of the story app to their own lives supported their involvement with the text and enhanced their reading motivation. The children's statements in the interviews and the learner texts showed they liked to be asked for their personal opinions and to develop their own ideas. This also helped them to establish a personal connection to the text and supported them in relating to the characters.

Summary and conclusion

In contrast to reading print picturebooks, story apps can make independent reading less formidable even in early ELT since the reading process is more individual and interactive. It is more individual through the amount of choices learners have in terms of language and content, as they can decide how much support and how much language input they would like and need. The interactive features have the potential to support comprehension, enhance reading motivation and develop reading strategies. However, they can also distract children from the plot if they do not accommodate both deep and hyper attention in a productive way. In this context, our data show the high relevance of agency even among young learners. Children can most benefit from the comprehension support through animation, oral rendition of the text or vocabulary support if this support is reader-activated, that is if they can decide when to use it and what to use.

As the data of this study show, the features of story apps significantly influence the reading process. In a classroom setting, it is therefore all the more important to develop suitable pre-, while-reading and post-reading activities that have the chance to impact the children's reading process as well. These should focus on the language of the stories, give young learners feedback on their understanding of the plot, model the use of comprehension strategies and leave room for personal reactions to the text.

RECOMMENDATIONS

- Early literacy events, such as story apps offer, play a significant role in literacy development. Sharing meaningful story apps with children may signal that their out-of-school learning has an important role to play and is being taken seriously.
- Extensive autonomous in-school or out-of-school reading is of great importance for acquiring a dynamic database of lexical knowledge and the practice needed to become an expert reader.

Bibliography

Jack and the Beanstalk (2015), [mobile application software] Ed Bryan and Nosy Crow.

Mud Monster (2013), [mobile application software] Chantal Bourgonje and Tizio Publishing.

Nash Smasher (2010), [mobile application software] Bill Doyler and Troy Cummings, Crab Hill Press.

Pete's Robot (2016), [mobile application software] Heartdrive Media LLC.

Snow White (2015), [mobile application software] Ed Bryan and Nosy Crow.

The Three Little Pigs (2015), [mobile application software] Ed Bryan and Nosy Crow.

References

Al-Yaqout, Ghada and Nikolajeva, Maria (2015), 'Re-conceptualising picturebook theory in the digital age', *Nordic Journal of ChildLit Aesthetics*, 6, http://www.childlitaesthetics.net/index.php/blft/article/view/26971 (accessed 14 February 2017).

Bircher, Katie (2012), 'What makes a good picture book app?' *The Horn Book Magazine*, 88: 72–8.

Bland, Janice (2013), *Children's Literature and Learner Empowerment*, London: Bloomsbury Academic.

Brewster, Jean and Ellis, Gail (2012), *The Primary English Teacher's Guide*, Harlow: Pearson.

Brunsmeier, Sonja and Kolb, Annika (2017), 'Picturebooks go digital – the potential of story apps for the primary EFL classroom', *Children's Literature in Language Education*, 5/1: 1–20.

Burns, Anne (2010), *Doing Action Research in English Language Teaching. A Guide for Practitioners*, New York: Routledge.

Bus, Adriana, Takacs, Zsofia and Kegel, Cornelia (2015), 'Affordances and limitations of electronic storybooks for young children's emergent literacy', *Developmental Review*, 35: 79–97.

Bus, Adriana, Verhallen, Marian and van der Kooy-Hofland, Verna (2009), 'Digital picture storybooks', *Better: Evidence-based Education Magazine*, 1/1: 16–17.

Cahill, Maria and McGill-Franzen, Anne (2013), 'Selecting "App"ealing and "App"ropriate book apps for beginning readers', *The Reading Teacher*, 1/67: 30–9.

Ciampa, Katia (2012), 'Electronic storybooks: A constructivist approach to improving reading motivation in grade 1 students', *Canadian Journal of Education*, 35/4: 92–136.

Day, Richard (2011), 'Extensive reading: The background', in OUP (eds), *Bringing Extensive Reading into the Classroom*, Oxford: Oxford University Press, pp. 10–21.

Ellis, Gail (2018), 'The picturebook in elementary ELT: Multiple literacies with Bob Staake's *Bluebird*', in Janice Bland (ed.), *Using Literature in English Language Education: Challenging Reading for 8–18 Year Olds*, London: Bloomsbury Academic, pp. 83–104.

Ertem, Ihsan (2010), 'The effect of electronic storybooks on struggling fourth-graders' reading comprehension', *Turkish Online Journal of Educational Technology*, 9/4: 140–55.

Grabe, William (2009), *Reading in a Second Language: Moving from Theory to Practice*, Cambridge: Cambridge University Press.

Hayles, Katherine (2007), 'Hyper and deep attention: The generational divide in cognitive methods', *Profession 2007*: 187–99.

Kolb, Annika (2013), 'Extensive reading of picturebooks in primary EFL', in Janice Bland and Christiane Lütge (eds), *Children's Literature in Language Education*, London: Bloomsbury Academic, pp. 33–43.

Korat, Ofra, Shamir, Adina and Segal-Drori, Ora (2014), 'E-Books as a support for young children's language and literacy: The case of Hebrew-speaking children', *Early Child Development and Care*, 184/7: 998–1016.

Manresa, Mireia (2015), 'Traditional readers and electronic literature. An exploration of perceptions and readings of digital works', in Mireia Manresa and Neus Real (eds), *Digital Literature for Children: Texts, Readers and Educational Practices*, Brussels: Peter Lang, pp. 105–20.

Mayring, Philipp (2014), Qualitative content analysis: Theoretical foundation, basic procedures and software solution. <http://nbn-resolving.de/urn:nbn:de:0168-ssoar-395173> (accessed 14 February 2017).

Miller, Elisabeth and Warschauer, Mark (2014), 'Young children and e-reading: Research to date and questions for the future', *Learning, Media and Technology*, 39/3: 283–305.

Mourão, Sandie (2015), 'The potential of picturebooks with young learners', in Janice Bland (ed.), *Teaching English to Young Learners. Critical Issues in Language Teaching with 3–12 Year Olds*, London: Bloomsbury Academic, pp. 199–218.

Paris, Scott, Wasik, Barbara and Turner, Julianna (1996), 'The development of strategic Readers', in Rebecca Barr, David Pearson, Michael Kamil and Peter Mosenthal (eds), *Handbook of Reading Research*, New York: Longman, pp. 609–40.

Smeets, Daisy and Bus, Adriana (2013), 'Picture storybooks go digital: Pros and cons', in Susan Neuman and Linda Gambrell (eds), *Quality Reading Instruction in the Age of Common Core Standards*, Newark, DE: International Reading Association, pp. 176–89.

Smeets, Daisy and Bus, Adriana (2014), 'The interactive animated e-book as a word learning device for kindergartners', *Applied Psycholinguistics*, 36/4: 1–22.

Stichnothe, Hadassah (2014), 'Engineering stories? A narratological approach to children's book apps', *Barnelitterært forskningstidsskrift/Nordic Journal of ChildLit Aesthetics*, 5, http://www.tandfonline.com/doi/full/10.3402/blft.v5.23602 (accessed 14 February 2017).

Takacs, Zsofia, Swart, Elise and Bus, Adriana (2015), 'Benefits and pitfalls of multimedia and interactive features in technology-enhanced storybooks: A meta-analysis', *Review of Educational Research*, 85/4: 698–739.

Verhallen, Marian and Bus, Adriana (2010), 'Low-income immigrant pupils learning vocabulary through digital picture storybooks', *Journal of Educational Psychology*, 102/1: 54–61.

Zheng, Yan (2016), 'Anything new here in story apps? A reflection on the storytelling mechanism across media', Libri & Liberi, 5/1: 55–76.

7

Transmedial reading: Tim Winton's LOCKIE LEONARD trilogy

Michael Prusse

Writing fiction is a challenging task, 'a bit like surfing', according to Tim Winton, the Australian author who is a keen surfer himself (Edemariam 2008: np). Thus it does not come as a surprise that surfing, which – in Winton's words – 'is a completely pointless exercise', has a special place in his fiction for children and adults (2016: 3). Learners in the ELT classroom usually feel that all the language skills are challenging, but reading is arguably the key skill when it comes to establishing a sound basis for lifelong learning. Publications such as Maryanne Wolf's *Proust and the Squid* (2007) or the paper issued by the American Federation of Teachers, *Teaching Reading Is Rocket Science* (Moats 2004) confirm the nature of reading as a challenge, not just for learners in the foreign or second language classroom but also for those reading in their first language. In the ELT classroom teachers tend to limit the linguistic input as closely as possible to the linguistic abilities of their learners and, by doing so, habitually neglect their cognitive needs and potential. However, learners of English ought to be challenged both by the language *and* the content, ideally by means of multifaceted texts that are characterized by ambiguity and indeterminacy and that support students in developing their critical reading abilities (Bland 2013: 8– 11). It is a challenge for the teacher to select literature that meets these criteria and is suitable for their classrooms. The range of media available for teaching purposes has risen exponentially in the past few years. Hence, in a world where literacy no longer simply refers to books but to an impressive array of formats, it is essential to foster critical media and information literacy in schools (Wilson et al. 2011: 17). In order to have a discerning appreciation of the various formats, the role of narrative is central. In the words of Ryan, 'it would be very difficult to assess the expressive ability of different media and types of signs' if one did not resort to 'narrative as point of comparison' (2014: 79). Adaptations of children's and young adults' novels for the screen are one instance where different formats of narrative can rewardingly be contrasted in the classroom.

Episodic narratives

Television series, frequently considered to be the most important narrative format in the twenty-first century, have gained a worldwide following of dedicated viewers. Complex narratives that are broadcast in episodes have reminded a number of critics of the heyday of the novel in the nineteenth century. This was the time when novels were initially published in instalments in newspapers and magazines, when the cliffhanger effect first acquired its name because of a specific scene in Thomas Hardy's *A Pair of Blue Eyes* (1873), and when entire narratives were resold at a later point in three-volume book editions. Similarly, contemporary television audiences sometimes watch episodes when they are first broadcast and subsequently buy the whole series on DVD (Fröhlich 2015: 17, Mittell 2015).

The adaptation of Tim Winton's *Lockie Leonard*, the award-winning young adult fiction trilogy from the 1990s, to a DVD box set (comprising twenty-six TV episodes), first broadcast in 2007, is one example of transferring narrative from one medium to another in order to provide viewers, as Reynolds puts it, with 'a satisfying aesthetic experience in its own right' (2011: 66). While each format has a distinct narratology there are 'common tracks or semiotic systems' they share (Ryan 2004: 34). The existence of both book and TV series permits English teachers to engage in training their learners' film literacy as well as critical cultural literacy by focusing both on book and film. The episodic nature of Tim Winton's books with short chapters – the novels have an established position in an Australian ELT context (Harders and Macken-Horarik 2008; Patterson 2011) – is mirrored in the relatively brief episodes of the TV series that are also promoted for classroom usage in Australia.

The potential of *Lockie Leonard*

The main focus of this chapter is on teaching *Lockie Leonard*, both the trilogy by Tim Winton and the TV series, with the example of a Swiss ELT context, bearing in mind such topics as interculturality, series and seriality and teaching narrative as cultural practice that is performed in a range of formats. In keeping with the rather summary definition in the *Common European Framework of Reference for Languages* (CEFR) – the teaching of *Lockie Leonard* fits under the heading of the aesthetic uses of language and there, more precisely, under 'the production, reception and performance of literary texts' (Council of Europe 2001: 56). The CEFR has rightly been criticized for its rather limited scope on teaching literature and culture, and its promotion of utilitarian and instrumental interpretations of the function of English language learning (Bland 2013: 6, Volkmann 2010: 8–9). School curricula, and the options with regard to teaching literature, vary considerably within German-speaking regions and countries. In a Swiss context and, more specifically, with reference to the scope for teachers who prepare secondary-school students, aged sixteen to nineteen, for the Federal Vocational Baccalaureate (such as the student teachers in my courses at the Zurich University of Teacher Education), the following very general phrasing in the curriculum outlines the aims of teaching literature and culture in English: 'Describe the content of a number of literary texts and situate them in their respective society, history and culture' (RLP 2013: 32–3 [author's translation]). Elsewhere in the curriculum it stipulates that students should be able to 'describe, classify and discuss representative works of art' and film is one of the arts explicitly referred to. Keeping these broad outlines of this particular ELT curriculum in mind, a sequence of lessons teaching *Lockie Leonard* across print and electronic media could strive towards achieving the following goals:

1   Students understand the difference between series and seriality.

2   Students become familiar with the quest structure and can identify it in various narrative formats.

3   Students gain an insight into the Australian way of life and Australian cultural history.

4   Students comprehend adaptation as a creative cultural practice.

After analysing series and seriality in more detail the ensuing discussion will provide a brief summary of the contents of the book trilogy and the TV series. Moreover, there will be a suggestion of how the teaching of series and seriality, adaptation, intertextuality and 'the hero's journey' could be envisaged. Last but not least, a painting illustrating an iconic moment in the history of Australia will be contrasted with the corresponding images relayed in both media, zooming in on an incident that recurs both in the trilogy and in the TV series.

Series and seriality

The notion of series and seriality is of particular relevance in the wide landscape of literature. The epic poems of Greek antiquity, the *Iliad* and the *Odyssey*, were sung or chanted in instalments; and if other literary-heritage narratives such as *One Thousand and One Nights* and *The Canterbury Tales* are considered, it is evident that experiencing tales in instalments is probably as old as storytelling itself. In the context of children's literature parents and teachers tend to read longer texts to young children in instalments. Furthermore, there exist innumerable examples of series – from Enid Blyton's *Famous Five* to J. K. Rowling's *Harry Potter*, from L. M. Montgomery's *Anne of Green Gables* to Suzanne Collins's *The Hunger Games* (to name but a few) – designed to capture the imagination of young readers not just once but several times over. The appeal of series to children and young adults is that many of them want to encounter, as Watson puts it, 'a room full of friends' rather than 'a room full of strangers' when they begin with a new book (2000: 6). The protagonists of such series may evolve in different ways. Blyton's famous five basically remain the same throughout a long succession of holidays, as does, to a lesser extent, Alex Rider in Anthony Horowitz's eponymous adventure series for boys (even though this protagonist acquires more scars and grows older). Alternatively, some characters grow and transform, as does Harry Potter, growing from child to teenager and adult. The plot can have a similar structure in the various volumes of a series or can definitely evolve and change. Even the format can change within a series, as evidenced by the addition of a playscript to the *Harry Potter* oeuvre (Bland 2018b, this volume).

Teachers who make use of series can advantageously draw on the resources available in the ELT classroom – the knowledge media-savvy students already possess in connection with series in electronic and print media. The learners, guided by their teacher, will soon detect that there is a distinction between series and serial. The former is by nature episodic – examples would be *The Famous Five* or *Alex Rider* – the latter continues and develops a wide-reaching narrative (Fröhlich 2015: 61). In episodic narratives we encounter a number of microtexts that can be part of a larger macrotext but follow the laws of individual narratives with closure (e.g. the numerous holidays that Blyton's *Famous Five* experience, or the various stories told in *The Canterbury Tales*). Each episode thus has its own plot with closure but the whole series may be linked by means of the frame story or by the development – or non-development – of the protagonist(s). In this sense, *series* refers to a repetition of similar plot and character constellations, a feature that appeals to young readers, as the point made by Watson above has established. In serial narration, by contrast, the reader, listener or viewer experiences microtexts as part of a macrotext that constantly develops the storyline and is characterized by an overall plot and closure. Hence the serial implies a future that has not yet been written whereas the series refers to a repetition of known schemata, in other words an expectable future (Ruchatz 2012: 81).

Many writers as well as producers of contemporary TV series combine the two forms, thus coming close to David Lodge's basic definition of narrative in his play *The Writing Game* where his writer-protagonist, Leo Rafkin, states that the magic formula of writing is that you have to know when to repeat yourself and when to differ from your previous texts (1991: 45). Regarding children's literature, Reimer et al. (2014: 1) have stated that research in general focuses much more on individual novels than series – a state of affairs they consider as 'curious'. This may well be due to the fact that many researchers in the field of literature are influenced by the romantic notion of utter originality, even if Eco considers this to be a recent notion: 'Much art has been and is repetitive. The concept of absolute originality is a contemporary one' (1990: 95). As Hutcheon points out in *A Theory of Adaptation*, the ideal of the original actually stems from the Romantic age while the practice of adaptation is probably as old as literature itself (2006: 4; see also Prusse 2014: 2).

Furthermore, the question of quality hovers persistently in the background: if it is popular, can it be literary? Fröhlich argues that serial narratives smack of industrial mass production, hence negative connotations are bound to arise in an audience that cherishes unique creations (2015: 51). However, it is evident that whether a text is published in episodes (and in the Victorian Age the novels of Dickens, for instance, were published in instalments, in other words as a serial) or in a stand-alone volume does not constitute a criterion of its literary quality as such. With regard to television it is certainly interesting to note that much like novels – nowadays securely in position as a serious art form – television series were originally perceived as junk, mainly for female consumption, and hence negligible for critics' serious attention (Allen 2004: 246). In the past, reading was regarded by many in the eighteenth century as a dangerous addiction, particularly for women, an attitude that has undergone a remarkable cultural metamorphosis. Today, in the light of the PISA test results that underline deficits in reading abilities among schoolchildren, binge reading carries positive connotations – libraries even organize literacy nights – while binge TV viewing is perceived as unhealthy and is harshly criticized. From a more enlightened critical perspective it could be argued that the 'particular appeal of a television series, for instance, may lie in ritualized viewing practices, in a long-term emotional engagement with fictional characters and their experiences, or in creative responses like fan fiction' (Loock 2014: 5).

Children's literature is – as several critics have noted – particularly suited for adaptation (Collins and Ridgman 2006: 9, Hutcheon 2009: 333–4). The frequent transmedial reworking of young adult fiction, for example, into formats such as film, drama (playscript adaptations for the theatre, television or radio), graphic novels or computer games testifies that adapting children's literature is a vibrant cultural practice. As Hutcheon points out, since children's literature is 'in a way, all about adaptation, about change, just like Ovid's Metamorphoses', this literary art form is predisposed to be adapted across the media (Hutcheon 2009: 335). She also suggests that the status of a book for children is enhanced by the adaptation – it acquires the aura of a 'classic' (Hutcheon 2009: 337). Children's literature therefore has an established tradition of being adapted from page to screen, a trend that has increasingly asserted itself in recent times, possibly as a result of the much criticized impact of the crossover novel (Falconer 2009: 2–3, Myerson 2001: np). While some critics analyse this phenomenon as a sign of the growing childishness of contemporary society, the true explanation of the appeal of young adult fiction to movie producers may well be much more straightforward: since children's and young adult literature is usually well plotted and addresses an audience in a transitory state, between childhood and adulthood, the narratives exert a pull on producers and directors who want to draw young audiences into the cinemas with well-told stories.

Evolving and adapting

The eponymous hero of *Lockie Leonard*, actually Lachlan Robert Louis Stevenson Leonard, is an Australian teenager who has just moved from Perth to Angelus in Western Australia (Winton's literary version of Albany, WA). His father, a policeman, is the sergeant of the local police station and this is why he is often simply referred to as Sarge. Lockie's mother, Joy, is a stay-at-home mom and looks after Lockie and his two siblings, his younger brother Phillip and his baby sister Blob (Barbara). The autobiographically inspired plot revolves around acclimatizing to life in a small town, beginning secondary school, falling in love and several further defining moments in the painful growing up process of a teenager (Edemariam 2008). Lockie's main passion is surfing and any free minute he has is spent on his board on the waves of the Indian Ocean. His nickname, the Human Torpedo, which also provides the title for the first book of the trilogy, is not due to his surfing skills, however, but an ironic reference to the fact that it takes Lockie ages 'to get out of bed in the mornings' (*Human Torpedo*: 6). The producers of the TV adaptation are great admirers of Winton's trilogy, arguing that the novels 'provide so much information about Australian culture, language, behaviours and beliefs that it is hard to find comparable stories about boys and growing up' (Cohen 2009: 57).

It is impossible to determine whether Winton wrote his trilogy with a potential future adaptation in mind. He is on record, though, describing how he has been influenced by television: 'I don't like reading books that are long and slow and wearisome. I haven't got that kind of patience. I was brought up in the sixties and I was a child of the television age [...]. I love nineteenth-century novels, but I like the ones that crack along like Dickens' (Winton, cited in Ben-Messahel 2006: 147). Thus it is perhaps logical that the aspects introduced above, namely the serial and the series, which are congruent with Dickens's mode of writing and publishing, can also be identified both in the *Lockie Leonard* trilogy and in the eponymous television series.

There exist two separate series with the title of *Lockie Leonard*: Series One (2007) is a highly awarded adaptation of Winton's trilogy; Series Two (2010) tries to continue along the same lines, based on the characters of the first series, but lacks the quality of Winton's original dialogue. It is this dialogue, written with an acute ear for how young adults express themselves, which gives the trilogy and the first TV series the feel of capturing authentic teenage experience. This does not mean that the screen adaptation of the three novels did not creatively recast certain aspects of the text. On the contrary, it did – and some of these changes are strikingly successful, such as the inspired idea of casting Egg as an Aboriginal Australian or the choice of the soundtrack: among others, Sting and Midnight Oil are quoted by Winton, whereas the TV series uses, for instance, Jebediah, Spiderbait or Little Birdy. These changes do indeed, as Cohen argues, give the TV series 'a more contemporary feel' (2009: 57), referring to 2007 when the TV series was first broadcast. Hutcheon argues in Darwinist terms about adaptation in general: 'Stories also evolve by adaptation and are not immutable over time. [...] In short, stories adapt just as they are adapted' (2006: 31). Therefore adaptation can be seen as a means of breathing new life into a narrative and reshaping it for a new audience.

Another positive feature of the television adaptation of Winton's trilogy is constituted by merging the first scene from the second book *Lockie Leonard, Scumbuster* (Winton 1993) with an early scene of surfing in *Lockie Leonard, Human Torpedo* (Winton 1990), which permits the directors to introduce most of the main characters in the very first TV episode and, hence, they are able to cast them in the consecutive episodes at liberty. For that reason, the most obvious difference between the trilogy and the TV series is that the characters appear in a different order and that, accordingly, the plot evolves in a different time sequence. In the trilogy, the first book *Human Torpedo* deals with Lockie and his relationship to Vicki while *Scumbuster* introduces Egg, his best mate, and Dot, Lockie's second girlfriend; by contrast, in the TV series, romance and 'mateship' compete for Lockie's attention immediately from the very first episode.

The quest narrative

The quest motif that Joseph Campbell identified in a large number of narratives across various cultures, and termed the monomyth in *The Hero with a Thousand Faces* (Campbell 1949), has influenced Hollywood as a template for the successful fashioning of film narratives. It is essentially the journey of the hero (more recently also the heroine, see Bland 2018c and Webb 2018: 213, this volume) with a particular focus on the stages of separation, initiation and return (Campbell 2004: 28). Christopher Vogler's *The Writer's Journey: Mythic Structure for Writers* (1998), an adaptation of Campbell's rather complex findings for screenplay writers, is a useful book for teachers who want to explore this structure and help their students understand its prominence and prevalence in numerous movies. Since the hero's or heroine's journey is a pervasive (if not omnipresent) pattern in narrative, it is ideally suited for classroom purposes to make students aware of how a large proportion of storytelling works. Teachers could, for instance, begin with a children's picturebook, such as *The Gruffalo* (1999). As Jonathan Bate points out (2010: 1), the underlying structure of Donaldson's best-known work is typical of a quest narrative, intimated already in the introduction of the hero on the opening page:

A mouse took a stroll through the deep dark wood.

A fox saw the mouse, and the mouse looked good. (Donaldson 1999: np).

The concept of the quest narrative is a pattern that learners can grasp. Furthermore, they can practise detecting it by tracing and identifying its aspects when they watch one of the episodes of *Lockie Leonard*. The whole series is structured according to the quest formula as Cohen writes, 'the central character (or hero) has to survive a number of challenges (physical and psychological) while striving to win some prize or reach a goal' (2009: 60). In the TV series the overall quest is to win the affections of Vicki Streeton ('the prize'). The dominance of heroes (rather than heroines) in storytelling across the media landscape, especially in formats written for a male audience, is an issue that certainly has to be addressed in the classroom (see Prusse 2014: 4–5). Thus Cohen's perception of Vicki as 'the prize' calls for the students to engage in critical reading of such perspectives in the novel and on screen, and to discuss gender issues. The quest for Vicki's love throughout the series constitutes the serial aspect of the TV adaptation of the *Lockie Leonard* trilogy. Furthermore, each episode tells a mini-quest story. The problem or struggle is usually revealed in the monologue at the opening of each episode whereas the wisdom gained is declared in the closing monologue of each episode (see Cohen 2009: 60). This repetitive structuring of each particular episode underlines the series aspect of the TV adaptation. Several critics in children's literature, among them Reimer et al. (2014: 8), have theorized about the centrality of repetition to numerous educational methods. Thus the countless repetitions in the young adult books and in the TV series are one aspect that makes them ideally suited for the classroom. Depending on the number of episodes they view, students have repeated opportunities to discern and analyse the pattern.

The opening of the first episode of the television series is, as outlined above, a thoughtful adaptation of Winton's trilogy. In this initial introduction to the setting and the characters there is a significant moment that is particularly relevant to the Australian context. In the classroom it can be used as a critical incident to foster an interest in reading culture through different narrative media. The scene alludes to several other texts and images, most importantly to Daniel Defoe's *Robinson Crusoe* (1719) and the famous footprint in the sand. This is generally considered to be one of the truly iconic moments in literature since it provides the point of reference for the tangled encounters of the colonialist with the Other – from the colonialist's perspective – the native inhabitant of the conquered realms. These days, many learners in the classroom at secondary school will no longer be familiar with *Robinson Crusoe*, and since the original text might be too great a challenge for them, the story of Friday and the moment Robinson discovers the footprint can be introduced by means of a graphic novel or graded reader. With the information gained from this tale in mind, the next step ought to involve an introduction to Australia. It may be advisable that the secondary-school students are first asked to note down in pairs what information they already possess about the Australian continent and the way of life of its inhabitants. This approach allows the teacher to glean the amount of knowledge, notions, fantasies and stereotypes that the learners bring to the classroom. Teachers may then proceed to supply further details on Australia with specific reference to Aboriginal Australians, for example by means of the award-winning autobiographical film *Rabbit-Proof Fence* (Noyce 2002).

After establishing the colonizers' depreciating stance towards Aboriginal Australians, the lost painting by John Alexander Gilfillan, entitled 'Captain Cook taking possession of the Australian continent, on behalf of the British Crown 1770' (1859), further illuminates colonial attitudes towards the indigenous people (see Figure 7.1, Samuel Calvert's 1865 engraving of Gilfillan's picture). It is most certainly a coincidence that Gilfillan is also the artist who created another well-known painting entitled 'Robinson Crusoe Landing Stores from the Wreck' (1836) and thus – in his painting career – links the iconic literary conquest of overseas territories with the actual claiming of the Australian continent by the British, in the person of Captain Cook.

The picture captures the moment of conquest: Captain Cook is at the centre of the painting, his officers and entourage around him, the Union Jack

FIGURE 7.1 *Samuel Calvert (1865), 'Captain Cook taking possession of the Australian continent, on behalf of the British crown, A.D. 1770', National Library of Australia.*

is firmly planted into the occupied ground. According to information given in the digital classroom of the National Library of Australia this flag is an anachronism since the Union Jack only came into use after the union with Ireland in 1801 (Endeavour Voyage 2015). The soldiers are firing a salute to celebrate the historic moment, the *Endeavour* in the background, anchored in Botany Bay. In the foreground on the right, two Aboriginal Australians are cowering in the bushes in an abject position, with their hands over their ears due to the thundering salute. Thus the picture can be used as an opportunity to foster critical literacy by having the students describe and discover how the conqueror and the conquered are represented.

Conquests and contrasts

In the first scene of the television series, Lockie is shown contemplating the surf and soon enjoying the waves of his new hometown, riding his board confidently and then, perhaps because he is overconfident, losing his balance and getting struck in the groin by his own surfboard. Next Egg is seen walking along the beach, dressed in the standard issue of a 'bogan': black boots, a red shirt, grimy black shorts. *The Macquarie Australian Slang Dictionary* defines a bogan as: 'a lout or hooligan, especially of a particular social group noted for wearing flannos [a shirt with printed patterns], black jeans and DBs [desert boots]' (Lambert 2005: 22). Initially, Lockie only notices Egg's feet – an obvious allusion to *Robinson Crusoe* and the protagonist's first encounter with indigenous visitors to his desert island. Crusoe at first only sees the footprint in the sand and, for the next two years, lives in continuous fear of cannibals before he actually succeeds in saving Friday and finds a companion and servant, establishing in fiction the prototypical representation of the presumed supremacy of the white man over indigenous peoples.

With regard to the television adaptation of *Lockie Leonard* the encounter on the beach is a comic situation in which the upright native comes across the white man who has just landed ungraciously in the sand after falling off his board. This meeting, right in the very first scene, is evidence of a change in white Australian sensitivity towards Aboriginal Australians, which can be further exemplified by Australian Prime Minister Paul Keating's 1992 Redfern Park Speech that for the first time publicly acknowledged the havoc the British conquest had wreaked on Aboriginal Australians.

Lockie's arrival on the beach thus imitates both ironically and iconically Captain Cook's landing in Botany Bay and the moment he takes possession of the Australian continent for the crown. Students will have the chance to discover the contrast between Calvert's engraving where the heroic conquerors dominate and celebrate their conquest with a gunfire salute while native figures cringe fearfully in the foreground, and the opening scene of the TV series where it is Lockie who is squirming in pain because he has been struck by his own surfboard whereas Egg swaggers along the beach in desert boots and a proud posture (see Figure 7.2). This comic opening of the TV programme sets the tone for the series and is coherent with the fine irony of the novels.

Language and culture

The statement that the television adaptation relies strongly on Winton's dialogue can be supported by comparing the exchange between Lockie and Egg in the book *Scumbuster* and the TV episode described above. Readers and viewers will rapidly become aware of how faithfully Series One adhered to the literary source. The scene introduced above opens both in the book and film with Lockie's thoughts at the sight of the billowing whitecaps down

FIGURE 7.2 *Lockie and Egg on the beach (movie still)* © *Goalpost Pictures (2007), reprinted with kind permission of Goalpost Pictures Australia.*

at the beach: 'The rumours were for real. The sea was fairly pumping. [...] It was demented out there' (*Scumbuster*: 1–2 and opening voiceover in the first episode of *Lockie Leonard* 2007). After successfully surfing for some time disaster strikes: 'Then he hit the sandbar feet first and the board hit too. And bounced up. Right up. Right, right up. Oh, he felt it alright. Right in the goolies' (*Scumbuster*: 5). By means of this scene, the class may learn about the difference between telling (*diegesis*) and showing (*mimesis*): What is narrated in the novel is shown as action on television (but again accompanied by the voiceover of Lockie, revealing his thoughts while he experiences this dramatic moment). Further on in this particular scene, namely when Egg comes strutting along the beach and encounters Lockie lying prostrate on the sand, again the dialogue is almost word for word the same as in the novel, with challenging, fast-paced, colourful and witty language that appeals to secondary-school students. There are a number of moments that capture the graphic expressiveness of teenagers, for instance when Lockie snaps at his brother and then immediately regrets his outburst: ' "You're as big a turd as anyone," Lockie told himself. He felt like sticking his head in a blender' (*Human Torpedo*: 73).

Winton's three young adult novels almost always begin and end with a scene that shows the protagonist surfing the waves. Boardriding provides Lockie with moments of peace and escape. These passages reflect Lockie's emotional experiences and represent the obstacles the teenager has to overcome on his way towards adulthood. Surfing challenging waves thus becomes a metaphor for adolescence. When Lockie is navigating breakers that are at times threateningly large or populated by lethal sharks, the symbolic meaning acquires an edge that may be perceived as exaggerated from an adult perspective but actually provides an accurate rendering of how teenagers tend to (over-) dramatize events they are confronted with. Lockie's victorious arrival on the beach then often has a touch of catharsis; the close avoidance of disaster ends in emotional peace that leaves the protagonist drained but ready to face the next challenge. The surfing also provides a repetitive motif that mirrors the character of the series: not only do readers learn about Lockie's growing up in the series, they also see him grow as a result of conquering the waves. And repetition in language (and literature) is 'not only persuasive but also pleasing' (Reimer et al. 2014: 7).

Comparing the text of the novels with the TV series will allow learners to gain some insights into the nature and practice of adaptation, nurturing perhaps an appreciation of what makes a convincing adaptation as well as an understanding of the benefits of each format. One of the consequences of the pictorial adaptation is, of course, that the imagined characters and settings in readers' minds are replaced by their representations on screen or, as Hutcheon puts it, 'Palimpsests make for permanent change' (2006: 29). This is an additional topic that teachers may want to discuss with secondary-school students. Furthermore, cultural elements can be compared in the ELT classroom: Lockie's surfing could – in another context – be skiing (a likely comparison in Switzerland) – or any other activity at which a teenager excels.

Conclusion

What is the challenge of reading across media with *Lockie Leonard*? Criss-crossing the different narrative formats, pre-adult students can acquire confidence in analysing the quest pattern and will, at the same time, deepen their knowledge of aspects of Australia and the Australian way of life. Most importantly, they will acquire notions of film literacy and critical literacy, how challenging race and gender analyses can deepen their reading of a book, a painting, a television series. Students in such a classroom will develop their intercultural competencies as a result of the kind of cultural studies approach advocated by Peel (2007: 87): 'Cultural products are seen as artefacts that now transcend national boundaries, and are located in the context of a global, technocultural economy' but without neglecting the relevant conditions of 'the historical moment, gender, class and race'.

RECOMMENDATIONS

- Whereas critical cultural literacy 'reads' cultures with a critical eye, critical pedagogy aims for social justice by means of education. This next step might begin by confronting contemporary Othering of minorities and making these issues available for discussion, for 'there are many groups in any society which are driven to the margins exactly because their political, behavioural, or belief systems are in conflict with those of the mainstream groups and they are consequently denied certain rights or opportunities' (Akbari 2008: 281).
- Critical pedagogy also means studying negative and positive features in the students' own local culture. This arguably shows more respect for local concerns than following the safe but possibly insipid topics of commercially produced graded readers and textbooks.

Bibliography

Calvert, Samuel (1865), Engraving of a historical painting by John Alexander Gilfillan (1859), *Captain Cook taking possession of the Australian continent on behalf of the British Crown 1770* for the *Illustrated Sydney News*, National Library of Australia: <http://nla.gov.au/nla.obj-135699884> (accessed 25 August 2015) (Out of copyright).

Donaldson, Julia, illus. Scheffler, Axel (1999), *The Gruffalo*, London: Macmillan.

Hardy, Thomas (1873), *A Pair of Blue Eyes*, Oxford: Oxford University Press.

Horowitz, Anthony (2000), *Stormbreaker: An Alex Rider Adventure*, New York: Penguin.

Lockie Leonard (2007), [TV series] Dir. Tony Tilse, Wayne Blair, Roger Hodgman, James Bogle and Peter Templeman, Goalpost Pictures. (Available through streaming video services)

Lodge, David (1991), *The Writing Game*, London: Secker and Warburg.

Rabbit-Proof Fence (2002), [Film] Dir. Phillip Noyce, Australia: Miramax Films.

Winton, Tim (1990/2007), *Lockie Leonard, Human Torpedo*, Camberwell, Victoria: Penguin.

Winton, Tim (1993/2007), *Lockie Leonard, Scumbuster*, Camberwell, Victoria: Penguin.

Winton, Tim (1997/2007), *Lockie Leonard, Legend*, Camberwell, Victoria: Penguin.

References

Akbari, Ramin (2008), 'Transforming lives: Introducing critical pedagogy into ELT classrooms', *ELT Journal*, 62/3: 276–83.

Allen, Robert (2004), 'Making sense of soaps', in Robert Allen and Annette Hill (eds), *The Television Studies Reader*, London: Routledge, pp. 242–57.

Bate, Jonathan (2010), *English Literature: A Very Short Introduction*, Oxford: Oxford University Press.

Ben-Messahel, Salhia (2006), *Mind the Country: Tim Winton's Fiction*, Crawley, WA: University of Western Australia Press.

Bland, Janice (2013), *Children's Literature and Learner Empowerment: Children and Teenagers in English Language Education*, London: Bloomsbury Academic.

Bland, Janice (2018b), 'Playscript and screenplay: Creativity with J. K. Rowling's Wizarding World', in Janice Bland (ed.), *Using Literature in English Language Education: Challenging Reading for 8–18 Year Olds*, London: Bloomsbury Academic, pp. 41–61.

Bland, Janice (2018c), 'Popular culture head on: Suzanne Collins's *The Hunger Games*', in Janice Bland (ed.), *Using Literature in English Language Education: Challenging Reading for 8–18 Year Olds*, London: Bloomsbury Academic, pp. 175–92.

Campbell, Joseph (1949/2004), *The Hero with a Thousand Faces*, Princeton: Princeton University Press.

Cohen, Deborah (2009), 'Lockie Leonard: Growing up can be a hairy business', *Idiom*, 45/1: 57–63.

Collins, Fiona and Ridgman, Jeremy (2006), 'Introduction', in *Turning the Page: Children's Literature in Performance and the Media*, Oxford: Peter Lang, pp. 9–16.

Council of Europe (2001), *Common European Framework of Reference for Languages: Learning, Teaching, Assessment*, Cambridge: Press Syndicate of the University of Cambridge, <http://www.coe.int/t/dg4/linguistic/Source/Framework_EN.pdf> (accessed 2 February 2016).

Eco, Umberto (1990), 'Interpreting serials', in *The Limits of Interpretation*, Bloomington: Indiana University Press, pp. 83–100.

Edemariam, Aida (2008), 'Waiting for the New Wave', *The Guardian*, 28 June 2008, <https://www.theguardian.com/books/2008/jun/28/saturdayreviewsfeatres.guardianreview9> (accessed 11 August 2016).

Endeavour Voyage (2015), Canberra: National Library of Australia, <https://www.nla.gov.au/digital-classroom/year-4/themes/endeavour-voyage> (accessed 28 August 2015).

Falconer, Rachel (2009), *The Crossover Novel: Contemporary Children's Fiction and Its Adult Readership*, New York: Routledge.

Fröhlich, Vincent (2015), *Der Cliffhanger und die serielle Narration: Analyse einer transmedialen Erzähltechnik*, Bielefeld: Transcript Verlag.

Harders, Pam and Macken-Horarik, Mary (2008), 'Scaffolding literacy and the year 9 boys: Developing a language-centered literacy pedagogy', *TESOL in Context*, 18/2: 4–20.

Hutcheon, Linda (2006), *A Theory of Adaptation*, New York: Routledge.

Hutcheon, Linda (2009), 'In praise of adaptation', in Janet Maybin and Nicola Watson (eds), *Children's Literature: Approaches and Territories*, Basingstoke: Macmillan, pp. 333–8.

Lambert, James (2005), *Macquarie Australian Slang Dictionary*, Macquarie University: The Macquarie Library.

Loock, Kathleen (2014), 'Introduction: Serial narratives', *Literatur in Wissenschaft und Unterricht*, 47/1–2: 5–9.

Mittell, Jason (2015), 'Why has TV storytelling become so complex?' *The Conversation*, 27 March 2015, <http://theconversation.com/why-has-tv-storytelling-become-so-complex-37442> (accessed 25 August 2015).

Moats, Louisa (2004), *Teaching Reading Is Rocket Science: What Expert Teachers of Reading Should Know and Be Able To Do*, Washington DC: American Federation of Teachers, <http://www.aft.org/sites/default/files/reading_rocketscience_2004.pdf> (accessed 29 January 2016).

Myerson, Jonathan (2001), 'Harry Potter and the sad grown-ups', *The Independent*, 14 November 2001, <http://www.independent.co.uk/arts-entertainment/books/news/harry-potter-and-the-sad-grown-ups-9131389.html> (accessed 24 February 2016).

Patterson, Annette (2011), 'Teaching English: Some remarks on the emergence of the sympathetic teacher in the English classroom', in Brenton Doecke, Larissa McLean Davies and Philip Mead (eds), *Teaching Australian Literature*, Kent Town (South Australia): Wakefield, pp. 319–23.

Peel, Robin (2007), 'The "Cultural Studies" model of English', in Wayne Sawyer and Eva Gold (eds), *Reviewing English in the 21st Century*, Melbourne: Phoenix Education.

Prusse , Michael (2014), '"Every story tells a story that has already been told": Intertextuality and intermediality in Philip Pullman's *Spring-Heeled Jack* and in Kevin Brooks' *iBoy*', *Children's Literature in Language Education*, 2/1: 1–21. <http://clelejournal.org/wp-content/uploads/2014/05/Prusse-Every-Story-Tells-a-Story-That-Has-Already-Been-Told.pdf> (accessed 18 December 2016).

Reimer, Mavis, Ali, Nyala, England, Deanna and Melanie Unrau (2014), *Seriality and Texts for Young People: The Compulsion to Repeat*, London: Palgrave Macmillan.

Reynolds, Kimberley (2011), *Children's Literature: A Very Short Introduction*, Oxford: Oxford University Press.

RLP (2013), *Rahmenlehrplan für die Berufsmaturität*, Bern: Staatssekretariat für Bildung, Forschung und Innovation SBFI.

Ruchatz, Jens (2012), 'Sisyphos sieht fern', *Zeitschrift für Medienwissenschaft*, 7: 80–9.

Ryan, Marie-Laure (2004), *Narrative across Media: The Languages of Storytelling*, Lincoln: University of Nebraska Press.

Ryan, Marie-Laure (2014), 'My narratology: An interview with Marie-Laure Ryan', *Diegesis: Interdisciplinary E-Journal for Narrative Research*, 3/1: 78–81. <https://www.diegesis.uni-wuppertal.de/index.php/diegesis/article/view/148/201> (accessed 21 February 2017).

Vogler, Christopher (1998), *The Writer's Journey: Mythic Structure for Writers*, Studio City, CA: Michael Wiese.

Volkmann, Laurenz (2010), *Fachdidaktik Englisch: Kultur und Sprache*, Tübingen: Narr.

Watson, Victor (2000), *Reading Series Fiction: From Arthur Ransome to Gene Kemp*, London: Routledge.

Webb, Jean (2018), 'Environmental havoc in teen fiction: Speculating futures', in Janice Bland (ed.), *Using Literature in English Language Education: Challenging Reading for 8–18 Year Olds*, London: Bloomsbury Academic, pp. 209–23.

Wilson, Carolyn, Grizzle, Alton, Tuazon, Ramon, Akyempong, Kwame and Cheung, Chi-Kim (2011), *Media and Information Literacy Curriculum for Teachers*, Paris: UNESCO, <http://unesdoc.unesco.org/images/0019/001929/192971e.pdf> (accessed 15 January 2017).

Winton, Tim (2016), 'The wait and the flow', *Underline*, 1: 2–6, <https://penguin.com.au/bonus/1248-underline-issue-1> (accessed 26 February 2017).

Wolf, Maryanne (2007), *Proust and the Squid: The Story and Science of the Reading Brain*, New York: Harper Perennial.

PART TWO

Provocative and compelling

8

Literature in language education: Challenges for theory building

Werner Delanoy

The central challenge faced in this chapter is to lay a foundation for a timely theory of literature teaching and literature learning in language education. To meet this challenge, a case is made for an open-ended dialogue between different positions in the light of current literary, language-related, educational and sociocultural demands. Engagement in dialogue implies a particular starting position, which is then questioned in the light of other concepts. In the following reflections this starting position is reader-response criticism (RRC). Indeed, RRC itself has undergone significant transformation through dialogue with other theories. Initially, therefore, the focus is on showing how RRC has continually widened its scope in the past fifty years. Subsequently, this conglomerate of theories is discussed in the light of the question why literature should still be included in (language) education. Again, rather than presenting one line of argumentation, a multiperspectival approach is chosen to justify the importance of literature from different language-related, utilitarian and sociocultural angles. Finally, a concrete teaching project is introduced with Beverley Naidoo's short story 'Out of Bounds' at its centre to link theory to concrete teaching practice. The title of this short story also serves as a motto for the approach to literature teaching and learning advocated in this chapter – *Out of Bounds*. In other words, border crossing is encouraged to bring the field up to date with present concerns, and to take it beyond the tried and tested.

Challenging reader-response criticism

In this section, a case is made for a dialogic approach to theory building, which is in essence post-theoretical. Whereas in the past different theories vied with each other for superiority over other positions, a post-theoretical stance aims to combine different perspectives. Such a stance stems from the belief that the multifarious complexities of literature and language learning demand a multi-perspectival approach. Furthermore, this approach is informed by a particular notion of dialogue. This understanding of dialogue rests on the assumption that viewpoints are always limited, but can be questioned, widened and transformed through ongoing, open-ended and (self)-critical engagement with other positions. Such a concept aims for respectful encounters between equal partners.

What makes reader-response criticism particularly relevant to the post-theoretical way of thinking is its commitment to dialogue, which excludes the belief in a single orthodoxy. Of course, RRC is a broad church with varied and conflicting positions (Bredella 2002: 34–45, Delanoy 2015: 21–4). The RRC approach that will be focused on in this chapter places at its centre the dialogue between the literary text and the reader. This approach is rooted in the concepts of literature teaching and learning as suggested by Michael Benton (1992), Lothar Bredella (2002) and Louise Rosenblatt (1994). For this 'interactive paradigm' (Bredella 2002: 43), reading is a process of text-guided meaning creation with literary texts challenging their readers' cognitive and affective faculties.

At the heart of the interactive paradigm lies a certain understanding of aesthetic experience. Such experience presupposes challenging literary texts that offer a critical perspective on sociocultural issues. Moreover, the reader adopts an aesthetically motivated stance. In the light of Benton's, Bredella's and Rosenblatt's comments the hallmarks of such a stance are as follows:

1 Readers can leave behind the pressures of their primary lifeworlds, and enter a relatively safe space to experiment with feelings and ideas (Bredella 1996: 2–5, Rosenblatt 1994: 31–2).

2 A holistic perspective is adopted: readers, rather than looking for specific information, ask themselves what a text means to them as a whole. Such whole-person and whole-text orientation permits the creation of manifold and unexpected links between text and reader (Bredella 2002:156, 160–3, Rosenblatt 1994: 22–5).

3 Reading is seen as a combination of intensive involvement and (self)-critical detachment (Benton 1992: 15, Bredella 1996: 18, Rosenblatt

1994: 27, 37). In other words, distance from primary worlds facilitates intensive affective and cognitive involvement in secondary worlds, or storyworlds. Simultaneously, readers are focused on the manifold feelings and ideas evoked by a text, thus asking themselves how the meanings created affect them in their understanding of themselves and others. Considering the critical sociocultural function of literature such a focus can lead to new critical literacy insights on the part of the reader.

RRC is a continually developing approach and has expanded its focus with the help of many schools. In terms of text analysis, RRC is mainly focused on the pragmatic dimension of meaning making. This is an important perspective since it looks at why and how certain texts attempt to have a particular impact on their readers. In its early realizations (Bredella 1980; Rosenblatt 1994), this approach, however, showed less interest in the linguistic make-up of literary texts, for example in their stylistic and narrative dimensions. Yet, through engagement with pedagogical stylistics and narratology, the narrow focus has been overcome (Nünning and Surkamp 2008: 194–244). As a reader-oriented concept, RRC originally did not engage with issues of text creation. However, RRC has incorporated this dimension through inclusion of creative writing approaches as suggested for literature teachers in ELT (see, e.g. Collie and Slater 1987, Duff and Maley 1990, Bland 2018b, this volume).

Another example concerns the critical literacy dimension of RRC. In its early phase, RRC mainly emphasized literature's power to give its readers new sociocultural insight without discussing literature's implication in hegemonic discourses. More recent approaches, however (e.g. Bland 2013a, Blau 2003, Delanoy 2002, Stephens 2010), have integrated both concerns, thus stressing the importance of appreciative *and* resistant, ideology-critical readings. Finally, RRC quite early made a case for integrating literary and cultural learning, the focus being on intercultural learning perspectives (Bredella 1996: 15–18 and 2002: Part 1). In the light of current sociocultural challenges, cosmopolitan and transcultural perspectives have been taken on board (Bredella 2002: 198–214, Delanoy 2006).

Further development includes moves beyond monomodal written texts and the single-text approach, plus the inclusion of new reader groups. In the past, the term literature stood for texts whose 'originating modality and final point of reference' is in written form (Widdowson 1999: 121). Increasingly, engagement with literature also includes multimodal practices such as picturebooks, comics, graphic novels, songs or hypertext literature. In theoretical terms, this shift has encouraged RRC to strengthen links with semiotic approaches and the multiple literacies movement to better understand how 'written-linguistic modes of meaning interface with oral, visual, audio, gestural, tactile, and spatial patterns of meaning' (Kalantzis and Cope 2012: 2). Previously, pedagogical concepts of RRC often focused on single literary texts to introduce their suggestions for literature learning. Wolfgang Hallet (2002: 6, 101, 105) is right when he criticizes such an approach as unsuited to the present time. Indeed, in an age of wide-ranging communication networks and mass data transfer, competencies need to be developed which allow students to successfully navigate in a vast body of texts both within and outside literary studies. In line with this aim, extensive reading in ELT has received more attention in recent publications (Hesse 2009: 120–30, Krashen 2013, Maley 2008, Strobbe 2013). This shift in focus, however, complements rather than replaces the deep reading, single-text approach, since this is where students still learn to focus intensively on a specific work. Finally, RRC approaches in ELT often had a model reader in mind who would attend the highest school grades, and who in principle would be motivated to engage with literature. In recent years scholars have developed concepts to include younger learners, from elementary school onwards, and reluctant readers with little or no interest in literature (Bland 2013a; Hesse 2009).

Why literature now?

The question as to whether and why literature should or should not be taught in language education has been asked over and again in the light of changing educational and sociocultural demands. For proponents of RRC the answer is that literature can challenge people in their established modes of thinking and feeling and guide them towards new insight, gained by the students as they activate the meaning structure of the text for themselves. Such insight implies a sharpening of critical abilities, the exploration of alternative perspectives and 'an expansion of sympathies that real life cannot cultivate sufficiently' (Nussbaum 1998: 111). Yet, how can such a programme be justified in the light of current educational and sociocultural development? This is a formidable challenge, which comes at a time where standardization threatens the inclusion of complex content in education, and where the motivation to read is in steady decline. Finding convincing arguments, therefore, may well decide about whether literature has a future in (language) education.

In this section, three different perspectives will be discussed which may help re-emphasize the importance of literature. The first perspective is focused on literature's language-related affordances. Second, concepts will be discussed which have foregrounded the utilitarian value of literature learning in (language) education. Third, a humanistic perspective will be presented which is cosmopolitan in orientation.

1. *Literary language involving the learner holistically*

In literature pedagogy, Geoff Hall (2015) offers a language-related defence of literature in the light of the recent shift towards standardization in language education. For Hall (2015: 37) this shift implies that undue preference is given to 'the literal and straightforward exchange of information', thus privileging forms of communication that exclude challenging content and personal learner involvement. In his reflections, Hall draws attention to the importance of language creativity in human communication. For Hall, such creativity includes playing with words, ideas and concepts in personally and socioculturally meaningful ways. Moreover, it is linked to the power of storytelling. Hall (2015: 10) argues that while such language creativity goes far beyond the confines of literature, literature is particularly rich in such activity, which makes it a treasure trove for language learning.

In his comments Hall brings together the two strands in second language acquisition (SLA) research which are most receptive to literature, namely those with a focus on language creativity (e.g. Cook 2000) and those concerned with the social dimension of language learning (e.g. Block 2003). Both aim for a broader conceptualization of SLA by including ludic, narrative and identity-related dimensions. Literature as a space for experimentation with feelings, ideas and language fits well into such concepts. Moreover, there is another pro-literature argument put forward by Hall (2015: 148) and Block (2003: 104), who make a case for looking at language learning as 'language participation', that is as learning to participate in new relationships and social contexts through language. For them, literature is a rich source for such language learning, since it permits personally meaningful participation in the lives of fictional characters within complex storyworlds.

In similar terms, Claire Kramsch has argued in favour of a concept of communicative competence that is multimodal and holistic in approach, and in tune with the challenges of a globalized modernity. For Kramsch 'symbolic competence' transcends established notions of communicative competence since it 'addresses students' subjectivity, not just the effectiveness of their information exchanges or their ability to satisfy the rules of grammar, play predetermined roles, or accomplish predesigned tasks' (Kramsch 2009: 202). Kramsch emphasizes that language learners are 'whole persons with hearts, bodies and minds, with memories, fantasies, loyalties, identities. Symbolic forms are not just items of vocabulary or communication strategies, but embodied experiences, emotional resonances, and moral imaginings' (2006: 251). Her position links back to the whole-person orientation of RRC approaches which stress literature's holistic appeal. Moreover, Kramsch (2006: 251) expresses a particular preference for literature by explaining that symbolic competence 'has to be nourished by a literary imagination at all levels of the language curriculum'. For her, literature can foster engagement with complex issues, openness to contradiction and insight into how form in its manifold dimensions helps construct meanings.

In line with Kramsch's perspective, Janice Bland (2013b: 87) gives a concrete example as to how multimodal literature can enrich language learning on symbolic levels. Bland discusses the difference between pictures in ELT coursebooks for young learners and in children's literature. She argues that while the former offer 'overdetermining, stylized, stereotyped and crude illustrations, [thus] limiting a creative response', picturebooks play with 'complex, naturalistic, untidy, ambiguous and thus partly determining' images. By doing so, such books invite deeper and more complex thinking processes.

2. *The utilitarian value of literature learning*

In his book *The Literature Workshop*, Sheridan Blau (2003) offers a utilitarian justification of literature learning. Arguing from a post-theoretical RRC position, Blau emphasizes that literature portrays a wide spectrum of different life experiences in complex and insight-inviting ways without presupposing the specialist knowledge required in many other fields. For him, literature learning is a workshop for developing interpretation competencies relevant to all subjects and professions (such as law, medicine, business) in which meaning must be negotiated and discussed. Also, he stresses the importance of literature learning for developing 'performative literacy' – becoming an active participant of the text – which is of transdisciplinary importance. For Blau, the following seven traits constitute the foundation for performative literacy:

1 Capacity for sustained, focused attention

2 Willingness to suspend closure

3 Willingness to take risks

4 Tolerance for failure

5 Tolerance for ambiguity, paradox, and uncertainty

6 Intellectual generosity and fallibilism

7 Metacognitive awareness. (Blau 2003: 211)

Blau's notion of a performative literacy, or participatory reading, has important implications for language learning. In line with Kramsch's position, such literacy draws attention to holistic language abilities permitting communication where the content is complex and the outcome is still open. Of course, this willingness to take risks poses a particular challenge to language learners when considering their developing interlanguage. Yet, such an active second language competence is indispensable in a globalized modernity where sociocultural and linguistic boundaries need to be crossed in order to engage with complex issues of transnational significance.

Another utilitarian justification comes from SLA research. A good example is Stephen Krashen (2013: 15) who refers to his case studies, which 'have all confirmed that more free reading results in better reading ability, better writing, larger vocabularies, better spelling and better control of complex grammatical constructions'. In a similar vein, Beniko Mason (2013: 31) points out that self-selected extensive reading, story listening and a combination of the two has proven an efficient method to well prepare language learners for TOEFL examinations. Studying young learners in Germany, Annika Kolb's (2013: 34, 39–41) picturebook project shows that extensive individualized reading supported through audio recordings and particular tasks, such as keeping a reading log, led to an increase in reading confidence, better understanding of, and reflective responses to texts.

3. Cosmopolitanism as a challenge for literature teaching and learning

Reader-response criticism is rooted in a humanistic philosophy which has been criticized by some postcolonial writers as serving Western hegemonic interests. Both humanism and postcolonial studies, however, have moved on, as can be seen in the work of Edward Said, one of the most eminent postcolonial critics to date. In his later work Said no longer wants to eliminate humanism. Instead, he argues for a humanism of cosmopolitan proportions which is based on careful, (self-)critical, and responsible engagement with oneself and others (Said 2003: 61–6). For Said, literature is a richly textured and multilayered discourse that can empower people to (self-)critically gain access to complex realities. Said (61–2) also argues for a return to philological – that is intensive or deep – readings. For him, both literature and such readings can act as a counterweight to one-sided and superficial media coverage.

Engagement with complex realities has become indispensable in a globalized modernity where local and global issues interpenetrate in complex ways. For Zygmunt Bauman (2000: 7–8), such a world is a 'liquid modernity' where rapid change is the norm, and where – because of the diminished role of collectives (the state, the family, the nation . . .) – the responsibility increasingly lies with the single subject, who is constantly faced with the need to make decisions. Reflective decision making, however, is hampered by the seductive and one-sided solutions suggested by popular media, populist politicians, or fundamentalist groups. Therefore, education is faced with the challenge of developing programmes where global interconnectedness is sufficiently acknowledged, where ongoing critical engagement with complex lifeworlds is fostered, and where issues are discussed in open-ended intercultural dialogue. Cosmopolitanism can offer such a perspective, since it has moved beyond Eurocentric concepts (Sobré-Denton and Bardhan 2013: 21), and since a case has been made for a complex dialogue of global proportions permitting 'multiple and conflicting evaluations' (Benhabib 2002: 40).

Communicative competence in twenty-first-century ELT is inextricably linked to coping with multiple and multimodal communication streams. In the light of Katherine Hayles's discussion of different cognitive modes (2007), therefore, a capacity for deep attention alongside the increasingly current hyper attention must be developed. While the former implies ongoing concentration on a text, the latter stands for switching between multiple information streams. In other words, Said's focus on philological readings, or deep reading, must be complemented by engagement with multiple communication streams. Thus, concepts of literature must be widened in scope to include, for example, multimodal texts and screen media 'for building bridges between deep and hyper attention' (Hayles 2007: 195). Also, extensive reading practices need to be fostered which permit discovery of and (self-)critical reflection upon intertextual connections in larger text corpora. Finally, such corpora should be transnational in design to firmly embed literature learning in global and cosmopolitan perspectives. Indeed, Anglophone literary studies provides an excellent reference frame for such learning because of its global reach.

Together, these three perspectives permit a language-related, utilitarian and sociocultural justification of literature teaching and learning in ELT contexts. In a nutshell, literature is a rich resource for language and sociocultural learning because of its complexity, creativity and social comment. Also, literature learning can foster a performative literacy. As aesthetic discourse, literature learning invites safe, personally meaningful and creative experimentation with feelings, ideas and language. Finally, a cosmopolitan imagination can be fostered by exploring the transnational character of Anglophone literatures.

Out of Bounds – A multimodal literature project

'Out of Bounds' is the final short story in the eponymous collection by Beverley Naidoo, first published in 2001 (see Figure 8.1). *Out of Bounds* is also the title of a multimodal literature project design comprising short stories,

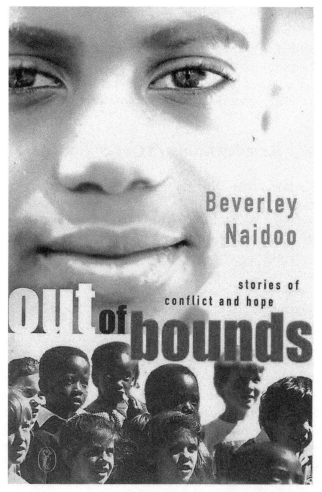

FIGURE 8.1 *Cover of* Out of Bounds *by Beverley Naidoo (London: Puffin, 2001). Cover design copyright © Penguin Books Ltd., 2001. Reproduced by permission of Penguin Books.*

picturebooks and a graphic novel. In the following, first, some of the teaching and learning challenges posed by Naidoo's short story will be discussed, and some suggestions will be presented as to how they can be met in the ELT classroom. Second, the focus is on the construction of a multimodal text corpus inspired by certain principles for text selection. This reading project must not be mistaken for the type of extensive reading suggested by proponents of SLA research such as Krashen (2013) or Mason (2013). While their research has focused on self-selected pleasure reading, the texts in the present project have been preselected in the light of certain criteria. This approach does not call into question the benefits of individualized pleasure reading for language learning. However, with reference to a dialogic, power-critical and cosmopolitan agenda such pleasure reading may not go far enough. Indeed, pleasure reading may imply reading the same type of text again and again, thus fostering entrenchment in certain modes of feeling and thinking. On the other hand, the project presented here is informed by criteria permitting (self-) critical and multiperspectival orientation in complex textual networks.

Beverley Naidoo's Out of Bounds

Out of Bounds is a short-story collection with seven stories spanning close to sixty years of South African history. In the introduction Naidoo (2001: xv) argues that South African history 'has been full of barriers – real walls and those in the mind. Some people have accepted these, while others have challenged them'. The stories show how young people have challenged apartheid and the barriers continuing to exist after its abolition. They often suffer defeat, yet they also sow the seeds for a more democratic future.

The setting for the final short story, also entitled 'Out of Bounds', is Durban at the beginning of the new millennium. In the story two worlds are contrasted, that of a multiracial middle-class community, and that of black displaced persons, who have set up camp as squatters in the immediate vicinity, their homes having been destroyed by devastating floods. By and large the story is told from a figural narrative perspective, the focus being on Rohan, the son of a middle-class Indian family living in a comfortable home overlooking the squatters' camp. The narration gives insight into Rohan's thought processes, his inner struggle between helping the squatters and shutting them out, and his courage to go out of bounds by giving water to a black boy (Solani) and by helping him carry the water to the squatters' camp. At the end of the story the two boys have started a friendship which must still be kept a secret due to the distrust the two communities feel for each other.

What makes 'Out of Bounds' a challenging text to read? The text gives insight into the complex thinking of a boy aged between twelve and thirteen, who is portrayed as a highly reflective, self-critical and empathetic individual struggling with inner conflict, yet capable of action in the interest of a more humane world. Indeed, Rohan can be seen as a role model for an educational programme where young people are taken seriously as thinking and feeling subjects, plus as change agents in a still divisive world. Moreover, the story addresses issues that echo some of the developments of the Syrian refugee crisis, with many countries first admitting and helping refugees before mental and real walls went up.

The precarious socio-economic situation of the squatters is shown vividly. For example, Rohan learns that – being barred from the local shopping malls – Solani's family has no chance to get a decent price for the arts and crafts they produce, which condemns them to the bottom of the social ladder. Indeed, the story interweaves personal, political and social dimensions, thus fostering complex and multidimensional thinking. Finally, the text has been hailed as one of the few children's books on Africa which is not steeped in a colonial and imperial mentality which aims to perpetuate social and racial divisions and imbalances (Maddy and MacCann 2009: 3, 136).

Teaching this text with, for example, fifteen-year-old language learners, can pose a series of form- and content-related, context- and language-related challenges. In its narrative structure the text only partly offers closure. Rohan and Solani have started a positive relationship, yet, they still find themselves in a world where their contact may turn out to be a one-off incident. This may cause a feeling of unease among readers who would prefer a more positive ending. Moreover, the text offers challenging content. In his actions the protagonist defies his parents' orders when he helps Solani. This raises serious moral questions as to when disobedience is justified both within the family and in wider social contexts. As for context, the setting is a South African city at the beginning of the millennium. Some of the references – the place of Indians in South African society, or the opening of non-black schools to all communities – may require some explanation or student research to facilitate learner involvement in the text. Finally, the text was written with a young adult audience in mind whose first language is English. While in an English-speaking context the intended audience may be readers between twelve and fourteen, in foreign language learning the text may be better suited for higher grades to make up for the students' more limited language proficiency.

How can these challenges be met in a classroom context? I will focus on what I see as the central teaching challenge in the light of the RRC-approach discussed, namely to foster both absorption and (self-)critical involvement in the text. To do so, I would read aloud the first eight pages in class – the story is twenty pages long – and stop at certain points to (1) check comprehension, (2) draw the students' attention to Rohan's thoughts, emotions and actions, (3) invite reflection upon the text in the light of the students' life experiences, (4) provide background information and (5) help remove some language barriers. In the first eight pages, the situation is explained why the squatters have come to Durban plus why and how the local community's attitude to them has changed. There is reference to a specific incident which Rohan repeatedly remembers as the story moves on. He watches on the news how a flood victim – a young mother giving birth – is rescued from a tree by the South African army. The first eight pages already give insight into Rohan's complex inner struggle, how he oscillates between his arguments for leaving the squatters to their fate and helping them. The squatter Solani asks Rohan for water for his mother, who is about to give birth. This is the break-off point where the students will first speculate about how the text may go on, and then read the remainder of the story for themselves. Individual readings can then be followed by a variety of post-reading tasks, such as writing a sequel, finding pictures to illustrate the text, discussing personal responses, or presenting the story as a newspaper article.

As for language learning, the preferred approach is interactionist in orientation. With reference to Lightbown and Spada (2013: 24–9, 114), language is made comprehensible through modified interaction. This means that scaffolding is provided throughout the interaction process, the teacher supplying the support needed to make the text intelligible and discussible.

A multimodal literature project

As stated in the first section, RRC has made attempts to move beyond the single text approach by shifting its focus to text ensembles, and by linking the concept to intertextual and intermedial approaches. A key concept here is Helene Decke-Cornill's (1994: 281, 2007: 254–5) notion of a *didaktischer Text*, by which she means pedagogically crafted text collections. Decke-Cornill argues that reading extensively is not enough, since people may read the same type of story again and again, and thus remain caught in a narrow understanding of themselves and others. For Decke-Cornill, pedagogically crafted text ensembles should include different positions, question established views, invite power-critical thinking and resist closure (1994: 281). From a postcolonial perspective, the writer Chimamanda Adichie (2009) holds a similar position, warning of 'the danger of a single story', which is told again and again, thus confirming and perpetuating patronizing, simplifying and negative images of African peoples.

As a single text Beverley Naidoo's 'Out of Bounds' is a good starting point for engaging in readings informed by Decke-Cornill's and Adichie's concerns. As mentioned above, the short story partly resists closure, it can foster critical literacy, and it goes beyond a stereotypical portrayal of South African people. The other texts included in the reading project all involve themes discussed in Naidoo's text, such as crossing borders, taking risks, experiencing homelessness, questioning stereotypes, or making friends coming from different backgrounds.

The text ensemble includes two picturebooks, namely *Friends from the Other Side/Amigos del Otro Lado* (1993) by Gloria Anzaldúa and illustrated by Consuelo Méndez and *Prietita and the Ghost Woman/Prietita y la Llorona* (1995) by Gloria Anzaldúa and illustrated by Maya Gonzalez. While in *Friends from the Other Side* the female protagonist helps an illegal immigrant family find their feet in her village, the same girl enters forbidden territory to help her sick mother in *Prietita and the Ghost Woman*. In addition, some more short stories were selected. One of the texts is Beverley Naidoo's 'The Playground', in which – after the end of apartheid – a black girl insists on her right to attend a formerly all-white school. Ovo Adagha's 'Homeless' and Ravi Mangla's 'Air Mail' are taken from the anthology *One World: A Global Anthology of Short Stories* (2009). In 'Homeless', losing one's home is presented from the perspective of a poor black Nigerian family. In 'Air Mail', two boys – one from the United States and the other one from India – become penfriends, and in their exchanges they manage to move beyond a stereotypical understanding of each other. Finally, one graphic novel is included in this text ensemble. Gene Luen Yang's *American Born Chinese* (2006) shows how going out of bounds may also result from attempts to fit into a new social environment.

The text selection was guided by Decke-Cornill's criteria. In order to facilitate the inclusion of different perspectives, the collection should give some insight into the cultural diversity of Anglophone literatures. Consequently the ensemble includes stories set in countries as diverse as South Africa, Nigeria, India, the United States or the Mexican-American borderlands with a special focus on cultural border crossing, hyphenated cultural identities and transformation through intercultural contact. Moreover, going out of bounds is treated differently in the texts selected: ranging from violating laws to demanding fulfilment of laws in the interest of a humanistic agenda, as well as hankering after the impossible because of the wish to conform. Many of the texts selected resist closure by presenting complex worlds, and endings where the conflicts – despite some temporary solution – have not disappeared. In addition, some of the texts are taken from anthologies of short stories. Thus, interest in one of these texts may motivate students to explore the anthology further. The texts address different power-related dimensions, such as questioning power divisions, giving a voice to marginalized groups, or succumbing to the power of the dominant culture. Also, the steps taken to resist and transgress power structures range from drastic action to first steps, like becoming penfriends, thus showing learners where they can make a start without risking too much. Going beyond Decke-Cornill's criteria, multimodal texts are included in this collection to bring literature learning up-to-date with current meaning-making practices. Finally, all the texts selected – even when aimed at younger first language speakers of English – are sufficiently complex in terms of form and content to challenge language learners at a relatively advanced level in their meaning-making capacities.

Conclusion

Summing up, a timely concept for literature learning must face a number of teaching challenges. First, suitable texts need to be selected inviting both engrossing and critical readings. Second, students need to be aided in developing an aesthetic reader stance that integrates intensive involvement and (self-)critical reflection. Third, competencies need to be fostered permitting deep reflection on single texts as well as navigation in complex textual networks. Fourth, such navigation is informed by quality criteria encouraging engagement with different perspectives and critical thinking. Fifth, the concept of literature is widened to include multimodal texts. Sixth, the language-related and utilitarian opportunities of literary discourse need to be stressed to firmly root literature in language education. Seventh, a transnational approach is chosen to link literature learning to a cosmopolitan agenda. Eighth, theories for literature teaching and learning must be inclusive of different positions to address the complexities involved in literature and language learning. Finally, the approach suggested in this chapter is open to critical inquiry and further development. In other words, as a theory-in-the-making it is intended as an invitation to its readers to highlight its shortcomings and to extend its possibilities for literature learning and teaching.

RECOMMENDATIONS

- Novelist Chimamanda Ngozi Adichie's stimulating TED talk entitled 'The Danger of a Single Story' is well worth watching in the secondary-school classroom, to inspire a meta-discussion of the different perspectives stories can reveal.
- Short story anthologies that represent global Anglophone literatures, like *One World: A Global Anthology of Short Stories*, allow language education to move away from a dominance of Anglo-American culture. This widening of focus is long overdue. English is now the global lingua franca, and spotlighting only Western cultures in language materials perpetuates the danger of the single story.

Bibliography

Adagha, Ovo (2009), 'Homeless', in Chris Brazier (ed.), *One World: A Global Anthology of Short Stories*, Oxford: New Internationalist, pp. 169–74.

Adichie, Chimamanda Ngozi (2009), 'The danger of a single story', *TEDGlobal*, 7 October 2009, https://www.ted.com/talks/chimamanda_adichie_the_danger_of_a_single_story (accessed 22 October 2017).

Anzaldúa, Gloria, illus. Méndez, Consuelo (1993), *Friends from the Other Side/ Amigos del Otro Lado*, San Francisco: Children's Book Press.

Anzaldúa, Gloria, illus. Gonzalez, Maya Christina (1995), *Prietita and the Ghost Woman/Prietita y la Llorona*, San Francisco: Children's Book Press.

Mangla, Ravi (2009), 'Air Mail', in Chris Brazier (ed.), *One World: A Global Anthology of Short Stories*, Oxford: New Internationalist, pp. 69–73.

Naidoo, Beverley (2001), *Out of Bounds. Stories of Conflict and Hope*, London: Puffin.

Yang, Luen Gene (2006), *American Born Chinese*, New York: Square Fish.

References

Bauman, Zygmunt (2000), *Liquid Modernity*, Cambridge: Polity Press.

Benhabib, Sayla (2002), *The Claims of Culture: Equality and Diversity in the Global Era*, Princeton/NJ: Princeton University Press.

Benton, Michael (1992), *Secondary Worlds: Literature Teaching and the Visual Arts*, Buckingham and Philadelphia: Open University Press.

Bland, Janice (2013a), *Children's Literature and Learner Empowerment: Children and Teenagers in English Language Education*, London and New York: Bloomsbury Academic.

Bland, Janice (2013b), 'Fairy tales with a difference: Creating a continuum from primary to secondary ELT', in Janice Bland and Christiane Lütge (eds), *Children's Literature in Second Language Education*, London and New York: Bloomsbury Academic, pp. 85–94.

Bland, Janice (2018b), 'Playscript and screenplay: Creativity with J. K. Rowling's Wizarding World', in Janice Bland (ed.), *Using Literature in English Language Education: Challenging Reading for 8–18 Year Olds*, London: Bloomsbury Academic, pp. 41–61.

Blau, Sheridan (2003), *The Literature Workshop: Teaching Texts and Their Readers*, Portsmouth/NH: Heinemann.

Block, David (2003), *The Social Turn in Second Language Acquisition*, Washington: Georgetown University Press.

Bredella, Lothar (1980), *Das Verstehen literarischer Texte*, Stuttgart: Kohlhammer.

Bredella, Lothar (1996), 'The anthropological and pedagogical significance of aesthetic reading', in Lothar Bredella and Werner Delanoy (eds), *Challenges of Literary Texts in the Foreign Language Classroom*, Tübingen: Gunter Narr, pp. 1–29.

Bredella, Lothar (2002), *Literarisches und interkulturelles Verstehen*, Tübingen: Gunter Narr.

Collie, Joanne and Slater, Stephen (1987), *Literature in the Language Classroom. A Resource Book of Ideas and Activities*, Cambridge: Cambridge University Press.

Cook, Guy (2000), *Language Play*, Oxford: Oxford University Press.

Decke-Cornill, Helene (1994), 'Intertextualität als literaturdidaktische Dimension: Zur Frage der Textzusammenstellung bei literarischen Lektürereihen', *Die Neueren Sprachen*, 3: 272–87.

Decke-Cornill, Helene (2007), 'Literaturdidaktik in einer "Pädagogik der Anerkennung": Gender and other suspects', in Wolfgang Hallet und Ansgar

Nünning (eds), *Neue Ansätze und Konzepte der Literatur- und Kulturdidaktik*, Trier: WVT Wissenschaftlicher Verlag Trier, pp. 239–58.

Delanoy, Werner (2002), *Fremdsprachlicher Literaturunterricht: Theorie und Praxis als Dialog*, Tübingen: Gunter Narr.

Delanoy, Werner (2006), 'Transculturality and (inter-)cultural learning in the EFL classroom', in Werner Delanoy and Laurenz Volkmann (eds), *Cultural Studies in the EFL Classroom*, Heidelberg: Carl Winter, pp. 233–48.

Delanoy, Werner (2015), 'Literature teaching and learning: Theory and practice', in Werner Delanoy, Maria Eisenmann and Frauke Matz (eds), *Learning with Literature in the EFL Classroom*, Frankfurt: Peter Lang, pp. 19–47.

Duff, Alan and Maley, Alan (1990), *Literature*, Oxford: Oxford University Press.

Hall, Geoff (2015), *Literature in Language Education* (2nd edn), Basingstoke: Palgrave Macmillan.

Hallet, Wolfgang (2002), *Fremdsprachenunterricht als Spiel der Texte und Kulturen: Intertextualität als Paradigma einer kulturwissenschaftlichen Didaktik*, Trier: WVT.

Hayles, Katherine (2007), 'Hyper and deep attention: The generational divide in cognitive modes', *Profession 2007*, 187–99.

Hesse, Mechthild (2009), *Teenage Fiction in the Active English Classroom*, Stuttgart: Klett.

Kalantzis, Mary and Cope, Bill (2012), *Literacies*, Cambridge: Cambridge University Press.

Kolb, Annika (2013), 'Extensive reading of picturebooks in primary EFL', in Janice Bland and Christiane Lütge (eds), *Children's Literature in Second Language Education*, London and New York: Bloomsbury Academic, pp. 33–43.

Kramsch, Claire (2006), 'From communicative competence to symbolic competence', *The Modern Language Journal*, 90: 249–52.

Kramsch, Claire (2009), *The Multilingual Subject*, Oxford: Oxford University Press.

Krashen, Stephen (2013), 'Free reading: Still a great idea', in Janice Bland and Christiane Lütge (eds), *Children's Literature in Second Language Education*, London and New York: Bloomsbury Academic, 15–24.

Lightbown, Patsy and Spada, Nina (2013), *How Languages are Learned* (4th edn), Oxford: Oxford University Press.

Maddy, Yulisa and MacCann, Donnarae (2009), *Neo Imperialism in Children's Literature about Africa: A Study of Contemporary Fiction*, London and New York: Routledge.

Maley, Alan (2008), 'Extensive reading: Maid in waiting', in Brian Tomlinson (ed.), *English Language Learning Materials*, London: Continuum, 133–56.

Mason, Beniko (2013), 'Efficient use of literature in second language education: Free reading and listening to stories', in Janice Bland and Christiane Lütge (eds), *Children's Literature in Second Language Education*, London and New York: Bloomsbury Academic, pp. 25–32.

Nünning, Ansgar and Surkamp, Carola (2008), *Englische Literatur unterrichten 1: Grundlagen und Methoden*, Stuttgart: Klett.

Nussbaum, Martha (1998), *Cultivating Humanity: A Classical Defence of Reform in Liberal Education*, Cambridge/MA: Harvard University Press.

Rosenblatt, Louise (1994), *The Reader, the Text, the Poem: The Transactional Theory of the Literary Work*, Carbondale/Edwardsville: Sothern Illinois University Press.

Said, Edward (2003), *Humanism and Democratic Criticism*, Basingstoke: Palgrave Macmillan.

Sobré-Denton, Miriam and Bardhan, Nilanjana (2013), *Cultivating Cosmopolitanism for Intercultural Communication: Communicating as Global Citizens*, London and New York: Routledge.

Stephens, John (2010), 'Ideology', in David Rudd (ed.), *The Routledge Companion to Children's Literature*, Abingdon: Routledge, pp. 192–3.

Strobbe, Johan (2013), 'Free space: An extensive reading project in a Flemish school', in Janice Bland and Christiane Lütge (eds), *Children's Literature in Second Language Education*, London: Bloomsbury Academic, 45–52.

Widdowson, Peter (1999), *Literature*, London and New York: Routledge.

9

Diversity in love-themed fiction: John Green's THE FAULT IN OUR STARS and David Levithan's PRINCES

Johanna Marks and Thorsten Merse

Choosing texts that challenge the practice of reading literature in the ELT classroom can in itself pose a challenge to the researcher, to the practising teacher and to the student teacher on several levels. In this chapter, we argue that at least three levels must be considered:

1 The question arises in how far the themes and issues negotiated in a literary text might be perceived as challenging not only by its teen readers but also by their teachers, in terms of content.

2 In how far can new literary texts in ELT challenge the established set of texts that have become canonized over time, possibly perpetuating what Adichie (2009) calls 'a single story'?

3 It needs to be taken into account how learners' practices of reading can be challenged, and how the reading of literary texts can be made a challenging experience for them, so that the exploration of literature can provide a unique and transformative learning experience.

This chapter challenges content, canon and methodology by exploring love-themed fiction in the context of diversity in ELT. The texts chosen – the novel

The Fault in Our Stars by John Green (2012) and the short story 'Princes' by David Levithan (2008) – negotiate the trajectories of love when closely intertwined with circumstances of illness and death (Green), and gay sexual orientation (Levithan). As we will illustrate, the legitimization for choosing these possibly controversial or taboo themes in literary texts is located in recent research developments in intercultural and global issues learning that seek to update and transform ELT pedagogy in terms of greater sociocultural diversity. We further argue that the topic of love provides an ideal locus for dialogic deep reading in that love is both a culturally universal phenomenon and a phenomenon contingent on discourse. Green's and Levithan's texts are then combined into a text ensemble (Decke-Cornill 2007) for the classroom, including methodological suggestions that illustrate how literary texts which negotiate love can be harnessed as a challenging learning experience.

Towards diversity: Renegotiations in intercultural learning

The *Common European Framework of Reference for Languages* (CEFR) (Council of Europe 2001: 1) highlights that '[i]n an intercultural approach, it is a central objective of language education to promote the favourable development of the learner's whole personality and sense of identity in response to the enriching experience of otherness in language and culture'. In Byram's (1997) five-dimensional model of intercultural communicative competence, learners are described as mediators who use their knowledge, their skills and their attitudes to negotiate meaning and communicate successfully between people from different cultural contexts. In negotiating meanings between the cultural self and the cultural other, learners relativize and decentre from their own deeply engrained cultural imprints and norms and open up to cultural otherness (Byram 1997: 3, 18, 35).

One key concern of current research into cultural learning is to renegotiate who or what is actually meant by the Other, by (socio-)cultural otherness. It appears that the pedagogy of cultural learning has had, and still continues to have, what Risager (2013: 145) calls a 'national shaping'. The tendency has been to equate culture with nation, and hence to focus on a nation's – frequently those of the so-called core countries UK and USA – institutions, artistic products, customs, traditions, geography or mentality. This has served to privilege a concept of nation as the core lens through which to view and carry out cultural learning (Eisenmann, Grimm and Volkmann 2010: vii). Liddicoat and Scarino (2013: 18) pointedly summarize why equating culture with nation in foreign language education is highly problematic:

Such a view of culture is an essentializing one that reduces culture to recognizable, often stereotypicalized, representations of national attributes. Identifying a culture as a national culture does not make reference to what culture is, but rather where culture is found: American culture resides in the essentialized attributes located in the territory of the United States, French culture in France, etc. Culture is an unproblematic and unproblematized construct that can be reduced to a label derived from political geography.

If this criticism is transferred to classroom practices, it follows that one needs to eschew the question 'what it truly means', say, to be British, and hence to avoid representing culture as nation in clearly monolithic or homogeneous terms. Furthermore, equating culture with nation – and hence to reduce the engagement with cultural otherness to national otherness only – does not mirror the transcultural realities of the twenty-first century, as Blell and Doff (2014: 80) argue:

Cultural realities for most people in the world are much more complex than simplistic notions of national 'cultures' as irreducibly different symbolic worlds of their own seem to suggest. The real challenge in coming to terms with this cultural complexity encountered in the social world lies in exploring the cultural practices of individuals and social groups that operate within a globally interlinked network of culture.

By taking up this call to mirror greater cultural complexities and realities in the ELT classroom, various researchers have worked towards updating and transforming cultural learning pedagogies for language education by expanding what is meant by cultural otherness to include a more diverse set of otherness*es* in the plural, as Alter (2015: 203) puts it. While this does not mean that nation must never again be a focal point of interest in cultural learning, it clearly indicates that an exclusive focus on nation is decidedly reductive in terms of representing inter- and intra-cultural diversity in English language education.

By now, several research and theory strands in ELT have responded to and taken up this tendency to further develop the diversification of the language classroom. Lütge (2013: 166–7), for example, suggests moving beyond the more established ethnic-national lines of demarcation and turning towards newly contoured explorations of difference categories such as gender, social class, or creed to shed a more nuanced light on identity constructions. One can observe a turn towards postcolonial studies (e.g. Lütge and Stein 2017) or gender studies (e.g. König 2014; König, Lewin and Surkamp 2016) as new theoretical sources for ELT. Additionally, both Nelson (2009) and Merse (2017) have engaged with queer theory and mapped out ways to increase the visibility of non-heterosexual identities in language education alongside challenging heteronormativity as a deeply engrained dominant cultural principle. Merse (2017) even argues in favour of a radical opening up and reorientation of ELT education, including its literature selection, under the heuristic rubric of 'other Others' and 'different differences' so as to achieve a more balanced representation of cultural diversity in the ELT classroom.

A similar thematic impetus for ELT education derives from the concept of Global Education, advocating global issues as content for the classroom, which then 'involves learning about those problems and issues that cut across national boundaries, and about the interconnectedness of systems – ecological, cultural, economic, political, and technological' (Lütge 2015: 7). These challenging thematic developments go beyond understanding language education in terms of a 'fact-based, conflict-avoiding and tourism-related approach' (Delanoy and Volkmann 2006: 12), and open up the arena for content that is a potential source of conflict and controversy. Alter and Merse (2014), for example, suggest using taboo topics in the classroom to explore cultural meanings. While they do not equate 'taboo' with an ontological state of absolute otherness (when in fact otherness emerges as relational to an assumed norm from which it allegedly deviates and becomes a 'hot-button topic'), they argue that taboos represent key sociocultural nodes of meaning which allow for particularly insightful, exciting and challenging classroom scenarios that may help to get students (and their teachers) out of their comfort zones and engage with truly relevant questions of our time. Bland describes the importance of sharing stories with young learners that mirror marginalized perspectives that are within the classroom: 'Literary texts reflecting diversity are enriching and enlightening for majority children as well as those being Othered, rendered invisible or suffering the pain of human migration' (2016: 45). Most certainly, as Showalter (2003: 125) points out, these 'controversial, dangerous, or explosive subjects' need to be introduced and taught in sensitive and non-intrusive ways. But still, the legitimization for exploring delicate issues such as illness, death, suicide, race or homosexuality lies in the educational mandate of schools 'to extend, not simply confirm, experience' (Humes 2012: 19) and to offer a 'supportive environment [that] can stimulate serious thinking and [...] deep learning'. In responding to these thematic considerations and the call for deep reading for deep learning, the literary texts presented below negotiate issues of illness, death and sexual orientation within the universal phenomenon of love.

What is this thing called love?
– Love, culture and discourse

The call for focusing on global or universal topics such as love, growing up, or the environment in ELT (see Bland 2018c and Webb 2018, this volume) is often voiced in the discussion of global issues. This is because universalities, characteristics that all of humanity shares, are considered to be especially suitable for evoking in students feelings of empathy, respect and understanding. Learners are meant to realize that cultures and subcultures may differ in many areas, but that there are essential commonalities which make us all human and which, in Volkmann's (2012: 125) words, 'unite us in a common struggle for co-existence in globalized societies on an endangered planet'. At the same time, the fact that societies have things in common does not, as Antweiler argues, simultaneously imply the absence of diversity (2009: 32–4). Nor does it mean that a certain feature can be found in every individual of every society. When universalities are investigated, researchers look at whole societies, not at their individual representatives.

While love has always been considered a universal, romantic love (or passionate love, as some researchers prefer to call it), which is defined as an intense, erotic attraction involving the idealization of the loved one and the expectation of a lasting relationship, used to be thought of as a typically Western construct that emerged in Europe during the times of industrialization (Antweiler 2009: 221, Jankowiak and Fischer 1992: 149–50). It was not until Jankowiak and Fischer's cross-cultural anthropological study (1992), which took into consideration the folklore of 166 societies, that romantic love could be proven to be a near universal. The authors attribute the fact that romantic love could not be found in some societies to their lack of folklore or their disapproval and thus silencing of the experience rather than the lack of the phenomenon itself (1992: 153, Jankowiak 1995: 13). Jankowiak and Fischer also distinguish between passionate love and what they call 'companionship love', the latter of which is, to them, 'characterized by the growth of a more peaceful, comfortable, and fulfilling relationship' (1992: 150). Our capacity to fall in love is said to be based on biological factors; for reasons of species survival, two people must be willing to stay together long enough to raise a child (Fisher 1995, 2004). Biology, however, is only one of three factors that determine the complex way in which individuals experience romantic love; a further two factors, self and society, are equally important (Jankowiak 1995: 4). The latter two might, for example, determine if and how we articulate our love for someone in public, whether romantic love is likely to be inside or outside of marriage or the freedom to self-select one's partner (1995: 8, 11). To summarize, romantic love is a universal but culturally unique phenomenon.

Apart from the experience of romantic love, gender differences in selecting a lover also seem to be based on biological factors. Heterosexually informed research conducted in this area suggests that for men signs of fertility, such as youth and health, are the primary incentive for falling in love while women are attracted to a high social status and income in a man (Jankowiak 1995: 10). This would also explain why men usually fall in love quicker than women: physical attraction can be more easily appraised than social standing (1995: 10). The factors identified in this anthropological research are not intended to suggest, however, that love only follows biological determinisms, nor do they imply that love is acultural.

Philosophical positions in Foucault's *The History of Sexuality* (1978) or Butler's *Gender Trouble* (2006 [1990]), for example, indicate that sexuality, desire and love are highly regulated social practices that are culturally contingent. What counts as legitimate and proper – or deviant and improper – forms of love or sexual expression is deeply enmeshed in power hierarchies and a society's 'regimes of truth' (Foucault 1977: 13). Such regimes of truth, then, work to regulate love and sexuality as primarily heterosexual, monogamous and reproductive, while other forms of love and sexual expression, such as same-sex love or other 'peripheral sexualities' (Foucault 1978: 42), are discursively produced as deviant. Butler takes Foucault's argument further and introduces the concept of the heterosexual matrix to describe the specific ways in which desire is socially and discursively regulated as heteronormative practice. Given the logic and function of this matrix, everything that falls outside its highly regulated realm appears as 'developmental failures or logical impossibilities' (Butler 2006: 24), for example gay or lesbian love, transgender identities or intersexuality. Yet Butler (2006: 105) remarks that '[t]he "unthinkable" is fully within culture'. It is with positions such as Butler's and Foucault's that the notion of love as a human universality receives an additional important nuance as also being culturally contingent and produced in and through discourse.

While romantic love has received the most attention in research, the psychoanalyst and philosopher Erich Fromm (1956) calls to mind that this is only one out of four forms of love, the others being brotherly love (or the gender neutral term, goodwill), motherly (and, as we would add, fatherly) love, self-love and the love of God. In the context of this chapter, the first two are of special relevance. Goodwill is defined by Fromm (1956: 47) as follows:

> The most fundamental kind of love, which underlies all types of love [...]. By this I mean the sense of responsibility, care, respect, knowledge of any other human being, the wish to further his life. [...] Brotherly love is love for all human beings; it is characterized by its very lack of exclusiveness. [...] The differences in talents, intelligence, knowledge are negligible in comparison with the identity of the human core common to all men. In order to experience this identity it is necessary to penetrate from the periphery to the core. If I perceive in another person mainly the surface, I perceive mainly the differences, that which separates us. If I penetrate to the core, I perceive our identity, the fact of our brotherhood.

Goodwill, as defined by Fromm, strongly resembles the goals promoted in intercultural learning, such as respect for the Other. To initiate these attitudes, universalities such as love could be investigated in class. In contrast to goodwill, which in essence is universal, romantic love is only given to one person and therefore characterized primarily by its exclusiveness. According to Fromm (1956: 53), romantic love is 'the craving for complete fusion, for union with one other person' and thus the exact opposite of maternal and paternal love, which is marked by the challenge to accept and encourage separation from oneself once the child becomes older and more independent: 'In erotic love, two people who were separate, become one. In motherly love, two people who were one become separate' (1956: 51). To sum up, goodwill, romantic love, maternal and paternal love are central constituents of the taxonomy of love, and, as they are found across the globe, they are particularly suitable topics for the ELT classroom, which aims to further cross-cultural understanding and counteract ethnocentricity. The following analysis will illustrate how romantic love, goodwill as well as love between family members are negotiated in two literary texts suitable for the middle to higher grades in the ELT classroom. Our suggestion is reading these two texts in combination as a text ensemble on a shared theme.

Love in the context of illness and death: John Green's *The Fault in Our Stars*

Green's hugely popular young adult novel centres on the star-crossed love of two American teenagers. Just as for the young lovers Romeo and Juliet, a future together is impossible for Hazel and Augustus, not because their families disapprove but because at least one of them will die of cancer in the not-so-distant future. The title of the novel, *The Fault in Our Stars*, is taken from Cassius's lines in Shakespeare's *Julius Caesar*: 'The fault, dear Brutus, is not in our stars, / But in ourselves, that we are underlings' (Act I, Scene 2), suggesting that we are ourselves responsible for what happens to us, not fate. The novel, however, seems to express rather the opposite, as the author highlights on his website: 'There is plenty of fault in our stars. The world is a profoundly unjust place in which suffering is unfairly distributed' (Green 'FAQ').

The fate of having had cancer for years has left Hazel with a breathing device that she has to permanently attach to her nostrils and Augustus with an artificial limb. The emotional pain this causes them seems to exceed the physical limitations as Hazel illustrates:

> I looked away, suddenly conscious of my myriad insufficiencies. I was wearing old jeans, which had once been tight but now sagged in weird places, and a yellow T-shirt advertising a band I didn't even like anymore.

Also my hair: I had this pageboy haircut, and I hadn't even bothered to, like, brush it. Furthermore, I had ridiculously chipmunked cheeks, a side effect of treatment. I looked like a normally proportioned person with a balloon for a head. (Green 2013 [2012]: 9)

Physical attraction, as was outlined earlier, is a universal expectation for falling in love and thus caring about our outward appearance in the context of sexuality is part of our humanity. Therefore, it is not atypical for Hazel to reflect on her looks. For one, she is bothered by things that are particularly important for teenagers such as the style of clothes and hair. Apart from this, however, she is unhappy that the illness has left its mark on her body – in her weight loss and her unnaturally puffy face. In a similar manner, she cannot help being bothered by Augustus's missing limb: 'I kept glancing over at his leg, or the place where his leg had been, trying to imagine what the fake leg looked like. I didn't want to care about it, but I did a little. He probably cared about my oxygen. Illness repulses' (2013: 36). Despite these insecurities, the two are – as the text strongly suggests – physically as well as mentally attracted to each other and become a romantic and sexually active couple.

While their self-image is painful, other people's perception of them is even more irritating: 'Any attempts to feign normal social interactions were just depressing because it was so glaringly obvious that everyone I spoke to for the rest of my life would feel awkward and self-conscious around me' (2013: 47). Later Hazel summarizes: 'We were irreconcilably other, and never was it more obvious than when the three of us [she, Augustus and her mother] walked through the empty plane' (2013: 144). Hazel's and Augustus's outward appearance is an indicator of their illness and both the cancer and the changes it has caused to their bodies have an impact on their romantic relationship as well as their relationships with others.

Every day, teenagers are confronted by physical challenge, severe sickness, even death. Otherness marked by disease or disability is thus a worthwhile subject of investigation for the ELT classroom. As both may be temporary, long-term or terminal, cause physical and psychological pain, require medical treatment and mean restrictions in everyday life, disease and disability cannot always be clearly distinguished. *The Fault in Our Stars* invites learners to see the person behind the ever-present sickness, not least because of the protagonists' objection to be solely defined by their state of health. The novel challenges common stereotypes associated with disease and disability such as the heroic fighter who never complains or the wise blind person, while at the same time not camouflaging the ugly side of death such as depression and humiliation. In so doing, it makes a contribution to 'rectify the conception of the disease, to de-mythicize' cancer, as Susan Sontag (1978: 7) demands in her classic essay *Illness as Metaphor*.

It is well established that the readership of young adult fiction does not restrict itself to teenagers. *The Fault in Our Stars* is no exception to this. One reason why the novel is so popular with adults, too, might be because it not only describes the psychological and emotional distress the cancer causes the two protagonists but also their parents. Hazel's mother, for example, had to give up her job to care for her daughter, which Hazel finds both annoying and worrisome. The novel successfully portrays the challenge the parents of terminally ill children face to tolerate a permanent separation from their children that goes far beyond the acceptance of the teenager's ever-growing independence defined by Fromm as the essence of motherly and fatherly love. From the viewpoint of a young adult, who has been ill ever since childhood, Hazel understands that her mother needs to accept her wish for independence despite her alarming illness: 'I don't need you like I used to. *You're* the one who needs to get a life' (2013: 255, emphasis in the original) she yells at her mother. Thus, she is relieved to discover towards the end of the novel that her mother has secretly been working on a degree in counselling so she might help families in crisis after Hazel's death. As much as Hazel is annoyed by her mother's perceived overprotection, she is also troubled by the pain the cancer inflicts on the people who love her. Because Hazel thinks of herself as a grenade that is going to blow up and hurt the people around her (2013: 99) she does not like meeting new people and is hesitant to start dating Augustus (2013: 101). At a funeral, she makes the conscious decision to spare her parents the sight of the coffin being lowered into the ground for fear this might remind them of their own fears for their daughter and tells white lies in her eulogy for the deceased because she understands that 'funerals [...] are for the living' (2013: 273). Thus, *The Fault in Our Stars* not only portrays a romantic relationship complicated but at the same time made possible by disease and disability but it also illustrates the emotional impact of severe illness on loved ones, especially parents. 'Cancer is a rare and still scandalous subject for poetry; and it seems unimaginable to aestheticize the disease', writes Sontag in 1978 (20). *The Fault in Our Stars* achieves just that.

Love in the context of coming of age and coming out: David Levithan's 'Princes'

The short story 'Princes' is part of the story collection *How They Met, and Other Stories* (2008) written by David Levithan, arguably the best-known author of young adult fiction with LGBTQ (lesbian, gay, bisexual, transgender, queer) protagonists and content. 'Princes' represents a multifaceted exploration of gay teenage coming-of-age – and coming out – that successfully evades the reductionist problem-laden paradigm typically found in much LGBTQ young adult fiction which deterministically connects being LGBTQ with immense life struggles or feelings of shame and guilt (Cart and Jenkins, 2006: xix–xx). Jon, the story's 17-year old protagonist, is a self-determined teenager who feels accepted by his queer-friendly circle of friends from a Manhattan dance school, who experiences the ups and downs of being in love with his dance instructor, and who struggles to reconcile his sexual orientation with his family which, as Jon says, is not yet 'a part of that part of my life' (Levithan 2008: 132). It is in this context that Jon, present to the reader as an I-narrator, constructs a life of his own, 'a kingdom that was still being defined' (2008: 137).

Jon's great passion in life is dancing. He sets the scene at the outset: 'My parents never really discussed the subject with me. They came to the *Nutcrackers*, they came to the big recitals, and they came to the conclusion that I was gay. Not every boy dancer is gay, or grows up to be gay. But come on. A whole lot of us are' (Levithan 2008: 132). Thereby 'Princes' plays with one of the many clichés associated with gayness. For Jon, both dancing and his sexuality are inextricably linked with New York City – this particular space stands in sharp contrast to his suburban home and his family, which he tries to avoid. His homosexuality has never been openly aired with his parents and thirteen-year old brother Jeremy because 'that part [of his life] resided in the city' (2008: 132). Even though his family context is not constructed as homophobic, Jon prefers to keep up this spatial division as his 'parents' voices didn't belong anywhere near this world' (2008: 147). One night at a family dinner, though, the spatial division collapses as Jon unexpectedly comes out to his family, who are busy planning his brother's Bar Mitzvah:

'All your cousins are bringing their boyfriends,' my mother said with a sigh. [. . .]

I don't know what started me thinking. [. . .] But suddenly I had something to say. [. . .]

'What about *my* boyfriend?' I found myself asking.

Pure silence at the table, loud shouting in each of our heads. Except Jeremy's. He just watched, transfixed.

'He doesn't have a boyfriend,' my father answered. 'He's just being stubborn.'

'His name is Graham,' I said. 'He's in my dance class.'

It was the name that did it. The name that made it real. For all of us.

'Jesus Christ,' my father said, pushing his plate away.

'There are already too many people,' my mother added quickly, somewhere between diplomatic and petrified. 'There isn't enough room.' (Levithan 2008: 140–1, emphasis in the original)

His parents' reactions to his coming out are, sadly, somewhat typical: his father is in denial while his mother, though acknowledging the facts, tries to keep it a family secret by arguing that there is no room for yet another guest. It is only after Jeremy insists on Jon being allowed to invite his boyfriend Graham that his parents relent, which indicates that their initial scepticism – evident in the Othering of Jon and his sexual orientation: 'It's not appropriate' (2008: 143) – gives way to a growing acceptance of their son's homosexuality.

However Jon is now faced with a new problem since his dance instructor Graham is not in love with him and therefore not really his boyfriend. Luckily for Jon, his good friend and dance partner Miles is willing to stand in for Graham, acting as Jon's boyfriend at the Bar Mitzvah. In a romantic twist, the two dancers become an actual couple on the Bar Mitzvah dance floor:

> When his feet started to move, there was no guarantee that my steps would match his.
> But they did.
> As if we had rehearsed. As if our bodies were meant to be this. As if we were meant to be this. Together. [...] I looked over his shoulder. My mother smiled at me and nearly cried. My aunt and uncle smiled. (2008: 159)

Like *The Fault in Our Stars*, 'Princes' is as much about the teenage troubles of being in love – falling for someone you look up to, being hurt by unrequited love, suddenly falling for somebody you have always considered to be just a friend – as it is about love in the family. As his mother and brother, his aunt and uncles, and possibly even his father accept Jon's sexual orientation, Jon finally feels part of this family again:

> I stayed up for the final candle, for my parents at their proudest. The love I felt for them then – I knew I meant that, too. It wasn't something I had to think about. It was there, unexpectedly deep. I hadn't been running away from that, or even from them. I had been so focused on my destination that I'd forgotten all the rest. (2008: 158)

What becomes evident here is that the story shows the typical elements of a coming-of-age narrative, elegantly mirrored in the Bar Mitzvah theme, the Jewish passage into adulthood, and the reference to Tchaikovsky's ballet *The Nutcracker*. It deconstructs the literary representation of LGBTQ identities and their coming out as problem-laden. Ultimately, Jon grows into an accepted member of his family and is completely at ease with himself. It appears that the love exchanged between Jon, his parents, his brother, his friends and his 'not-quite-but-maybe-so-boyfriend' (2008: 160) Miles, provides a welcoming context to 'stay, and stay, and stay' (2008: 161) rather than escaping from his home or leaving certain parts of his life 'blank' (2008: 135).

Reading 'Princes' in the ELT classroom gives voice to a hitherto underrepresented class of sociocultural difference, that is LGBTQ identities and experiences, and thus to overcome what Nelson (2009) has time and again criticized as the monosexuality and entrenched heteronormativity of ELT. Learners engaging with the story can experience a normalization of the feeling of romantic love that unfolds irrespectively of sexual orientation. Sentences such as 'he asked me to join him for a drink. I knew it wasn't a date. I knew he wasn't asking me out. But what my mind knew, my hope ignored' (Levithan 2008: 138) are probably more indicative of the general rollercoaster experience of teenagers seeking and finding love than they are of a 'true' or 'unique' 'gay way' of being in love. At the same time, Levithan's story is not insensitive to the struggles and experiences LGBTQ teenagers might be facing. Even though Levithan does not overemphasize an emerging gay identity as problematic, he nonetheless portrays how a gay teenager copes with the implications of coming out and gaining full recognition for who he is in the heart of his family. It will be instructive for students to experience how 'Princes' discursively and literarily constructs a genuine love story vis-à-vis its protagonist's gay identity and coming out, without reverting to problem-laden stereotypes of LGBTQ fiction or depicting difference from the heterosexual norm as ontological and ultimately Other.

Outlook: Methodological considerations

So what is this thing called love? While a definitive answer to this question will most likely forever remain elusive, both literary texts discussed in this chapter can invite learners – and their teachers – to explore specific literary representations of love as a universal, yet culturally contingent, human experience. Students' engagement with Green's The Fault in Our Stars and Levithan's 'Princes' becomes a challenging reading experience, we have argued, for the texts map various spheres of love onto the often silenced contexts of illness and homosexuality. As we believe, however, students will eagerly take up this challenge because of the intensive, accessible and often humorous insights into teenage love that these texts mediate. Thus, both stories serve to provide alternatives to the assumed canon of established literary texts, or what one could call the single story of love told in ELT classrooms – polished and glossy depictions of heteronormative love as opposed to love that intersects with 'imperfect' bodies or 'abnormal' sexualities. The text ensemble collated here serves to engage with cultural diversity within a cultural universality.

To facilitate this engagement and to ease students' passage into these both challenging and appealing texts, we conclude with proposals from a task typology for literary and cultural learning in ELT developed by Britta Freitag-Hild (2010). Of the variety of potential tasks this typology offers for challenging classroom practice, the following seem especially fruitful:

- *Tuning-in and self-awareness*: By working with specific fragments from the texts (quotes, title, blurb), learners can pre-construct a storyline that predicts what the love stories could be about, and then compare their hypotheses with the actual story lines to raise awareness of their own preconceived notions of how a love story should be, or normally is. With 'Princes', for example, it would be interesting to see what the quote 'I wanted to kiss him. I wanted him to want to kiss me' (Levithan 2008: 139) – which is potentially open to all kinds of meanings and relationship constellations – has learners predict, and in particular, if they fall for a love story in the vein of 'compulsory heterosexuality' (Rich 1980: 632).

- *Interpretation and empathy*: In order to train interpretation and empathy, learners could be invited to take on the parents' perspective, which the texts make only partly accessible through the protagonists' (Hazel's, Jon's) narration. For example, they can engage in creative writing tasks, such as writing the dialogue of how Hazel's mother describes her experience of Hazel's illness to a mother she counsels.

- *Analysis*: In close readings, learners can analyse how the themes of love, illness and sexual orientation are constructed aesthetically in the literary texts, for example the 'normalizing' of gay love in 'Princes', or the witty commentary on illness in *The Fault in Our Stars*.

- *Reflection*: On a meta-level, learners express their experience of otherness while engaging with both texts and reflect on their processes towards, and potential difficulties of, understanding the particular othernesses negotiated in the texts.

These methodological suggestions to deepen the engagement with Green's and Levithan's texts can invite learners to explore Fromm's (1956: 56) statement that '[t]o love somebody is not just a strong feeling – it is a decision, it is a judgment, it is a promise' (Fromm 1956: 56) – and by extension, that love is also an elaborate and challenging literary literacy experience.

RECOMMENDATIONS

- It is important to select books that reflect marginalized groups as well as the mainstream. Trying to avoid sensitive issues means taking sides: 'Because the books we as teachers choose to use *or decide not to use* is a pervasive and subtle form of censorship' (Leland, Lewison and Harste 2013: 13, emphasis in the original).
- Above all other topics, the theme of love belongs both to the world of literature, and to the world of teenagers. Such texts turn non-reading youth into readers.

Bibliography

Green, John (2012), *The Fault in Our Stars*, London: Penguin.

Levithan, David (2008), 'Princes', in *How They Met, and Other Stories*, New York: Alfred. A. Knopf, pp. 131–61.

References

Adichie, Chimamanda Ngozi (2009), 'The danger of a single story', *TEDGlobal*, 7 October 2009, https://www.ted.com/talks/chimamanda_adichie_the_danger_of_a_single_story (accessed 19 March 2017).

Alter, Grit (2015), *Inter- and Transcultural Learning in the Context of Canadian Young Adult Fiction*, Münster: LIT Verlag.

Alter, Grit and Merse, Thorsten (2014), 'Das Potenzial tabuisierter und kontroverser Texte für das literarisch-ästhetische Lernen innerhalb der pluralen Bildung', in Christiane Fäcke, Martina Rost-Rot and Engelbert Thaler (eds), *Sprachenausbildung, Sprachen bilden aus, Bildung aus Sprachen. Dokumentation zum 24. Kongress für Fremdsprachendidaktik der Deutschen Gesellschaft für Fremdsprachenforschung (DGFF)*, Baltmannsweiler: Schneider Verlag Hohengehren, pp. 161–71.

Antweiler, Christoph (2009), *Was ist den Menschen gemeinsam?: Über Kultur und Kulturen*, 2nd edn, Darmstadt: WBG.

Bland, Janice (2016), 'English language education and ideological issues: Picturebooks and diversity', *Children's Literature in English Language Education*, 4/2: 41–64.

Bland, Janice (2018c), 'Popular culture head on: Suzanne Collins's *The Hunger Games*', in Janice Bland (ed.), *Using Literature in English Language Education: Challenging Reading for 8–18 Year Olds*, London: Bloomsbury Academic, pp. 175–92.

Blell, Gabriele and Doff, Sabine (2014), 'It takes more than two for this tango: Moving beyond the self/other-binary in teaching about culture in the global EFL-classroom', *Zeitschrift für interkulturellen Fremdsprachenunterricht*, 19/1: 77–92.

Butler, Judith (2006/1990), *Gender Trouble: Feminism and the Subversion of Identity*, New York: Routledge.

Byram, Michael (1997), *Teaching and Assessing Intercultural Communicative Competence*, Clevedon, Philadelphia: Multilingual Matters.

Cart, Michael and Jenkins, Christine (2006), *The Heart Has Its Reasons: Young Adult Literature with Gay/Lesbian/Queer Content, 1969–2004*, Lanham: Scarecrow Press.

Council of Europe (ed.) (2001), *Common European Framework of Reference for Languages: Learning, Teaching, Assessment*, Cambridge: Cambridge University Press.

Decke-Cornill, Helene (2007), 'Literaturdidaktik in einer "Pädagogik der Anerkennung": Gender and other suspects', in Wolfgang Hallet und Ansgar Nünning (eds), *Neue Ansätze und Konzepte der Literatur- und Kulturdidaktik*, Trier: WVT Wissenschaftlicher Verlag Trier, pp. 239–58.

Delanoy, Werner and Volkmann, Laurenz (2006), 'Introduction: Cultural studies in the EFL classroom', in Werner Delanoy and Laurenz Volkmann (eds), *Cultural Studies in the EFL Classroom*, Heidelberg: Winter, pp. 11–21.

Eisenmann, Maria, Grimm, Nancy and Volkmann, Laurenz (2010), 'Introduction: Teaching the new English cultures and literatures', in Maria Eisenmann, Nancy Grimm and Laurenz Volkmann (eds), *Teaching the New English Cultures & Literatures*, Heidelberg: Winter, pp. vii–xii.

Fisher, Helen (1995), 'The Nature and Evolution of Romantic Love', in William Jankowiak (ed.), *Romantic Passion – A Universal Experience?* New York: Columbia University, pp. 23–41.

Fisher, Helen (2004), *Why We Love: The Nature and Chemistry of Romantic Love*, New York: Henry Holt and Company.

Foucault, Michel (1977), 'The political function of the intellectual', *Radical Philosophy*, 17: 12–14.

Foucault, Michel (1978), *The History of Sexuality*, vol. I: *An Introduction*, New York: Pantheon Books.

Freitag-Hild, Britta (2010), *Theorie, Aufgabentypologie und Unterrichtspraxis inter- und transkultureller Literaturdidaktik: 'British Fictions of Migration' im Fremdsprachenunterricht*, Trier: WVT.

Fromm, Erich (1956), *The Art of Loving*, New York: Harper & Row.

Green, John, 'FAQ', http://www.johngreenbooks.com/the-fault-in-our-stars-faq (accessed 4 November 2016).

Humes, Walter (2012), 'Democracy, trust and respect', in Paula Cowan and Henry Maitles (eds), *Teaching Controversial Issues in the Classroom: Key Issues and Debates*, London: Continuum, pp. 13–23.

Jankowiak, William and Fischer, Edward (1992), 'A Cross-Cultural Perspective on Romantic Love', *Ethnology* 31/2: 149–55.

Jankowiak, William (1995), 'Introduction', in William Jankowiak (ed.), *Romantic Passion – A Universal Experience?* New York: Columbia University, pp. 1–19.

König, Lotta (2014), 'Schlüsselthemen der Anglistik und Amerikanistik in der Schule: Gender-orientierte Literaturdidaktik im Englischunterricht', in Ansgar Nünning and Elizabeth Kovach (eds), *Key Concepts and New Topics in English and American Studies. Schlüsselkonzepte und neue Themen in der Anglistik und Amerikanistik*, Trier: WVT, pp. 363–80.

König, Lotta, Lewin, Sonja and Surkamp, Carola (2016), 'What does it mean to teach about gender? Gender studies and their implications for foreign language teaching', in Daniela Elsner, Daniela and Viviane Lohe (eds), *Gender and Language Learning: Research and Practice*, Tübingen: Narr Francke Attempto, pp. 19–36.

Leland, Christine, Lewison, Mitzi and Harste, Jerome (2013), *Teaching Children's Literature. It's Critical!* New York: Routledge.

Liddicoat, Anthony and Scarino, Angela (2013), *Intercultural Language Teaching and Learning*, Chichester: Wiley-Blackwell.

Lütge, Christiane (2013), 'Sprachenlernen und Identität(en) im Fremdsprachenunterricht', in Eva Burwitz-Melzer, Frank Königs and Claudia Riemer (eds), *Identität und Fremdsprachenlernen. Anmerkungen zu einer komplexen Beziehung*, Tübingen: Narr, pp. 163–70.

Lütge, Christiane (2015), 'Introduction: Global education and English language teaching', in Christiane Lütge (ed.), *Global Education: Perspectives for English Language Teaching*, Münster: LIT Verlag, pp. 7–16.

Lütge, Christiane and Mark Stein (eds) (2017), *Crossovers: Postcolonial Studies and Transcultural Learning*, Münster: LIT Verlag.

Merse, Thorsten (2017), *Other Others, Different Differences: Queer Perspectives on Teaching English as a Foreign Language*, Münster: LIT Verlag.

Nelson, Cynthia (2009), *Sexual Identities in English Language Education: Classroom Conversations*, New York: Routledge.

Rich, Adrienne (1980), 'Compulsory heterosexuality and lesbian existence', *Signs* 5/4: 631–60.

Risager, Karen (2013), 'Introduction: Intercultural learning, raising cultural awareness', in Maria Eisenmann, Maria and Theresa Summer (eds), *Basic Issues in EFL Teaching and Learning*, 2nd edn, Heidelberg: Winter, pp. 143–55.

Showalter, Elaine (2003), *Teaching Literature*, Malden, MA: Blackwell Publishing.

Sontag, Susan (1978), *Illness as Metaphor*, New York: Farrar, Straus and Giroux.

Volkmann, Laurenz (2012), 'The "transcultural moment" in English as a foreign language', in Sabine Doff and Frank Schulze-Engler (eds), *Beyond 'Other Cultures': Transcultural Perspectives on Teaching the New Literatures in English*, Trier: WVT, pp. 113–28.

Webb, Jean (2018), 'Environmental havoc in teen fiction: Speculating futures', in Janice Bland (ed.), *Using Literature in English Language Education: Challenging Reading for 8–18 Year Olds*, London: Bloomsbury Academic, pp. 209–23.

10

Popular culture head on: Suzanne Collins's THE HUNGER GAMES

Janice Bland

Dystopias have been a major part of the literary landscape for the best part of a century. Although classics such as Huxley's *Brave New World* (1932), Orwell's *Nineteen Eighty-Four* (1949) and Bradbury's *Fahrenheit 451* (1953) were all first published well over sixty years ago, their relevance and urgency has not dimmed, so that they can be read alongside the plethora of more recent dystopias now demanding attention. The banning of books is a key element of despotic control in most dystopias, and yet, as Ray Bradbury himself urged in an interview with the *New Seattle Times*, 'You don't have to burn books to destroy a culture. Just get people to stop reading them' (Berson 1993: np).

A concern among educators is ensuring that teenagers read and enjoy their core texts, the books they are expected to study, rather than employ avoidance strategies such as reading summaries and interpretations on the Web. Therefore the opportunities of the adult canon must wait, I argue, until teenagers have metamorphosed into readers – a step-by-step process that should begin well before the age of twelve while children are generally still excited by books. When reading in a foreign language, this slow but indispensable apprenticeship into literary literacy (learning to read the aesthetic nature of a literary text) is too often ignored by the curriculum. Frequently the curriculum insists on the reading of highly challenging adult texts with advanced secondary-school students without their having any gradual preparation. The teacher may suggest graded readers – for example simplified versions of classics – at earlier stages, which are widely considered to be effective for linguistic gains through extensive reading. However literary literacy cannot be gained in this way (see Bland 2013: 1–28). Unfortunately, increasingly the curriculum dispenses with reading a literary text entirely, effectively banning books from the classroom.

Award-winning author John Green (see discussion in Marks and Merse 2018, this volume) has reviewed *The Hunger Games* in an article he entitled 'Scary New World' (Green 2008) – a clear allusion to *Brave New World*. Green's argument is in line with that of the American-Dominican writer Junot Díaz, who claims that the dystopia has become 'the default narrative of the generation [...] We are making the genre in which we are living, and we are making it at such an extraordinary rate' (2016: np). The promise of education must surely be that critical literacy and a critique of the sociopolitical present can equip teenagers to evaluate their world and realistically help create a more auspicious politics for the future. The dystopia genre addresses larger existential questions, and has often breathtakingly foreshadowed the fears and realities of the twenty-first century. Díaz, significantly, emphasizes the regenerative nature of the critical dystopia: 'It is something that maps, warns, and *hopes*' (2016, my emphasis).

In the popular cultural landscape of today young people are increasingly unsettled, and many reasons for this are addressed in Suzanne Collins's trilogy, *The Hunger Games* (2008), *Catching Fire* (2009) and *Mockingjay* (2010). Referring to recent dystopian films, as well as President Trump's withdrawing the United States from the Paris climate accord, Fleishman points to 'the anxieties of a new century marked by wars and multiplying images of environmental degradation. The planet seemed to be shrinking, and every click of the screen – every YouTube rant, beheading, cyclone and story uttered – made us intimate with the ills that for so long seemed foreign and safely beyond our borders' (2017: np). *The Hunger Games* trilogy has struck a chord with huge numbers of young adult readers, for feelings of unease, helplessness and fear for the future have fuelled an appetite for dystopias. Recent UK research, for example, has revealed that a frighteningly high percentage of fourteen-year-old girls – as many as one in four – are now experiencing high levels of depressive symptoms (Patalay and Fitzsimons, 2017). Significantly, in the Hunger Games reality show, it is the young who must be sacrificed. The spirit of the age, according to cultural critic Ziauddin Sardar, is characterized by rapid change leading to uncertainty and upheaval:

> We live in an in-between period where old orthodoxies are dying, new ones have yet to be born, and very few things seem to make sense. Ours is a transitional age, a time without the confidence that we can return to any

past we have known and with no confidence in any path to a desirable, attainable or sustainable future. (Sardar 2010: 435)

This points to bewilderment and lack of trust in authority; consequently education must bestow a stronger confidence that students themselves are fit and able to make necessary changes. The potential of confidence giving but also confidence stealing in English teaching is discussed in Blau: 'I want to emphasize the danger and opportunity that English classes offer for convincing students not of their capacity and potential as readers, but of their intellectual insufficiency' (2003: 91). This is particularly relevant in ELT, where students have a linguistic disadvantage, less experience as readers, as well as – when teenagers in school settings – less background knowledge of the world. Quite apart from the suitability of *The Hunger Games* trilogy as a dystopia in advanced ELT, the *advantage* it gives students who probably know aspects of popular culture of the twenty-first century better than their teachers (social media, celebrity culture, reality television and Western consumerism) should be embraced, welcomed and exploited.

Connecting *The Hunger Games* to out-of-school literacy practices

The immense popularity of *The Hunger Games* trilogy teaches us about the emotional climate of the world outside the book, for the postmodern disconnect felt by many to those in power is mirrored and magnified in the series. The trilogy resonates with teenagers' troubling concerns 'in an age of war and economic upheaval coupled with an intense interest in entertainment – even when it comes at others' expense' (Karras 2012: np). Thus the series is excellently positioned to involve students' out-of-school literacy practices. By means of group work and projects students can bring their knowledge of popular culture to bear, and even take the lead in dialogic learning. As Connors (2014: 139) writes,

> authors of dystopias aim to construct a deeper understanding of the human condition by exaggerating its flaws and imagining the consequences of their being taken to an extreme. In this way, though the genre ostensibly presents stories that are set in the future, young adult dystopian fiction is best understood as inviting readers to wrestle with, and interrogate, contemporary problems and issues.

This contemporary real-world relevance is very much a part of *The Hunger Games*, and offsets the fantasy elements, enhancing the depth of the trilogy as well as suggesting a wealth of topics to explore further. For tactical reasons, I recommend concentrating on the second book, *Catching Fire* (Collins 2009), for deep, in-class discussion. This will ensure that many students read the first and third books in their own time – contributing to out-of-school extensive reading. To encourage the students to fulfil each home reading assignment of *Catching Fire* thoughtfully, group hot seating can become a regular post-reading task:

- For group hot seating, several students take on the role of the characters in the reading assignment, sitting at the front of the class, while the remaining students ask them questions.

- The students playing characters must answer in role, and they also communicate with each other consistently in role.

This is extremely effective, for as Katniss Everdeen narrates the story, and certain characters such as Katniss's mother express little in the dialogue reported, we often need to fill in gaps, interpret the actions and feelings, and guess the thoughts of the other characters. The teacher should also volunteer to be hot-seated as a character from time to time, as students may be inspired by the opportunity to interrogate their teacher. This activity – a well-known drama convention – is not only more interactive and motivating than traditional comprehension questions but also encourages deep reading of the text. A further task that encourages thoughtful reading is to ask the students to create titles for each of the chapters read at home, and to justify their chosen titles. While reading *Catching Fire*, students should be encouraged to keep a reading log, which will be an excellent support for them during talk around the text. All students should at least view the films of the entire series in the original version as they will need some knowledge of the complete trilogy to focus on several of the themes for project work, as discussed below. In-class film viewings could be organized as a Friday afternoon extracurricular activity. Students can be encouraged to view the films a number of times outside of school – extensive listening is an oft-neglected but highly effective strategy in second language acquisition (Mason 2013, Tomlinson 2015).

Connecting to young people with relevant topics and themes

Elsewhere I have suggested three stepping-stones for a gradual literary apprenticeship through children's literature – like real stepping-stones the three are equally necessary, and not hierarchical (Bland 2013: 113–20). The first is 'engaged reading', or reading with commitment, which is addressed in this chapter. The second is 'participatory reading', exemplified in this book by Arizpe and Ryan (2018), for example, and the third is 'reading against the text', a key skill for critical literacy, illustrated in Bland, this volume (2018b: 45–51).

After first considering the accessibility of the texts for the ELT classroom, the serious themes of the trilogy – and how they can be exploited for engaged reading in the classroom – will be considered: reality television and celebrity culture, the theme of social justice, the theme of education and mental enslavement, idealism and realism and the theme of the environment.

1. *The Hunger Games* trilogy: Language and accessibility

The Hunger Games trilogy combines challenging topics and themes for ELT with accessible language for teenage learners. Accessibility is an essential consideration when choosing a text for ELT. Texts that are too difficult linguistically for a target group shut down the opportunities that literature offers, such as exercising deep attention, language and literacy acquisition, talk around the text and widening horizons. Katniss is a first-person narrator and the focalizing character in the series. Consequently the books consist of her thoughts and fears throughout her traumatic experiences as well as extensive dialogue between the characters. Katniss is sixteen when the story begins, and her narration gives the impression of being her unedited reflections, addressing directly the discourse community of teenagers. In the following extract from *Catching Fire*, Katniss's thinking is staccato and abrupt while she is hurtling through the jungle, for she is sure she can hear her younger sister Prim screaming:

> Vines cut into my face and arms, creepers grab my feet. But I am getting closer to her. Closer. Very close now. Sweat pours down my face, stinging the healing acid wounds. I pant, trying to get some use out of the warm, moist air that seems empty of oxygen. (Collins 2009: 410)

The language is characterized by a marked use of repetition; in this extract, for example: 'close' and 'closer', and also parallelisms: 'Vines cut into my face and arms, creepers grab my feet'. There are frequent ellipses, when subjects and finite verbs are omitted: 'Closer. Very close now'. The effect is of direct access to the protagonist's thought processes, which may be repetitive, hesitant and contemplative, or rushed and desperate. The ellipses suggest spontaneity and incompleteness – allowing the reader to contribute to the story.

Apart from the flashbacks, the novels are narrated in the present tense, which would be far less common in adult fiction. According to John Stephens (2005: 79–80): 'The function of present tense narration is to convey an illusion of immediacy and instantaneity, suppressing any suggestion that the outcome is knowable in advance'. Thus the young adult reader vicariously experiences the fear, the heartbreak, the humour, the human warmth and love as well as the cruelty together with Katniss. This immediacy strongly draws the reader in, who, in ELT, is likely to be of a similar age to Katniss, Peeta and Gale (between sixteen and eighteen years old at the beginning of the series).

Storytelling in the present tense is relatively easy and compelling to read when well executed – due to the urgency and suspense. However this seeming simplicity is deceptive, for present tense narration is not easy to write, it requires an exceptional command of tense and grammatical aspect. ELT students composing their own creative texts should be encouraged to write using past tense narration, which is the usual tense for stories in English. Past tense narration includes all aspects of the past – past perfect and past progressive – but excludes all aspects of the present, such as present perfect and present progressive, except in dialogue. As the present perfect cannot be used when the story is told in the past, a common confusion in the ELT context – present perfect or past tense? – is easy to resolve.

A lively and communicative activity that can help students learn unusual terminology in the series is the *Circumlocution Circle*. For this the students stand in two large concentric circles, facing each other. Students on the outside describe a concept they have been given without naming the term to their partners on the inside – for instance *Capitol, reaping, Hunger Games, tributes, mentor, Avox, Careers, prep team, Peacekeepers, bloodbath, force field, Gamemakers, cornucopia, Remake Room, jabberjay, mockingjay, tracker jacker, mutts*. Their partners, on hearing the explanation, must try to discover the exact term. After one minute the students rotate to new partners and new concepts.

2. *Theme of reality television and celebrity culture*

The real coup of *The Hunger Games* trilogy is managing to combine the sociocultural with the political – the menace of a celebrity-obsessed culture directed by a brutal centralized government. Among other targets, the trilogy strongly challenges and critiques the reality contestant-elimination show. The setting of *The Hunger Games* is the post-apocalyptic nation of Panem, recalling the *panem et circenses* of Ancient Rome, for the pampered but ignorant citizens of the ruling district, the Capitol, are constantly distracted by luxurious food and shows. The sadistic Capitol Gamemakers have established the annual Hunger Games show as a prolonged battle lasting a number of weeks, in a specially built, sprawling arena with omnipresent cameras providing for intense media coverage, until only one contestant survives. For the show one boy and one girl are randomly selected from each of the twelve fenced-in districts, large areas of what used to be North America, and that are now all subjugated to the Capitol. The selected teenagers are trained and groomed to perform for the pampered Capitol citizens, who may sponsor their favoured tribute by sending gifts of food or medicine into the arena.

Muller (2012: 54) suggests: 'In our current times, violent video games and reality television shows serve much the same purpose; they are our modern bread and circuses and they are potentially dangerous detractors from what might really matter in terms of humanity's greater goals or the truths that their virtual mode so entertainingly conceals'. This is strong condemnation of a global society that is in some ways over scrutinized (particularly adolescents often suffer from lack of privacy due to the nature of social media) and saturated with self-promotion. The very culture critiqued by *The Hunger Games* is of course adapting the narrative to its own ends, for example with many video games now available and a growing collection of Barbie Dolls based on the movies (see Bland and Strotmann 2014). This development offers numerous opportunities for practising critical cultural literacy in the classroom, in other words reading contemporary culture critically.

In shows such as *Big Brother*, a 'preplanned group surveillance within a "game frame" that permits a measure of viewer intervention through the regular voting-off of participants' (Corner 2002: 261), the performance space is fabricated but unscripted. This is far from the educationally beneficial construct of story as cognitive play, which is said to tone neural wiring and train 'our capacity to see from different perspectives, and this capacity in turn both arises from and aids the evolution of cooperation and the growth of human mental flexibility' (Boyd 2009: 176). While Boyd is referring to the importance of narrative in human evolution, the kind of shows critiqued in *The Hunger Games*, in contrast, have been termed antinarrative, as artistic integrity and carefully crafted story patterns are lacking in favour of what many call crass entertainment. Antinarrative, according to Rose (2012: np), is 'a nonform that eschews such conventions as plot, character development, and resolution'. She further argues that 'traditional narrative forms demand certain cognitive propensities – attention, focus, discipline, and the willingness to defer gratification – that individuals who spend much of their time traveling the information slipstream tend increasingly not to possess'.

Not only are young adults' cognitive abilities in all probability influenced by hyper stimulation but young adults today must also make distressing decisions as to how far they allow the image-based media culture determine the way they live their lives. This is reflected in the predicaments of Katniss and fellow-tribute Peeta, both of whom desperately try to maintain some minimal agency and sense of self-worth. Katniss, extremely self-aware amid the voyeurism of the Capitol and potential sponsors, initially becomes a proficient performer. Throughout the trilogy, however, her resilience is weakened as she is progressively traumatized by the enforced role playing, violence and orchestrating of her appearances, which increase the cumulative effects of the cruelty of the Capitol (and later District 13).

A suitable project for a student expert team focusing on Reality TV and celebrity culture could be the introduction of a number of twenty-first century reality shows for discussion, in the light of critical comments such as: 'These shows do indeed traffic in suffering and humiliation' (Ungar-Sargon 2016: np). Furthermore, the rise of a celebritocracy in the political arena, with celebrated actor-politicians such as Eva Perón, Ronald Reagan, Arnold Schwarzenegger and Donald Trump, might be examined. In addition, the award-winning films *The Truman Show* (Weir 1998) and *Slumdog Millionaire* (Boyle 2008) offer excellent further material for an examination of the topic of popular reality shows and grave manipulation of both contestants and viewers.

3. *Theme of social justice*

The Hunger Games series is filled with rage against the tyrannical and arbitrary power of authority, coupled with a strong criticism of consumerism and consumer manipulation. Teenagers relate to the powerful sense of injustice that permeates the trilogy, which plants 'a mirror before readers, challenging them to examine the world they inhabit and the obstacles it places on the path to social justice' (Rodríguez 2014: 157). The three central characters, Katniss Everdeen, Peeta Mellark and Gale Hawthorne, are politically passionate in different ways that are as complex and muddled as real-life issues of war and peace. Their fury is initially directed against President Snow and the grotesque consumerism of Capitol citizens, but as the characters mature so does their resentment – particularly in the case of Katniss – for President Coin, the leader of the rebels in the newly rising District 13, is gradually revealed to use propaganda and violence to an equally deadly extent. Katniss's tragic realization that no matter how hard she tries, people will always get hurt, resonates with the anger of contemporary teenagers as they discover the complexity of the way things are.

The districts suffer through despotic colonization, mass poverty and starvation, disenfranchisement and enslavement. Consequently there are many potential project topics that students could investigate in connection to the theme of exploitation and injustice. Student teams might, for example, research and prepare poster presentations on the following real world topics:

- Contemporary slavery and child labour (the Avox are mutilated slaves; Rue and Bonnie are named victims of child labour)

- Sex slavery (Finnick is a named victim)

- Class society and economic disparity

- Hunger and starvation

- Refugees and post-traumatic stress disorder (Katniss and Finnick suffer from PTSD in District 13)

- Military use of children as child soldiers, in propaganda and as human shields (Katniss, Peeta and Prim are among many that are exploited although still under eighteen years of age; in District 13, children over the age of fourteen are addressed as 'Soldier')

- Human rights such as free speech, freedom of movement and a safe work environment

As Christensen writes on English Language Arts (2009: 8): 'Teaching students to write with power and passion means immersing them in challenging concepts, getting them fired up about the content so that they care about their writing, and then letting them argue with their classmates as they imagine solutions'.

4. *Theme of education and mental enslavement*

The school curriculum for the population of Panem is entirely under the control of the totalitarian dictatorship. In addition, the broadcasts are wholly government controlled, and many bulletins and shows are mandatory viewing. The Capitol is technologically advanced, however beyond television indoctrination and school textbooks there seems to be no media use throughout Panem, no books or alternative print or screen media at all. The thoughts of the hedonistic Capitol centre on luxury, food, fashions and surgical enhancements, they are so feckless that Katniss at times feels sorry for them. The districts, on the other hand, must focus on their struggle for survival, and have no resources to widen or deepen their education. School prepares the citizens of the twelve districts for their life-long servitude in providing for the Capitol. The children of District 2 are raised with a warrior mindset and many join the army of Peacekeepers protecting the Capitol, District 4 learns about fishing, District 7 about lumber and the children of coal-mining District 12 learn about coal. Thus all narratives, whether through formal education or the media, are state-controlled and state-sanctioned and fit a widely accepted definition of propaganda: '*Propaganda is the deliberate and systematic attempt to shape perceptions, manipulate cognitions, and direct behavior to achieve a response that furthers the desired intent of the propagandist*' (Jowett and O'Donnell 2006: 7, italics in the original).

Propaganda through the media – which is unquestioned by the majority of Capitol citizens – might be compared to unscrupulous tabloid journalism in the real world. However, the tabloid press seems to be losing its excessive sway on popular opinion as the influence of social media and information flooding via the Web takes over the business of creating public moods, as exemplified in the Facebook–Cambridge Analytica stolen personal data scandal. Scenarios are swiftly manufactured through the 24-hour news cycle and social media, further increasing sensationalism at the expense of verification, rigour and quality of interpretation. Journalistic speed is now essential due to the competition for audience and revenue through advertising. On the one hand there are now many voices on the Web shouting to be heard, which may be less elitist, but on the other hand there are fears regarding fake news. As Delanoy writes (2018: 147–8), cautious and reflective decision making 'is hampered by the seductive and one-sided solutions suggested by popular media, populist politicians, or fundamentalist groups'.

For democracy to work well, students must learn to research and investigate using the Web wisely and skilfully for information – they need to practise information literacy. As the Web is for the most part in English, clearly this should belong to the remit of ELT and the English Language Arts classroom. Texts on the Web referring to *The Hunger Games* include young adult literature fandom, online newspaper articles, book reviews on the Goodreads site, blogs, merchandise advertising as well as open access peer-reviewed articles. In order to help students distinguish these, they can be invited to write different text types themselves. Writing tasks could include the following:

- Students write a Capitol tabloid newspaper article, beginning with an explosive headline, such as COULD SNOW CANCEL THE HUNGER GAMES? or WHO WILL BE THE VICTOR OF VICTORS?

- Students write a brief review of *Catching Fire*, noting what makes it unique

- Students write a blog on the importance of story in their life

- Students write a quality newspaper article on the significance of education for democracy

5. Idealism and realism: The characters

Katniss is a hugely popular heroine. Made both strong *and* vulnerable by happenings beyond her control, she seems to symbolize the inner conflicts of adolescence. Her fearsome survival tactics brought on by bitterly unfair odds, and her attempts to always aim higher than is humanly possible under the circumstances, ring true for idealistic teen readers. Her thoughts are dominated by her protective relationship to her sister Prim and fellow victim Rue, her confusing relationships to Gale and Peeta, her relationship to her own body, which is severely compromised by the manipulative Capitol, and her attempt to maintain some control of her concept of self, even when thoroughly abused by the Gamemakers and later also in District 13. For her very survival she is forced to kill others, although she dwells on the aftermath, and 'how they never leave you' (Collins 2010: 81). Apart from her self-appointed role as provider and carer for her family, Katniss must play a number of imposed roles to survive: as the fairy-tale princess dressed up in wedding gowns, as a lethal warrior, as a 'star-crossed lover', and, in the final book, as the symbol of the revolution. The impossible weight of her responsibility as female protector in a brutal world nearly destroys her in *Mockingjay*. In the films her characterization is more popular and conventional, both as a warrior and in her performance of femininity. The damage to her body and mind is less pronounced in the films, and her vulnerability less revealed: she appears, as a critic maintains, to shoot 'a flaming arrow across a cultural landscape barren of images of young, self-contained female strength' (Moore 2013: np). In the trilogy it is Gale who finally chooses a warrior role; neither Katniss nor Peeta are comfortable performing as rebels able to kill.

Katniss is thus a complex character, and seen in very contrasting ways by those around her. This provides an opportunity for students to explore her character and that of others with the following tasks:

- Students create an entirely subjective characterization of Katniss from the perspective of another character, such as Peeta, Gale, Haymitch, President Snow, Madge Undersee, the District 8 runaways Bonnie and Twill, Effie Trinket, Cinna, Caesar Flickerman, Finnick Odair, Johanna Mason, Plutarch Heavensbee, the prep team Octavia, Venia and Flavius or Prim's cat Buttercup.

- Students explore Katniss's relationship to Gale and Peeta by scripting, rehearsing and then performing an intrapersonal role play (see Bland 2018b: 47–8): One student performs the Katniss that loves Peeta, the other performs the Katniss that loves Gale.

- As a thoughtful task on characterization, students write acrostics on different characters' names, as the following examples show:

Killer by coercion, protective by nature
Armed and angry, at war with herself
Torn by her love for others
Needing healing herself
Instinctive and on fire, inspiring revolution
Strong survival skills, socially conscious,
Sincere by nature

Ready to take flight across the treetops
Understands birdsong and herbs that heal
Everything beautiful brings her to mind.

6. *Environmental theme*

The Hunger Games is usually discussed in the sociocultural and sociopolitical context of its storyworld. However, there is ample opportunity to practise ecocriticism and consider the relationships between culture and nature in the series. The agenda of ecocriticism includes education towards global citizenship and emphasizes critical thinking, in a world that is linked socially, culturally, politically, economically and environmentally. Ecocriticism has been defined as 'an ethical discourse that focuses on the interconnections between nature and culture as these are expressed in language, literature and the plastic arts' (Stephens 2010: 168), and 'seeks social change as well as deeper understanding of literature' (Garrard 2014: 8). Due to the seriousness of environmental degradation, and teenagers' existential interest in the topic, it should be considered whether the change of perspective that is central to intercultural learning in ELT might include a moving way from an anthropocentric, towards an ecocentric perspective (see also Bland and Strotmann 2014). *The Hunger Games* trilogy speaks directly to the teen reader when Katniss blames their ancestors, who did not 'seem much to brag about. I mean, look at the state they left us in, with the wars and the broken planet. Clearly, they didn't care about what would happen to the people who came after them' (Collins 2010: 99).

Three tropes can be highlighted in an ecocritical discussion of *The Hunger Games*: the apocalypse, the pastoral and the wilderness. The apocalyptic narrative implies that the very fate of our world 'hinges on the arousal of the imagination to a sense of crisis' (Buell 1995: 285); one must be able to imagine a disastrous future in order to take measures to avert it (see also Webb 2018, this volume). The country of Panem 'rose up out of the ashes of a place that was once called North America', destroyed by 'the disasters, the droughts, the storms, the fires, the encroaching seas that swallowed up so much of the land' (Collins 2008: 21). At the end of *Catching Fire*, it is Katniss's home, impoverished District 12, that she has longed to return to, that has been obliterated. Paradoxically, despite concerns of 'overemphasized hopelessness in young adult literature' (Thacker 2007: 17), the representation of apocalypse is not hopeless: 'Only if we imagine that the planet *has* a future, after all, are we likely to take responsibility for it' (Garrard 2012: 116, emphasis in the original).

Pastoral, on the other hand, tends to evoke a rural idyll, far from city consumerism. At the end of the trilogy, it is the recovered pastoral utopia of the Meadow in District 12 that symbolizes Katniss's kernel of hope for the future: 'The bright yellow [dandelion] that means rebirth instead of destruction. The promise that life can go on, no matter how bad our losses. That it can be good again' (Collins 2010: 453). The empathetic, intuitive characters Katniss, Rue and Primrose (Prim) are all named after plants:

> (. . .) I noticed the plants growing around me. Tall with leaves like arrowheads. Blossoms with three white petals. I knelt down in the water, my fingers digging into the soft mud, and I pulled up handfuls of the roots. Small, bluish tubers that don't look like much but boiled or baked are as good as any potato. 'Katniss,' I said aloud. It's the plant I was named for. (Collins 2008: 63)

Aside from the tropes of pastoral and apocalypse, the idea of wilderness belongs to the most influential of North American traditions. The woodland wilderness surrounding District 12, where Katniss and Gale hunt illegally in order to feed their starving families, serves as a wild space for temporarily escaping the corrupt power of the Capitol. The peril of the arena's wilderness, on the other hand, lies additionally in its artificial nature, described by Curry (2013: 105) as 'a hostile space of ecological extremes: a grotesque instantiation of our anthropogenically changing climate'.

The ecofeminist Val Plumwood (2006) writes we should distrust any model or tradition that does not integrate the human narrative with narratives of the land, illustrating 'rounded and embodied ways of knowing the land, for example, by walking over it, or by smelling and tasting its life, from the perspective of predator or prey' (Plumwood 2006: 123). In her narration, Katniss personifies nature as a nurturing parent: 'The woods became our saviour, and each day I went a bit further into its arms' (Collins 2008: 62), and both Katniss and Gale show a deep connection to the woodland, which is the source of their families' sustenance. In contrast to mass industrial food production, which renders animals for food production invisible to most humans, hunting for food relies on rapport with the animals, and can be understood as 'participation in normal ecological processes that celebrates and respects the value of the natural world, including the quarry' (Goodbody 2007: 157).

Katniss learned hunting from her father and herbalism from her mother, she is skilled in trapping and hunting for food, which gives her the edge in the arena. She can melt into the wilderness, where she finds shelter, food and herbs that heal. This aligns with the ecofeminist perspective, which rejects the androcentric tradition of conqueror of the wilderness, instead choosing 'immersion rather than confrontation, "recognition" rather than "challenge"' (Garrard 2012: 84). Gale too immerses himself in the woods: 'I think of Gale who is only really alive in the woods, with its fresh air and sunlight and clean, flowing water' (Collins, 2009: 5).

An *Unofficial Hunger Games Wilderness Survival Guide* (Stewart 2013) has appeared, which is very useful as a source of information and clear illustration for in-depth study leading to students' presentations on survival strategies. The guide supports environmental literacy, and potentially life-saving skills, like finding water and edible plants, setting up snares like Gale, stalking, hunting and building shelters like Katniss and even camouflage techniques like Peeta's. The nonfiction handbook could serve students who prefer inquiry projects and active tasks – as many male teenagers do (Smith and Wilhelm 2002). Stewart manages to capture the mood of the books: 'The human spirit is strongest when it's fighting for something or someone else. Katniss fights for Prim. Peeta fights for Katniss. Gale fights for freedom. None of them fight for themselves' (2013: 14). The storyworld of the trilogy carries the message that food gathered in nature can be delicious or life saving. Students might further prepare presentations on wild greens, herbs, nuts, edible mushrooms, fruits and berries collected for food or medicines in their own local culture. This idea is modelled on the family book that Katniss and Peeta work on together in *Catching Fire* (Collins 2009: 194–5).

Ecocriticism is more than raising awareness about environmental issues – it rather takes an ethical stand by questioning the anthropocentric perspective that is the cause of the environmental crisis. Ecocriticism is about broadening perspectives, highlighting anthropocentrism and developing empathy for human and nonhuman nature.

Conclusion

Although not all students in our classrooms are immediately keen to talk around their most treasured texts with their teachers, this option is still far more attractive than the sole use of the textbook. The factor of appeal is decisive: 'one of the key ways that teachers in our study tried to manage or negotiate the challenges posed by literature was through choosing texts that they felt would appeal to their students, that is texts they felt students would enjoy, be interested in or motivated by' (Duncan and Paran 2018: 249). The decisive aspect in choosing a challenging text for teenagers is the number of opportunities it offers for transactional, deep reading and meaningful literacy events. With *The Hunger Games* the class is spoilt for choice.

RECOMMENDATIONS

- The environmental theme woven within *The Hunger Games* can be further investigated with Jeff Orlowski's awe-inspiring and emotional eco documentary *Chasing Coral* (2017). Students might compare the effectiveness of the visual proof of non-fiction film with the power of mental imagery evoked by print narrative.
- *The Hunger Games* encourages students to view screen-based media with a critical eye. Students can consider whether the overuse of social media – their being constantly compared to others – affects their sense of self-worth and resilience as well as their reading practices, which may become fragmentary rather than focused and deep.

Bibliography

Bradbury, Ray (1953), *Fahrenheit 451*, New York: Ballantine Books.
Collins, Suzanne (2008), *The Hunger Games*, London: Scholastic.
Collins, Suzanne (2009), *Catching Fire*, London: Scholastic.
Collins, Suzanne (2010), *Mockingjay*, London: Scholastic.
Huxley, Aldous (1932), *Brave New World*, London: Chatto and Windus.
Orlowski, Jeff (director) (2017), *Chasing Coral*, US: Netflix.
Orwell, George (1949), *Nineteen Eighty-Four*, London: Secker and Warburg.
Slumdog Millionaire (2008), [Film] Dir. Danny Boyle, UK: Fox Searchlight Pictures.
The Truman Show (1998), [Film] Dir. Peter Weir, US: Paramount Pictures.

References

Arizpe, Evelyn and Ryan, Sadie (2018), 'The wordless picturebook: Literacy in multilingual contexts and David Wiesner's worlds', in Janice Bland (ed.), *Using Literature in English Language Education: Challenging Reading for 8–18 Year Olds*, London: Bloomsbury Academic, pp. 63–81.

Berson, Misha (1993), 'Bradbury still believes in heat of *Fahrenheit 451*', *New Seattle Times* 12 March 1993 <http://community.seattletimes.nwsource.com/archive/?date=19930312&slug=1689996> (accessed 25 June 2017).

Bland, Janice (2013), *Children's Literature and Learner Empowerment: Children and Teenagers in English Language Education*, London: Bloomsbury Academic.

Bland, Janice (2018b), 'Playscript and screenplay: Creativity with J. K. Rowling's Wizarding World', in Janice Bland (ed.), *Using Literature in English Language Education: Challenging Reading for 8–18 Year Olds*, London: Bloomsbury Academic, pp. 41–61.

Bland, Janice and Strotmann, Anne (2014), '*The Hunger Games* Trilogy: An Ecocritical Reading', *Children's Literature in English Language Education*, 2/1: 22–43.

Blau, Sheridan (2003), *The Literature Workshop: Teaching Texts and Their Readers*, Portsmouth/NH: Heinemann.

Boyd, Brian (2009), *On the Origin of Stories: Evolution, Cognition, and Fiction*, Cambridge, MA: Harvard University Press.

Buell, Lawrence (1995), *The Environmental Imagination*, Cambridge, MA: Harvard University Press.

Christensen, Linda (2009), *Teaching for Joy and Justice: Re-imagining the Language Arts in the Classroom*, Milwaukee, WI: Rethinking Schools.

Connors, Sean (2014), '"I try to remember who I am and who I am not": The subjugation of nature and women in *The Hunger Games*', in Sean Connors (ed.), *The Politics of Panem: Challenging Genres*, Rotterdam: Sense, pp. 137–56.

Corner, John (2002), 'Performing the real. Documentary diversions', *Television & New Media*, 3/3: 255–69.

Curry, Alice (2013), *Environmental Crisis in Young Adult Fiction*, Basingstoke: Palgrave Macmillan.

Delanoy, Werner (2018), 'Literature in language education: Challenges for theory building', in Janice Bland (ed.), *Using Literature in English Language Education: Challenging Reading for 8–18 Year Olds*, London: Bloomsbury Academic, pp. 141–57.

Díaz, Junot (2016), 'Global dystopias, critical dystopias: A podcast with Junot Díaz', *Boston Review*, 31 October 2016 http://bostonreview.net/podcast/global-dystopias-critical-dystopias-podcast-junot-d%C3%ADaz (accessed 25 June 2017).

Duncan, Sam and Paran, Amos (2018), 'Negotiating the challenges of reading literature: Teachers reporting on their practice', in Janice Bland (ed.), *Using Literature in English Language Education: Challenging Reading for 8–18 Year Olds*, London: Bloomsbury Academic, pp. 243–59.

Fleishman, Jeffrey (2017), 'Dystopia has emerged as "the default narrative of the generation"', *Los Angeles Times*, 25 June 2017 http://www.pressherald.com/2017/06/25/hollywood-dystopia-or-a-lens-into-future-all-those-apocalyptic-films-are-looking-pretty-prescient-after-president-trumps-exit-from-the-paris-climate-pact/ (accessed 25 June 2017).

Garrard, Greg (2012), *Ecocriticism*, London: Routledge.

Garrard, Greg (2014), 'Foreword', in Roman Bartosch and Sieglinde Grimm (eds), *Teaching Environments: Ecocritical Encounters*, Frankfurt/Main: Lang, pp. 7–9.

Goodbody, Axel (2007), 'The hunter as nature-lover: Idyll, aggression and ecology in the German animal stories of Otto Alscher', in Fiona Becket and Terry Gifford (eds), *Culture, Creativity and Environment: New Environmentalist Criticism*, Amsterdam: Rodopi, pp. 135–59.

Green, John (2008), 'Scary New World', *The New York Times*, 07 November 2008 http://www.nytimes.com/2008/11/09/books/review/Green-t.html (accessed 5 July 2017).

Jowett, Garth and O'Donnell, Victoria (2006), *Propaganda and Persuasion* (4th edn), California: Sage.

Karras, Christy (2012), 'Jennifer Lawrence: *Hunger Games* important for "our generation"', *New Seattle Times*, 17 March 2012 http://old.seattletimes. com/html/movies/2017750534_hungergames18.html (accessed 27 June 2017).

Marks, Johanna and Merse, Thorsten (2018), 'Diversity in love-themed fiction: John Green's *The Fault in Our Stars* and David Levithan's *Princes*', in Janice Bland (ed.), *Using Literature in English Language Education: Challenging Reading for 8–18 Year Olds*, London: Bloomsbury Academic, pp. 159–74.

Mason, Beniko (2013), 'Efficient use of literature in foreign language education free reading and listening to stories', in Janice Bland and Christiane Lütge (eds), *Children's Literature in Second Language Education*, London: Bloomsbury Academic, pp. 25–32.

Moore, Suzanne (2013), 'Why *The Hunger Games*' Katniss Everdeen is a role model for our times', *The Guardian*, 27 November 2013 https://www. theguardian.com/commentisfree/2013/nov/27/why-hunger-games-katniss-everdeen-role-model-jennifer-lawrence (accessed 27 June 2017).

Muller, Vivienne (2012), 'Virtually real: Suzanne Collins's *The Hunger Games* trilogy', *International Research in Children's Literature*, 5/1: 51–63.

Patalay, Praveetha and Fitzsimons, Emla (2017), 'Mental ill-health among children of the new century: Trends across childhood with a focus on age 14', London: Centre for Longitudinal Studies. https://www.ncb.org.uk/sites/ default/files/uploads/documents/Research_reports/UCL%20-%20NCB%20-%20Mental_Ill-Health%20FINAL.pdf (accessed 22 September 2017).

Plumwood, Val (2006), 'The concept of a cultural landscape. Nature, culture and agency in the land', *Ethics and the Environment*, 11/2: 115–50.

Rodríguez, Rodrigo (2014), '"We end our hunger for justice!" Social responsibility in *The Hunger Games* trilogy', in Sean Connors (ed.), *The Politics of Panem: Challenging Genres*, Rotterdam: Sense, pp. 157–65.

Rose, Ellen (2012), 'Hyper attention and the rise of the antinarrative: Reconsidering the future of narrativity', *Narrative Works*, 2/2. https:// journals.lib.unb.ca/index.php/NW/article/view/20173/23270 (accessed 4 December 2017).

Sardar, Ziauddin (2010), 'Welcome to Postnormal Times', *Futures* 42/5: 435–44.

Smith, Michael and Wilhelm, Jeffrey (2002), *Reading Don't Fix No Chevys: Literacy in the Lives of Young Men*, Portsmouth: Heinemann.

Stephens, John (2005), 'Analysing texts. Linguistics and stylistics', in Peter Hunt (ed.), *Understanding Children's Literature* (2nd edn), London: Routledge, pp. 73–85.

Stephens, John (2010), 'Ecocriticism', in David Rudd (ed.), *The Routledge Companion to Children's Literature*, London: Routledge, pp. 168–9.

Stewart, Creek (2013), *The Unofficial Hunger Games Wilderness Survival Guide*, Wisconsin: Living Ready.

Thacker, Peter (2007), 'Growing beyond circumstance: Have we overemphasized hopelessness in young adult literature?' *English Journal*, 96/3: 17–18.

Tomlinson, Brian (2015), 'Developing principled materials for young learners of English as a foreign language', in Janice Bland (ed.), *Teaching English to Young Learners: Critical Issues in Language Teaching with 3–12 Year Olds*, London: Bloomsbury Academic, pp. 279–93.

Ungar-Sargon, Batya (2016), 'The pleasure of their pain. Why the punishment and humiliation of reality TV contestants provides such a satisfying and deep pleasure', *Aeon*, 5 April 2016 https://aeon.co/essays/is-reality-tv-a-kind-of-bite-size-greek-tragedy (accessed 4 July 2017).

Webb, Jean (2018), 'Environmental havoc in teen fiction: Speculating futures', in Janice Bland (ed.), *Using Literature in English Language Education: Challenging Reading for 8–18 Year Olds*, London: Bloomsbury Academic, pp. 209–23.

11

Thought experiments with science fiction: Ursula Le Guin's THE ONES WHO WALK AWAY FROM OMELAS

Jürgen Wehrmann

Science fiction has long been a valued guest as well as a disturbing alien in the English-language classroom. Teachers and educationalists have regularly welcomed this popular genre as a medium to reflect on futurity and alterity (Lütge 2007), as an instrument to 'confront and often overturn passive acceptance of contemporary conditions' (Sawyer and Wright 2011: 1) or, simply, as incentive to make reluctant male readers tackle literature in English. Yet, at the same time, most teachers have a low opinion of and little experience with science fiction, as the genre is widely neglected at universities and in teacher education. The specific challenges posed by reading science fiction in ELT are not always taken into consideration.

Modes of reading science fiction

Science fiction is a protean genre, encompassing a multitude of subgenres, styles, motifs and themes, which invite different modes of reading. The most common mode might be the one focusing on the 'sense of wonder' evoked. It seems that science fiction is, above all, popular among young people because it can be experienced as 'romantic fiction' (Mendlesohn 2003: 9–10), in which heroines and heroes with whom students can empathize cross boundaries of space, time, knowledge and biology.

The mode of the romantic reading (Bredella and Burwitz-Melzer 2004: 93–7) tends to clash with the goals teachers traditionally set when discussing literary texts in advanced ELT. If they do not aim specifically at extensive reading for language development that sidelines deep reading, most teachers will promote a close reading of science fiction: they will use analytical tasks exploring relations between content and literary form, looking for complexities and hidden meanings under the textual surface. Most likely, this is the reason why, for example, Ray Bradbury's early short stories and his novel *Fahrenheit 451* (1953) have so frequently been discussed in the German EFL classroom for decades, because they can be read in such a manner with satisfying results. Many science-fiction novels and short stories are much more daring as far as their main ideas are concerned, but written conventionally or even sloppily, with little effort devoted to composition, style or characterization.

While a *close* reading searches for 'messages' in science fiction – usually satirical or allegorical comments on current problems or tendencies – a *wide* reading traces intertextual references. Wolfgang Hallet (2007), for example, has shown how intertextual tasks can be used to foster an understanding as to how science-fiction short stories like Philip K. Dick's 'The Minority Report' (1956) allude to and play with elements of contemporary political and social discourses. Nevertheless, both close and wide reading have in common that they 'normalize' science fiction by transforming the fantastic text into a realistic one describing the world we live in today.

In contrast, a *speculative* reading, understood as experimenting with thoughts, anticipating, following and varying the plot of science-fiction texts, can preserve the important element of wonder in the genre. It is not a new idea that science fiction resembles or even consists of thought experiments, that is: tests of scientific or philosophical hypotheses in experimental arrangements of counterfactual ideas (Engels 2004: 14–17). Already during the decade when H. G. Wells wrote his classic 'scientific romances', arguably the founding texts of the genre, Ernst Mach, in the first systematic discussion of thought experiments in the philosophy of science in 1897, pointed out that the 'author of social or technological utopias', like the scientist, experiments in thoughts (1976: 136). Since then, philosophers and authors as well as critics of science fiction have frequently made this connection, most famously perhaps Ursula Le Guin in her reflections on her novel *The Left Hand of Darkness* (1969) as a 'messy' thought experiment (1989: 10) or in Roy Sorensen's (not completely serious) description of thought experiments as 'small-scale science fiction' (1992: 15).

I would like to argue that, although science-fiction texts are significantly different from thought experiments, experimenting with thoughts can be described as *one* mode of reading science fiction, which should be fostered together with other modes in ELT education, such as the romantic, close and wide reading modes described above. I will first compare thought experiments and science-fiction texts with an emphasis on textual rather than logical analysis. The results will, then, allow me to develop some suggestions for thought experiments based on science fiction in ELT, focusing on three important types: utopian thinking, heuristics of fear and dilemma discussion.

From thought experiment to science fiction

What could be a better example to discuss the relationship between science fiction and thought experiments than a science-fiction text openly declaring that it was inspired by a thought experiment? Ursula Le Guin's short story 'The Ones Who Walk Away from Omelas' (1973) has the subtitle 'Variations on a theme by William James', which is a reference to William James's essay 'The Moral Philosopher and the Moral Life' (1891). Le Guin's introductory remarks even cite James's thought experiment that her story develops:

> Or if the hypothesis were offered us of a world in which Messrs Fourier's and Bellamy's and Morris's utopias should all be outdone, and millions kept permanently happy on the one simple condition that a certain lost soul on the far-off edge of things should lead a life of lonely torment, what except a specific and independent sort of emotion can it be which would make us immediately feel, even though an impulse arose within us to clutch at the happiness so offered, how hideous a thing would be its enjoyment when deliberately accepted as the fruit of such a bargain? (Le Guin 2004: 275, citing William James)

James's thought experiment is typical of this philosophical device in many respects. It is very short and integrated in a much longer argumentation: James wants to convince the reader of the anthropological thesis that our moral sense is also based on some innate ideas and not simply derived from our experiences with pleasure and pain. For this reason, James asks us to imagine an almost perfect society in which the great majority lead a happy life at the price that one person far away is continuously tortured. Would we accept to live in such a utopia? James assumes that we would not – he concludes that we hold an idea of what is good, independent from our experience, and that we are not only interested in maximizing the pleasure and minimizing the pain in this world (1912: 189).

Philosophical thought experiments are usually very short narratives strategically reduced to the essentials and framed by longer argumentations. In James's case, the narrative is hardly noticeable because experiment and interpretation are merged. Still, a situation is sketched as an experimental arrangement, and the reader is involved in the only reaction to this situation that James believes to be possible. Thus, the reader, like in many thought experiments, is cast both as co-protagonist and co-author of the thought experiment. The reader is asked to adopt the perspective of somebody who experiences a certain situation, and she is also supposed to imagine what happens next.

Typical plot elements of science fiction and thought experiments

What both science-fiction texts and many thought experiments have in common are typical plot elements. There is at least one radical, counterfactual assumption that not only introduces fictitious people or places but breaks with more fundamental conditions of the world as it was seen and understood at the time of writing. The most influential critic of science fiction, Darko Suvin, calls such significantly different elements that constitute the science-fiction storyworld *nova* (1979: 7–8, also Csicsery-Ronay 2008: 47–75). Another similarity is the specific connection to science. Thought experiments are supposed to be constructed in analogy to scientific experiments, and the *nova* of science fiction must be, to some extent, reconcilable with a scientific world view. As soon as a text depicts a complete magical world order or simply describes the irruption of something dark and irrational into everyday life, it moves into the realms of fantasy or horror respectively. A thought experiment puts forward a scenario that is supposed to be thought through with all its consequences and implications. Suvin demands the same as far as science fiction is concerned, the *novum* 'can be methodically developed against the background of already existing cognitions, or at the very least as a "mental experiment" following accepted scientific, that is cognitive, logic' (1979: 66).

Although many science-fiction texts do not develop their *nova* as consistently as Suvin considers necessary, there is obviously a deep affinity between science-fiction *nova* and the test arrangement of philosophical and scientific thought experiments. Thus, Le Guin can easily adopt the situation proposed by James's thought experiment as the *novum* of her science-fiction story. She also depicts a society in which the vast majority are perfectly happy on the condition that one person has to suffer permanently, and she describes the reactions of various citizens to this situation.

Disparity in discourse

Yet although Le Guin's science-fiction short story is very similar to James's thought experiment on the level of plot, the narratives differ hugely on the level of discourse. This already becomes evident at the very beginning of Le Guin's story:

With a clamor of bells that set the swallows soaring, the Festival of Summer came to the city of Omelas, bright-towered by the sea. The rigging of the boats in harbour sparkled with flags. In the streets between houses with red roofs and painted walls, between old moss-green gardens and under avenues of trees, past great parks and public buildings, processions moved. Some were decorous: old people in long stiff robes of mauve and grey, grave master workmen, quiet, merry women carrying their babies and chatting as they walked. In other streets the music beat faster, a shimmering of gong and tambourine, and the people went dancing, the procession was a dance. (2004: 276–7)

One immediately notices that the speed of narration is much slower and the narrative accordingly much more detailed. There is no argumentative frame (apart from the introductory notes, which concentrate on the description of the writer's creative process and were only added when the story was republished in a compilation of short stories), nor is the *novum*, the basic hypothesis, openly mentioned. Instead, the reader is immediately immersed into the utopian world and has to understand how it differs from ours. Finding out what the *nova* actually are and how they have emerged is usually central to the process of reading science fiction and often dramatized in the narrative. While many thought experiments are written in the present tense or the conditional, Le Guin's uses the past tense, which is interestingly typical of a narrative genre whose actions are so often set in the future. In contrast to thought experiments, science fiction confronts the reader with a seemingly finished world and action – the storyworld – though, of course, in fact offering many gaps to be filled in during the reading process.

The differences in discourse reflect different functions. In philosophical texts, thought experiments are part of an argument; they are used to support a theoretical position or refute other opinions (Sorensen 1992, Engels 2004). Science-fiction texts and films might contain a serious speculation on possible futures, but they need not. Many science-fiction texts can be better understood as allegories or satires on current facts and trends, others are all about the aesthetic experience. The best and most efficient serve all three functions – serious speculation, allegory, aesthetic experience – at one and the same time.

From science fiction to fostering experimenting with thoughts

Having compared thought experiments and science-fiction texts, it seems clear that in order to use science fiction as thought experiments the reader or community of readers has to make selections, fill gaps and embed the text into a reflective discourse. I will differentiate these three acts of reading as selection, immersion and framing.

Selection means that science-fiction readers as experimenters with thoughts, first of all, have to find texts or isolate plot elements that offer interesting hypotheses. Short science-fiction narratives recommendable for thought experiments in advanced ELT, which combine speculative relevance with high literary quality, are, for example, William Gibson's 'Burning Chrome' (1986) on love, media and self-promotion, Ted Chiang's 'Understand' (2016) on brain enhancement and the meaning of life, Ursula Le Guin's 'The Matter of Seggri' (1994) on intercultural communication and gender politics, Octavia Butler's 'The Book of Martha' (2005) on freedom and ecology, and Paolo Bacigalupi's 'The People of Sand and Slug' (2008) on technological enhancement and the relationship between humanity and non-human nature.

Immersion requires that the readers engage in the speculation by conducting the experiment in their mind while reading. As we have seen, this usually involves taking on the role of a co-author of the narrative, possibly coming up with an alternative story and a different outcome. Moreover, the reader must often adopt the perspective of the protagonist who is mainly interesting as the subject of experience, a representative of mankind rather than as a specific character with an individual background.

Framing entails that the readers must construct their own argumentative frame: they have to look for questions related to the *novum* and evaluate the outcome of the experiment as well as its wider reaching implications.

Experimenting with thoughts can be supported by numerous classroom activities, most of which are well known but might be accentuated differently. For example, it is common practice to introduce the main theme or problem of a text before reading it by a visual impulse, or a quotation. Yet experimenting with thoughts necessitates a certain depth and reflexivity already at the pre-reading phase in order to establish a frame for the experiment. Some teachers let students write their own texts about the dilemma of the narrative as a lead-in. Conducting the isolated central thought experiment of a given science-fiction text before reading is a similar activity, but it is more clearly defined because a thought experiment has to be logical and probable. Perspective change in thought experiments focuses on imagining possible reactions to a counterfactual *situation*, rather than on understanding another *person's* view of the world. Thus, perspective change here uses extreme circumstances to explore one's own moral ideas and feelings directly, instead of adopting the perspective of a person with a different cultural background and coordinating this perspective with one's own as in the intercultural approach developed by Lothar Bredella, Ansgar Nünning, Britta Freitag-Hild and others (Freitag-Hild 2011). Within the wide range of post-reading activities that have been developed over recent decades, framing the thought experiment can be

TABLE 11.1 *Activities fostering thought experiments*

	Selection	Immersion	Framing
Pre-reading activities	Involving students in the selection of texts	Conducting the central thought experiment before reading the narrative	Introducing the problem/ question. Formulating hypotheses
While-reading activities	Identifying *nova*. Looking for key passages to be discussed	Comparing one's thought experiment with the story. Reading log, creative tasks	Comparing hypotheses with the events of the storyworld. Focusing on certain aspects of the thought experiment
Post-reading activities		Alternative thought experiments with changed premises	Discussion of the outcome. Intertextual tasks. Essays on implications

fostered most efficiently by discussions in class (also formal debates or dilemma discussions), by intertextual tasks and by writing argumentative essays (see Table 11.1, or overview in Nünning and Surkamp 2006: 78–80).

Science-fiction *nova* can be used for all kinds of thought experiments. However, many language teachers and students will not be interested in scientific, metaphysical and anthropological thought experiments or will lack the knowledge to engage with them, while moral and political questions concern everybody and are much less difficult to discuss. Le Guin's short story suggests thought experiments that belong to the types most relevant to ELT.

Types of thought experiment:
1. Utopian thinking

What is special and striking about 'The Ones Who Walk Away from Omelas' is how explicitly the text reflects on processes of writing and reading science fiction. After the first description of the 'Festival of Summer' the narrative is interrupted. The narrator ponders how to convince readers that the citizens of Omelas were joyous, and points out how difficult it is to depict a believable utopia. Without mentioning it explicitly, the short story alludes to the well-known problem that if human beings are profoundly determined by the society they have grown up in they can hardly have gained the ability to imagine an optimal, radically new alternative to this society. Utopian texts are always marked by the times in which they were composed, full of errors and shortcomings absurdly evident to their know-all posterity. Yet, the narrator of Le Guin's short story perceives an even deeper disillusionment with the possibility of human fulfilment. Today, it seems, complete happiness can only be placed in a distant legendary past or naive fantasy world with 'the King, mounted on a splendid stallion and surrounded by his noble knights' (Le Guin 2004: 277):

> The trouble is that we have a bad habit, encouraged by pedants and sophisticates, of considering happiness as something rather stupid. Only pain is intellectual, only evil is interesting. This is the treason of the artist: a refusal to admit the banality of evil and the terrible boredom of pain. If you can't lick 'em, join 'em. If it hurts, repeat it. But to praise despair is to condemn delight, to embrace violence is to lose hold of everything else. (Le Guin 2004: 278)

This is a plea for imagining utopias instead of writing only dystopian texts: the challenge is to continue hoping and to believe in happiness as something realistic, realizable. The difficulty of representing utopias is solved by Le Guin's heightening reflexivity and involving the reader as co-author. Various alternatives are presented as to how Omelas could be organized and what the 'Festival of Summer' might look like. In the end, the narrator lets the reader decide: 'Or they could have none of that: it doesn't matter. As you like it' (Le Guin 2004: 279). These are strategies typical of utopias of the 1970s onwards, Tom Moylan's 'critical utopias', which were no longer meant as 'blueprints' for constructing a perfect state but as tools for imagining better alternatives to contemporary society (Moylan 2014: 9–11). I think such critical utopias allow teachers in ELT to shift the emphasis, in Fredric Jameson's terms, from 'utopian closure' to 'utopian impulse' (2005: 4–5): it is less important and interesting to analyse in detail how utopian texts present allegedly perfect states than to encourage students to imagine alternative ways of living together. Without including utopian thinking, political education could only aim at fostering understanding and accepting societal arrangements and not at shaping them and developing them further.

Utopian thinking in the classroom

Utopian thinking differs from the thought experiments discussed so far in that it cannot be described as speculative deductions from a given set of assumptions. It is a much more open, creative, not completely rational process which resembles daydreaming rather than academic work. One could consider it a reverse direction of thought: the utopian thinker does not set out from a specific situation and think through its consequences and implications. Instead, she attempts to come up with a situation in which specific problems are solved or specific needs are fulfilled.

How can utopian thinking be fostered and integrated in the classroom? The moderation technique 'workshop of the future' developed in order to help organizations in democratic future planning provides a lot of interesting ideas for this (Kuhnt and Müllert 1996). Such workshops consist of three main phases:

- Critique phase

- Fantasy or visionary phase

- Implementation phase

A closer look shows that, in her treatment of her readers, Le Guin uses many of the techniques that Müllert and Kuhnt recommend. She sets out with criticisms of our society – the critique phase – having her narrator name things that this utopia should not know, such as kings, clergy, soldiers, cars and helicopters. By positively reversing them, these criticisms can already be starting points for utopian alternatives, the visionary phase. Through the narrator, Le Guin adopts a humorous tone that establishes a playful distance from the pressure of reality and invites readers to imagine everything they might need in order to create a happy society, regardless of its costs or improbable technological prerequisites. Similarly, Müllert and Kuhnt suggest playing games, decorating the room or creating funny hats as means to create a protective zone for utopian imagination. Discussions as to which of the utopian ideas could actually be realized are explicitly forbidden in the visionary phase and postponed until later since they would unquestionably stifle the imagination. According to Müllert and Kuhnt, utopian visions should be approached indirectly and artistically instead of being constructed in an abstract manner (Kuhnt and Müllert 1996: 78–89). They recommend first having participants draw a sketch and later write a narrative describing an encounter or relevant situation, like Le Guin's 'Festival of Summer'. The utopian ideas in such pictures and stories are then discussed in the implementation phase, selected or sorted out and, finally, translated into concrete and detailed requests how the organization should work in the future in order to realize the vision (Kuhnt and Müllert 1996: 95–106). Of course, an implementation of utopian ideas is not possible in the ELT classroom except, perhaps, for utopias of teaching and learning. However, creative products can be discussed and evaluated, forming the frame of the thought experiment together with the critique phase.

Utopian thought experiments with higher-grade students based on Le Guin's short story could begin with an independent critique phase or could select one of the criticisms in the text for positive reversals. Either the students collect reasons why people are not happy in the society they live in and then choose an aspect to focus on, or they try to imagine a society in which, for example, cars do not exist. In both cases, they work on a central creative product, for instance a description of one citizen's life in a carless, but happy and functional society. While listening to the presentations, the students immerse in the thought experiments of their classmates and ask themselves whether they would like to live in such a society and why (or not). The discussion evaluates the potential of the utopian ideas. In order to think through possible consequences and implications, it can be helpful to include intertextual tasks involving additional fictional or non-fictional texts on the subject. The result might be that the utopian idea could actually contribute to a better society, but it is also possible that the thought experiment convinces the thinker that its realization would be disastrous, thus turning an instrument to attain utopia into something dystopian. However, as Ernst Bloch has pointed out, utopian imagination is not only important because it might provide us with new practical insights but also because utopian thinking is as much about clarifying one's aims and values as about finding a way to change (Bloch 1980: 103).

Types of thought experiment:
2. Heuristics of fear

The last utopian promise most students still believe in – at least in Europe – is technology improving the world. Looking at the narrator's suggestions for creating a happy Omelas in Le Guin's story, only one relevant technology appears:

> I thought at first there were no drugs, but that is puritanical. For those who like it, the faint insistent sweetness of *drooz* may perfume the ways of the city, *drooz* which first brings a great lightness and brilliance to the mind and limbs, and then after some hours a dreamy languor, and wonderful visions

at last of the very arcana and inmost secrets of the Universe, as well as exciting the pleasure of sex beyond all belief; and it is not habit-forming. For more modest tastes I think there ought to be beer. (2004: 279)

Le Guin's *drooz* seems to meet quite divergent demands typical of different ages of drug abuse: on the one hand, in the later stages of its influence, *drooz* is supposed to trigger metaphysical visions and heighten the experience of sex, everything alternative culture in the 1960s and 1970s could wish for; on the other hand, it appears to first enhance the abilities of body and mind, giving them 'a great lightness and brilliance' that might facilitate a better work performance for a manager of today. Genetic engineering and cloning are the branches of biotechnology frequently discussed in ELT textbooks. However, neuroenhancement is arguably more topical than ever since especially many young people already try to improve their work performance or change their personality by using drugs like Ritalin and Prozac. It is also probable that other enhancing drugs will be developed over the next few decades (Fukuyama 2002: 41–56).

Science-fiction narratives on neuroenhancement, like on any technology, will regularly suffer from the shortcoming that their *nova* are sensational but not really probable or scientifically consistent. Nonetheless, the genre can still be used for what philosopher Hans Jonas calls 'the heuristics of fear'. Jonas argues that technology radically questions traditional ethics and forces us to become morally speculative: new technological options appear for which traditional ethics do not provide answers, and our actions have far more significant long-term consequences than they used to have two hundred years ago. In order to find principles that could orient us, future projections are central, according to Jonas. By understanding how technology might change human existence and experience, we can find out what is valuable and significant for us, and the fallibility of our future projections thus does not render them useless (Jonas 2003: 67–8).

ELT students confronted with a neuroenhancing drug like *drooz* could be asked to write several creative texts that vary aspects of the thought experiment. For example, they could write two diary entries each, one about the first and one about the hundredth time their protagonists take *drooz*. Half of the class assumes that their protagonists live in a storyworld in which they are one of very few people using the drug, while the other half imagines a storyworld where everybody uses it. Probably, comparing the diary entries will highlight that the experience of the drug significantly changes depending on time and the social environment: obviously, the effect cannot remain as strong as at the beginning. And in a society in which perceptions and performances enabled by the drug are generally expected, there would not be any special rewards for using it. Again, references to other texts and media can deepen the thought experiment, for instance to the film *Limitless* (2011) by Neil Burger, in which a failed writer stumbles upon a large number of pills giving him, for a time, superhuman memory, intelligence and creativity. On the drug, the writer is like another person, and he succeeds in winning back his former girlfriend, who had left him disappointed by his self-centredness and lack of initiative – but does she now love him or his drug personality (see Wehrmann 2014: 280–5)? Even if such a drug is impossible, imagining a world in which it exists might still teach us something about the value of authentic emotions as well as authentic self and world perceptions.

Types of thought experiment: 3. Dilemma discussion

After suggesting a lot of aspects that might make Omelas a happy city, the narrator returns to the depiction of the 'festival of summer', ending with the following remarks: 'Do you believe? Do you accept the festival, the city, the joy? No? Then let me describe one more thing.' (Le Guin 2004: 280). The narrative that follows is no longer humorous, but painfully detailed and vivid:

> In a basement under one of the beautiful public buildings of Omelas, or perhaps in the cellars of one of its spacious private homes, there is a room. [...] In the room a child is sitting. It could be a boy or a girl. It looks about six, but actually is nearly ten. It is feeble-minded. Perhaps it was born defective, or perhaps it has become imbecile through fear, malnutrition, and neglect. It picks its nose and occasionally fumbles with its toes or genitals, as it sits hunched farthest from the bucket and the two mops. [...] It is so thin there are no calves to its legs; its belly protrudes; it lives on a half-bowl of corn meal and grease a day. It is naked. Its buttocks and thighs are a mass of festered sores, as it sits in its own excrement continually. (Le Guin 2004: 281)

Regularly, people visit the abused child in order to witness its suffering. Knowing unhappiness allows the inhabitants of Omelas to deepen and enrich their own happiness so that one person's pain turns out to be the basis of the huge majority's joy:

> If the child were brought up into the sunlight out of that vile place, if it were cleaned and fed and comforted, that would be a good thing, indeed; but if it were done, in that day and hour all the prosperity and beauty and delight of Omelas would wither and be destroyed. (Le Guin 2004: 282)

In contrast to James in his philosophical article, the narrator tells us that almost everybody in Omelas accepts sacrificing one child for the benefit of the many. Only occasionally, there are individuals who leave Omelas because they cannot live with the deal on which Omelas is built. The narrator recounts that those who go away from Omelas have a destination that cannot be described: 'I cannot describe it at all. It is possible that it does not exist. But they seem to know where they are going, the ones who walk away from Omelas' (Le Guin 2004: 284).

The central thought experiment of Le Guin's short story is thus based on the same situation that James used for his. Yet without James's argumentative frame the question that arises is a variation of the classic moral dilemma between the human rights of an individual and the interests of an overwhelming majority. The dilemma is in fact independent of the science-fiction setting; it is only radicalized, made more obvious by the science-fiction frame.

There are many science-fiction narratives that focus on moral dilemmas without presenting any original or productive *novum*. At the same time, of course, utopian thinking and heuristics of fear might also lead to two conflicting values. The model character of science fiction enables the construction of interesting moral dilemmas, which can be used for dilemma discussions in ELT. The emphasis of this method, based on the moral psychology of Lawrence Kohlberg (Blatt and Kohlberg 1975) and developed further by, among others, Georg Lind (2016: 103–13), is on the development and testing of ethical arguments as an alternative to the literature in language education focus on empathy and perspective change.

Conclusion

Ursula Le Guin's short story 'The Ones Who Walk Away from Omelas' illustrates the variety of thought experiments that can be conducted with advanced school students in ELT while reading science fiction. Thought experiments are not only an engaging, activating way of reading science fiction, illuminating specific qualities of the popular genre, but equally they foster moral and political judgement as well as speaking and writing skills. However, Le Guin's text, like the other narratives mentioned above, also clearly demonstrates how limiting a purely speculative approach to science fiction would be. The humorous tone, the many metafictional elements or the subtle way in which the beginning of the story communicates details so that readers understand they have entered an alternative world (*heinleining* after one of the most famous representatives of this technique, Wolfe 2011: 52) are an invitation to an analytic approach and closer reading. Le Guin's reflections on cars, drugs and technology as a whole suggest intertextual tasks, connecting the text to political and ecological discourses. Especially the story's ending is too intense to simply perceive it as a speculative model; the starving child and the happy city become too recognizable for the reader, and gain allegorical energy. Already in the introductory notes, Le Guin comments on James's thought experiment with the words: 'The dilemma of the American conscience can hardly be better stated' (2004: 275). She could also have called it *the dilemma of Western conscience*, as all over the Western world individual and collective happiness are built on the acceptance of suffering elsewhere. Thus, only an integration of romantic, close, wide and speculative reading in ELT will foster a competent deep reading of science fiction. Experimenting with thoughts based on science fiction should be incorporated in process-oriented task sequences that include rational-analytical as well as creative approaches and, while concentrating on the speculative dimension, do not neglect the formal, allegorical and intertextual dimensions of science fiction.

RECOMMENDATIONS

- Women writers are deeply involved in science fiction, from the early masterpiece Mary Shelley's *Frankenstein* (1818), now celebrating its bicentenary year, to Alice Sheldon (pen name James Tiptree Jr.), Octavia Butler, Joanna Russ, Ursula Le Guin and Margaret Atwood. And J. K. Rowling's *Harry Potter and the Goblet of Fire* was awarded the Hugo Award in 2001 by the World Science Fiction Society. It is worth examining whether science fiction is truly a genre particularly for boys.
- Students might attempt to define fantasy and science fiction narratives, and discuss to what extent the genres can be distinguished.

Bibliography

Bacigalupi, Paolo (2008), 'The People of Sand and Slag', in *Pump Six and Other Stories*, San Francisco: Night Shade, pp. 49–67.
Bradbury, Ray (1953), *Fahrenheit 451*, New York: Ballantine.
Butler, Octavia (2005), 'The Book of Martha', in *Bloodchild and Other Stories*, New York: Seven Stories Press, pp. 187–213.
Chiang, Ted (2016), 'Understand', in *Arrival*, London: Picador, pp. 35–84.
Gibson, William (1986), 'Burning Chrome', in *Burning Chrome*, London: Gollancz, pp. 179–205.
Le Guin, Ursula (1994/2003), 'The Matter of Seggri', in *The Birthday of the World and Other Stories*, London: Gollancz, pp. 23–68.
Le Guin, Ursula (1975/2004), 'The Ones Who Walk Away from Omelas', in *The Wind's Twelve Quarters: Stories*, New York: Perennial, pp. 275–84.
Limitless (2011), [Film] Dir. Neil Burger, USA: Virgin Productions.

References

Blatt, Moshe and Kohlberg, Lawrence (1975), 'The effects of classroom moral discussion upon children's level of moral judgement', *Journal of Moral Education*, 4/2: 129–61.

Bloch, Ernst (1980), 'Antizipierte Realität – Wie geschieht und was leistet utopisches Denken?', in Hanna Gekle (ed.), *Abschied von der Utopie?: Vorträge*, Frankfurt (Main): Suhrkamp, pp. 101–15.

Bredella, Lothar and Burwitz-Melzer, Eva (2004), *Rezeptionsästhetische Literaturdidaktik (mit Beispielen aus dem Fremdsprachenunterricht Englisch)*, Tübingen: Narr.

Csicsery-Ronay, Istvan (2008), *The Seven Beauties of Science Fiction*, Middletown: Wesleyan University Press.

Engels, Helmut (2004), *'Nehmen wir an ...' Das Gedankenexperiment in didaktischer Absicht*, Weinheim: Beltz.

Freitag-Hild, Britta (2011), 'Searching for new identities: Inter- and transcultural approaches to Black and Asian British literature and film', in Sabine Doff and Frank Schulze-Engler (eds), *Beyond 'Other Cultures': Transcultural Perspectives on Teaching the New Literatures in English*, Trier: Wissenschaftlicher Verlag Trier, pp. 65–78.

Fukuyama, Francis (2002), *Our Posthuman Future: Consequences of the Biotechnology Revolution*, London: Profile.

Hallet, Wolfgang (2007), 'Teaching literature and cultural history in a unit on Philip K. Dick's "Minority Report"', *Amerikastudien*, 52/2: 381–97.

Jameson, Fredric (2005), *Archaeologies of the Future: The Desire Called Utopia and Other Science Fictions*, New York: Verso.

James, William (1912), 'The moral philosopher and the moral life', in *The Will to Believe and Other Essays in Popular Philosophy*, New York: Longmans, Green, pp. 184–215.

Jonas, Hans (2003), *Das Prinzip Verantwortung: Versuch einer Ethik für die technologische Zivilisation*, Frankfurt (Main): Suhrkamp.

Kuhnt, Beate and Müllert, Norbert (1996), *Moderationsfibel Zukunftswerkstätten*, Neu-Ulm: AG SPAK.

Le Guin, Ursula (1989), 'Is gender necessary? Redux', in *Dancing at the Edge of the World: Thoughts on Words, Women, Places*, New York: Grove Press, pp. 7–16.

Lind, Georg (2016), *How to Teach Morality: Promoting Deliberation and Discussion, Reducing Violence and Conceit*, Berlin: Logos.

Lütge, Christiane (2007), 'Philosophieren mit Science-Fiction? "The Matrix" im fortgeschrittenen Englischunterricht', *Praxis Fremdsprachenunterricht*, 4/6: 39–43.

Mach, Ernst (1976), 'On Thought Experiments', in *Knowledge and Error*, Dordrecht: Reidel, pp. 137–47.

Mendlesohn, Farah (2003), 'Introduction: Reading science fiction', in Edward James and Farah Mendlesohn (eds), *The Cambridge Companion to Science Fiction*, Cambridge: Cambridge University Press, pp. 1–12.

Moylan, Tom (2014), *Demand the Impossible: Science Fiction and the Utopian Imagination* (new edn), Bern: Peter Lang.

Nünning, Ansgar and Surkamp, Carola (2006), *Englische Literatur unterrichten: Grundlagen und Methoden*, Seelze-Velber: Kallmeyer.

Sawyer, Andy and Wright, Peter (2011), 'Introduction', in Andy Sawyer and Peter Wright (eds), *Teaching Science Fiction*, Basingstoke: Palgrave Macmillan, pp. 1–20.

Sorensen, Roy (1992), *Thought Experiments*, New York: Oxford University Press.

Suvin, Darko (1979), *Metamorphoses of Science Fiction: On the Poetics and History of a Literary Genre*, New Haven: Yale University Press, 1979.

Wehrmann, Jürgen (2014), 'Utopien, Dystopien und Science-Fiction im Englischunterricht: Probleme und Perspektiven', in Wolfgang Gehring and Matthias Merkl (eds), *Englisch lehren, lernen, erforschen*, Oldenburg: BIS, pp. 267–90.

Wolfe, Gary (2011), 'Theorizing science fiction: The question of terminology', in Andy Sawyer and Peter Wright (eds), *Teaching Science Fiction*, Basingstoke: Palgrave Macmillan, pp. 38–54.

12

Environmental havoc in teen fiction: Speculating futures

Jean Webb

The current problems and concerns emanating from global warming, climate change, the depletion of natural resources and damage to the environment are not going to end with the current generation that is responsible for decision-making, but are going to continue and will become the problems and responsibilities of the youth of today, with which they will have to grapple in the future. The responsibility of how they learn and think about such matters lies with teachers and educators who formulate programmes of education. There are various approaches which can be taken such as directly addressing environmental matters from scientific and experiential perspectives, but these do not allow for projection into future states which include the complexities of societies and how the individual might be positioned under these circumstances. Fiction is, however, a space where these matters can be contemplated; where awareness can be raised and possible futures can be posited in creative and imaginative ways unrestricted by reality but related to actual conditions. It also opens up ways that students may be critically engaged through discussion, role play, projects and problem solving.

This chapter therefore considers how the reader is placed by a range of contemporary texts in the umbrella genre of speculative fiction which reflect upon potential problems arising from the consequences of contemporary social and scientific attitudes and developments projected into imagined futures where the environment is under threat or has been corrupted by irresponsible practice. Furthermore, the selected texts all question what it is to be human by placing their protagonists in extreme circumstances which test their physical and moral character. These works of speculative fiction place the responsibility with teenagers and young adults as they mature into the decision makers who can affect the course of the world. They implicitly raise questions for the reader such as 'What would I do in this situation?'

Speculative fiction

Speculative fiction has various definitions. Robert Heinlein's 1947 definition, which I employ in this discussion, is particularly clear. For him it is:

> the story embodying the notion 'just suppose—' or 'What would happen if—.' In the speculative science fiction story, accepted science and established fiefs [areas of control] are extrapolated to produce a new situation, a new framework for human action. As a result [...] new human problems are created—and [the story] is about how human beings cope with those new problems.

Speculative fiction is the ideal vehicle for contemplating these matters in a future to which readers can relate current circumstances. It is increasingly being employed by contemporary authors of teenage and young adult fiction to present problems and scenarios, raising the awareness of their readers through speculation. There are extensive reading lists available on the Web such as 'Goodreads' and librarians' sites, in addition to sites dedicated to ecological or environmental science fiction (e.g. 'Ecological Science Fiction'), although to date there is limited critical consideration of speculative fiction for young adults. For purposes of this discussion I am using the overarching term of speculative fiction as it encompasses all aspects of the range of these texts.

In my preparation I surveyed a considerable number of texts, although I have only selected a few as exemplars in the discussion. The pattern which emerged can be described as a spectrum from being grounded in the reality of the circumstances of the contemporary era to dystopian fiction set in a speculative/science-fiction/fantasy future. I suggest that employing this spectrum could be used to provide the basis for a programme of environmental studies for teenage readers to stimulate talking around texts, and set up scenarios for deep reading leading to speculative problem solving, for example in a Content and Language Integrated Learning programme (CLIL).

I have broadly identified three stages of development along this spectrum that reflect the concerns of the authors from raising awareness to different ways of living: some of the texts are clearly within my categorizations, while others shift across boundaries. The first stage, 'Extreme weather', is comprised of texts which are intent upon raising consciousness in the reader of the devastating effects of global warming. These texts interrogate experiences of surviving increasingly difficult situations emanating from changing weather patterns, resulting in extreme heat and drought, or flooding due to rising sea levels. In each circumstance the dangers are exacerbated by the effects of the shortages of water and food. The second stage, 'Cityscapes', is comprised of more hypothetical scenarios which consider post-industrial and post-technological societies and the reimagining of the city as a physical and social environment. The third stage 'Posthuman future', considers the possibilities of life affected by climate change and adapted beyond the boundaries of the normal body. All of the works discussed pose a further range of questions, for example about the nature of humanity, power relations and social organization. In all of them the adolescent is central, placing the teenage reader in a direct relationship with the texts. The following sections consider exemplars from each of these stages and what these texts offer to the adolescent reader.

Stage one: 'Extreme weather'

One of the effects of climate change is extremes of weather experienced in areas thought to have moderate climates. In the UK flooding is an increasing problem: November to January of 2015–16 in the UK were the wettest months since records began in 1910. In 2007, for example, severe flooding across a considerable area of England and Wales caused disruption to thousands of people who were forced to leave their homes, plus the loss of life for four unfortunate souls (BBC News 2007). *Floodland* (Sedgwick 2010) directly addresses the problems of flooding as a consequence of global warming. Sedgwick gives a sense of veracity to his work by setting it against a real context. As far back as the 1960s scientists were recognizing the problems associated with global warming and rising sea levels (Weart 2008, 2017). Sedgwick's novel becomes a fictional playing out of the predicted effects of rising sea levels.

Floodland raises the awareness of readers to the fact that these potential circumstances are not at all restricted to countries far away. Significantly Sedgwick sets his novel in East Anglia, a quiet rural area of England which would not feature in the international consciousness alongside major world cities, yet it is equally as vulnerable. Norfolk and the Fens of Cambridgeshire are areas particularly susceptible to rising sea levels as they are principally comprised of land reclaimed from the sea. These counties are low-lying and protected by dykes; however it is neither practical nor possible to keep increasing the height of the seawalls against considerable rising sea levels. Following the floods in 2014, there were serious considerations to abandon reclaimed land in Norfolk as the Environmental Agency warned that these were not going to be rare events to be expected once in a century, but regular occurrences as part of the changing weather patterns and rising sea levels due to global warming (Hope 2014). Researchers warn of the long-term consequences of abuse of the environment and global warming. Peter Clark, Oregon State University, recently raised the matter of the effect of global warming on settlement: 'People need to understand that the effects of climate change won't go away, at least not for thousands of generations. (...) Entire populations of cities will eventually have to move' (Carrington 2016: np).

Marcus Sedgwick's *Floodland*

In *Floodland* sea levels have risen drastically as a result of global warming resulting in catastrophic flooding. In his compact novel (first published in 2000), Sedgwick has pre-empted the warnings of scientists for the need for populations to relocate to safer environments. Zoe and her parents live in Norwich, a city founded in the tenth century. It is in reality situated thirteen miles from the coast with a population of circa one hundred and thirty-five thousand. However, in Sedgwick's speculative future, rising sea levels and erosion of the coastline have resulted in the city becoming reduced to an island with a population of about one hundred. Norwich is increasingly threatened by submersion forcing this small population to evacuate despite their efforts to stay: 'After the water came, Zoe and her parents had tried for years to stick it out in Norwich, along with another hundred or so. After a while, they realised they were fighting a losing battle, and that the sea was not going to stop rising' (Sedgwick 2010: 9). Initially this is not a circumstance which the reduced population had to endure without support as:

> Back then, there were still fairly regular supply trips from the mainland. A big ship used to bring as much food as could be spared, and anchor half a mile offshore. After rowing in with the supplies and sharing them out, the captain would ask if anyone wanted to leave. Usually there would be one or two more people ready to go to the mainland. (Sedgwick 2010: 9)

Under extreme pressure with reduced resources and an ever threatening and threatened environment, social cohesion and order begin to break down resulting in marauding bands who roam in search of food and drinking water. Finally Zoe's parents decide to abandon what has now become the island of Norwich along with others who see no hope in staying, as the supply boats have become less and less frequent. The pressure to escape the sinking land means that when the rescue boat does come it is dangerously overcrowded. Zoe therefore responsibly decides to take another boat enabling her father to escape with her sick mother. Catastrophically Zoe misses the other boat and is thus alone, separated from her family. Not yet a teenager, Zoe has to make decisions by herself and to work out what she is going to do and how she can escape.

The character of Zoe is one of an increasing number of proactive, brave, adventurous heroines who feature in works of teen and young adult fiction, such as Suzanne Collins's *The Hunger Games* (2008) and Veronica Roth's *Divergent* (2011). Alice Curry's groundbreaking study from an ecofeminist perspective (Curry 2013) analyses the phenomenon of the rise of powerful girls who confront the circumstances of environmental disaster in contemporary young adult dystopian fiction. Like her fictional contemporaries such as Katniss Everdeen, Zoe is a role model for female readers. Initially Zoe waits months for her father to come back for her or for another rescue boat, but those options failing Zoe decides to make her own way. She refurbishes an old rowing boat and makes the dangerous and demanding journey across the sea in search of land, but exhausted after hours of rowing she comes across an even smaller island that a local gang call Eels Island. This seems to be the monumental tenth-century Ely Cathedral, sometimes called 'the ship of the Fens', as it towers above the surrounding flat landscape – which in the story has now become seascape. Traditionally a place of sanctuary, the cathedral has been taken over by an aggressive gang of youths. Instead of finding safety Zoe is attacked by the gang members who then ask to which gang she belongs. Under adversity these survivors have become highly territorial, protective of their space and resources and guarding against intruders who would deplete their supplies. Teenagers and children themselves, they have little or no knowledge of other settlements. Their function is to survive.

Sedgwick has the reader consider what happens when social order breaks down under conditions of duress. The weather and the environment are extreme, violent and, as it were, out of control, and the implication is that human society is also affected, losing structure, predictability and a sense of civilization, resorting to violence and self-protection. The vital factor which can save lives and the quality of life is someone showing empathy and extending a sense of humanity, being willing to share and to help. The protagonist is fighting not only against the weather but also against the savagery into which society has descended. Yet human connections win out. Zoe is befriended by Munchkin, a character somewhat out of kilter with the rest of the gang. They escape and finally make it in Zoe's rowing boat to a larger tract of land called 'Hope' where Zoe finds her parents. They have a week-old baby, and, reunited with Zoe and accepting of Munchkin, are intent upon making a new life, growing their own food and living in harmony with nature. What is clearly emerging through these texts is the importance of the family unit, and that the quest for humanity and survival is linked with bonds of loyalty and kinship.

Floodland in the classroom: Script-writing task[1]

In addition to talking around texts and environmental projects on the content matter of the teen fiction discussed in this chapter – for example in the mid-secondary CLIL classroom – speculative fiction offers creative opportunities for language work. The boat scenes are tense and full of drama in *Floodland*, for Zoe's little rowing boat is symbolic of her resistance to adversity while also highlighting the helplessness of those who have no boat and cannot escape. This suggests opportunities for the methods of drama and creative writing, which are popular with students. The following pivotal scenes offer scenarios for group work such as script writing – writing the dialogues of the characters involved – followed by acting out the scripts in small groups and finally comparing the interpretations:

- Zoe rowing away from Norwich into the unknown, and the desperate shouts of the children being left behind.

- Zoe landing on Eels Island (Ely Cathedral), and the conflict this causes among the children stranded there – who believe she is from a rival gang.

- Dooby's brutal attempt to kidnap Zoe and steal her boat to save himself.

- Zoe's dangerous but finally successful escape in her rowing boat with Munchkin.

Stage two: 'Cityscapes'

Floodland is set within a recognizable reality, whereas Jeanne DuPrau's *The City of Ember* and Julie Bertagna's *Exodus* move into more speculative hypothetical worlds, which have all been affected by environmental disaster due to human behaviour.

Jeanne DuPrau's *The City of Ember*

The City of Ember has been built following what one projects to be a nuclear disaster. The builders of the city speak of the future before it is inhabited:

'They must not leave the city for at least two hundred years,' said the chief builder. [. . .]

'And when the time comes,' said the assistant, 'how will they know what to do?'

'We'll provide them with instructions, of course.' (DuPrau 2005: 1)

The instructions are to be within the safe keeping of the mayor; however, as time goes on the box is lost. The city is enclosed like a great nuclear shelter or bunker: 'In the city of Ember, the sky was always dark. The only light came from great flood lamps mounted on the buildings and at the top of poles in the middle of the larger squares' (DuPrau 2005: 4). The inhabitants are no longer aware of any life outside of Ember, for the city was planned this way. What the inhabitants fear, or preferred to ignore, is 'that some day the lights of the city might go out and never come back on' (DuPrau 2005: 5). This is a place run on ageing technology with resources which are progressively becoming depleted. Despite their situation the city is well organized under the control of the mayor. Information about their city is contained in *The Book of the City of Ember* which lays out the philosophy of the community without giving anything of a factual history: 'The citizens of Ember may not have luxuries, but the foresight of the Builders, who filled the storerooms at the beginning of time, has ensured that they will always have enough, and enough is all that a person of wisdom needs' (DuPrau 2005: 34).

On completing their education the children serve the city by taking on jobs for which they draw lots. It might be working in the supply rooms where furniture, clothing, light bulbs and so forth are kept and allocated: the stores that were put aside over two centuries ago. Another possibility is to work on the maintenance of the tunnels and pipeworks under the city, which deal with the water and sewage systems and serve the water-powered electricity generator. Communication is also devoid of sophisticated technology since it is provided by messengers who run throughout the city delivering orally communicated messages. This is a city working on minimal technology and minimal resources. The two protagonists, Lina and Doon, take on work as a messenger and in the pipeworks. Lina is an athletic girl, bright, articulate and with a good memory. Doon is keen to find out how the generator works, for he has a scientific curiosity and is afraid for the future of this crumbling city. Over the course of time the technological know-how has been forgotten and all that is done is makeshift maintenance, minimalizing the use of power and conserving resources, as they are limited to what they have stored and the vegetables they can grow within the city under less than ideal conditions. Unlike *Floodland*, this is a community that principally works together, except that the current mayor has taken more than his share of the stores, leading to their rapid depletion.

The box of instructions left by the Builders is accidentally found by Lina, having been in the possession of her family who were mayors at one time. It contains the instructions for when the people have to leave the city and make their way onward. Unfortunately the papers have been partially destroyed and Lina and Doon have to decipher and unlock what seems essentially a secret code. Their ingenuity and determination drive them onwards to overcome the central hurdle: that there is no record of their history and they are trapped within a darkened existence of diminishing well-being due to their own limited knowledge. Lina and Doon finally discover a journal of the original group of two hundred people who had entered the bunkered city. They also discover the way out of Ember, initially thinking they perceive an electric light in the darkness, which is actually, unbeknown to them, the moon. For them this is an 'other' world of wonder and nature, greenness and light into which they go to make their future. The question which remains unanswered at this stage in the series is whether the people of the upper community of Sparks will welcome them.

The City of Ember in the classroom: Think, pair, share activities

A highly accessible read, told from the perspective of the two 12-year-old-protagonists Lina and Doon, *The City of Ember* offers excellent opportunities for considering the implications of the *novum* (see Wehrmann 2018, this volume) of living in complete ignorance of the past or present of any other human culture. For example think, pair, share activities on being 'in the dark' in the City of Ember could be:

- When is the recurrent image of being in the dark literally true due to lack of light? What do the citizens of Ember miss?

- Where in the story is being in the dark a leitmotiv for ignorance? The builders wanted the people of Ember to be in the dark about life outside their city: 'The babies must grow up with no knowledge of a world outside, so that they feel no sorrow for what they have lost' (DuPrau 2005: 260). Do students consider the consequences of ignorance always bad?

- Although likewise in the dark about the past, Lina and Doon are different because they ask searching questions. What dangers might result from their total disconnect to the past and any civilization outside Ember?

Julie Bertagna's *Exodus*

The texts discussed thus far have a common trope of acceptance and rejection of environmental responsibility. *Exodus* (Bertagna 2011), is no exception. The problem being faced by the community on a small Scottish island is that of fast rising sea levels due to global warming. The catastrophe has arisen from the irresponsible use of resources, as the prologue makes clear:

Once upon a time there was a world . . .

[. . .]*The people feasted upon their ripe world. Endlessly, they harvested its lands and seas. They grew greedy, ravaging the planet's bounty of miracles. Their waste and destruction spread like a plague until a day came when this plague struck* [. . .]

The globe grew hot and fevered, battered by hurricanes and rain. [. . .] *Earth raged with a century of storm.* [. . .] *Imagine the vast, drowned ruin of a world* [. . .] *Imagine survivors scattered upon lonely peaks, clinging to the tips of skyscrapers, to bridges and treetops.*

[. . .] *Is this where we stand now, right here on the brink?* (Bertagna 2011: np, italics in the original)

The reader is given the scenario of devastation due to irresponsible treatment and use of the earth's resources. The phrase '*Once upon a time ...*' suggests that the world as we know it could become a fantasy, a fairy tale, far removed from a ravaged present reality. It is this kind of reality where the story of Mara's venturing to a safer place begins. The island is all that remains, the mainland having been drowned by the rising sea levels and ravaging storms. Old Tain, the wise man of the island, tells her that she must find a new home elsewhere in the world for the sea level is rising still further. He has long ago heard of New World cities which are built in the sea, towering above the ocean. However Tain refuses to leave, as space is limited on the boats, so it is Mara's quest to find such a place when the islanders are forced off the island because of the worsening conditions. The exodus begins. Eventually they find 'New Mungo', a city rising out of the sea, yet there is no access, for this supposed haven is guarded by Sea Police who will fire on refugees. The city sits above the ocean on great steel legs around which gather refugee boats. This is a mobile refugee camp. *Exodus* is a more complex text, for here matters are being raised about the treatment of refugees and of the dispossessed by those in power, and about the conditions in camps, which are all situations extant in today's world.

Some of the refugees are taken by Pickers who select those who look fit enough for work. These people become slaves until they are no longer of use and then they disappear. This is a harsh socially differentiated world to which some have become adapted and in which others fail to survive. There are bands of urchins who live in the muddy area around the huge legs of the city structure. They have become physically adapted with the development of thicker, almost scaly skin, however, they have also lost the capacity for language and are savage survivors. There is a strong element of Social Darwinism included here, akin to the Eloi and Morlocks in H. G. Wells's *The Time Machine* (Wells 1895). However, Mara is not a time traveller but a sea survivor. Again she is an adventurous, brave heroine who intelligently manages to enter the city and adapt to the behaviour of its inhabitants. Those living in New Mungo travel around on the equivalent of powered skates. They eat artificially produced food which is highly coloured and the equivalent of junk food. The upper level inhabitants are interested only in immediate unchallenging satisfaction, either with their food or in their entertainment. As with Wells's Eloi, society has deteriorated because they have not had to strive. Those who keep the city going, like Morlocks, are from the netherworld; however they do not feed upon the upper level dwellers as the Morlocks on the Eloi, but work in the slime and mud. Mara finally escapes New Mungo, having found the information she required, which was the possibility of reaching Greenland. She ventures forth with those she has gathered together and sets off with courage and hope. Perhaps they will find a utopia, or at least a safe haven away from this nightmarish dystopia.

Exodus in the classroom: Creative writing task and fact-finding project

There are hoards of refugees trying to survive the global warming catastrophe in *Exodus*. The refugee groups include:

- Boat people, who maintain a precarious fringe existence in the filthy water around New Mungo.

- Treenesters, who build nests in trees and live on the dwindling natural resources still above water near Glasgow Cathedral and Glasgow University, in the shade of towering New Mungo.

- Urchins – nameless orphans – who scavenge and fight in gangs in the polluted waters, without any language, and destined to die young.

- Slaves, selected or kidnapped by the Pickers, who are worked to death on New Mungo construction sites.

As the story of *Exodus* is told entirely from Mara's perspective, the dire circumstances of these various refugee groups are less well known. The experience of one of these refugees, a named character or possibly a newly invented character, told from their perspective, could be a challenging but compelling creative writing task. Student groups might also research groups of people in the contemporary world or in history who have lived under similar circumstances.

Stage three: 'Posthuman Future'

What might be called a final stage in the projection of the possibilities of life affected by climate change and the consequences of damage to the environment is the adaptation of the human beyond the boundaries of the normal body. In a study analysing fiction for adults, Adam Trexler comments on the limitations of literary realism: 'When literary authors have tried to depict climate change, disasters disassemble the illusion of realism, rupturing quotidian experience, devastating towns, fracturing the economy' (Trexler 2015: 223–4). I would take his arguments further in my discussion of young adult fiction to propose that current speculative fiction for young adults has moved further into more fantastic realms in order to explore the positioning and possibilities for teenage protagonists. Authors have moved beyond the limitations of realism, to create imagined worlds and imagined forms of the human, or posthuman, producing situations where human existence depends on the young who have to create the new world of the future. The young protagonists may themselves be posthuman subjects, that is modified humans or having to deal with posthuman beings.

Jay Kaplan's *Earth 1: Return* (Kaplan 2015) oscillates between a future that is having to live with the effects of global warming and contemporary times. The environment was destroyed in the twenty-first century as a result of nuclear war and continued abuse with, for instance, the burning of fossil fuels. The humans of the year 2223 lead a restricted life on a polluted Earth, living on chemical substitutes instead of food and water and surviving within buildings protected from the hostile exterior. Their existence is further impoverished by a restrictive totalitarian government which has removed access to the arts, music and literature. The familiar dystopian tropes of totalitarianism – both the repression of culture, and the suppression of historical knowledge as one finds in George Orwell's *Nineteen Eighty-Four* (1949) or Ray Bradbury's *Fahrenheit 451* (1953) – are used to structure Kaplan's plot. This is a world where robots are deployed by the government to control the populace; however, Rebekka, a renegade human-friendly robot, gives the teenage protagonists access to their history. Without posthuman assistance humanity is doomed. Their mission is then to go back in time and warn the people of the twenty-first century in order to change events, by convincing scientists and politicians of the devastation of humanity which their future holds unless they change the course of history and work with nature instead of destroying it. Although this is a text which lacks sophistication in literary terms it does strongly express concerns for the environment and the future of humanity, opening up questions of who the responsible parties are and how they could be persuaded to avert environmental disaster.

Isobelle Carmody's *Obernewtyn Chronicles*

There are currently a number of sophisticated and challenging texts for young adults with posthuman protagonists. Set in worlds where the ravaged environment is the backdrop, and the focus is on the problems of society, the implication is that scientific development has resulted in both human adaptation and environmental destruction. For example, the *Obernewtyn Chronicles* series (Carmody 1987–2015) is set in a future where the world has been ravaged by a nuclear holocaust thought to have come about as a punishment for an overly materialistic society. The few survivors form a governing Council and are determined to protect themselves. However, what it is to be human has changed in this polluted environment, for mutants are born. It falls to Elspeth, a mutant Misfit, who has telepathic powers, and other Misfits with enhanced mental powers, to save the world. Their powers are all related to the mind and forms of communication, such as the ability to manipulate others' minds without their knowing, healing through mental intervention and communication with animals. Carmody's perspective could be interpreted as a pessimistic view of humanity for in its present state it is incapable of saving the future, or perhaps this is another way of saying that humans both have to evolve and adapt to produce a future where there is a harmony and a communication with the natural environment.

Obernewtyn in the classroom: Create a presentation on an historical, legendary or literary figure with an invented telepathic power

The first book of the series introduces a number of characters, including the first-person narrator, Elspeth Gordie, who are identified as Misfits – and adolescent readers are likely to strongly empathize with some of them. The Misfits have a variety of telepathic powers. These include:

- Farseeking – a mind-reading ability over distance
- Coercion – the ability to manipulate others through mind control
- Empathy – the deep experience of others' emotions and feelings
- Beastspeaking – communication with animals by telepathy.

Students can be given the task, working in small groups, to associate one or more of these abilities with an historical, legendary or literary figure. The group creates an invented episode in their chosen figure's life story, and presents it to the class, illustrating how the figure made use of their special power of the mind.

Conclusion

In conclusion, these works of speculative fiction all have a strong moral perspective which circulates around the responsibility mankind has for the well-being of the environment and the animal kingdom. Technology can be used to create what is yet thought of to be marvellous, but there are elements where irresponsibility and misuse can deplete the quality of life for both human and non-human animals, and impinge upon what it is to be human. These dystopian speculative texts imagine and warn, for as William Blake (1790) wrote: 'What is now proved was once only imagined'. These texts raise questions and problems and confront the reader with challenges as to how they would or might deal with such matters: such reading takes them on the adventurous journey into contemplating the future.

RECOMMENDATIONS

- These texts offer exciting reads for young teenagers; however, those students with as yet limited language skills in English are likely to struggle. To help them, the teacher could perform dramatic readings of key passages. Following this the students might read on silently, at their own pace, or practise reading the same passage aloud in groups, combining reading and performing.
- Duncan and Paran's research into the strategies of experienced teachers with literature (this volume) found that reading aloud was a surprisingly popular activity among advanced students. The teachers reported on 'reading aloud to scaffold understanding, reading aloud as a tool for close reading or reflection, and reading aloud as literary experience' (2018: 254).

Note

1 Suggestions for classroom tasks and activities on *Floodland*, *The City of Ember*, *Exodus* and *Obernewtyn* were devised by Janice Bland.

Bibliography

Bertagna, Julie (2002/2011), *Exodus*, London: Macmillan Children's Books.
Bradbury, Ray (1953), *Fahrenheit 451*, New York: Ballantine.
Carmody, Isobelle (1987/2010), *Obernewtyn*, London: Bloomsbury.
Collins, Suzanne (2008), *The Hunger Games*, London: Scholastic.
DuPrau, Jeanne (2003/2005), *The City of Ember*, London: Corgi Books.
Kaplan, Jay (2015), *Earth 1: Return*, Austin: Greenleaf Publishers.
Orwell, George (1949), *Nineteen Eighty-Four*, Harmondsworth: Penguin.
Roth, Veronica (2011), *Divergent*, London: HarperCollins.
Sedgwick, Marcus (2000/2010), *Floodland*, London: Orion.
Wells, Herbert George (1895), *The Time Machine*, London: Penguin Books.

References

BBC News, 26 June 2007 <http://news.bbc.co.uk/1/hi/uk/6239828.stm>
(accessed 27 April 2017).
Blake, William <http://www.blakesociety.org/about-blake/gilchrists-life-of-blake/
chapter-x/> (accessed 28 February 2017).
Carrington, Damian, 'Sea-level rise "could last twice as long as human history"',
The Guardian, 8 February 2016. <https://www.theguardian.com/environment/
2016/feb/08/sea-level-rise-could-last-twice-as-long-as-human-history>
(accessed 28 February 2017).
Curry, Alice (2013), *Environmental Crisis in Young Adult Fiction*, Basingstoke:
Palgrave Macmillan.
Duncan, Sam and Paran, Amos (2018), 'Negotiating the challenges of reading
literature: Teachers reporting on their practice', in Janice Bland (ed.), *Using
Literature in English Language Education: Challenging Reading for 8–18 Year
Olds*, London: Bloomsbury Academic, pp. 243–59.
Ecological Science Fiction. <http://bestsciencefictionbooks.com/ecological-
science-fiction.php> (accessed 28 February 2017).
Explore Norfolk <http://www.explorenorfolkuk.co.uk/norwich-cathedral.html>
(accessed 28 February 2017).
Heinlein, Robert (1947), 'On the writing of speculative fiction', <http://www.
mab333.weebly.com> (accessed 28 February 2017).
Hope, Christopher, 'Parts of Britain to be abandoned to the sea after December
tidal surge', *Telegraph*, 24 January 2014. <http://www.telegraph.co.uk/news/
earth/environment/10592746/Parts-of-Britain-to-be-abandoned-to-the-sea-after-
December-tidal-surge.html> (accessed 28 February 2017).
Trexler, Adam (2015), *Anthropocene Fictions: The Novel in a Time of Climate
Change*, Virginia: University of Virginia Press.
Weart, Spencer (2008), *The Discovery of Global Warming*, Cambridge, MA:
Harvard University Press.
Weart, Spencer (2017), 'Impacts of climate change', *The Discovery of Global
Warming*, <http://history.aip.org/climate/impacts.htm> (accessed 28
February 2017).

Wehrmann, Jürgen (2018), 'Thought experiments with science fiction: Ursula Le Guin's *The Ones Who Walk Away from Omelas*', in Janice Bland (ed.), *Using Literature in English Language Education: Challenging Reading for 8–18 Year Olds*, London: Bloomsbury Academic, pp. 193–208.

13

Hamlet, Ophelia and teenage rage: Michael Lesslie's PRINCE OF DENMARK

Tzina Kalogirou

The one-act play *Prince of Denmark* (2012), by the British playwright and screenwriter Michael Lesslie, commissioned by the London National Theatre and first staged there in 2010, is suitable for reading and performing by all age groups within the teenage spectrum. Originally conceived as a prequel of *Hamlet*, it is set a decade before the action of Shakespeare's foremost play, and presents teenagers Hamlet, Ophelia and Laertes revolting against the roles handed down to them by their parents and other empowered adults at court. In their struggle for liberation from parental authority and for personal fulfilment, they are learning to cope, as contemporary adolescents may do, with the power hierarchies, the inherent contradictions and the painful anxieties of their world.

Based upon a general conception of adolescence in psychology as a 'time of internal turmoil, of storm and stress' (Hilton and Nikolajeva 2012: 2), the play by Lesslie employs an apposite spectrum of themes, confronting young people with situations of political injustice, violence, oppression and emergent sexuality. By its elaborated poignant social critique and deep awareness of the problems of youth, the play meets unequivocally some of the most fundamental characteristics of a *challenging text*, which is not only 'truly polysemic and worthy of in-depth analysis' (Evans 2015: 4) but also an intrinsically nuanced and unconventional text that opens up a vast array of interpretative affordances, thus pluralizing the ontological monolith of the original play. Challenging texts can, I will argue in this chapter, produce challenging readings.

Prince of Denmark is a shrewdly written, challenging adaptation of the Shakespearean play that can be fruitfully analysed through a wide range of critical and pedagogical perspectives. Foregrounding issues of social urgency as well as the adolescents' apparent instabilities in relation to multiple societal and personal anxieties, the play challenges young readers to 'read the world critically, constructively and purposefully' (Bland 2013: 111–12) or, in other words, to think actively about 'the word and the world' (Macedo and Freire 1987), and therefore can be successfully implemented in a critically oriented reading and teaching project.

The three main characters of the play, namely Hamlet, Ophelia and Laertes, are sketched as energetic and intense adolescents that embody the archetype of the teenager, often to be found in young adult literature, as performing acts of rebellion against authority figures (Seelinger-Trites 2000: xi) and learning in a painful way 'their place in the power structure' (Seelinger-Trites 2000: x). As fictional characters, they are represented as both powerful – in their youth and vigour – and disempowered, destined to fulfil an unfathomable and inscrutable fate. They yearn for love and erotic fulfilment and yet they are fascinated by violence, as represented in the play by swords and fencing. Violence is the key theme of the play according to Lesslie (2012: 199) and a way for adolescents to enter into the adult world.

The rotten state of Denmark

Everything is rotten in the state of Denmark, which is represented as a murky place, characterized by political oppression, violence and ruthless militarism. Accordingly, the court is a place of concealed feelings, secrets and lies where only devious people can be found and where no one can be really trusted. The young Hamlet detests his father, the King, who is determined to banish him to Wittenberg, a dull place, according to Rosencrantz, 'a place for monks and midwives, not princes' (Lesslie 2012: 173). The King, Hamlet claims, is so totally preoccupied by war and indifferent to his wife that he murdered old Fortinbras on the same day Gertrude gave birth to their son. Hamlet condemns his father's cruelty and pursuit of royal glory as a vain and shallow reason for slaying thousands of people. His soliloquy in Scene 2 (2012: 172–3) challenges the obsolete and frail heroic ideal of war and at the same foreshadows the future conquest, however without an actual fight, of the kingdom by the young Fortinbras who is already 'charged with the fury of filial vengeance' (Lesslie 2012: 173). This last statement foregrounds a core thematic element in the original play, which is actually overwhelmed by sons avenging the murders of their fathers: from Hamlet to Pyrrhus (in the play-within-the-play, *Hamlet*, Act 3, Scene 2; also Lesslie 2012: 184–6) to Laertes to young Fortinbras.

The state is in turmoil in both Shakespeare's and Lesslie's plays. It has been said that '*Hamlet* is about Denmark as well as its prince' (Edwards 2003: 41). However, a correspondence between the private and the public sphere is also masterfully articulated in Lesslie's play in the parallelism between turmoil in the individual, with the teenagers' furious behaviour and impassioned speeches, and turmoil in the state, with ongoing war. The adolescent protagonists rage against a rotten state that demands their obedience; their agitated behaviour serves as a metaphor for the broader turmoil of their country.

Prince of Denmark as a challenging adaptation of *Hamlet*

Lesslie's *Prince of Denmark* interrogates the pre-text (Shakespeare's *Hamlet*) by posing grand questions about power, politics, sexuality and fate, and does so insightfully in a way that mirrors anxieties of contemporary readers. Several explicit or implicit intertextual references to Shakespeare's play are woven into the text, subtly taking cues from details in the original while inferring motives that reflect some of the uncertainties of young adults today. Thus the play by Lesslie can lead – according to Linda Hutcheon's theoretical position – to an intertextual reading and ongoing dialogic process in which adolescent readers compare the work they may already know (e.g. through film or reimaginings) to the prequel they are experiencing (2006: 21).

Prince of Denmark links to a vast territory of overt prequels and sequels of *Hamlet*. Many authors have engaged with the play, imagining events both before and after the original, or filling the gaps in the offstage lives of characters, while others have been prolific in the creation of transmedial and multimodal adaptations, which renew and invigorate Shakespeare's cultural capital (Lanier 2010: 104–13, Hateley 2009) and worldwide appeal. A huge variety of texts succeed in unveiling the Bard's work to a young audience with diverse cultural interests: from comics retellings (Williams 2000), to animation, manga and graphic novels (Müller 2013: 95–111 and Rokison 2013), to a retelling based on the coded language of texting and emojis (Carbone 2015).

In the field of young adult literature, contemporary female authors (e.g. Fiedler 2003, Klein 2008, Ray 2011 and Zindel 2014) have produced radical rewritings of *Hamlet* as young adult fiction primarily from Ophelia's perspective, drawing attention to 'the similarity of experiences between early modern girls and the girls of today' (Tosi 2013: 20). Already in the nineteenth century

Mary Cowden Clarke in her pioneering tales *The Girlhood of Shakespeare's Heroines* (1852/2009) highlighted Ophelia's emotional instability and her early experiences of loneliness and trauma. John Marsden's *Hamlet* (2008) is another compelling and insightful reimagining of Shakespeare's play that is characterized by psychological complexity and erotic tension (MacLeod 2013: 81).

According to Desmet and Sawyer (1999: 3–4), the play by Lesslie can be described as what might be termed 'small-time Shakespeare' appropriation, that is an individual act of revision that arises from a desire to play with Shakespeare, to subvert, destabilize and demystify the Shakespearean characters, offering a challenging rethinking of the text from a political, feminist or other perspective. The play can also be considered a 're-vision' (the term associated with Adrienne Rich) that succeeds in 'looking at the initial text with fresh eyes, entering it from a new direction' (Desmet and Sawyer 1999: 7).

Lesslie's play is in many ways a subversive retelling of *Hamlet* that enriches considerably the original by opening up its potential meanings through intertextual play and echoing. It is also a skilful text written in a faux Elizabethan idiom that sounds, however, neither formal nor grandiloquent. As the writer contends: 'the faux-Elizabethan idiom seemed the only option – these characters would one day speak in Shakespearean English, after all, but as yet would still be green and so only able to approximate the brilliant later language' (2012: 199). Lesslie also recasts the play-within-the play using iambic pentameter, and – according to Kate Godfrey of the National Theatre Voice Department – 'this means it is written with the rhythm of the heartbeat' (Godfrey 2012: 202). The final sword fighting between Hamlet and his eternal foil, Laertes, is complex, carefully designed and choreographed.

Lesslie shapes the subject positions of the heroes and heroine so as to develop their adolescent actions in such a way that they adequately foreshadow the pre-text. However, the play also offers subversive twists and compelling rearrangements of meaning that can be found to shed new light on the original. The structural device of the dramatic foil is maintained, for instance, while the antagonism between Hamlet and Laertes is reinterpreted. The latter, despite being scheming and manipulative, has a no less fascinating characterization than the Prince of Denmark. It is surely no coincidence that the most elaborate and significant soliloquy of the play (2012: 177–8) is bestowed on him. Laertes echoes the 'To be or not to be?' soliloquy as he considers killing Hamlet and meditates on the dilemma between revolutionary action and passive acceptance of fate. Ready to take arms against the injustice of his world, he denounces the arbitrariness of elective monarchy (fictional Elsinore's regime) according to which the son of the king is, to be sure, the prime candidate for the throne. Laertes, who has strong ambitions to gain the power he believes he deserves, accuses the royal heir, born to be king, of incapacity and cowardice. Hamlet, on the other hand, contrasts sharply with the pensive and melancholic 'sweet' prince of the original: he is rather domineering and often takes advantage of the sovereign power he possesses, in order to control other people's lives (even Horatio's and Ophelia's). Irony can be detected in the portrayal of the rival characters, as adolescents who react to circumstances quickly and even fiercely, with a minimum of reflection on the meaning and possible outcome of their actions.

The female characters, Ophelia more prominently than Gertrude, serve also as a critical focus of the play, opening up multiple interpretative paths. The play endows them with psychological complexity despite their lack of agency at court. Seen through Hamlet's eyes, the queen is neglected, unhappy in marriage to a stern and gloomy king, who is preoccupied with war. Tension is thus created for an extramarital affair with a seemingly tender and caring Claudius (Lesslie 2012: 173). This echoes other reimaginings, such as John Updike's *Gertrude and Claudius* (2000), and contrasts with the suggestion of 'flagrancy' (Rose 2002: 97). Ophelia, as a main character, is by far more principled and trustworthy than the two reckless male heroes who either try to manipulate (Laertes) or impose authority over her (Hamlet). She says forebodingly: 'I pray that none of these men are ever king' (Lesslie 2012: 196). Another significant aspect in the representation of Ophelia is her traditional symbolic association with water within the broader archetypal association of the element with the feminine: 'with female fluidity as opposed to masculine aridity' (Showalter 1985: 80). The text also sustains the trope of drowning as the female death par excellence. Ophelia (Scene 7) considers the pale reflection of her face in the brook, singing a modified version of her mad sing-song language (*Hamlet* 4.5). It is the same brook where her mother died and where Ophelia spotted the queen bathing 'white as the moon' (Lesslie: 169). The figurative language connects the three women, associating them with profound and organic symbols of femininity (water and moon), pointing at the same time to female abjection.

Reading and teaching *Prince of Denmark*: To read or not to read *Hamlet*?

I set up the long-term teaching project entitled 'From *Prince of Denmark* to *Hamlet*: The many faces of an adolescent hero' during autumn/winter 2015–16 in an ELT oriented secondary school located in Athens, located in a predominantly middle to high socioeconomic area of the city. The fourteen- to sixteen-year-old students (male and female) who volunteered to participate were all Athenians, advanced readers of English literature and competent speakers of English. They had participated in several ELT activities (e.g. English Theatre and School Forensics Tournament, which had given them the opportunity to be involved in various forms of public speaking in English) through which they had become proficient. They were experienced in oral communication and writing essays in English and in studying effectively not only the plays themselves but also the rich material of print and audiovisual resources I provided (see the Bibliography of this chapter).

The main goal of this *Hamlet*-centred project was for students to engage in a critical reading of the two texts, both Shakespeare's and Lesslie's, by placing them in a dialogue and thus producing different interpretative readings through oral and written responses and other activities. In other words, the main goal of the project was for the students to be actively involved in 'grand conversations' (Peterson and Eeds 1990) about the two chosen texts. According to Banks (2012: 206), the National Theatre director of *Prince of Denmark*, the one-act play is undoubtedly a stand-alone piece. In ELT it could certainly be treated as such, and in most contexts this would offer an excellent introduction to Shakespeare without over-challenging the students. However, I considered it fundamental for the goal of my project to have the students study both plays in order for them to interrogate and scrutinize more genuinely the puzzling questions and dilemmas arising from the texts, so as to enable them to feel the 'intertextual pleasure' in adaptation, a pleasure that is both aesthetic and intellectual (Hutcheon 2006: 117). I thus opted for a deeper, more insightful reading of both works leading to a profound understanding of the intertextual reading process itself. The students were encouraged to delve into the Shakespearean pre-text so as to examine more profoundly its contemporary adaptation.

The underlying framework of the project is critical pedagogy combined with reader-response criticism (RRC). In general, both critical theories have had a significant impact on the practice of teaching today and they have radically changed the ways we conceive, read, interpret and finally *teach* literature in the classroom. While RRC encourages students to articulate their personal engagement with texts and stay attuned to their reading, critical pedagogy helps students develop critical consciousness through reading and empowers them to interrogate authority. Both theories, however, allow readers to understand that literature cannot be explained ontologically, but only in terms of how it functions within different audiences and cultural contexts, bearing eloquent witness to the fact that the literary text is multifaceted and therefore cannot be considered as a preconceived and stable entity but as a space that offers multiple pathways for exploration. In Roland Barthes's words, our goal in teaching reading is not any more 'to find *the* meaning, nor even *a* meaning of the text [. . .]. Our goal is ultimately to conceive, imagine, to experience the plurality of the text, the open-endedness of its *signifying process*' (Barthes 1988: 262, emphasis in the original).

Reader response: A first step towards a deep reading

I modified Probst's concept for structuring a dialogue with a text (1988: 35–6 and 2004: 81–3) as a frame for eliciting student's responses to *Prince of Denmark* and fostering their ability to develop a personal response to the literary work. Only a brief sense of the students' responses can be provided here, summarized for the purposes of this chapter:

- *First reaction*: What was your first reaction or response to the text?

Do Hamlet / Laertes / Ophelia seem like real teenagers to you? Why or why not? Do you feel that you can relate to them? Why or why not?

- *Feelings*: What feelings did the text awaken in you?

How do you feel about Laertes / Hamlet / Ophelia and their situation? What emotions do Laertes / Hamlet / Ophelia experience in the story? How do you know? With which character do you empathize more?

- *Perceptions*: What did you see happening in the text?

What are the main / most important incidents for you? Could the events described in the play happen today?

- *Visual images*: What images were called to mind by the text?

Which locations can you see in the representation of Elsinore? Can you describe your mental model of the storyworld?

- *Associations*: What memories does the text call to mind?

What other texts have you read or seen depicting adolescents in anger or in repressive situations?

- *Thoughts, ideas*: What ideas or thoughts were suggested by the text?

- *Selection of textual elements*: Upon what, in the text, did you focus most intently as you read?

- *Judgements of importance*: What is the most important word / line / aspect of the text for you?

- *Identification of problems*: What is the most puzzling aspect in the text?

- *Author*: What sort of person do you imagine the author of this text to be?

Search the Web to find information about Michael Lesslie. Why do you think he wrote this play?

- *Literary associations*: What other texts / movies does the text remind you of?

From reader response to critical pedagogy

Critical pedagogy is one of the most illuminating of recent epistemological innovations in the field of education. It brings powerful insights to the understanding of education, raising questions about the sociocultural spaces where learning takes place. The classroom, as seen from this theoretical perspective, is a sociocultural space where we can critically examine our condition in the world, raising challenging questions about issues of race, social power, gender, sexuality, justice, oppression and so forth (Darder, Baltodano and Torres 2009).

This theory, namely that education actually constitutes a 'discourse' through which identifiable social groups and individuals historically have framed themselves and their relation with others, is closely related to the very practice of teaching and learning in the everyday classroom. Discourse is considered as a form of power embedded in the social fabric, framing social subjects through strategies of regulation and exclusion. Critical pedagogy asks students and teachers to become aware of themselves as social subjects who have power, that is 'power to become more inclusive of others or to marginalize them, to construct themselves and others' (Johnson and Freedman 2006: 30). In the frame of critical pedagogy, texts can be used in the classroom as a means of discussing the complex social realities that surround the issues of power and social injustice. By negotiating the meanings of literature, students can gain a deeper understanding of social issues in relation to themselves as students, citizens and human beings sharing a planet with others.

Prince of Denmark appears to fit ideally the agenda of critical pedagogy; it creatively reimagines a canonical masterpiece and challenges its dominant interpretations in literary criticism or as it is taught in schools and universities. Critical pedagogy in theory and practice lends itself to such texts that highlight, often in an audacious and bold manner, demanding issues related to social agency, political conflict and personal or political struggle against domination and towards emancipation (Christensen 2000; 2009).

Lesslie's play not only encourages students to stand outside any 'model reading' of the pre-text, allowing the conjuring of new interpretative perspectives, but it also enables students to embrace multiplicity in reading literature. According to Tyson (2014: 1–10), students can and should be accustomed to using multiple perspectives in order to read and interpret literature effectively and, more importantly, to enrich their vision on different dimensions of human experience. The comparative reading of the two plays can help students construct a sustained plurality of perspectives, and empower their interpretive skills, helping them to overcome any single, super-imposed, authoritarian meaning. They will have chances for meaningful and engaging encounters with literature and opportunities to view literary texts, including the canon, in ways never thought of before.

Challenging texts and challenging readings

Challenging texts may produce challenging readings – for instance when readers engage in intellectual practices such as experimenting with new ideas, seeking different perspectives and ultimately challenging dominant readings or stereotyped beliefs. Undoubtedly, this kind of questioning reading is not only an activity but also a competence that can be learned, although we need to keep a sense of freedom and play in reading itself, hence readers should be encouraged to read actively as well as deeply, keeping their enthusiasm and mental freshness. Challenging reading may be described as a kind of reading that shows engagement with and resistance to literature. Engagement with literature means that readers should be able to move beyond mere solipsistic reading (Rabinowitz and Smith 1988) in order to take into account the particular conventions of the literary text, linked to its medium, format and genre, for example, while being able to become reflexive, fully engrossed in the arguments the literary text implies. Challenging reading also includes resisting reading, a notion signifying an empowered and vigorous reading stance (Rabinowitz and Smith 1988). Resisting readers are capable of questioning arguably the dominant interpretation of the text or what others see as the single textual meaning. They are encouraged to read literature using the cultural values and belief systems of their own era (or even against them), and thus they are able to question and critique the ideology proposed by the text. This kind of reading involves 'a New Historicism's perspective' (Johnson and Freedman 2006: 49–51) that allows readers to interpret a classic or a canonical text according to current beliefs and attitudes towards the premises of the text. The literary work is seen not merely as an artefact of a certain time period but as a product eventually open to new interpretations through space and time. In the project it was noticeable that students adopted almost instinctively this revisionist stance in their readings of both plays.

Four dimensions of challenging texts: Implications for the classroom

How may we define the fundamental characteristics of a challenging text? In what ways could we implement them in the classroom, reshaping them as questions, topics of discussion and activities for the students? I have followed a four-dimensional taxonomy influenced by the basic tenets of critical pedagogy (Groenke and Scherff 2010: 105–8), slightly adapted for the purposes of this project and applied to *Prince of Denmark*. Below are given four cardinal characteristics of a challenging text, followed by some representative examples of the coordinating activities and topics for discussion.

1. Disrupting the commonplace

In what ways does *Prince of Denmark* disrupt, problematize or deconstruct the conventional image of Ophelia as the silenced, betrayed and marginalized woman? In what ways does the adolescent Ophelia cause the revision of her standard image in the Shakespearean play? In what ways might Ophelia, either Shakespeare's or Lesslie's, be seen as a girl of the twenty-first century? What might be meant by the 'Ophelia-ization' of contemporary teenage girls (Hulbert 2010: 199)? What messages about femininity and masculinity are conveyed by Lesslie's text? Do you see Lesslie's Elsinore as a prison for young Hamlet? Do you see Shakespeare's Denmark as a prison for Hamlet? How would you interpret Horatio's lines: 'I am a scholar [...] As my brain is my Elsinore, I have nothing to gain from you but the approval of my own conscience' (Lesslie 2012: 183). What messages about political power, oppression and violence are conveyed by the text?

2. Interrogating multiple viewpoints

Discuss in what ways *Prince of Denmark* expands or contradicts the original play. Is young Hamlet a royal heir or a false master? Is it mankind's duty to accept the future as handed down, or to arm oneself against the will of fate and carve out one's own fortune? What role might *Prince of Denmark* play in (re)conceptualizing Hamlet's relationship with his father and with his uncle? Playing the game of 'what if' (Shepherd 1991: 99): What if Hamlet had not gone to Wittenberg? What if Gertrude and Ophelia had had a scene together? (See also Bland 2018b: 51, on scripting missing scenes between female characters.)

3. Focusing on sociopolitical, cultural and anthropological issues

Discuss in class the contemporary nuances of the lines 'whoever comes to power, there shall be no escape from bloodshed' or 'The rest [...] is always violence' (Lesslie 2012: 197). In the light of both plays, consider the following phrase: 'If thought kills action, then action must be thoughtless' (Critchley and Webster 2013: 11). Is there a moral for us to draw from the *Prince of Denmark*?

4. Taking action

This is the ultimate goal of reading according to critical pedagogy discourse. By reading challenging texts, the reader gains an enlightened consciousness and therefore seeks taking active part in the world, interrogating conditions of injustice, oppression, or social malevolence. Common teaching practices in this category culminate in several activities for the students such as:

- Write an article for a popular women's magazine, or create an audio or video clip, reversing and deconstructing the stereotyped icons of Ophelia as predominantly represented in painting, photography, psychiatry, and literature, as well as in theatre.

- Watch singer-songwriters and bands perform recent songs inspired by Ophelia (e.g. Natalie Merchant, Marika Hackman and Kula Shaker). How does the interpretation in each song compare with Lesslie's or Shakespeare's Ophelia? Listen to the lyrics, get inspired by the visual images, and try to write your own song for Ophelia.

'Speak to me': Students' responses to *Prince of Denmark*

The ELT students, both male and female, felt deeply impressed by the way Lesslie represented Ophelia as a clever and sensible teenager in love. Many students articulated the idea that Ophelia is actually the only figure in the play that is truly high-spirited and independent-minded. She stays true to her feelings and loyal to herself while struggling with the constraints of her 'boyish' times (Lesslie 2012: 182). The reading of the play led students to a thorough reconsideration of Ophelia as a character in *Hamlet*. Even in Shakespeare, they said, Ophelia is more courageous than Hamlet who is not able to kill himself, nor can he kill the usurper king, all the while hesitating 'and dreaming of a redeeming, cataclysmic violence' (Critchley and Webster 2013: 5).

The bravura of Hamlet and Ophelia at the brook, where Ophelia sees herself in the watery mirror, generated interesting discussion between students. This scene is heavily invested with metafictional playfulness, breaking the ontological borders between theatrical illusion and reality, and thus alerting the reader to the artifice of the characters. What Ophelia sees in the mirror seems to be her long-lasting afterlife as iconic subject matter of artistic imagination. The reflecting surface of the water multiplies her mise-en-abyme image endlessly, regenerating and reinventing her as the par-excellence figure of girlhood, innocence, mermaid-like beauty and female malady.

Furthermore, *Prince of Denmark* offered many cues to the students for speculation and deep reading on the gap between action and thought, and Hamlet's famous procrastination that students felt were at the core of both plays. Some students endorsed the phrase of Laertes that some people (as well as ironically Laertes himself) are 'brooding solipsists [...] paralysed by soliloquy' (Lesslie 2012: 178). Some students favoured the opinion that Hamlet's infinite self-reflexivity in the original is a real gift that privileges the individual with extraordinary insight into themselves and the genuine knowledge of the world. On the whole, the students were highly stimulated by the fact that Lesslie complicated the readers' empathy for Hamlet, diffusing it among the other characters.

The ending of the play: 'The rest [...] is always violence' and 'whoever comes to power, there shall be no escape from bloodshed' (Lesslie 2012: 197) was considered by the students as the epitome of Lesslie's poignant re-vision of the Shakespearean play, a reimagining that penetrates by its awareness of mortality and constant sense of inexorable fate. However the play is not only about the tragic fate of the heroes and heroine; it somehow raises them above any conjuncture of circumstances, providing a variation on the theme of eternal rottenness and human suffering. The play points to the same ineluctable violence that comes and returns persistently every time history itself is repeated. Not, of course, as farce but always as tragedy.

Conclusion

This chapter brought together two texts very close and at the same time very different to each other, namely the masterpiece of *Hamlet* and its radical contemporary adaptation for a young audience by Michael Lesslie. Students were invited to offer interpretative and intertextual readings to these texts in order to find as many nuances as possible, in the texts themselves and in other associated discourses as well, gaining additional pleasure in seeking this variety. The students in the project were already profoundly experienced and proficient as readers; during the project they blended idiosyncratic and more systematic and articulated ways of reading to achieve a fuller, rich interpretation, that does justice to the artistic complexity of the texts. However, when reading a challenging piece like *Prince of Denmark*, less proficient students will also have the chance to encounter a vast array of concepts, notions and perspectives that shape our understanding of life, and to negotiate reading as an enterprise of encountering the world from a number of different, even contradictory perspectives, and making sense of it. *Prince of Denmark* raises its own set of challenging questions that very often resist or enrich interpretations of the canonized original. The powerful one-act play displays unique characteristics: its artistic complexity, its openness to interpretation, its responsiveness to contemporary problems, and its vivid depiction of adolescent psychology, makes it an ideal choice for innovative work with secondary students.

Challenging works like *Prince of Denmark* can have a potentially liberating effect on the lives and minds of teenagers. Spiritual deprivation and indifference, even intellectual idleness, may be prevented, transforming readers into actively thinking individuals with a purpose in life, and preparing them to be free and autonomous members of society. Challenging texts can also help students maintain their curiosity, keeping themselves in a state of mental vividness. Burke (2010), citing Neil Postman, refers to the aphorism: Children enter school as question marks and leave as periods. This is why it is essential for them to acquire 'an intellectual flexibility that allows them to generate a range of questions as well as possible answers' (Burke 2010: 3). Challenging texts can undoubtedly offer readers panache and audacity, suggesting to them how to position themselves in the world and making them ready to leave a bold, distinctive imprint in the world; to pose and live with many questions, such as: *To be, or not to be?*

RECOMMENDATIONS

- Most great actors have performed Hamlet, and his best known soliloquy 'To be, or not to be, that is the question' can be watched on YouTube, performed by Laurence Olivier, Richard Burton, Mel Gibson, Kenneth Branagh, Ethan Hawke, David Tennant, Benedict Cumberbatch and Adrian Lester. Students might review the performances, compare the actors' interpretations, and try out for themselves.

- Ophelia is one of the best known literary female victims of all time. Students might consider whether hashtag activism, such as the Me Too campaign, can be truly empowering for women in similar situations.

Bibliography

Carbone, Courtney (2015), *srsly Hamlet (OMG Shakespeare)*, New York: Random House.

Clarke, Mary Cowden (1850–52/2009), *The Girlhood of Shakespeare's Heroines* (3 vols), Cambridge: Cambridge University Press.

Fiedler, Lisa (2003), *Dating Hamlet: Ophelia's Story*, New York: Flamingo Collins Books.

Klein, Lisa (2008), *Ophelia. A Novel*, New York: Bloomsbury.

Lesslie, Michael (2012), 'Prince of Denmark', in *Connections 2012: Plays for Young People, National Theatre*, London: Methuen Drama: pp. 163–201.

Marsden, John (2008), *Hamlet*, Melbourne: Text Publishing.

Ray, Michelle (2011), *Falling for Hamlet*, New York: Poppy.

Shakespeare, William (2006), *Hamlet*, edited by Ann Thompson and Neil Taylor, The Arden Shakespeare, London: Cengage Learning.

Updike, John (2000), *Gertrude and Claudius: A Novel*, New York: Random House.

Williams, Marcia (2000), *Mr. William Shakespeare's Plays*, London: Walker.

Zindel, Lizabeth (2014), *A Girl, a Ghost and the Hollywood Hills*, New York: Viking.

References

Banks, Anthony (2012), 'Ideas for staging and production', in *Connections 2012: Plays for Young People, National Theatre*, London: Methuen Drama: pp. 205–206.

Barthes, Roland (1988), *The Semiotic Challenge*, trans. Richard Howard, Oxford: Blackwell.

Bland, Janice (2013), *Children's Literature and Learner Empowerment: Children and Teenagers in English Language Education*, London: Bloomsbury Academic.

Bland, Janice (2018b), 'Playscript and screenplay: Creativity with J.K. Rowling's Wizarding World', in Janice Bland (ed.), *Using Literature in English Language Education: Challenging Reading for 8–18 Year Olds*, London: Bloomsbury Academic, pp. 41–61.

Burke, Jim (2010), *What's the Big Idea? Question-Driven Units to Motivate Reading, Writing, and Thinking*, Portsmouth, NH: Heinemann.

Christensen, Linda (2000), *Reading, Writing, and Rising Up: Teaching about Social Justice and the Power of the Written Word*, Milwaukee, Wisconsin: Rethinking Schools.

Christensen, Linda (2009), *Teaching for Joy and Justice: Re-imagining the Language Arts in the Classroom*, Milwaukee, Wisconsin: Rethinking Schools.

Critchley, Simon and Webster, Jamieson (2013), *The Hamlet Doctrine*, London: Verso.

Darder, Antonia, Baltodano, Marta and Torres, Rodolfo (2009), *The Critical Pedagogy Reader* (2nd edn), New York: Routledge.

Desmet, Christy and Sawyer, Robert (1999), *Shakespeare and Appropriation*, London: Routledge.

Edwards, Philip (2003), 'Introduction' in Philip Edwards (ed.), *Hamlet, Prince of Denmark*, (updated edn), Cambridge: Cambridge University Press, pp. 1–82.

Evans, Janet (2015), 'Picturebooks as strange, challenging and controversial texts', in Janet Evans (ed.), *Challenging and Controversial Picturebooks: Creative and Critical Responses to Visual Texts*, London and New York: Routledge, pp. 3–32.

Godfrey, Kate (2012), 'Exercises for use in rehearsal', in *Connections 2012: Plays for Young People, National Theatre*, London: Methuen Drama, pp. 201–3.

Groenke, Susan and Scherff, Lisa (2010), *Teaching YA Lit Through Differentiated Instruction*, Urbana, IL: National Council of Teachers of English.

Hateley, Erica (2009), *Shakespeare in Children's Literature: Gender and Cultural Capital*, New York: Routledge.

Hilton, Mary and Nikolajeva, Maria (2012), 'Introduction. Time of turmoil', in Mary Hilton and Maria Nikolajeva (eds), *Contemporary Adolescent Literature and Culture: The Emergent Adult*, Farnham, Surrey: Ashgate, pp. 1–16.

Hulbert, Jennifer (2010), '*Adolescence, thy name is Ophelia*': The Ophelia-ization of the contemporary teenage girl', in Jennifer Hulbert, Kevin Wetmore and Robert York (eds), *Shakespeare and Youth Culture*, New York: Palgrave/Macmillan, 199–220.

Hutcheon, Linda (2006), *A Theory of Adaptation*, New York: Routledge.

Johnson, Holly and Freedman, Lauren (2006), *Developing Critical Awareness at the Middle Level: Using Texts as Tools for Critique and Pleasure* (2nd edn), Newark, DE: International Reading Association.

Lanier, Douglas (2010), 'Recent Shakespeare adaptation and the mutation of cultural capital', *Shakespeare Studies*, 38: 104–13.

Macedo, Donald and Freire, Paulo (1987), *Literacy: Reading the Word and the World*, Westport, CT: Bergin and Carvey.

MacLeod, Mark (2013), 'Adapting and parodying Shakespeare for young adults: John Marsden's *Hamlet* and Andy Griffiths' *Just Macbeth!*', in Anja Müller (ed.), *Adapting Canonical Texts in Children's Literature*, London: Bloomsbury, pp. 77–93.

Müller, Anja (2013), 'Shakespeare comic books: Visualizing the Bard for a young audience', in Anja Müller (ed.), *Adapting Canonical Texts in Children's Literature*, London: Bloomsbury, pp. 95–111.

Peterson, Ralph and Eeds, Maryann (1990), *Grand Conversations: Literature Groups in Action*, New York: Scholastic.

Probst, Robert (1988), 'Dialogue with the text', *English Journal*, 77/1: 32–8.

Probst, Robert (2004), *Response and Analysis: Teaching Literature in Secondary School* (2nd edn), Portsmouth, NH: Heinemann.

Rabinowitz, Peter and Smith, Michael (1988), *Authorizing Readers: Resistance and Respect in the Teaching of Literature*, New York: Teachers College Press.

Rich, Adrienne (1972), 'When we dead awaken: Writing as re-vision', *College English*, 34/1: 18–30.

Rokison, Abigail (2013), *Shakespeare for Young People: Productions, Versions and Adaptations*, London: Bloomsbury.

Rose, Jacqueline (2002), 'Sexuality in the reading of Shakespeare: *Hamlet* and *Measure for Measure*', in John Drakakis (ed.), *Alternative Shakespeares* (2nd edn), New York: Routledge, pp. 97–120.

Seelinger Trites, Roberta (2000), *Disturbing the Universe: Power and Repression in Adolescent Literature*, Iowa City: Iowa University Press.

Shepherd, Simon (1991), 'Acting against bardom: Some utopian thoughts on workshops', in Lesley Aers and Nigel Wheale (eds), *Shakespeare in the Changing Curriculum*, London: Routledge, 88–107.

Showalter, Elaine (1985), 'Representing Ophelia: Women, madness, and the responsibilities of feminist criticism,' in Patricia Parker and Geoffrey Hartman (eds), Shakespeare *and the Question of Theory*, London: Methuen, pp. 77–94.

Tosi, Laura (2013), 'Shakespeare for girls: Victorian versus contemporary prose versions of *Hamlet* and *The Merchant of Venice*', in Anja Müller (ed.), *Adapting Canonical Texts in Children's Literature*, London: Bloomsbury, pp. 95–111.

Tyson, Lois (2014), *Critical Theory Today: A User-Friendly Guide* (3rd edn), New York: Routledge.

PART THREE

Embracing the challenges

14

Negotiating the challenges of reading literature: Teachers reporting on their practice

Sam Duncan and Amos Paran

Scholars examining the role of literature in language teaching have, over the years, pointed out the paucity of empirical research in this field. Carter (2007: 11) suggests that one of the 'challenges for future work at the interfaces of pedagogy, language and literature' is the need 'to address the absence of empirical classroom-based research and to begin to ensure that very proper concerns with pedagogic process are better rooted in verifiable evidence of classroom practice'. Paran (2008) points out that the need for additional research has been highlighted both by supporters of using literature in language teaching (e.g. Shanahan 1997) and by its critics (see Edmondson 1997). He goes on to observe that much of the empirical research extant is in tertiary settings, with little of it conducted in secondary settings, which is where most language teaching in the world is carried out.

The situation has not changed considerably in the decade since Carter (2007) and Paran (2008). Although recently there have been a number of publications of empirical studies into the way literature plays out in the foreign or second language (L2) classroom and with L2 learners and teachers (Jones and Carter 2011, Nguyen 2016, the chapters in Part II of Teranishi, Saito and Wales 2015, Thoms 2014), including secondary school settings (Bloemert, Jansen and van de Grift 2016, Bloemert, Paran, Jansen and van de Grift 2017, Mourão 2013), such studies are in fact still infrequent. Paesani (2011), in an article examining the language–literature interface in foreign language (FL) teaching in the United States, highlights that 'very little of the existing scholarship on language–literature pedagogy is empirical in nature; most published articles provide examples of pedagogical and curricular best practices and policy statements' (2011: 164–5). And although Hall (2015) surveys the main areas in which literature in language teaching developed between 2005 and 2015, many of the developments seem to have actually been in teaching and resources rather than empirical research. Indeed, in a systematic review of studies of stylistics in language teaching, Fogal (2015) was able to find only thirteen empirical studies since 1997.

Our chapter is therefore intended as a contribution to empirical research in this area, based on the research project, 'The Effectiveness of Literature on Acquisition of Language Skills and Intercultural Understanding in the High School Context' (Duncan and Paran 2017).[1] This project looked at the use of literature in language teaching in the frame of the International Baccalaureate Diploma Programme (IB DP), a school leaving/university preparation programme designed for secondary school students aged between 16 and 19 and delivered worldwide. As part of the programme, students are required to take both a Language A, which is defined by the International Baccalaureate Diploma Programme Subject Brief as the student's 'best language' (IB DP SB 2014: np), which focuses on literary study, and a Language B, characterized as an 'additional language'. Language B courses are 'designed for students who possess a degree of knowledge and experience in the target language' (IB DP SB 2014: np). They are available at either Standard or Higher Level, which differ in that students taking a Language B at Higher Level are required to read at least two literary texts. The two texts are assessed by a creative assignment in which students have to write a creative piece based on one of the two literary texts, as well as append an explanation and a rationale for their own creative output. This study was commissioned by the International Baccalaureate Organization (IBO) and involved a mixed-methods research design. Crucially, although we include possible implications for practice in our discussion section, this study did not seek to produce recommendations for best practice: rather, we aimed to develop a more nuanced, empirically based understanding of how literary texts are actually used with IB DP Language B students.

The study

One element in our study was a 118-item online questionnaire, completed by 264 respondents from across the globe, teaching seventeen different languages. The second element consisted of case studies of three IB schools, two private and one state school, located in three different European countries (because we identify the educational context, we do not identify the countries in order not to compromise anonymity). In two of these schools the teaching language was English, and in the third the teaching language was French. The data for the case studies was generated through school visits consisting of lesson observations, student focus groups (including qualitative questionnaires) and semi-structured interviews with teachers. In this chapter we report on the findings from the teacher interviews in the three case studies.

To date, only a few studies have looked at teachers' views of using literature in language teaching. Harlow and Muyskens (1994), a survey of fifty-four teachers of Spanish and French in US universities, only touched on literature tangentially, showing that it was ranked very low, in eleventh place, in the list of goals for language teaching. Gilroy (1995) and Jones and Carter (2011), two small-scale studies investigating the views of English language teachers in the UK Higher Education sector, both document overall positive views of literature as a resource in language teaching.

The main aim of our own study was to explore the factors that teachers take into account when choosing literary texts for use in their classrooms; the ways in which teachers use literary texts and the types of activities they employ; and the views of teachers and learners on the impact of literary texts on language learning. For this chapter we took a fresh look at the data from our teacher interviews to understand the way in which teachers negotiated the challenges of reading literary texts.

In a combination of group and individual interviews, we interviewed twelve teachers at School A, fourteen teachers at School B and nine teachers at School C. The thirty-two teachers we interviewed taught a variety of languages: English, French, German, Italian, Japanese, Mandarin, Russian and Spanish. Although obviously our interviewees cannot be taken to represent the wider population of Language B teachers on IB programmes, they did represent the range of languages represented in the responses to our questionnaire (where English, French, Mandarin, Spanish and German were the most widely taught languages). However, it is important to remember that there was a strong self-selection element in this study as the teachers who teach Literature B Higher Level are likely to be a priori more enthusiastic about literature and teaching literature (as was the case with our questionnaire respondents, who responded with means of above five on a six-point Likert scale when asked about the importance of literature in their own lives and the importance of enjoying literature).

Interviews lasted between twenty and forty minutes. Our interviewees mostly spoke English with a high degree of fluency and accuracy, and most of the interviews were held in English. Two interviews were conducted in French, and one in Spanish. Some of the individual interviews included reflection by the teacher on a lesson we had observed, and in some cases incorporated an element of stimulated recall (Gass and Mackey 2000). Our semi-structured interview schedule consisted of a number of specific questions (e.g. 'Tell me about your favourite or most successful lesson which involved literature') as well as a list of general points, such as vocabulary, length of text and so forth, which we raised as and when appropriate. This flexibility allowed us to probe areas of interest to our study while improvising and moving with teachers' particular interests and preoccupations.

The interviews were audio-recorded and transcribed verbatim. The interview transcripts were then analysed through a process of data immersion, listening and reading repeatedly (Becker 1986), followed by inductive thematic coding (Braun and Clarke 2006), supported by NVivo software.

We now turn to a presentation of the main findings of our interviews regarding the ways in which teachers negotiated the challenges of reading and studying literature in their Language B classrooms. We first explore how the teachers in our study conceptualized the challenges of reading literature and then present the ways in which they used text choice, organization of reading and reading aloud to negotiate these challenges.

The challenges

The teachers we interviewed identified clear challenges in reading literary texts with their secondary-school language B students, particularly around 'difficulty' in various forms. Teachers felt that many literary texts are 'too difficult' (B3J)[2] either conceptually or in terms of language – the breadth and depth of vocabulary as well as language structures. They also expressed their sense of the challenge posed by limited class time, feeling that literature can be 'too time consuming', taking time which they may need to prioritize for other work, such as 'revising grammar' (A6G). A number of teachers also felt that a challenge is presented by their learners' expectations or experiences of reading in a foreign language, which have created a fear of unfamiliar vocabulary. This necessitates 'changing their reading habits' so students grasp that they may not always 'need to understand every word' (B8FS).

In terms of language, one teacher emphasized the potential 'scary'-ness of authentic texts for those used to reading highly graded, controlled texts (B10FS). A different type of fear was expressed by several teachers who felt that a key challenge is the reputed nature of canonical literature, or rather what we would call Literature with 'a capital L' (McRae 1991: vii), which for many teachers is characterized by conceptual and linguistic difficulty and (arguably) admired precisely for a lack of accessibility. For this reason, one teacher explained, some students see literature as 'too big, too "I can't access that" ' (A8G).

One teacher discussed a challenge which was not raised by other teachers, but is nevertheless worth pointing out here, in order to highlight the multiplicity of challenges perceived. This teacher (A2G) felt that discussion around literary texts may get students so animated that they move into their mother tongues or more familiar languages (such as the school's teaching language) to discuss the topic, rather than speaking in the target language. This point highlights the complexity of analysing the potential challenges posed by literary texts, as every aspect of challenge literature presents is also an opportunity, if negotiated well, as we will explore below.

Negotiating challenges through text choice

The main way in which our interviewees negotiated the challenge of reading literature was through their choice of which texts to read. Since the IB DP curriculum does not list any specific texts for study, teachers are free to choose whichever text they thought would suit their learners and would lend itself well to the assessment. In this respect there was a strong washback effect – influence of assessment on teaching (Alderson and Wall 1993) – noticeable in our interviews. In some cases teachers would change their choice from year to year, though in other cases we found that teachers in different schools had all chosen the same pieces. Teachers searched for texts on particularly engaging topics, texts they were passionate about themselves, texts that they felt students, or particular groups of students, would relate to or enjoy. They chose shorter texts, texts written in 'less difficult' language, texts they felt students may already be partially familiar with, texts that had been made into films or were currently being performed in the theatre. Teachers also allowed students to choose their own texts.

Importantly, teachers made choices related to the nature of the challenge they perceived that literature poses. Some teachers felt that for some of their groups, literature presented a challenge primarily because of the lower or limited language level of the students; the teachers therefore made choices driven by the desire to make literature as accessible as possible. Others felt that literature was a challenge primarily because literature was not attractive to their students (because of past experience or perceptions of conceptual difficulty or density) and so made choices driven by the desire to make literature as appealing as possible.

One teacher (C9FE) highlighted the distinction between these two priorities, speaking of his (stronger) English class and his (weaker) French class: 'So for English I adapted it more to the contents and that the work would trigger their interests and for French I adapted it to their level and how the work would enhance their linguistic skills [...] bearing in mind they have only been speaking French for a year or a year and a half'. This teacher thus conceptualizes the challenge and the solution as two poles: accessibility on the one hand and appeal on the other. In the sections below, we explore teacher choices as related to these two poles.

Text choice: Accessibility

Teachers chose texts that they felt would be more accessible (frequently using this term) for their students. They spoke of texts of shorter length, lower linguistic difficulty, potential familiarity and more relatable. Several teachers noted the importance of finding texts that are 'not too long or fairly approachable linguistically' (C9FE) as part of the search for something that students 'are not going to find too overwhelming' (B8FS). Teacher B8FS highlights the decision-making process in such cases, speaking about *Une femme* (Ernaux 1987), which was the first book she had read with her class: 'that's why with the first book, it's only about 100 pages and the style of writing [...] is quite straight-forward in terms of tense, but it's quite interesting [...] because it's all about whether, how you can get to the truth' (B8FS). Crucially, this teacher notes the inseparability of accessibility and appeal: there is no point in something being accessible if it does not also appeal. Similarly, another teacher spoke about her preference for short stories 'that could be appealing to them and not too difficult to read' (A5S). She went on to note that shorter texts are also a way to try something out and get a better sense of student preferences, suggesting that more accessible texts can help you discover what students find more - or less - appealing.

Attention to length and linguistic difficulty, however, was not the only way that teachers felt they could choose accessible texts. A teacher of German (C5G) explained that he chose to read the Brothers Grimm's fairy tales because of 'the length, the cultural importance, the general – all students will know lots of the stories already so maybe then – at some point in their life they have loved them so they have some sort of connection to them already, and as well quite interesting'. Another German teacher (B1G) argued that she chose *Der Vorleser* (Schlink 1995) not primarily because of its length or the existence of a film version (though this was also a factor; see below), but because the teenage narrator makes the text easier for young people to relate to: 'the narrator is a fifteen-year-old and it's quite nice for students who have never been faced with literature before to deal with something they find reasonably accessible, so that seemed to be quite an obvious choice'.

A teacher of Spanish (A5S) also felt that texts which are about young people were more accessible to her secondary school students.

Text choice: Appeal

The teachers above stressed that texts with a teenage narrator or teenage characters make it easier for their teenage students to 'get it', which also potentially makes the texts more appealing. Certainly one of the key ways that teachers in our study tried to manage or negotiate the challenges posed by literature was through choosing texts that they felt would appeal to their students, that is texts they felt students would enjoy, be interested in or motivated by. Several Spanish teachers, for example, chose *La casa de Bernarda Alba* (Lorca 1945) because they felt the topic would appeal: 'it's about women and it's about wives, so they have a lot to say' (A5S). A teacher of French (A7F) explained that he also chooses text types that he feels will appeal to his students, not just topics. If a group expresses an interest in the theatre, for example, he will choose a play. Teachers also reported making choices by considering the overall experience across a year or two of study, and so chose texts that would appeal in contrast to each other or meet a wider range of student preferences, for example choosing contrasting genres or time periods.

Rather than trying to anticipate what students would find appealing, some teachers encouraged their students to have an input in text choice, allowing students to select texts they find more appealing and getting students more motivated in the process. Teacher A7F explained: 'I presented five or six books to them and I explained what kind of books they were, what were the main themes, the main topics, and we had a class discussion about what kind of topics they would like to cover. I also told them about how difficult the books were to study.' Similarly, teacher A5S spoke of a time when 'I offered them two possibilities of books. And the girls by themselves chose one and the boys chose the García Márquez one [...]. They had to explain one to each other, I mean the girls to the boys and the boys to the girls, what was going on in their books and why they were feeling that this book was much more interesting than the other'. Teacher A7F also noted that giving students a choice of text is 'a lot more work but I find the class works so much better when they have some sort of decision to make, when they are involved in the process of choosing a book, it makes a massive difference'.

One issue that was raised by the majority of teachers was the theme or the topic of the text. This too played a part in creating appeal: A7F noted that choosing books that match topics students are already studying, such as stereotypes, also potentially increases accessibility and appeal.

Text choice: Ways into texts

In addition to choosing texts which they felt were accessible and appealing to their students (and allowing students to make their own choices), we found that teachers chose some texts because they had identified ways into these texts that would make them either more appealing or more accessible. Several teachers noted the importance of choosing texts that the teacher loves and knows well. They felt that teachers must love the literature they are teaching in order to make the text more appealing to their students, 'they've got to be convinced by your passion and your enjoyment' (B9I); 'I could talk about it (*The Master and Margarita*, [Bulgakov 1967]) as something I enjoyed, and that would help as well to enthuse students' (B6R). Just as important, though, was the idea of knowing the text very well in order to make the text more accessible to their students: Teacher B8FS suggested that 'it's always important to have something that the teacher themselves is (*sic*) very confident with and familiar with and knows very well' and is therefore better placed to identify 'ways in' to the reading of challenging texts. In this way, teacher 'passion' and teacher knowledge of or confidence with a text becomes a valuable tool for negotiating challenge.

Finally, several teachers argued that the availability of a film of the literary work provides an important tool for both accessibility and appeal. A German teacher (B1G) who chose *Der Vorleser* (Schlink 1995) summed this up: 'and then you've got the film for support, in terms of just quickly understanding what happens, it's a short cut in a way, if you want, they watch it and then they are au fait with the storyline such as it is and they can then access the text'.

Text choice: An interplay of factors

Overall, then, our data provides a picture of teachers choosing texts in ways that they feel will work against the potential difficulties of literature, both linguistic and motivational. We see teachers choosing texts that they feel will be more accessible or more appealing, involving students in the choice of texts and teachers choosing texts because of the tools presented by their own existing knowledge or passions, and existing film versions. But this is still a complex picture, where every teacher interviewed expressed multiple motivations for their choices, weighing up accessibility with appeal and student choice of text with practicalities like availability of materials and teacher preparedness. It is also a picture where decisions were made based on teacher assessments of the nature of a group and its particular challenges and preferences.

Negotiating challenges through the organization of reading

Teachers also negotiated challenges through the way they organized the reading of the literary texts. While, as previously, many practices were common to different teachers, there were also some notable differences in what teachers presented as the ideal way to organize the reading in order to support student understanding and wider language development.

The ideal of 'read it all together'

Two teachers explained that they preferred to read the whole of the literary text together in class time, and a third suggested that she would like to if time allowed. Yet another, teacher A9G, made a distinction between plays and novels: she would read most of a play in class, but organize the reading differently for novels (see below). Teacher A1E explained: 'in the past I told you I used to make them read the text at home because I didn't want to waste class time'; however, she found that students did not actually do the reading, and so 'it's the first time that I'm doing it like that. It feels like you are cheating – you're being paid to teach and yet you're reading a text. But, to be honest, if I have to compare the way I used to do it and the way we're doing it this time, I think this time is much more effective'. This teacher went on to clarify that in this way she knows that the students have actually read the whole text. Similarly, teacher C8S also aims to read the entire literary text together in class, 'because I want to make sure that they understood everything. Or they can ask me questions'. She reads aloud, gets students to read aloud and asks students to read silently together in class time. In both cases, what these teachers prioritized was ensuring that their students read all of the text, often by reading aloud together; in other cases it seemed that teachers were using reading aloud as a form of scaffolding: teachers used the advantages of the shared process of reading aloud, in the same physical space, where questions could be asked and where intonation and body language would clarify meaning and aid comprehension. For all of these teachers, reading the literary text in class usually meant reading it aloud.

The ideal of 'read at home and spend class time doing activities with it together'

A different ideal was expressed by teacher C5G, who aimed for students to do the reading at home so they could devote their time together in class to activities, presentations and other work around the text. This teacher's argument was not just that class time is better spent on what students cannot do alone at home (talk around the text) but also that reading together, particularly aloud, 'doesn't work'; with one particular class he felt 'half of the class just wandering or sniggering away'. He also felt that 'reading is an individual experience rather', to be done at the student's own pace, elsewhere. What Teacher C5G wants to be shared, then, is not the reading but the work on what has been read.

Other teachers, too, seemed to aim for students to read most of the text at home, with class time spent on activities which develop, foster and encourage an understanding of what was read, including the understanding of words and phrases; the understanding of plot and characters; and understandings of larger themes. These activities include discussions, debates, student presentations, creation of mind-maps around characters, describing scenes, themes and characters and sharing student writing based on the texts, such as reviews or blogs. Teachers would read, or ask students to read, short extracts in class but mainly used class time to support the understanding of text already read at home.

Reading at home and in class: 'It's a balancing act'

Many teachers, unsurprisingly, aimed for a mixture, organizing the reading so that some was done together in class and some done at home, and ensuring that their time together was spent both reading together (silent and aloud) and discussing or exploring what was read. Teacher A7F provided a rationale for this, based on the idea of variety: 'At home, in the classroom, reading silently, reading aloud. We just vary because if you were doing the same thing all the time it would be boring.' Teacher B1G described the nature of the balance she is looking for:

> To some extent, it's a question of getting the balance right between getting them to read enough, and also in enough detail. [...] It's good to get them to do reading outside class and then to come back and go over bits that they've read so they have time to see things, so we'll take key moments from the text [...] we'll look at those in particular over the course of the term rather than just going over rigorously chapter by chapter [...] I'd give them each a chapter to read for homework and they are then responsible for giving the others a summary of what happens and the others take notes.

Some teachers felt that this balance shifted as they progressed through a text, with more reading together earlier in the process, and less later.

Using film as an organizational factor

The use of film also emerged as a factor in how teachers organized reading to negotiate the challenges of using literature. Two teachers of Russian (B6R and B5R) discussed how they had used a film of the story *The Lady with the Little Dog* (Chekhov 1899), chosen because 'every single scene is in the film' (B6R). Teacher B5R said, 'we didn't literally read [...] the whole thing, I'd pick paragraphs and they'd read at home but the film filled in all the gaps' (B5R). Likewise, a teacher of Italian (B9I) explained that to read the novel *Il giorno della civetta* (Sciascia 1961) they started reading it together, stopping to talk through vocabulary, themes and history, but in a few weeks when they are all more 'into' the book, and when she can see 'that they are doing fine', she will get them to do more of the reading at home, using the film for support:

> We will read it, we will read it, we will read it and then [...] if I'm running short of time, I might gain some time in the middle with [the film]. You have to read the beginning and you have to read the end, but if you need to gain some time it's there [the film].

The use of film, for these teachers, is not only as a potential tool for scaffolding understanding, as noted above, but also a tool in organizing the reading, or 'getting through' the text itself.

Negotiating challenges through reading aloud

An important factor in how teachers organized their reading was the use, or not, of reading aloud. Many teachers spoke of reading aloud as one of the tools at their disposal as teachers, with one teacher (A1E) noting that although she feels that reading aloud is something generally disapproved of, or disapproved of in teacher education circles, it was something she has come round to because her students 'insist on it [...] they are fighting over who gets to read,' and so feels 'maybe there needs to come a rethinking about this whole reading aloud'. Teachers spoke of using reading aloud to develop students' reading automaticity and pronunciation skills but also emphasized reading aloud as a way to create a shared experience supporting the reading of literature: 'on a basic level, have we all read it properly, can I say that they've all read it properly?' (B9I). Only one teacher (C5G) argued that reading aloud was not useful, both because students' attention would wander and because he saw silent reading as more natural (see above). These uses of reading aloud were presented as consisting of three interrelated aspects: reading aloud to scaffold understanding, reading aloud as a tool for close reading or reflection and reading aloud as literary experience, as we discuss below.

Reading aloud to scaffold understanding

Teachers certainly used reading aloud as a way to scaffold or support understanding of words, plot, character and themes, through creating a shared experience of everyone hearing the same words at the same time, stopping to talk together about those words, asking and answering questions:

> I know that people say that if you read aloud you don't remember what you've read but I have actually not found that to be true and it means that I know I can go through vocabulary with them when it comes up [...] lots of people [colleagues] do it so they can check pronunciation, understanding as they go along (A1E).

Teacher A8G describes how students read aloud 'to each other, to the whole group, without pressuring'; the class would then 'discuss what we just read, what is happening there [...] to give them a kind of global experience [...] trying to recap what happened in the last bit that we read maybe a page, two pages, three pages'. Teacher C8S echoes this: 'I like reading it aloud. And there are some bits I read them myself so they listen. I think it's also very important that they listen sometimes – they pay more attention [...] I want to make sure that they understand everything. Or they can ask me questions. Or there are doubts about something'. This use of reading aloud for concentrated, collective development of understanding is apparent in several teachers' increased use of reading aloud to start off a book and create a shared initial understanding: 'at the beginning definitely [we read aloud]. Because we need to get a sense of what the book is about, the language, the structure, so we do a lot of explaining' (A7F).

Reading aloud for close reading or reflection

Teacher A9G also explained that her classes only read the beginnings of novels aloud and then the reading is done by students at home alone, although they do sometimes 'just take little passages and reflect on them'. Teacher C9FE reads aloud 'for specific parts [...] particularly meaningful parts of books. Reading aloud would be one of the activities to identify, to study main passages, so to speak, of importance of the works'. An Italian teacher (B9I) notes that her class read particular 'extracts' aloud to capture 'what happens, what is he getting at, the writer, what is he trying to convey here, what is the purpose of this section of the book [...], the overarching thing I wanted them to take away, the one main thing'. Here, the desired shared experience is not the working through the whole text but a shared experience of a particular passage, a focused close reading.

Reading aloud as literary experience

Several teachers identified reading aloud as something they would do only or mainly with drama or poetry. Teacher A1E spoke about reading *An Inspector Calls* (Priestley 1945):

> ... they loved reading, they're fighting over who gets to read which part [...] I think actually reading aloud gives them a sense of security so that even kids who are very very shy feel that they can participate and join in and have a voice but don't need to worry about what they're going to say. (A1E)

Similarly, Teacher A9G described reading Ödön von Horváth's (1931) play *Geschichten aus dem Wiener Wald*:

> ... they very much enjoy reading it [...] [the characters] purport to be very nice people but the way they speak it turns – they show they're not. And they enjoy reading it. They enjoy each other – hearing how this person reads the character and how the other person . . .

In these examples, the reading aloud is a way of providing students with a more authentic experience of these plays, something potentially motivating as well as something that could scaffold understanding.

Discussion and conclusion

Our study is different from the previous studies exploring teachers' views of literature in foreign language teaching (Gilroy 1995, Harlow and Muyskens 1994, Jones and Carter 2011) in a number of ways. One is that all three previous studies were conducted in tertiary settings. Another difference is that in the context we were researching literature was part of the curriculum, rather than an option that teachers could choose (though the actual pieces that they taught were not prescribed, as we pointed out above). Most importantly, we were able to explore teachers' views and practices in greater detail than these studies, though in this chapter we have focused only on one aspect of their teaching: the way they conceptualized challenges in their classroom and the way they dealt with these challenges.

Our interviewees very clearly saw the challenges they faced and were constantly engaged in addressing them. Indeed, in addition to negotiating the challenge inherent in the use of literary texts, they also needed to negotiate the challenge of teaching literary texts for an external assessment, an issue that concerned all of them and which they addressed in a variety of ways.

As we have shown, one of the most important ways of addressing challenges was choice of text. It is important to stress that this was possible because the educational system that the teachers were working in enabled them to be flexible in their choices. Thus the autonomy of teachers plays an important part in the way in which challenges were negotiated, and in the fact that each of our interviewees negotiated their own way through these challenges. The teacher's own 'curricular heritage' (Bloemert et al. 2016) was thus able to come into play and interact with other factors in the choice of texts as well as in the choice of activities for these texts (Duncan and Paran 2017).

The implications from our study can be viewed from both a policy angle and a practical angle. In terms of policy, the picture that emerged suggests that affording teachers the autonomy to choose the literary texts that they use and teach in the language classroom enables them to balance accessibility and appeal, tailoring their choice to the specific class that they are working with. Our interviewees were all extremely passionate about literature, and an essential aspect was the possibility of choosing whichever piece they wanted (within the constraints of the assessment). Many of them discussed at length specific choices with specific classes, illustrating the care they took with these choices, which they viewed as crucial to success in the classroom. From a practical point of view, what came to the fore as important was the possibility of changing pedagogic approaches, balancing reading at home and in class, the different types of activity that teachers spoke about, and using reading aloud as a judicious tool for scaffolding learning. Perhaps most of all, the accounts we have gathered of teachers' uses of literature in foreign language teaching present the complex bundles of factors that influence teachers' choices of texts and activities, exposing the in- and out-of-class deliberations and decisions which are part of teachers' daily struggles and yet all too often not shared. It is our hope, as we have noted, that these will provoke reflection and discussion among teachers and managers that will challenge and develop practice.

One element of our study that is not apparent here is the views of the learners, and the way in which the teachers' own passion transfers to the learner, and is in fact another important way in which the challenge is negotiated. We therefore end with a quote from one of the learners we interviewed, talking about reading *The Master and Margarita* (Bulgakov 1947). This summarizes what we feel is the main reason for using literature in language teaching, and, indeed, shows how it is possible to overcome the challenges we have spoken about:

Author A: Should a teacher use literature as part of teaching a language?
Student: (…) it makes learning the language different. It changes the subject.
Author A: OK, how does it change the subject?
Student: Well, rather than talking about the weather you are talking about *Master and Margarita* in Russian, it's talking about whether God exists and Jesus and the devil being in Moscow. It's more interesting than the weather.

RECOMMENDATIONS

- The present study showed a large difference between teachers who had had training in using literature in the classroom and those who had not, including differences in the choice of format and genre for negotiating challenges of literary texts. Initial teacher education programmes should therefore expose student teachers to a range of literary texts, including poetry and plays, and to exploring how these materials can be used creatively. Initial teacher education should also devote time to focused work on how such texts can be used in a language education context.

- Reading aloud emerged as an important pedagogical tool when used creatively and flexibly. Initial teacher education should however devote time to exploring and demonstrating different activities for reading aloud and understanding the different affordances of this tool, to prevent teachers from just asking young learners and teenagers to read aloud round the class without preparation.

Notes

1 This study was funded by the International Baccalaureate Organisation. We would like to thank Heike Schröder, Research Manager at the IB Global Centre and Mary Garland, former Diploma Programme Curriculum Manager (Language Acquisition) for their invaluable support and contribution to this study. We would also like to thank the schools we visited and our interviewees for their willingness to take part in our study.

2 We identify each teacher according to their school (A, B or C), an ordinal number within the school, and the language or languages they teach. Thus

Teacher B3J taught in school B, was the third teacher we interviewed there, and teaches Japanese; teacher B10FS teaches in school B, was the tenth interviewee there, and teaches French and Spanish.

Bibliography

(The years given refer to date of first publication or first performance.)

Bulgakov, Mikhail Afanasievich (1967), *The Master and Margarita*, Paris: YMCA Press.
Chekhov, Anton (1899), *The Lady with the Little Dog*, Moscow: Russkaya Mysl.
Ernaux, Annie (1987), *Une Femme*, Paris: Gallimard.
Lorca, Federico García (1945), *La casa de Bernarda Alba*, Buenos Aires: Teatro Avenida.
Priestley, John Boynton (1945) *An Inspector Calls*, Moscow: Kamerny Theatre.
Schlink, Bernhard (1995), *Der Vorleser*, Zürich: Diogenes.
Sciascia, Leonardo (1961), *Il giorno della civetta*, Torino: Einaudi.
von Horváth, Ödön (1931), *Geschichten aus dem Wiener Wald*, Berlin: Deutsches Theater.

References

Alderson, Charles and Wall, Diane (1993), 'Does washback exist?' *Applied Linguistics*, 14/1: 115–29.
Becker, Howard (1986), *Writing for Social Scientists*, Chicago, IL: University of Chicago Press.
Bloemert, Jasmijn, Jansen, Ellen and van de Grift, Wim (2016), 'Exploring EFL literature approaches in Dutch secondary education', *Language, Culture and Curriculum*, 29/2: 169–88.
Bloemert, Jasmijn, Paran, Amos, Jansen, Ellen and van de Grift, Wim (2017), 'Students' perspective on the benefits of EFL literature education', *The Language Learning Journal*. On line pre-publication Open Access.
Braun, Virginia and Clarke, Victoria (2006), 'Using thematic analysis in psychology', *Qualitative Research in Psychology*, 3/2: 77–101.
Carter, Ronald (2007), 'Literature and language teaching 1986–2006: A review', *International Journal of Applied Linguistics*, 17/1: 3–13.
Duncan, Sam and Paran, Amos (2017), *The effectiveness of literature on acquisition of language skills and intercultural understanding in the high school context*. A research report for the International Baccalaureate Organisation. Available at: <http://www.ibo.org/contentassets/1fcefe0df17448bebe6781ea0396adff/effect-of-literature-on-language-acquisition-final-report.pdf> (accessed 29 August 2017).
Edmondson, Willis (1997), 'The role of literature in foreign language learning and teaching: Some valid assumptions and invalid arguments', in Anna Mauranen and Kari Sajavaara (eds), *Applied Linguistics across Disciplines*, *AILA Review*, 12: 42–55.

Fogal, Gary (2015), 'Pedagogical stylistics in multiple foreign language and second language contexts: A synthesis of empirical research', *Language and Literature*, 24/1: 54–72.

Gass, Susan and Mackey, Alison (2000), *Stimulated Recall Methodology in Second Language Research*, Mahwah, NJ and London: Lawrence Erlbaum.

Gilroy, Marie (1995), 'An investigation into teachers' attitudes to using literature in the language classroom', *Edinburgh Working Papers in Applied Linguistics*, 6: 1–17.

Hall, Geoff (2015), 'Recent developments in uses of literature in language teaching', in Teranishi, Masayuki, Saito, Yoshifumi and Wales, Katie (eds), *Literature and Language Learning in the EFL Classroom*, Basingstoke: Palgrave Macmillan, pp. 13–25.

Harlow, Linda and Muyskens, Judith (1994), 'Priorities for intermediate-level language instruction', *The Modern Language Journal*, 78/2: 141–54.

IB DP SB (2014), *International Baccalaureate Diploma Programme Subject Brief: Language Acquisition: Language B – Higher level*. Available at: <http://www.ibo.org/globalassets/publications/recognition/2_langbhl.pdf> (accessed 29 April 2017).

Jones, Christian and Carter, Ronald (2011), 'Literature and language awareness: Using literature to achieve CEFR outcomes', *Journal of Second Language Teaching and Research*, 1/1: 69–82.

McRae, John (1991), *Literature with a Small 'l'*, London and Basingstoke: Macmillan.

Mourão, Sandie (2013), 'Response to the *The Lost Thing:* Notes from a secondary classroom', *Children's Literature in English Language Education*, 1/1: 81–95.

Nguyen, Ha Thi Thu (2016), 'How does an interactive approach to literary texts work in an English as a foreign language context? Learners' perspectives in close-up', *Innovation in Language Learning and Teaching*, 10/3: 171–89.

Paesani, Kate (2011), 'Research in language-literature instruction: Meeting the call for change?' *Annual Review of Applied Linguistics*, 31: 161–81.

Paran, Amos (2008), 'The role of literature in instructed foreign language learning and teaching: An evidence-based survey', *Language Teaching*, 41/4: 465–96.

Shanahan, Daniel (1997), 'Articulating the relationship between language, literature and culture: Toward a new agenda for foreign language teaching and research', *Modern Language Journal*, 81/2: 164–74.

Teranishi, Masayuki, Saito, Yoshifumi and Wales, Katie (eds) (2015), *Literature and Language Learning in the EFL Classroom*, Basingstoke: Palgrave Macmillan.

Thoms, Joshua (2014), 'An ecological view of whole-class discussions in a second language literature classroom: Teacher reformulations as affordances for learning', *The Modern Language Journal*, 98/3: 724–41.

15

Afterword: Thoughts on the way ahead

Geoff Hall

In this final chapter I attempt to review some salient themes and issues raised by this volume from my own partial perspective, and also to challenge a little the challengers, to take the debate on to further research, books, articles and most importantly to further worthwhile activities in uses of literature in ELT classrooms. The challenge is to move students and teachers to value and seek out challenge, the rewards and difficulties of moving 'out of the comfort zone', when it is easier and more comfortable not to be challenged.

The pleasures and sometimes also the disappointments of rereading are discussed by Spacks (2011) in her informal autobiographical reflections on rereading. For successful readers, it is clear that a book or text that is worth reading is likely to be worth the effort of reading more than once. We discover more about the text, but also about ourselves and our worlds, as we read the same text again over time and in different contexts. Something that can be read once and wholly understood, and which does not prompt a reader to take a second look, is not challenging and for the experienced reader barely worthwhile, except perhaps as information for a specific utilitarian purpose. In such cases, the reading is not the thing. Such purely instrumental reading is not challenging, nor do we learn from it, even if it may help us achieve some more worthwhile end (assembling furniture, following a recipe, troubleshooting troublesome equipment). It is what Rosenblatt (1994) called 'efferent' rather than 'aesthetic' reading, where aesthetic reading is all about process and interaction rather than a take away benefit.

For some, difficulty is the paradigm of literary reading, though the difficulty can lie in the ideas as much as in any unusual uses of language. The language of a literary text can be difficult (vocabulary, grammar, style or other variations) but so too can be narrative devices such as flashback or flashforward in plot, tellings as perspectives (free indirect speech for example), or indeed a whole gamut of unfamiliar cultural practices and events. Some like to travel, some stay at home and avoid those challenges. Challenging reading may be thought of as some kind of travel into a wider world than we are familiar with just as much as (in its other sense) challenging reading may involve a resistant reading to a familiar story or other text with familiar yet questionable values.

While reimaginings or transmedial retellings of stories we know can discomfort, schema refreshment may be the beneficial and challenging result. Engaging literature and engaging language–literature lessons prompt questions to which the answers are not clear or simple and thus encourage deep communication around issues that participants feel matter in a significant way (race, gender, matters of life and death, values and beliefs). There are no right answers for such issues for a comprehension test to assess. Inferencing is a clear challenge of deep reading including literary and critical reading: not what is going on here, but what is 'really' going on here? Yet the mantra throughout this volume is that already elementary children can inference, predict and think deeply about their books. Children will bring their own experience and that of others to understanding and may not be able to formulate a worthwhile response immediately, but the challenging reading stays with them, in some cases for years to come, even across a lifetime. Lack of clarity, we must remember in a sometimes simplistic world, is not lack of value, never mind lack of validity. Literary understanding is contingent and provisional and dynamic – which is challenging.

Texts – as this collection amply illustrates – are no longer simply 'books' as I have been tending to suggest, but increasingly come to us through a variety of formats and manifestations or indeed as complex multimodal experiences often through a screen or other ever-proliferating new technologies. As we once had to adjust our reading practices to the arrival of the codex and, much later, print, so now new hardware and software is prompting new and, yes, challenging ways of reading, and artefacts to read, if not to challenge the very paradigm of what 'reading' might mean. Thus Gee (2015), for example, writes on the demands and satisfactions of computer gaming, arguing for the educational value of the 'challenges' of gaming (a word used three times in his Conclusion). Even before the recent presidential election in the United States, Gee writes that 'human beings are much better at seeking and finding confirmation of their own views than they are at challenging those views' (Gee 2015: 111). Stronger readers are needed. The affordances of different and ever more innovative media for reader agency, participation and learning are still being investigated by Gee and others (see also Brunsmeier and Kolb 2018, this volume, on the affordances of story apps, including embedded games) but are legitimately seen as extensions of 'reading' in a broad semiotic and communicative sense, with active and creative participation in the construction of the story. Part One of this book most explicitly addresses this final kind of challenge.

Definitions

It is worth pausing at this point to consolidate some of the multiple possible meanings of the title of this collection, *Using Literature in English Language Education: Challenging Reading for 8–18 Year Olds*. Challenging reading is first an activity: we want readers to read critically, to challenge texts, for many educators the final aim of reading development. Then second, challenging texts are *difficult* in some way for a reader to read, a kind of text that can challenge someone in some way – although this will clearly depend on the age of the reader. Ideally, to bring both senses now together, a text that challenges can or should provoke a challenging reading rather than a shrug of the shoulders and a turning away, and it is one of the English teacher's jobs to promote and afford the opportunities for such challenging readings in both senses.

The challenge for teachers is to get younger and less experienced readers to read in ways that more proficient readers know to be among the most satisfying ways to read, and to build the capacities and attention spans and even strategies to read complex texts. Ellis (2018: 97, this volume) introduces the concept of 'learning' literacy with elementary children. She describes challenging reading at this young age as learning to learn in ways that are 'linked to metacognitive strategies and to learner autonomy. It involves developing awareness and understanding of one's own learning processes, personal cognitive preferences and learning strategies. Learning literacy is also about developing an inquisitive mindset and using resources that ignite curiosity and enable experimentation'. An interesting recent study of college-age foreign language readers reading literary texts in Vietnam notes that readers found 'challenging' texts, those difficult to understand and interpret, often to be the most 'useful' for their learning, particularly language learning (Nguyen 2016: 183). This is a paradox, but then again a paradox is precisely an utterance that at first sight does not seem to make sense but yields more insight on closer consideration ('a little learning is a dangerous thing'). Paradox may indeed stand as the epitome of challenging reading. These readers in Vietnam learned more than a little.

In sum then, challenging reading means:

1   Texts can be challenging. However this will be dependent on the language competence, age-related schemata, world experience, cultural background, previous reading experience and so forth of the reader: 'If we know one thing about understanding and learning processes, we know that they are subject to their social context, and even if reading often happens in isolation, the various possible EFL contexts can be expected to have some effect on the reading' (Reichl 2013: 111).

2   Texts can be challenged – through deep reading, critical reading and possibly resistant reading. A number of chapters have referred to 'text ensembles' (Delanoy 2018; Marks and Merse 2018) – reading several works from different perspectives. The idea is, as far as possible, 'to include many experiences from around the world, so that no one particular perspective predominates' (Bland 2018a: 3).

3   Reading itself is an ever more challenged activity for our age due to widespread access to high-speed media in childhood and beyond. This challenge to concentration spans and deep reading has been widely recognized by educators, and the trend towards a hyper attention cognitive style (Hayles 2007) is referred to in several chapters in this volume (Bland 2018b, Brunsmeier and Kolb 2018 and Delanoy 2018).

This collection

So how far do the readings in this book discuss the educational and ELT affordances of challenging reading? And in what ways should those challenging readings be still further challenged? Such challenges generate an unfinalizable project as Bakhtin would have it (see Morson and Emerson 1990).

Part One addresses 'Multimodal challenges'. Necessarily some of the weighty thematic issues that follow in Part Two are also foreshadowed in these first chapters that are more focused on children and younger teen readers. Oziewicz launches the discussion in Chapter 2 by attempting to bring terminological clarity into the field – no easy undertaking as the inventiveness of today's author–artists is outstripping scholars' efforts to categorize their work. Brian Selznick is a case in point. Clearly destined to be a canonical author of the twenty-first century, and ideal for teaching visual literacy as this chapter shows, his innovative works according to the current state of the art are actually extremely challenging to define. The participatory nature of teaching with multimodal texts, and thus their suitability also for young readers, is emphasized throughout Part One. In Chapter 3 Bland writes on creativity in ELT, making use of Rowling's Wizarding World, the use of the recent *Harry Potter* play and screenplay for critical literacy and creative writing. Important effects of creative writing for reading as highlighted by Bland are also mentioned, if not always fully implemented, in the Council of Europe's Framework of Reference for Languages (CEFR 2001: 62).

In Chapter 4, Arizpe and Ryan deal with literacy and language learning in multilingual contexts with reference to the affordances of wordless picturebooks such as Shaun Tan's (2006) *The Arrival*, a book that fascinates adults as well as children. Such crossovers are an increasingly common phenomenon (Reynolds 2011: 17). Traditional notions of 'proper reading' are contested in the researchers' contexts of Glasgow EAL language and culture learning, including storytelling through David Wiesner's (2013) *Mr Wuffles!* with its evocations of migration and communication issues. Postmodern features are shown as affordances for negotiating cultural identities and reflection, using students' words and bringing their own world experience to bear, active engagement in short.

Gail Ellis in Chapter 5 shows the value of such picturebooks in supporting children's learning and potential, which must not be underestimated just because their English is limited. The compelling nature of apparently simple tales – wordless in picturebooks like Briggs's (1978) *The Snowman* and Lamorisse's (1956) film classic *Le Ballon Rouge* – that have caught the imagination of generations, as well as Staake's (2013) contemporary classic *Bluebird*, are referenced in this chapter with ample proof that the challenge of texts does not rely on the linguistic mode of communication. Beyond core linguistic learning goals, Ellis refers to multiple literacies (with specific reference to Cope and Kalantzis 2000), including film literacy, emotional literacy (in this case, empathy and understanding the feelings of a victim of bullying), nature literacy ('reading' the environment) and the widest educational aims.

Brunsmeier and Kolb investigate how children's reading can benefit from story apps. Beyond the intrinsic interest of the topic, the most salient point for me here was the importance of teacher mediation of story apps as of other software for the most fruitful educational outcomes and experiences. The findings are reminiscent of research on tertiary modern foreign language learners in the United States who are consistently shown to have more worthwhile group discussions of literary texts when a teacher mediates the discussion rather than just leaving the group to work on questions by themselves (Zyzik and Polio 2008).

In Chapter 7 Prusse explores media and critical literacy teaching through the TV series *Lockie Leonard* and Tim Winton's book trilogy. Particularly interesting is the exploration for educational purposes of the features of series (episodic and relatively self-contained) and the building of seriality as a plot principle in these works, an instance of tensions between repetition and creativity. Prusse rightly reminds us – a recurring finding of history of reading studies from Eisenstein (1979) on – that reading itself as now established in its mainstream meaning (taking meaning from print in a book) was once seen as a rather suspicious activity of dubious value – not suitable for women or servants at least! New formats and media only slowly come to be recognized fully for what they can and cannot do well. Prusse's approach and example will help teachers and students understand the historical point more concretely and should prompt us all to work harder at the creative workings between his two *Lockie Leonard* media. Adaptation is a creative cultural practice, with different plot organization and presentation choices, which are shown to promote classroom interaction and engagement, but also in this case offering insights into modern and historical Australian culture and society.

Part Two is titled 'Provocative and compelling': the texts themselves are the main focus though it will always be impossible to divorce a text from how that text is experienced, in the classroom or elsewhere. There follows a set of chapters illustrating the kind of material and the ways in which challenges can be precipitated, including migration debates, disability, sexual orientation and gender, utopian and dystopian thinking and further non-mainstream ways of being and encountering the world.

In Chapter 8 Werner Delanoy precisely illustrates my earlier truism that the world is not a simple place with his examples of diaspora and migration literature, a particularly controversial issue recently, and of growing magnitude and seriousness globally. He argues rightly that multiperspectivism, 'a cosmopolitan imagination' (Delanoy 2018: 148), is needed for global citizens to appreciate such issues and challenges in the contemporary world, evidently lacking in much recent activity and debate around this topic in cafes, bars, parliaments and news media. Dialogue is recommended, the essence of educational method, including a methodology of intertextuality in which the literary text, here the short story 'Out of Bounds' (Naidoo 2001), is to be read in the context of other relevant texts, with developing and complex degrees and range of participation in difficult contemporary debates which students would be encouraged to join. A wider point raised by Delanoy through his chosen short story is the 'global reach' of English-language literature which can afford educators and students access to an unusually wide range of human experience in search of the desired cosmopolitan values and attitudes through critical engagement with a story and then the anthology it is taken from. Further anthologies of short stories from multiple cultural contexts are introduced in the annotated bibliography (Bland 2018d: 291–3).

Marks and Merse in Chapter 9 suggest extending the experience of readers through non-canonical narratives of cultural otherness, in this case to bring to the fore the still relatively taboo subjects in many educational systems that focus on reduced or one-dimensional models of romantic love and exclude for example LGBTQ identities or disability. Romantic love can, of course, be pursued in many ways, and can be validated and normalized where needed with positive representations offered. Again, the tenor is that identities are never as straightforward as convention would have us believe and so convention should be challenged through education, and that as far as possible all readers should have the chance to see themselves in the texts they read. This is a familiar current in young adult or children's literature criticism. Bland (2016), Gray (2016) and Paran and Wallace (2016), for example, have argued that ELT has been slow and ineffective in responding to more subtle understandings of diversity like these, with the development of bland international materials. Teacher intervention can be effective in such instances, but poses a new challenge of course.

Bland's contribution in Chapter 10 is devoted to the challenges of Suzanne Collins's *The Hunger Games*. The study of dystopia is now mandated in numerous education regimes, and Bland gives many reasons why, in ELT settings with teenagers, this twenty-first-century text might be chosen over the more canonical adult literature *Brave New World*, *Nineteen Eighty-Four* or *The Handmaid's Tale*. With *The Hunger Games*, readers can research the contemporary themes – sex slavery, child labour, starvation, refugees, child soldiers and propaganda – and thus, Bland argues (2018c: 182–3), they can become more truly involved in 'engaged reading'. An added challenge is that, with texts not yet canonized, there are fewer published explications and interpretations, the use of which is questionable though still widespread. This is a critical point in the introduction to this volume: 'In ELT, there still seems to be a dominant belief among teachers and their students that there are absolute meanings in texts that must be taught' (Bland 2018a: 9).

Wehrmann argues in Chapter 11 for moving students out of their comfort zones by using science fiction to 'cross boundaries of space, time, knowledge and biology' (2018: 194). Utopian thinking and 'thought experiments' are advocated to prompt readers in our imperfect world to imagine better alternatives to society and 'demand the impossible' as one of the references for the chapter has it (Moylan 2014). This important point, on the cognitive challenge and usefulness of imagining fantasy worlds, has by now been made across the academic disciplines. A function of speculative fiction may, for example, 'be to create greater flexibility and adaptability in unforeseen circumstances. Imaginary worlds allow experimentation with possible eventualities which the mind, locked in its routines, might otherwise not have seen' (Cook 2000: 58). In Chapter 12, Webb illustrates how closely themes of speculative fiction are related to our twenty-first century; the author introduces several exemplars of young adult fiction that address urgent environmental issues. There is a continuum with topics and concerns of earlier chapters, such as anthropocentrism, migration and refugees, education and literacy, Othering, apocalypse, corrupt regimes – as well as, fatally, the human propensity of turning a blind eye.

Part Two ends with Chapter 13 and Kalogirou on adaptations and reimagining as new challenges to literary readers and performers, in this case Lesslie's 'Prince of Denmark' drama in combination with *Hamlet*, Shakespeare's gem so familiar to many educators, as taught in Athens, Greece. This is a valuable study of the uses of a new version of an old tale for engaging fresh generations of learners in the tradition of making the difficult language and historical stagecraft more accessible, when Shakespeare is still a required author on many curricula for advanced learners.

Part Three opens with a strong empirical study of teachers' views on using literature in language teaching. Duncan and Paran's data relate to the International Baccalaureate Diploma Programme, with findings reported from teacher interviews in three case studies. The main aim of the study

> was to explore the factors that teachers take into account when choosing literary texts for use in their classrooms; the ways in which teachers use literary texts and the types of activities they employ; and the views of teachers and learners on the impact of literary texts on language learning. For this chapter we took a fresh look at the data from our teacher interviews to understand the way in which teachers negotiated the challenges of reading literary texts. (Duncan and Paran 2018: 245)

Issues of 'difficulty' quickly came to the fore, foregrounding not only language but also conceptual accessibility, appeal, ways into texts including the availability of supplementary materials such as film, also personal advocacy or enthusiasm of individual teachers, and again the affordance of being able to relate to topics already being studied. Organization of reading (methodologies) including use of film and reading aloud are also reported here. In contrast to recommendations in other chapters in this volume, the teachers' use of film is however limited to 'a potential tool for scaffolding understanding [...] also a tool in organizing the reading, or "getting through" the text itself' (2018: 253). For further perspectives on transmedial adaptations see Ellis 2018 (film literacy and opportunities for comparative viewing of picturebook and film) and Prusse 2018 (the TV series of the popular *Lockie Leonard* books exemplifies adaptation as creative cultural practice that extends meanings). The investigation found that exam challenges were seen as constantly haunting the classroom and study beyond the classroom. Nevertheless, in a formulation which most of us working in this field would want to underline, a grateful IB student reports: 'Well, rather than talking about the weather you are talking about *Master and Margarita* in Russian, it's talking about whether God exists and Jesus and the devil being in Moscow. It's more interesting than the weather' (2018: 257).

Thoughts on the way ahead

I have presented – in a nutshell – the undoubted value and some points of particular interest raised by this collection. In closing let me suggest some issues for the field moving forward, beyond the remit of specific chapters but which came to my mind as I read through, and might inform future research developments.

1 The balance or tension between appealing to readers and challenging them

2 Related to this, the need for authentic reading, authentic communication

3 New understandings of reading in the world of the Web, and ever-proliferating new technologies in an ever more challenging world

4 The range of benefits from language to discourse that the reading of literature can bring.

1. *The balance or tension between appealing to readers and challenging them*

The best-loved children's books tend to challenge rather than uphold conventional adult values (Lurie 1998). Children, and thoughtful adults, love challenges. But challenges also change over time and according to contexts: Today's challenges are tomorrow's conventions or disappear into oblivion. British cultural critic Kenneth Tynan dared to use the word 'fuck' on British television in 1965 – which seems a pretty unremarkable thing to report today. Challenging to whom then? Engagement is a key word throughout this collection and this area of research and practice – no engagement, no challenge.

'Should Singapore children only or mainly read stories about growing up in Singapore?' I found I was asking myself after a recent seminar I attended. Adolescents are often dissatisfied already with who and what they are and their surroundings, and want to move on rather than celebrate being a 'teen'. There is a risk of constructing children or young adults as 'children' or 'teenagers' in a disempowering and limiting discourse. Teachers well know there is often resistance to invasion of in-group areas by establishment authority figures. 'Let's discuss a pop song now everybody' (cringe). Consider these wise words from a highly successful children's literature writer:

> Anyone who tries to write *down* to children is simply wasting his [sic] time. You have to write up, not down. Children are demanding. They are the most attentive, curious, eager, observant, sensitive, quick, and generally congenial readers on earth. [...] In *Charlotte's Web*, I gave them a literate spider, and they took that.
>
> Some writers for children deliberately avoid using words they think a child doesn't know. This emasculates the prose and, I suspect, bores the reader. Children are game for anything. [...] They love words that give them a hard time, provided they are in a context that absorbs their attention. (E. B. White, quoted in Haviland 1973: 140)

The treating of difficult subjects in all their complexity is found typically in the best and most successful young adult literature (e.g. *The Hunger Games*).

2. *Related to this, the need for authentic reading, authentic communication*

Let us consider some examples of successful uses of literary texts in a recent report from London secondary schools (Macleroy 2013). First a less challenging teacher: 'The Year 7 class really like doing really simple tasks. They really like doing comprehension because they understand how to do it and I think you kind of have to start really simple' (UK teacher data in Macleroy 2013: 306); '. . . but you do need for them to know how to use full stops and apostrophes' (2013: 307). David's students, meanwhile (twelve to thirteen-year-olds, mixed ability class with a Bangladeshi background), develop deeper word knowledge as they discuss phrases from a travel writing text: 'flat as a pancake; the blessing and the bane of Bangladesh; lazy meandering waters; water squeezes arthritically from the taps' (Macleroy 2013: 311). These students are demonstrably growing in plurilingual and pluricultural competence: 'They can visualise the flatness of the land and understand the concept of water being the blessing and the bane of Bangladesh in a country where drinking water is scarce, but the country is susceptible to flooding. The metaphorical language gives bilingual learners the possibility of imagining this familiar landscape in new ways' (2013: 311).

Macleroy (2013: 313) discusses the implications of her research as showing that 'emergent bilingual learners can be exposed to high levels of language from the outset and rich discussions around literary texts [... and] bilingual learners, at all levels of language, actively engaged with stories and longer pieces of text and were learning to interpret texts from different cultural perspectives'. As the research amply illustrates, 'a diet of engaging books works much better than a diet of worksheets and drills in developing reading comprehension and academic language' (Cummins 2001: 87).

3. New understandings of reading in the world of the Web, and ever-proliferating new technologies in an ever more challenging world

Multimodality has always been central and basic to children's literature: we may consider pop-up and pull-tab books, as well as animated films, even before the Web, television tie-ins, merchandising and the rest. Even so, growing interactivity is a salient feature of children's literature today. Jenkins (2006) writes on transmedial activities as a *socialisation of narrative*, with widening circles of participation rather than author-centred and delimited. Immersion is, it seems, being replaced by interactivity, creativity, or at least the acceptance of new forms. Reynolds (2011) notes the simultaneity rather than sequentiality of much versioning today, and the increasing interdependence of formats, such as the simultaneous release of films and novels.

Challenging the world through education means a search for better futures – critical literacy may reveal the world does not have to be this way. Younger people have the imagination, energy and open-mindedness in principle to lead initiatives to take on the challenges of our time. Some have suggested there may be too much challenge for young people today, for example eco-tragedies and apocalyptic literature pervade children's literature, though we note too the positive ethical features of *The Hunger Games* and others.

4. The range of benefits from language to discourse that the reading of literature can bring

Bloemert et al. (2017) analysed responses of 635 secondary-school students (fifteen to seventeen-year-olds) across 15 different schools and 28 different classes in the Netherlands, who were asked a simple open question: 'What do you think are the benefits of EFL literature lessons?' Their results showed 'the majority of the students consider literature in a FL primarily as language education' (Bloemert et al. 2017: 1). Mostly language approaches were being used rather than traditional literary approaches (study of genre, plot, theme, literary terminology). Students saw English vocabulary and idioms as their main benefit from reading literature – 'I learn synonyms of words I already know' (2017: 9), also some historical social and cultural contexts – 'you learn about how people thought in different periods' (2017: 9). Less than a third of the students seemed to consider critical thinking skills and personal development – 'It gives you time and space to think about topics that you would not look for on your own initiative' (2017: 9). Overall, however, the authors of the study felt that both teachers and students were missing the possible value of a more comprehensive approach to literature use in ELT. According to *Using Literature in English Language Education: Challenging Reading for 8–18 Year Olds*, a more comprehensive approach to language–literature education would include multiple literacies, reader response, intercultural learning and global issues approaches as well as creativity, transmedial and intertextual approaches.

We should close with another study that emphasizes the social and collective nature of reading and its challenges, this time for apprentice readers of literature in secondary education in the UK. Yandell's (2014) own challenge is against the doctrine, often implicit, that the best reading is private, silent and somehow takes place in a vacuum of independence and self-sufficiency. Against this view, Yandell assembles his data to show the reading of Shakespeare and others can be 'irreducibly social, collaborative, dialogic' (2014: 179) and pervasively challenging: 'Literature [...] is valuable precisely as a site of contestation, a site where new cultures and new meanings are produced' (2014: 179). This is the ultimate challenge and value for teachers and learners of literary literacy and deep reading.

Krashen has changed his well-known original 'comprehensible input' hypothesis to the *compelling* comprehensible input hypothesis (Krashen and Bland 2014). Literature, children's literature or otherwise, 'consists of texts which engage, change, and provoke intense responses in readers' (Hunt 2005: 1). From Shakespeare to Suzanne Collins, Tim Winton or David Wiesner, compelling examples are to be found throughout the present collection.

Bibliography

Briggs, Raymond (1978), *The Snowman*, Harmondsworth: Hamish Hamilton.

Collins, Suzanne (2008), *The Hunger Games*, London: Scholastic.

Le Ballon Rouge (1956), [Film] Dir. Albert Lamorisse, France: Films Montsouris.

Lesslie, Michael (2012), 'Prince of Denmark', in *Connections 2012: Plays for Young People, National Theatre*, London: Methuen Drama, pp. 163–201.

Lockie Leonard (2007), [TV series] Dir. Tony Tilse, Wayne Blair, Roger Hodgman, James Bogle and Peter Templeman, Goalpost Pictures.

Naidoo, Beverley (2001), *Out of Bounds. Stories of Conflict and Hope*, London: Puffin.

Staake, Bob (2013), *Bluebird*, New York: Random House.

Tan, Shaun (2007), *The Arrival*, New York: Arthur A. Levine Books.

Wiesner, David (2013), *Mr Wuffles!*, New York: Clarion Books.

Winton, Tim (1990/2007), *Lockie Leonard, Human Torpedo*, Camberwell (Victoria): Penguin.

References

Arizpe, Evelyn and Ryan, Sadie (2018), 'The wordless picturebook: Literacy in multilingual contexts and David Wiesner's worlds', in Janice Bland (ed.), *Using Literature in English Language Education: Challenging Reading for 8–18 Year Olds*, London: Bloomsbury Academic, pp. 63–81.

Bland, Janice (2016), 'English language education and ideological issues: Picturebooks and diversity', *Children's Literature in English Language Education*, 4/2: 41–64.

Bland, Janice (2018a), 'Introduction: The challenge of literature', in Janice Bland (ed.), *Using Literature in English Language Education: Challenging Reading for 8–18 Year Olds*, London: Bloomsbury Academic, pp. 1–22.

Bland, Janice (2018b), 'Playscript and screenplay: Creativity with J.K. Rowling's Wizarding World', in Janice Bland (ed.), *Using Literature in English Language Education*, London: Bloomsbury Academic, pp. 41–61.

Bland, Janice (2018c), 'Popular culture head on: Suzanne Collins's *The Hunger Games*', in Janice Bland (ed.), *Using Literature in English Language Education*, London: Bloomsbury Academic, pp. 175–92.

Bland, Janice (2018d), 'Annotated bibliography: Literary texts recommended for children and young adults in ELT', in Janice Bland (ed.), *Using Literature in English Language Education*, London: Bloomsbury Academic, pp. 277–300.

Bloemert, Jasmijn, Paran, Amos, Jansen, Ellen and van de Grift, Wim (2017), 'Students' perspective on the benefits of EFL literature education', *The Language Learning Journal*, online pre-publication Open Access.

Brunsmeier, Sonja and Kolb, Annika (2018), 'Story apps: The challenge of interactivity', in Janice Bland (ed.), *Using Literature in English Language Education*, London: Bloomsbury Academic, pp. 105–19.

Cook, Guy (2000), *Language Play, Language Learning*, Oxford: Oxford University Press.

Cope, Bill and Kalantzis, Mary (eds) (2000), *Multiliteracies: Literacy Learning and the Design of Social Futures*, Routledge: London.

Council of Europe (2001), *Common European Framework of Reference for Languages*, Strasbourg: Language Policy Unit.

Cummins, Jim (2001), *Negotiating Identities: Education for Empowerment in a Diverse Society*, Los Angeles: California Association for Bilingual Education.

Delanoy, Werner (2018), 'Literature in language education: Challenges for theory building', in Janice Bland (ed.), *Using Literature in English Language Education*, London: Bloomsbury Academic, pp. 141–57.

Duncan, Sam and Paran, Amos (2018), 'Negotiating the challenges of reading literature: Teachers reporting on their practice', in Janice Bland (ed.), *Using Literature in English Language Education*, London: Bloomsbury Academic, pp. 243–59.

Ellis, Gail (2018), 'The picturebook in elementary ELT: Multiple literacies with Bob Staake's *Bluebird*', in Janice Bland (ed.), *Using Literature in English Language Education*, London: Bloomsbury Academic, pp. 83–104.

Eisenstein, Elizabeth (1979), *The Printing Press as an Agent of Change: Communications and Transformations in Early-Modern Europe*, Cambridge: Cambridge University Press.

Gee, James Paul (2015), *Unified Discourse Analysis: Language, Reality, Virtual Worlds, and Video Games*, New York: Routledge.

Gray, John (2016), 'ELT materials: Claims, critiques and controversies', in Graham Hall (ed.), *The Routledge Handbook of English Language Teaching*, Abingdon, Oxon: Routledge, pp. 95–108.

Haviland, Virginia (ed.) (1973), *Children and Literature: Views and Reviews*, New York: Lothrop, Lee and Shepard.

Hayles, Katherine (2007), 'Hyper and Deep Attention: The generational divide in cognitive modes', *Profession 2007*, 187–99.

Hilton, Mary and Nikolajeva, Maria (eds) (2012), *Contemporary Adolescent Literature and Culture: The Emergent Adult*, Baltimore: Johns Hopkins University Press.

Hunt, Peter (2005) (ed.) *Understanding Children's Literature* (2nd edn), Abingdon: Routledge.

Jenkins, Henry (2006), *Convergence Culture*, New York: New York University Press.

Kalogirou, Tzina (2018), ' Hamlet, Ophelia and teenage rage: Michael Lesslie's Prince of Denmark', in Janice Bland (ed.), *Using Literature in English Language Education*, London: Bloomsbury Academic, pp. 225–40.

Krashen, Stephen and Bland, Janice (2014), 'Compelling comprehensible input, academic language and school libraries', *Children's Literature in English Language Education*, 2/2: 1–12.

Lurie, Alison (1998), *Don't Tell the Grown Ups. The Subversive Power of Children's Literature*, Boston: Little Brown.

Macleroy, Vicky (2013), 'Cultural, linguistic and cognitive issues in teaching the language of literature for emergent bilingual pupils', *Language, Culture and Curriculum*, 26/3: 300–16.

Marks, Johanna and Merse, Thorsten (2018), 'Diversity in love-themed fiction: John Green's *The Fault in our Stars* and David Levithan's *Princes*', in Janice Bland (ed.), *Using Literature in English Language Education*, London: Bloomsbury Academic, pp. 159–74.

Morson, Gary Saul and Emerson, Caryl (1990), *Mikhail Bakhtin: Creation of a Prosaics*, Stanford, CA: Stanford University Press.

Moylan, Tom (2014), *Demand the Impossible: Science Fiction and the Utopian Imagination*, (new edn), Bern: Peter Lang.

Nguyen, Ha Thi Thu (2016), 'How does an interactive approach to literary texts work in an English as a Foreign Language context?' *Innovation in Language Learning and Teaching*, 10/3: 171–89.

Oziewicz, Marek (2018), 'The graphic novel: Brian Selznick's *The Invention of Hugo Cabret*, *Wonderstruck* and *The Marvels*', in Janice Bland (ed.), *Using Literature in English Language Education*, London: Bloomsbury Academic, pp. 25–40.

Paran, Amos and Wallace, Catherine (2016), 'Teaching literacy', in Graham Hall (ed.), *Routledge Handbook of English Language Teaching*, London: Routledge.

Prusse, Michael (2018), 'Transmedial reading: Tim Winton's *Lockie Leonard*', in Janice Bland (ed.), *Using Literature in English Language Education*, London: Bloomsbury Academic, pp. 121–37.

Reichl, Susanne (2013), 'Doing identity, doing culture: Transcultural learning through young adult fiction', in Janice Bland and Christiane Lütge (eds),

Children's Literature in Second Language Education, London: Bloomsbury Academic, pp. 107–17.

Reynolds, Kimberley (2011), *Children's Literature. A Very Short Introduction*, Oxford: Oxford University Press.

Rosenblatt, Louise (1994), *The Reader, the Text, the Poem. The Transactional Theory of the Literary Work*, Carbondale: Southern Illinois Press.

Spacks, Patricia Meyer (2011), *Rereading*, Cambridge, MA: Belknap/ Harvard University Press.

Webb, Jean (2018), 'Environmental havoc in teen fiction: Speculating futures', in Janice Bland (ed.), *Using Literature in English Language Education*, London: Bloomsbury Academic, pp. 209–23.

Wehrmann, Jürgen (2018), 'Thought experiments with science fiction: Ursula Le Guin's *The Ones Who Walk Away from Omelas*', in Janice Bland (ed.), *Using Literature in English Language Education*, London: Bloomsbury Academic, pp. 193–208.

Yandell, John (2014), *The Social Construction of Meaning: Reading Literature in Urban English Classrooms*, London: Routledge.

Zyzik, Eve and Polio, Charlene (2008), 'Incidental focus on form in university Spanish literature courses, *Modern Language Journal*, 92/1: 53–70.

Annotated bibliography: Literary texts recommended for children and young adults in ELT

Janice Bland

This annotated bibliography introduces the literary texts in this volume briefly. Many further recommendable texts for ELT with eight to eighteen-year-olds have been added. Mostly recent texts for school-aged children and teenagers have been included, in preference to older classics such as those by Dr Seuss, Roald Dahl and other already widely known canonical texts for children.

The bibliography is divided into ten categories from short to longer formats suitable for ELT settings: story apps, picturebooks, poetry books, chapter books, graphic novels, short story collections, verse novels, playscripts, screenplays and young adult fiction. The categories are an attempt at organization; however many outstanding author-illustrators (e.g. Raymond Briggs) defy rigid classifications, and there is no clear boundary between, for example, picturebooks, graphic novels, and richly illustrated chapter books. Of course this list could have been far longer, but I hope nonetheless that it will be useful for teachers, teacher educators, parents and librarians. The recommendations are not all specifically for challenging reading, in some cases the suggestions are rather to challenge children to start reading in the first place in order to improve their life chances, for research studies have established that 'reading is actually linked to increased cognitive progress over time' (Sullivan and Brown 2013: 37).

The many graded readers that are produced for the international ELT market are mostly similar to the chapter book format (see below), but are typically less richly illustrated, with a less cohesively patterned text (Bland 2013: 8). The majority are also without child-focused or adolescent-focused content, as even beginner graded-reader titles are very often aimed at adult ELT. Graded readers frequently include comprehension questions and other activities intended to support the teacher, and are offered for particular language levels with the vocabulary and grammar correspondingly controlled. In many ELT classrooms, this is considered an essential aid, although answering comprehension questions does not in most cases support the joy of playful language, intercultural awareness and deep reading, as outlined in the introduction (Bland 2018a: 6–8). In ELT curricula with young learners and teenagers, for example in Europe, acquiring intercultural competence is often considered to be as important as learning the language. Graded readers are not usually written by stellar writers, are far thinner than the original versions of classic texts yet are often twice as expensive and they are unlikely to be given a place on home bookshelves to be reread in the future. Many students in school settings are prepared to tackle texts in the more challenging original, *as long as the texts are sufficiently motivating.*

Sadly school libraries do not exist in most countries worldwide, and even those countries that do have school libraries seldom have a children's literature scholar or librarian with an understanding of ELT to advise them. Consequently, the issue of access to texts is a global concern. In an extensive reading programme aimed at pleasure reading and language enrichment, the usually unrealizable ideal is that teachers are in a position to offer titles of all possible formats for wide reader choice. Access and the opportunity to enjoy self-selected material is particularly important with children who are in danger of losing the love of reading, which happens frequently at around the age of 12 (Harmgarth 1999: 18). For, as Bamford and Day express it: 'Only by discovering the rewards of reading through actually engaging in it will students become people who both *can* and *do* read' (1997, emphasis in the original). The main focus of the following list is on texts for *shared* reading in the ELT classroom rather than extensive reading, texts that afford excellent opportunities for language-dependent activities leading to deep reading. However the first category introduces a format that can be useful for encouraging independent reading at the outset with young learners.

1. Story apps

Story apps offer multimodal reading with reader-activated animation, music and background noises as well as audio narration that can be activated by the reader. Integrated choices and tasks activated by the learner clicking on an action hotspot ensure high involvement, sometimes with a choose-your-own-way-forward format and feedback given on the action taken. For young learners in ELT, any autonomous reading is a challenge – if tablet computers are available in the classroom, story apps may help pave the way to book reading.

Jack and the Beanstalk (2015), [mobile application software] Ed Bryan and Nosy Crow (Chapter 6, in detail). This is a lively, inventive and motivating version of the story. Usefully, there is also a picturebook version of the app, which provides opportunities for shared activities around the pages of the book: Bryan, Ed (2015), *Jack and the Beanstalk*, London: Nosy Crow Fairy Tales.

Mud Monster (2013), [mobile application software] Chantal Bourgonje and Tizio Publishing (Chapter 6, mentioned).

Nash Smasher (2010), [mobile application software] Bill Doyler and Troy Cummings, Crab Hill Press (Chapter 6, mentioned).

Pete's Robot (2016), [mobile application software] Heartdrive Media LLC (Chapter 6, mentioned).

Snow White (2015), [mobile application software] Ed Bryan and Nosy Crow (Chapter 6, mentioned).

The Three Little Pigs (2015), [mobile application software] Ed Bryan and Nosy Crow (Chapter 6, mentioned).

2. Picturebooks

The picturebook has received in-depth critical attention from literary and education scholars, to the extent that it has been called 'one of the richest and potentially most rewarding of literary forms' (Hunt 2001: 291). Due to the richness of this format, this category has the longest list of recommended titles for ELT. The picturebook is essentially defined by the interaction between the words and pictures as being vital to the meaning. This leads to complex opportunities for discovery and interpretation of meanings that are created by the pictures as well as the combination of pictures, verbal text, creative typography and design. Consequently, to emphasize its compound nature, the format is now frequently spelled as a compound noun: *picturebook*. For the most part excellent for younger grades, there are some extremely complex and darker picturebooks more suitable for the secondary school.

Ahlberg, Allan, illus. Amstutz, André (1998), *Monkey Do!* London: Walker Books.
A book that is just perfect for chorusing with the youngest grades.

Alexie, Sherman, illus. Morales, Yuyi (2016), *Thunder Boy Jr.* New York: Little, Brown.
A book that is highly suitable for the youngest grades, vividly illustrated and featuring a touching father–son relationship.

Amnesty International (2008), *We Are All Born Free: The Universal Declaration of Human Rights in Pictures*, London: Frances Lincoln.
This is an important book that celebrates human rights in pictures by well-known artists. The book can be used on different levels with different age groups.

Andreae, Giles, illus. Parker-Rees, Guy (1999), *Giraffes Can't Dance*, London: Orchard Books.
This is a book that is sure to get all the children dancing and joining in, for younger grades.

Anzaldúa, Gloria, illus. Méndez, Consuelo (1993), *Friends from the Other Side/ Amigos del Otro Lado*, San Francisco: Children's Book Press (Chapter 8, mentioned).
This and the following Gloria Anzaldúa picturebook are bilingual English-Spanish. Both are suitable for lower secondary-school language learning. The picturebooks centre on aspects of Hispanic culture and Mexican–US border crossing.

Anzaldúa, Gloria, illus. Gonzalez, Maya Christina (1995), *Prietita and the Ghost Woman/Prietita y la Llorona*, San Francisco: Children's Book Press (Chapter 8, mentioned).
A version of a Mexican legend, the picturebook features strong female protagonists.

Baldacchino, Christine, illus. Malenfant, Isabelle (2014), *Morris Micklewhite and the Tangerine Dress*, Toronto: Groundwood Books.
A book with gorgeous pictures and a poetic text, this is a moving story about a young boy who loves cross-dressing.

Baker, Jeannie (1987), *Where the Forest Meets the Sea*, Julia MacRae Books.
With inspiring artwork, this environmentally committed book appeals to different age groups and invites us to fall in love with an ancient setting of Australia.

Briggs, Raymond (1978), *The Snowman*, Harmondsworth: Hamish Hamilton (Chapter 5, mentioned).
This is a timeless classic, a wordless picturebook that generations of British families have loved.

Brown, Ken (2001), *What's the Time Grandma Wolf?* Atlanta: Peachtree.
Ideal for sharing with the youngest grades, this book is a richly detailed visualization of the favourite children's game, with a clever twist at the end.

Browne, Anthony (1986), *Piggybook*, London: Julia MacRae Books.
This is a clever and beautifully illustrated book that focuses on gender issues, with a story that appeals to children.

Browne, Anthony (1989), *The Tunnel*, London: Julia MacRae Books.
This book invites children to discover the fascinating hidden secrets in the images.

Browne, Anthony (1992), *Zoo*, London: Random House Children's Books.
As in all Anthony Browne's books, the illustrations are complex and magnificent. The meaningful story invites deep thinking on keeping animals in zoos. This book won the Kate Greenaway Medal, and is highly suitable for Art lessons through the medium of English: Content and Language Integrated Learning (CLIL).

Browne, Anthony (1998), *Voices in the Park*, London: Random House.
This is another beautifully illustrated and complex book, and might be shared with lower grades in secondary school ELT. The story is told from four different perspectives and focuses on social class issues.

Browne, Anthony (2009), *Me and You*, London: Doubleday.
This is a version of the Goldilocks and the Three Bears tale. Social class issues are cleverly woven within the story.

Browne Eileen (1994), *Handa's Surprise*, London: Walker Books.
This is a favourite in ELT with the youngest grades. The language is extremely simple, and the gorgeous pictures tell a happy story of a friendship between two village girls in Kenya.

Burningham, John (1989), *Oi! Get off our Train*, London: Jonathan Cape.
This is an environmentally conscious, rhythmical story for younger grades.

Child, Lauren (2000), *Beware of the Storybook Wolves*, London: Hodder Children's Books.
A funny, postmodern fairy tale, it is ideal for young, autonomous readers in ELT.

Child, Lauren (2002), *Who's Afraid of the Big Bad Book?* London: Hodder Children's Books.
A riotous and complex picturebook that plays with fairy tales, upsets expectations and creates countless opportunities for retelling tales and discovering how the tales are outrageously disrupted.

Daywalt, Drew, illus. Jeffers, Oliver (2013), *The Day the Crayons Quit*, New York: Penguin Group.
This is a hilarious book that is wonderful for encouraging creativity. It is particularly suitable for Art in English (CLIL).

Demi (1997), *One Grain of Rice: A Mathematical Folk Tale*, New York: Scholastic.
This beautiful book, inspired by traditional Indian miniature paintings, is ideal for both Maths CLIL and Art CLIL.

Donaldson, Julia, illus. Scheffler, Axel (1999), *The Gruffalo*, London: Macmillan (Chapter 7, mentioned).
Julia Donaldson needs no introduction – all her picturebooks appeal to elementary school children through their clever stories, rhythmical texts and bright illustrations.

Donaldson, Julia, illus. Scheffler, Axel (2000), *Monkey Puzzle*, London: Macmillan.
This charming tale can be shared with the youngest learners.

Donaldson, Julia, illus. Scheffler, Axel (2001), *Room on the Broom*, London: Macmillan.
This is another favourite, full of clever rhymes.

Donaldson, Julia, illus. Scheffler, Axel (2002), *The Smartest Giant in Town*, London: Macmillan.
This is the rhythmical tale of a very humane giant.

Donaldson, Julia, illus. Scheffler, Axel (2003), *The Snail and the Whale*, London: Macmillan.
This beautiful tale of the oceans has an environmental theme.

Donaldson, Julia, illus. Scheffler, Axel (2008), *Stick Man*, London: Scholastic.
A lovely tale, this one is perfect at Christmas.

Donaldson, Julia, illus. Ogilvie, Sara (2016), *The Detective Dog*, London:
    Macmillan Children's Books.
This is a clever book on the pleasures of books and libraries.

Graham, Bob (2011), *A Bus Called Heaven*, Somerville: Candlewick Press.
This is a delightful story of a community bus: intercultural learning for young
learners.

Greder, Armin (2007), *The Island*, Crows Nest: Allen and Unwin.
This symbolic picturebook has already become a classic. More suitable for
secondary ELT, it shows in striking pictures and few but troubling words
the hostility shown by islanders towards a helpless refugee due to his alien
appearance.

Gregory, Nan, illus. Lightburn, Ron (1995), *How Smudge Came*, New York:
    Walker.
A brave young woman, Cindy, who has Down syndrome, adopts a stray puppy in
this moving story.

Horáček, Petr (2006), *Silly Suzy Goose*, London: Walker Books.
This is a perfect story, with a helpfully repetitive text, for the youngest grades.

Jenkins, Steve and Page, Robin (2003), *What Do You Do with a Tail Like This?*
    Boston: Houghton Mifflin.
This is a nonfiction picturebook for younger grades, ideal for modelling mini
writing activities.

Kitamura, Satoshi (1987), *Lily Takes a Walk*, London: Blackie Children's Books.
This book is bewitching, with simple text for the youngest grades but hugely
amusing pictures that demand to be talked and talked about.

Lewis, Kim (2003), *Goodnight Harry*, London: Walker Books.
This book of cuddly toys at bedtime is beautifully drawn – for early grades.

Levine, Ellen, illus. Björkman, Steve (1989), *I Hate English!* New York: Scholastic.
This is a must-read for classes with migrant and refugee children.

McKee, David (1980), *Not Now, Bernard*, London: Andersen Press.
A simple text, but this is a story to give the youngest grades plenty to puzzle over.

Macaulay, David (1990), *Black and White*, Boston: Houghton Mifflin.
A Caldecott Medal winner, this is a complex puzzle of a book. The reader must
unravel four interrelated stories.

Macaulay, David (1995), *Shortcut*, Boston: Houghton Mifflin.
An extremely convoluted story, this picturebook will get young learners
puzzling.

Martin, Rafe, illus. Shannon, David (1992), *The Rough-Face Girl*, New York:
    Putnam Books.
This is a story from Algonquin Indian folklore, a haunting version of the Cinderella
tale.

McKee, David (1989), *Elmer*, London: Andersen Press.
This is a picturebook classic for young children and the celebration of difference.

Meddaugh, Susan (1997), *Cinderella's Rat*, Boston: Houghton Mifflin.
This clever picturebook with lively illustrations tells of the rat that took Cinderella to the ball.

Monks, Lydia (2004), *Aaaarrgghh, Spider!* London: Egmont Books.
This entertaining picturebook tells a delightful story of a spider that wants to become a family pet. It has very striking illustrations and an easy text for young language learners to follow and enjoy.

Munsch, Robert, illus. Martchenko, Michael (1980), *The Paper Bag Princess*, Toronto: Annick Press.
This picturebook centres on a brave and resourceful princess and her rescue of a superficial and ungrateful prince, and is an early revision of the 'happily every after' tale.

Munsch, Robert, illus. Martchenko, Michael (1985), *Mortimer*, Toronto: Annick Press.
This book is suitable for the youngest ELT grades, and just perfect for reading aloud.

Nye, Naomi Shihab, illus. Carpenter, Nancy (1994), *Sitti's Secrets*, New York: Simon and Schuster.
The story is detailed and beautiful and the illustrations are stunning. The picturebook tells of a visit to a special grandmother, who lives in a Palestinian village on the West Bank.

Parr, Todd (2003), *The Family Book*, New York: Little, Brown.
This is non-fiction, and on a favourite topic for the youngest grades.

Pattison, Darcy, illus. Cepeda, Joe (2003), *The Journey of Oliver K. Woodman*, San Diego: Harcourt.
A brilliant story, written in letters, this book illustrates a fantastic journey from the east to the west US coast.

Rathmann, Peggy (1994), *Good Night, Gorilla*, New York: Penguin Group.
There are plenty of visual jokes for the youngest learners to discover and enjoy, and opportunities to tell the simple story of this nearly wordless picturebook.

Reynolds, Peter (2004), *Ish*, London: Walker Books.
Amazing in its simplicity and wonderful message, this book about the 'ishness' of things is ideal for Art in English (CLIL) in the elementary school.

Rosen, Michael, illus. Oxenbury, Helen (1989), *We're Going on a Bear Hunt*, London: Walker Books.
A luxurious rendering of English landscapes and weathers to accompany a rhythmic campfire chant, with its singsong pattern and beat.

Say, Allen (1993), *Grandfather's Journey*, Boston: Houghton Mifflin Company.
A Caldecott Medal winner, the breathtaking illustrations with few words evoke the powerful emotions of emigration.

Scieszka, Jon, illus. Smith, Lane (1989), *The True Story of the 3 Little Pigs! By A. Wolf*, London: Puffin.
An excellent postmodern version of the story, this is highly suitable for secondary students.

Shannon, David (1998), *No, David!* New York: Scholastic.
This picturebook is nearly wordless, but offers manifold opportunities for creative language work with the youngest learners.

Smith, Lane (2010), *It's a Book*, New York: Roaring Brook Press.
This is a humorous glance at new and old kinds of storytelling, for young language learners.

Snicket, Lemony, illus. Klassen, Jon (2013), *The Dark*, New York: Little, Brown.
With amazing illustrations, this is a story for the youngest grades, ideal for class trips away from home.

Staake, Bob (2013), *Bluebird*, New York: Random House (Chapter 5, in detail).
A silent picturebook that speaks powerfully through the images, and gently expresses the serious themes of love, bullying and death.

Steptoe, John (1987), *Mufaro's Beautiful Daughters – An African Tale*, London: Penguin Group.
This is a lusciously illustrated and complex African Cinderella.

Swain, Gwenyth (1999), *Carrying*, Minneapolis: Lerner Publishing.
This non-fiction picturebook shows how people all around the world carry different objects – a picturebook for the youngest grades with one sentence per picture.

Tan, Shaun (2000), *The Lost Thing*, Sydney: Hachette Australia.
Tan's work is usually complex, dark and more suitable for secondary ELT students. An Oscar-winning short film exists that compliments the picturebook: *The Lost Thing* (2010), [Film] Dir. Shaun Tan and Andrew Ruhemann, Australia: Passion Pictures.

Taylor, Clark, illus. Dicks, Jan Thompson (1992), *The House that Crack Built*, San Francisco: Chronicle Books.
This is a dark and angry picturebook with a rhythmical text, for secondary students.

Van Allsburg, Chris (1985), *The Polar Express*, London: Andersen Press.
Not an easy verbal text for young learners in ELT, but with amazing illustrations and justly a Caldecott Medal winner. It is a must read at Christmas time.

Van Allsburg, Chris (1986), *The Stranger*, Boston: Houghton Mifflin Company.
In this picturebook, with a more difficult text, nature is not a mere backdrop to more important human-centred concerns, nature herself becomes a character in the story.

Waddell, Martin, illus. Benson, Patrick (1992), *Owl Babies*, London: Walker Books.
Children in the first grade can join in this beautiful picturebook from the very beginning.

Wallace, Karen, illus. Bostock, Mike (1993), *Think of an Eel*, London: Walker Books.
An excellently written and illustrated nonfiction picturebook, this story of the eel highlights the mystery of life.

Ward, Helen, illus. Anderson, Wayne (2001), *The Tin Forest*, London: Templar Publishing.
A lovely environmental story, this book will enchant young learners in ELT from the third grade upwards.

Wiesner, David (1992), *Tuesday*, New York: Clarion Books (Chapter 4, mentioned).
David Wiesner is another grandiose, multiple prizewinning picturebook artist. His books are surreal, multilayered and can be read on many levels. *Tuesday* is Wiesner's first Caldecott Medal winner.

Wiesner, David (2002), *The Three Pigs*, New York: Clarion Books (Chapter 4, mentioned).
Another Caldecott Medal winner, this amazing retelling of the traditional tale is a must for young learners who can manage a complex story.

Wiesner, David (2006), *Flotsam*, New York: Clarion Books (Chapter 4, in detail).
Yet again, this book earned a Caldecott Medal for Wiesner.

Wiesner, David (2010), *Art and Max*, New York: Clarion Books (Chapter 4, mentioned).
This book with its desert setting is perfect for Art lessons in English (CLIL).

Wiesner, David (2013), *Mr Wuffles!* New York: Clarion Books (Chapter 4, in detail).
A wonderful book for intercultural learning with young learners, the wordless story is also a fine opportunity to train creative teacher talk.

Wild, Margaret, illus. Vivas, Julie (1994), *Our Granny*, Boston: Houghton Mifflin.
A picturebook that celebrates diversity of body shapes and life styles, this has a patterned and rhythmical text and is suitable for younger grades. It works effectively against stereotyping grannies.

Williams, Karen and Mohammed, Khadra, illus. Doug Chayka (2007), *Four Feet, Two Sandals*, Michigan: Eerdmanns Publishing.
This is a moving refugee story with rather more text, so not for the youngest learners in ELT.

Williams, Karen and Mohammed, Khadra, illus. Stock, Catherine (2009), *My Name is Sangoel*, Michigan: Eerdmanns Publishing.
This is a refugee story about a clever boy, suitable for lower secondary grades.

Willis, Jeanne, illus. Ross, Tony (1999), *Susan Laughs*, London: Andersen Press (Chapter 5, mentioned).
This picturebook is perfect for the youngest language learners. The topic of disability is beautifully handled.

Willis, Jeanne, illus. Ross, Tony (2009), *Big Bad Bun*, London: Andersen Press.
This is a fantastic story, hilariously funny pictures and words, and ideal for inspiring creative writing.

3. Poetry books

Well-known contemporary poets who write for children, such as Roger McGough and Michael Rosen, have successfully emulated the strong rhythms, fun and naughtiness of playground rhymes. The vibrant poetry in the following anthologies works well for classroom performance, and some also plunge into serious themes that are highly meaningful for teachers as well as their students.

Cookson, Paul (ed.) (2014), *The Works: Every Kind of Poem You Will Ever Need At School* (new edn), London: Macmillan Children's Books.
This excellent anthology covers the huge breadth of poetry, but also many glimpses of the depth of poetry for children.

Crebbin, June (ed.) (2000), *The Puffin Book of Fantastic First Poems*, London: Penguin Books.
This is a wonderful anthology suitable for young learners, organized by topic, and each topic colourfully illustrated by a well-known illustrator.

Heppermann, Christine (2014), *Poisoned Apples*, New York: HarperCollins Children's Books.
Feminist poetry inspired by fairy tales, this collection is dark and angry.

Matterson, Elizabeth (1969/1991), *This Little Puffin: A Treasury of Nursery Rhymes, Songs and Games*, London: Penguin Books.
This anthology for the youngest grades has become a classic.

McGough, Roger, illus. Monks, Lydia (2004), *All the Best. The Selected Poems of Roger McGough*, London: Penguin Books.
Every elementary and secondary ELT class should have the opportunity to share in the delight of Roger McGough's poetry.

Rosen, Michael (ed.) (2009), *A to Z: The Best Children's Poetry from Agard to Zephaniah*, London: Penguin Books.
This is a delightful anthology of short and mostly funny poems.

Wright, Blanche Fisher (illus.) (1916/1994), *The Real Mother Goose*, New York: Scholastic.
This book has been in print for over a hundred years, and is excellent value. With nearly 300 rhymes to choose from, the ELT teacher is bound to find some that are suitable for the youngest grades, while others contain archaic language and are less suitable. Blanche Fisher Wright's boldly colourful illustrations are as timeless as the anonymous nursery rhymes.

4. Chapter books

The chapter book (called middle-grade fiction in the United States) is a format for those pre-teens who are now reading independently. The books consequently have far more text than a picturebook, and have protagonists in the eight- to twelve-year-old age range who have very different experiences in the storyworld from teenagers. Chapter books have short chapters 'for children who have mastered basic reading skills but still require simple, illustrated texts' (Agnew 2001: 139). Although typically quite richly illustrated, the pictures are not essential for the meaning of the story, in contrast to the graphic novel and the larger-formatted picturebook.

Applegate, Katherine (2012), *The One and Only Ivan*, New York: HarperCollins Children's Books.
A Newbery Medal winner, this book 'stops time' with its soul-touching story.

Blackman, Malorie (2012), *Hostage*, Edinburgh: Barrington Stoke.
The publisher Barrington Stoke has created an excellent list for young readers who are reluctant, dyslexic or – for whatever reason – not yet into books: children who can read, but are not readers. This story by a first-rate author is action-packed, gripping and truly moving.

Blackman, Malorie (2015), *Robot Girl*, Edinburgh: Barrington Stoke.
This is thought-provoking science fiction, highly suitable for teenagers still not into reading.

Deary, Terry (2015), *The Vampire of Groglin*, Edinburgh: Barrington Stoke.
This is humorous (Terry Deary of *Horrible Histories* fame) and horrible – just right for young secondary-school students.

Ellis, Deborah (2009), *The Breadwinner Trilogy*, Toronto: Groundwood Books.
A reminder of how courageous children around the world in war-torn settings must be, this well-researched trilogy about a sixth-grade girl's life in Afghanistan is devastating and utterly unforgettable.

Fine, Anne (1990), *Bill's New Frock*, London: Mammoth Books.
This is a hilarious story of a boy who wakes up one day as a girl.

Foxley, Janet (2011), *Muncle Trogg*, Frome: Chicken House.
Plenty of action and fun, this is the first of a promising series for young readers.

Gleitzman, Morris (2002), *Boy Overboard*, Victoria: Penguin Books.
With this sad and funny book, readers can gain an understanding of some of what refugees and asylum seekers must go through to survive.

Gleitzman, Morris (2005), *Once*, Victoria: Penguin Books.
This Holocaust book for young readers is heart breaking, but with a touch of hope.

Horowitz, Anthony (2000), *Stormbreaker: An Alex Rider Adventure*, New York: Penguin.
The first in the Alex Rider series, this is is a stereotype enforcing rather than a challenging read. The series is hugely popular among boys, so the reluctant young-teen readers who love the nonstop action should not be denied the books, but I suggest they should be challenged to practise critical literacy (Chapter 7, mentioned).

Hughes, Ted (1968/2005), *The Iron Man*, London: Faber and Faber (Chapter 3, mentioned).
This is a poetic text for young readers.

Kinney, Jeff (2007), *Diary of a Wimpy Kid*, New York: Amulet Books.
This is a hugely popular series, funny and richly illustrated.

Morpurgo, Michael (2008), *Animal Tales*, London: Egmont Press.
Three stories, richly illustrated and suitable for younger grades, told in the persuasive voice of the master storyteller and animal lover, Michael Morpurgo.

Morpurgo, Michael (2012), *Who's a Big Bully Then?* Edinburgh: Barrington Stoke.
A simple yarn, but the book covers an issue that concerns most children.

Pilkey, Dav (1997), *The Adventures of Captain Underpants*, New York: Scholastic.
For young pre-teens, easy to read, this is the first of a funny and popular, comic-like series.

Pullman, Philip (1995), *The Firework-Maker's Daughter*, London: Corgi Yearling Books.
Philip Pullman's books are all wonderfully written, and offer endless opportunities as an inspiration for creative writing.

Pullman, Philip, illus. Bailey, Peter (1996), *Clockwork*, London: Doubleday.
This is a darker story – but children in this age group just love horror stories.

Pullman, Philip (2000), *I was a Rat!*, London: Corgi Yearling Books.
This is a postmodern fairy tale – a highly amusing version of Cinderella.

Rowling, J. K. (2017), *Fantastic Beasts and Where to Find Them, Newt Scamander* (2nd edn), London: Bloomsbury (Chapter 3, mentioned).
J. K. Rowling has created an entire intertextual world of her own which fascinates and motivates young readers.

Walliams, David, illus. Blake, Quentin (2008), *The Boy in the Dress*, London: HarperCollins.
The drawings of the great illustrator Quentin Blake perfectly complement this seriously funny, sensitive book. This is a brilliant, feel-good read about a twelve-year-old, and written in an easy style.

5. Graphic novels

This format is swiftly gaining attention due to a sudden surge in high quality, seriously themed, award-winning graphic novels in recent years. Whereas the picturebook is mostly, but not exclusively, aimed at children in elementary school or even younger, the graphic novel is more likely to be shared with higher grades. The potential of the graphic novel in the ELT classroom stretches from a support for reluctant readers to a challenge for high-level readers (Ludwig and Pointner 2013).

Almond, David, illus. McKean, Dave (2008), *The Savage*, London: Walker Books.
David Almond is well known for his magic realist texts. This small book is beautiful, both in language and (sometimes disturbing) illustration – suitable for challenging booktalk with pre-teens.

Almond, David, illus. McKean, Dave (2013), *Mouse Bird Snake Wolf*, Somerville, MA: Candlewick Press (Chapter 3, in detail).
There is much more to this book than first meets the eye. As a challenging book for the pre-teen years, it is best for shared reading.

Baum, Frank, adapt. Cavallaro, Michael (2005), *The Wizard of Oz: The Graphic Novel*, New York: Puffin Graphics.
There are ever more retellings of classics in graphic-novel format such as this one. The text is shortened, however the details that are not expressed in words are expressed in the panels. Thus most of the layers of the original are retained, with opportunities for meaningful language-dependent activities around the pictures.

Bechdel, Alison (2006), *Fun Home: A Family Tragicomic*, Boston: Houghton Mifflin.
An autobiographical graphic novel, this book shows once again how intense feelings can often be best expressed in images with few words.

Briggs, Raymond (1982), *When the Wind Blows*, London: Hamish Hamilton.
This is a graphic novel for advanced secondary students – the message is dark and haunting.

Briggs, Raymond (1998), *Ethel and Ernest, a True Story*, London: Jonathan Cape.
There is much twentieth-century cultural history of the UK in this poignant autobiographical story, suitable for higher grades.

Dickens, Charles, adapt. Viney, Brigit, illus. Stokes, John (2010), *Great Expectations, The ELT Graphic Novel*, Andover: Heinle Cengage Learning.
Although this version of Dickens's classic is shortened and adapted, the story still shines through due to the vivid settings and characterization in the colourful panels.

Gaiman, Neil, illus. Russell, Craig (2008), *Coraline Graphic Novel*, New York: HarperCollins.
This graphic novel has become a classic horror story for young teens.

Gaiman, Neil and Craig Russell (2014), *The Graveyard Book Graphic Novel*, New York: HarperCollins Children's Books (Chapter 2, mentioned).
This is the multiple prize-winning, spellbinding read by Neil Gaiman, as a graphic novel.

Gaiman, Neil, illus. Riddell, Chris (2014), *The Sleeper and the Spindle*, London: Bloomsbury.
This is a darkly magical, postmodern version of Sleeping Beauty, magnificently illustrated.

Garland, Sarah (2012), *Azzi In Between*, London: Frances Lincoln.
This is unusual as it is a graphic novel suitable for elementary school, a moving refugee story.

Hale, Shannon and Hale, Dean, illus. Nathan Hale (2008), *Rapunzel's Revenge*,
London: Bloomsbury.
A swashbuckling heroine, this Rapunzel is very definitely not waiting for rescue.

Hosseini, Khaled, illus. Andolfo, Mirka and Celoni, Fabio (2011), *The Kite
Runner: Graphic Novel*, London: Bloomsbury.
This graphic novel version of the prizewinning bestseller set in Afghanistan is
stunning.

Horowitz, Anthony, adapt. Johnston, Anthony, illus. Kanako, Damerum and
Yuzuro, Takasaki (2012), *Alex Rider – The Graphic Novel – Stormbreaker*,
London: Walker Books.
This *Alex Rider* graphic novel has action scenes like watching a movie – so
will be very helpful for the many girls and boys for whom any kind of book is a
challenge.

Marois, André and Patrick Doyon (2013), *The Sandwich Thief*, San Francisco:
Chronicle Books (Chapter 2, mentioned).
A short, rather unique Canadian graphic novel, this book with a school setting
is hugely popular with children for its Gallic humour, cartoon-like images and
typography. In ELT for the pre-teen years, the stereotyping of classroom
characters provides opportunities for critical literacy.

Ness, Patrick, illus. Jim Kay (2011), *A Monster Calls*, Massachusetts:
Candlewick Press.
This Carnegie Medal *and* Kate Greenaway Medal winner offers storytelling within
a story, a complex read about a 13-year-old boy whose mother is terminally ill.
The words as well as the illustrations are powerful and poetic.

Riddell, Chris (2007), *Ottoline and the Yellow Cat*, London: Macmillan
Children's Books.
This is an imaginative wacko tale, the first in a series, for young readers.

Satrapi, Marjane (2007), *The Complete Persepolis*, New York: Pantheon Books.
This is an unforgettable autobiographical coming-of-age story about a girl growing
up in Iran and as a teenager in Austria, suitable for the higher grades.

Selznick, Brian (2007), *The Invention of Hugo Cabret*, New York: Scholastic
(Chapter 2, in detail).
A Caldecott Medal winner, this inventive book and the following amazing works
by Brian Selznick can be an inspiration in the mid- to higher secondary ELT
classroom.

Selznick, Brian (2011), *Wonderstruck*, New York: Scholastic (Chapter 2, in detail).

Selznick, Brian (2015), *The Marvels*, New York: Scholastic (Chapter 2, in detail).

Sewell, Anna, adapt. Brigman, June and Richardson, Roy (2005), *Black
Beauty: The Graphic Novel*, New York: Puffin Graphics.
This is one of many graphic novel retellings of the classic tale. Readers are truly
spoilt for choice.

Shakespeare, William, adapt. Appignanesi, Richard, illus. Kate Brown (2008),
Manga Shakespeare: A Midsummer Night's Dream, New York: Abrams.

Similarly, there are very many retellings of Shakespeare as graphic novel or manga. This version is dynamically and dramatically illustrated.

Skye, Obert (2011), *Wonkenstein: A Creature from My Closet*, New York: Henry Holt (Chapter 2, mentioned).
This is the first in a series around a twelve-year-old and a fantastic closet creature. With comic-like illustrations it is ideal for reluctant readers.

Stevenson, Robert Louis, adapt. Hamilton, Tim (2005), *Treasure Island: The Graphic Novel*, New York: Puffin Graphics.
Treasure Island is another timeless classic that does very well as graphic novel.

Tamaki, Mariko, illus. Tamaki, Jillian (2008), *Skim*, Toronto: Groundwood Books.
This is a gripping graphic novel for girls – set in the emotional world of female teenagers.

Tan, Shaun (2007), *The Arrival*, New York: Arthur A. Levine Books (Chapters 2 and 4, mentioned).
Difficult to define, this wordless graphic novel (picturebook?) speaks volumes on refugees and asylum.

TenNapel, Doug (2012), *Cardboard*, New York: Scholastic.
With a clever and quite moving story, this is a dynamically executed graphic novel. The action scenes are fast paced, though predictably dominated by male characters, so also suitable for reading against the text.

Tolstikova, Dasha (2015), *A Year Without Mom*, Toronto: Greenwood Books (Chapter 2, mentioned).
A coming of age story set in the Soviet Union, poignant and gripping.

Wilde, Oscar, illus. Russell, Craig (2012), *The Fairy Tales of Oscar Wilde, The Happy Prince*, New York: NBM Graphic Novels.
These favourite tales are enlivened by an expert illustrator.

Yang, Luen Gene (2006), *American Born Chinese*, New York: Square Fish (Chapter 8, mentioned).
The theme of cultural identity has already turned this graphic novel into a classic for the advanced ELT classroom.

6. Short story collections

There are short stories in all possible genres: science fiction, fantasy, realism and so forth. This is a favoured format in the ELT classroom due to the brevity of the stories. However, short stories are also very condensed, and thus only the very best can be as compelling as longer fiction. The storyworlds, being so very concise, are not generous panoramas inviting the reader into a new world, but rather brief but significant glimpses of another world. Thus short stories are generally more suitable for the higher grades in ELT.

Amnesty International (2009), *FREE? Stories Celebrating Human Rights*,
    London: Walker Books.
This anthology, by expert children's authors from all around the globe, conjures
inspiring stories around themes of human rights.

BAME authors (2017), *A Change is Gonna Come*, London: Stripes.
This excellent anthology is united by the theme of change. Leading British BAME
voices (Black, Asian, and minority ethnic) cover in unsettling, thought-provoking
ways urgent and often sensitive issues that young people are currently facing.

Bardugo, Leigh, illus. Kipin, Sara (2017), *The Language of Thorns: Midnight Tales
    and Dangerous Magic*, New York: Macmillan.
This collection presents enthralling, otherworldly and dark dreamscapes by a
bestselling author and with stunning illustrations.

Bradbury, Ray (1952/1997), *Golden Apples of the Sun and Other Stories*,
    New York: HarperCollins (The story 'A Sound of Thunder' is mentioned in
    Chapter 3).
These classic science-fiction short stories speculate on the human condition with
clarity and apprehension.

Brazier, Chris (ed.) (2009), *One World: A Global Anthology of Short Stories*,
    Oxford: New Internationalist (Chapter 8, mentioned).
This is a truly global anthology. Each expert author manages to bring the reader
right inside their very different, sometimes heart-breaking world.

Butler, Octavia (2005), *Bloodchild and Other Stories*, New York: Seven Stories
    Press (The story 'The Book of Martha' is mentioned in Chapter 11).
This is a captivating and intelligent collection that uses the allegorical cloak of
science fiction accessibly.

Erdrich, Heid and Tohe, Laura (eds) (2002), *Sister Nations: Native American
    Women Writers on Community*, Minnesota: Minnesota Historical
    Society Press.
This anthology of contemporary Native American women's voices weaves a
fascinating tapestry of different perspectives and visions.

Gaiman, Neil (2007), *M Is for Magic*, New York: HarperCollins.
Stories for young adults, told with Neil Gaiman's characteristic magic and mystery.

Le Guin, Ursula (1975/2004), *The Wind's Twelve Quarters: Stories*, New York:
    Perennial (The story 'The Ones Who Walk Away from Omelas' is in
    Chapter 11, in detail).

Le Guin, Ursula (1994/2003), *The Birthday of the World and Other Stories*,
    London: Gollancz (The story 'The Matter of Seggri' is mentioned in
    Chapter 11).
Ursula Le Guin, Grandmaster of Science Fiction, tests her deeply insightful ideas
on the present through her speculative storyworlds.

Levithan, David (2008), *How They Met, and Other Stories*, New York: Alfred.
    A. Knopf (The story 'Princes' is in Chapter 9, in detail).
This compilation of stories on the universality of love is heart-warming and eye
opening.

Morpurgo, Michael (2006), *Singing for Mrs Pettigrew – A Storymaker's Journey*, London: Walker Books.
Morpurgo always paints amazing pictures with his words, his stories are beautiful and among the most accessible in this list.

Naidoo, Beverley (2001), *Out of Bounds: Stories of Conflict and Hope*, London: Puffin (Chapter 8, in detail).
This collection contains powerfully moving stories that cover the decades of apartheid and post-apartheid in South Africa.

7. Verse novels

The verse novel is a fairly new format that is extremely promising for ELT, and should be introduced in every classroom. The word scenery of verse novels and the musicality of the language often reflect the fierce emotions of adolescence – as in poetry, feelings reverberate in the omissions, lingering in the moment of what can be said and what can only be felt. The slower reading of poetry works well for deep reading: the most successful verse novels not only offer the vivid depth of feeling that poetry can deliver but they are also convincing as stories. And readers are forced to pay attention to every word.

Alexander, Kwame (2014), *The Crossover*, New York: Houghton Mifflin Harcourt.
A Newbery Medal winner, this book has reportedly already turned countless male mid-secondary students into readers. It is rhythmic, playful, visually appealing, exciting and poetic.

Applegate, Katherine (2007), *Home of the Brave*, New York: Square Fish.
This is a beautiful and very accessible refugee story, with humour and humanity, as well as wonderfully strange images of Minnesota from the puzzled perspective of a Sudanese boy.

Creech, Sharon (2001), *Love that Dog*, New York: HarperCollins.
A charming verse novel, and one of the few that is suitable for pre-teens and younger.

Crossan, Sarah (2011), *The Weight of Water*, London: Bloomsbury.
The verse novel format works extremely well with gently poetic, introspective stories such as those by Sarah Crossan. With this Polish girl's moving tale of migration to England, we experience the alienation that many immigrants face. The absence of wordiness creates images that are all the more evocative in their expression of prejudice, as well as the sweetness of first love.

Crossan, Sarah (2015), *One*, London: Bloomsbury.
This Carnegie Medal winner is a powerful story of conjoined twins – heart breaking and unforgettable.

Engle, Margarita (2009), *Tropical Secrets: Holocaust Refugees in Cuba*, New York: Henry Colt.
History interwoven with poetry, the quietly intense verse creates the heartbeat of this holocaust story.

Frost, Helen (2006), *The Braid*, New York: Frances Foster.
At the time of the Highland Clearances, two Scottish sisters symbolically braid their hair. Throughout this exquisite verse novel, the braided hair is echoed by the poetry of the sisters' alternating voices when one of them must emigrate to Nova Scotia and the other stays behind on the ruggedly beautiful Western Isles of Scotland.

Frost, Helen (2009), *Crossing Stones*, New York: Farrar, Straus and Giroux.
This is another beautiful, poetic and passionate book in verse, WW1 historical fiction.

Herrick, Steven (2000), *The Simple Gift*, Brisbane: University of Queensland Press.
Powerful and passionate, this is the experience of a sixteen-year-old who befriends a homeless man, told in short gem-like scenes of free verse.

Lai, Thanhha (2011), *Inside Out & Back Again*, New York: HarperCollins.
This is an absorbing autobiographical story in any format. Yet the verse is exactly right to vividly express the conflicting emotions of Há, who becomes a refugee when Saigon falls during the Vietnam War.

Woodson, Jacqueline (2003), *Locomotion*, New York: Puffin Books.
This lovely and accessible verse novel is in the voice of an eleven-year-old orphan, who expresses his pain through poetry.

8. Playscripts

Drama conventions can be used with or without a literary text, and can support all dimensions of learning: cognitive, affective, sociological and physiological (Bland 2015). Guy Cook (2000: 196) particularly highlights using a playscript as strongly supporting attention to language: 'The rehearsal and performance of an appropriate play combines the best of both structural and communicative syllabuses: rote learning and repetition of a model, attention to exact wording, practice in all four skills, motivating and authentic language and activity, instances of culturally and contextually appropriate pragmatic use, and integration of linguistic with paralinguistic communication.' Half of the texts listed below are original plays for young people, and half are successful young adult novels that have been dramatized for the stage. Through the medium of theatre and multisensory learning, these plays can potentially afford all the advantages of rehearsal and performance (even when only in the classroom) that Cook describes.

Almond, David (2002), *Wild Girl, Wild Boy*, London: Hodder Children's Books.
Once again, this time as a play, Almond has created a poetic and magical text, suitable for lower to mid-secondary ELT. The chorus scenes of schoolmates, teachers and neighbours are wonderful to act out.

Bland, Janice, illus. Lottermoser, Elisabeth (2009), *Mini-Plays, Role-Rhymes and other Stepping Stones to English. Book 2: Legends and Myths* and *Book 3: Favourite Festivals*, California: Players Press.
These are very brief, illustrated plays with many roles for elementary children in ELT – the lines are short and rhythmical.

Bland, Janice (2013), *Allie's Class*, California: Players Press.
A one-act play for lower secondary ELT, the focus is on a new girl in class, and the playground bullying and friendships she experiences.

Connections (2012), *Plays for Young People, National Theatre*, London: Bloomsbury Methuen Drama (Michael Lesslie's 'Prince of Denmark', an exciting one-act prequel to *Hamlet*, is in Chapter 13, in detail).
Every year for the last two decades, an anthology of newly commissioned one-act plays, *Connections*, has been published for performance by teenagers. The plays ('ten plays about the world' in the 2012 anthology) are accompanied by notes on rehearsal and staging, and are suitable for the highest grades in ELT.

Cooper, Susan, dramatized by Mitchell, Adrian (2011), *King of Shadows*, Oxford: Oxford University Press.
With this time-slip play students are brought right into the mucky, smelly yet vital world of Shakespeare. The gripping play introduces *A Midsummer Night's Dream* and Shakespeare himself, as a practical, paternal and deeply humane actor-playwright.

Haddon, Mark, dramatized by Stephens, Simon (2013), *The Curious Incident of the Dog in the Night-Time*, London: Bloomsbury.
The young adult novel that offers a unique window into the mind of an unusual boy works very well as a play, providing excellent opportunities for interactive ELT in higher grades.

Hales, Ben (2013), *There's a leak!*, Cheltenham: Nelson Thornes.
Satirical and dramatic, with very funny crowd scenes, this is a brief and lively play suitable for mid-secondary ELT.

Kemp, Gene (2003), *The Turbulent Term of Tyke Tiler*, Oxford: Oxford University Press.
This is a clever play, based on Kemp's successful novel, which stages the school life of twelve-year-old children in the UK, with a surprising twist at the end.

Lewis, C. S., dramatized by Mitchell, Adrian (2000), *The Lion, the Witch and the Wardrobe*, London: Oberon Plays for Young People.
This favourite story works perfectly as a play and will be a joy to act out with children in mid-secondary ELT.

Rushdie, Salman, dramatized by Supple, Tim and Tushingham, David (1998), *Haroun and the Sea of Stories*, London: Faber and Faber.
The young hero Haroun has a quest to fulfil, to protect his father and the power of the imagination that his father represents. Despite the seriousness of the themes, the exuberance of Rushdie's language sustains a light-hearted tone throughout.

Thorne, Jack (script), Rowling, J. K. and Tiffany, John (story) (2016), *Harry Potter and the Cursed Child*, London: Little, Brown Book Group (Chapter 3, in detail).
This compelling and accessible play is thankfully gaining new readers across the world for the playscript format.

Zephaniah, Benjamin, dramatized by Sissay, Lemn (2013), *Refugee Boy*, London: Methuen Drama.
This powerful story of the refugee experience in the UK can be wonderfully brought alive in the classroom with the playscript format.

9. Screenplays

It is possible to download screenplays of many favourite films from the Web, for aficionados painstakingly transcribe the full script of films and upload them to sites such as http://www.awesomefilm.com/. This is a very useful aid – particularly for non-native speakers of English – and it is really helpful to be able to refer to the screenplay in the classroom after having watched a film. Many screenplays of films that are quite popular in ELT settings can be downloaded free of charge and are not listed here, such as *Dead Poets Society*, *Gandhi*, *Schindler's List*, *Shakespeare in Love*, *Ten Things I Hate About You*, *The Cider House Rules* and *The King's Speech*.

It is to be welcomed that now in addition, publishers are publishing the screenplays (also called shooting scripts) of highly successful films.

Beaufoy, Simon (2008), *Slumdog Millionaire: The Shooting Script*, New York: Newmarket Press.
This won the Best Adapted Screenplay Oscar – reading the screenplay, and enjoying stills of the film in the publication, enriches the experience of the film.

Kureishi, Hanif (2002), *Collected Screenplays*, London: Faber and Faber.
Kureishi's witty and deep screenplays include *My Beautiful Laundrette*, a film that cleverly explores postcolonial identity in Britain.

Logan, John (2012), *Hugo: The Shooting Script*, New York: Newmarket Press.
The graphic novel *The Invention of Hugo Cabret*, the screenplay *Hugo*, and Martin Scorsese's film – together these texts offer a wonderful opportunity to study the process of adaptation.

Niccol, Andrew (1998), *The Truman Show*, New York: Newmarket Press.
This is an amazing movie, and the gripping screenplay reminds us why.

Rowling, J. K. (2016), *Fantastic Beasts and Where to Find Them, Original Screenplay*, London: Little, Brown (Chapter 3, in detail).
Hopefully this J. K. Rowling screenplay will help reveal the huge potential of this under-exploited format.

10. Young adult fiction

These titles are books that resonate with teenagers, their concerns and often their anger at being troubled, ignored, permanently on display or generally left at the mercy of helpless or useless adults. The themes are thought provoking, sometimes humorous and often gritty or dark, more suitable for higher grades in secondary school ELT.

Alexie, Sherman (2008), *The Absolutely True Diary of a Part-Time Indian*, London: Random House.
Hilarious and heartbreaking, this young adult novel is irresistible.

Almond, David (1999), *Kit's Wilderness*, London: Hodder Children's Books.
For slightly younger teens, this magic realist text is a beautifully written portrayal of a young writer, a young artist and their troubled times.

Bauer, Michael Gerard (2006), *Don't Call Me Ishmael*, Dorking: Scholastic Australia.
Many teen readers love humour, and this story is one of the funniest.

Bertagna, Julie (2002), *Exodus*, London: Macmillan Children's Books (Chapter 12, in detail).
Countless ethical questions are raised by this adventure story in a drowning world.

Brooks, Kevin (2003), *Lucas*, London: Chicken House.
This is a haunting, unforgettable read.

Carmody, Isobelle (1987), *Obernewtyn*, Melbourne: Penguin Books (Chapter 12, in detail).
The Obernewtyn Chronicles is a series of seven books, which was written over almost four decades. Set in a fantasy world, it is hugely popular and compelling, though less well known in Europe.

Chandler, Kristen (2010), *Wolves, Boys, and Other Things that Might Kill Me*, New York: Penguin.
This is realist fiction based on environmental issues concerning wolves, environmentalists, and ranchers – as well as young love.

Collins, Suzanne (2008), *The Hunger Games*, New York: Scholastic (Chapter 10, in detail; Chapter 12, mentioned).
The trilogy is young adult fiction par excellence.

Collins, Suzanne (2009), *Catching Fire*, New York: Scholastic (Chapter 10, in detail).

Collins, Suzanne (2010), *Mockingjay*, New York: Scholastic (Chapter 10, in detail).

Cooper, Susan (1999), *King of Shadows*, London: Penguin.
This is a moving time-slip story, embedded in a detailed tapestry of Elizabethan England.

Doherty, Berlie (2007), *Abela: The Girl Who Saw Lions*, London: Andersen Press.
A beautifully told, moving story which manages to cover adoption, female circumcision, child slavery, AIDS and the foster care system – an outstanding book.

DuPrau, Jeanne (2003), *The City of Ember*, New York: Random House (Chapter 12, in detail).
This is exciting fantasy for younger fluent readers, who will want to solve the mystery along with the young protagonists.

Gavin, Jamila (2000), *Coram Boy*, London: Mammoth.
A brilliantly woven and complex story for higher grades, the darkness of eighteenth-century England is shocking and gripping, while a light shines through of music, love and charity.

Fiedler, Lisa (2003), *Dating Hamlet: Ophelia's Story*, New York: Flamingo Collins Books.
Empowering Ophelia, the book is an engaging story for teen readers (Chapter 13, mentioned).

Gaiman, Neil (2008), *The Graveyard Book*, London: Bloomsbury.
This is a Carnegie Medal winner, a Newbery Medal winner and the Hugo Award winner, which says it all.

Gino, Alex (2015), *George*, New York: Scholastic.
This is a heart-warming story about George, a fourth grader who knows she is really a girl. The poignant story reveals the difficulties George faces with clarity and grace.

Green, John (2012), *The Fault in Our Stars*, London: Penguin (Chapter 9, in detail).
While Hazel and Augustus are consumed by their cancer, their lives signify so much more than their illness. The book is powerful and tragic, but often exquisitely funny.

Laird, Elizabeth (2017), *Welcome to Nowhere*, London: Macmillan Children's Books.
An emotionally involving and compelling read about young people caught up in the Syrian civil war and forced to flee – a moving call to action.

Lowry, Lois (1993), *The Giver*, Boston: Houghton Mifflin.
A Newbery Medal winner, the prose is simple, clear and suitable for younger teens, with a thought-provoking story.

McCormick, Patricia (2006), *Sold*, New York: Hyperion.
Written from the perspective of a Nepalese thirteen-year-old girl sold into sex slavery, this well-researched book paints a vivid picture of the horrors of contemporary sex trafficking.

Marsden, John (2008), *Hamlet: A Novel*, Melbourne: Text Publishing.
This is a lyrical and engaging reimagining of *Hamlet* (Chapter 13, mentioned).

Morpurgo, Michael (1990), *Waiting for Anya*, Portsmouth: Heinemann.
There are wonderful historical novels among young adult fiction, and Morpurgo's works are among the best. This is a compelling story of courage when Jewish children are sheltered from the Nazis on the French-Spanish border in WW2.

Morpurgo, Michael (2003), *Private Peaceful*, London: HarperCollins.
This WW1 story has the moving and awe-inspiring quality of war poetry of the era.

Naidoo, Beverley (2000), *The Other Side of Truth*, London: Puffin Books.
This is a Carnegie Medal winner. The refugee story of Nigerian children lost in London expertly brings home the monstrous challenges that face families that lose everything when they must flee from the country of their birth.

Palacio, Raquel (2012), *Wonder*, New York: Alfred. A. Knopf.
This poignant story tells of friendship and kindness, and a young boy who is a wonder of courage.

Pitcher, Annabel (2011), *My Sister Lives on the Mantelpiece*, London: Orion Publishing Group.
Jamie's youthful optimism inspires in this tale of resilience and hope when parents become dysfunctional through grief.

Reeve, Philip (2001), *Mortal Engines*, London: Scholastic.
For those who love science fiction, this is a page-turner set in a futuristic London.

Rushdie, Salman (1990), *Haroun and the Sea of Stories*, London: Penguin Books.
A political background to a wonderfully fantastic story by a genius with words – the book is complex and creative, significant and fun.

Sachar, Louis (1998), *Holes*, New York: Farrar, Straus and Giroux.
Already a classic in ELT, this multilayered book, a Newbery Medal winner, creates multifaceted historical and contemporary characters, and is both exciting and highly satisfying.

Sedgwick, Marcus (2000), *Floodland*, London: Orion (Chapter 12, in detail).
This qualifies as young adult fiction due to the dark theme of a drowning world and gang violence. The book is however very short with a ten-year-old heroine, suitable for younger teens.

Sutcliffe, William (2013), *The Wall*, London: Bloomsbury.
This is an intriguing story that symbolically reflects the complexities of the West Bank and Israeli-Palestinian conflicts.

Welford, Ross (2016), *Time Travelling with a Hamster*, London: HarperCollins.
This is a gem that focuses on family relationships, time travel and science – at once suspenseful, adventurous and deep.

Winton, Tim (1990), *Lockie Leonard, Human Torpedo*, Camberwell (Victoria): Penguin (Chapter 7, in detail).
The series provides a riotously funny story of teen life in Australia.

Winton, Tim (1993), *Lockie Leonard, Scumbuster*, Camberwell (Victoria): Penguin (Chapter 7, in detail).

Winton, Tim (1997), *Lockie Leonard, Legend*, Camberwell (Victoria): Penguin (Chapter 7, mentioned).

Zusak, Markus (2005), *The Book Thief*, Sydney: Picador.
A multiple award-winning book that is rich and remarkable – it creates the magic of hope while telling of war and devastation.

References

Agnew, Kate (2001), Chapter books, in Victor Watson (ed.), *The Cambridge Guide to Children's Books in English*, Cambridge: Cambridge University Press, p. 139.

Bamford, Julian and Day, Richard (1997), Extensive reading: What is it? Why bother? *The Language Teacher*, 21/5. Available from: http://www. jalt-publications.org/tlt/articles/2132-extensive-reading-what-it-why-bother (accessed 17 August 2017).

Bland, Janice (2013), *Children's Literature and Learner Empowerment: Children and Teenagers in English Language Education*, London: Bloomsbury Academic.

Bland, Janice (2015), 'Drama with young learners', in Janice Bland (ed.), *Teaching English to Young Learners. Critical Issues in Language Teaching with 3–12 Year Olds*, London: Bloomsbury Academic, pp. 219–38.

Bland, Janice (2018a), 'Introduction: The challenge of literature', in Janice Bland (ed.), *Using Literature in English Language Education: Challenging Reading for 8–18 Year Olds*, London: Bloomsbury Academic, pp. 1–22.

Cook, Guy (2000), *Language Play, Language Learning*, Oxford: Oxford University Press.

Harmgarth, Friederike (1999), *Das Lesebarometer – Lesen und Umgang mit Büchern in Deutschland*, Gütersloh: Bertelsmann Stiftung.

Hunt, Peter (2001), *Children's Literature*, Oxford: Blackwell.

Ludwig, Christian and Pointner, Frank (eds) (2013), *Teaching Comics in the Foreign Language Classroom*, Trier: Wissenschaftlicher Verlag Trier.

Sullivan, Alice and Brown, Matt (2013), *Social Inequalities in Cognitive Scores at Age 16: The Role of Reading*, London: Centre for Longitudinal Studies, Institute of Education.

Index